THE FRIGHT FILE

DUSTIN PUTMAN

Haunted Sideshow Press
Ashburn, Virginia
www.HauntedSideshow.com

LIBRARY OF CONGRESS CATALOGING-IN-PUBLICATION DATA
Putman, Dustin.
The fright file : 150 films to see before Halloween / Dustin Putman.
p. cm.
ISBN: 978-0-61577-402-2
1. Horror films — History and criticism. 2. Media — Film Studies. 3. Film Criticism I. Title.

First Printing, September 2013

FIRST EDITION
10 9 8 7 6 5 4 3 2 1

Portions of this book contain material previously published and syndicated, in a slightly different form, by the author via *dustinputman.com*.

Cover Photo: Mykola Velychko/Photos.com
Design and Layout: Patrick Jennings

For Rudy,
Who inspired my love of movies,

and

For Mom and Dad,
Who were cool enough to let their
5-year-old son rent Halloween.

CONTENTS

"Well, kiddo, I thought you outgrew superstition."

Laurie Strode
Haddonfield, Illinois
October 31, 1978

INTRODUCTION

When did I fall in love with movies, and, more specifically, the horror genre? That is a tough question to answer. Growing up, there were a lot of different factors that likely informed my fascination with the darker shades of cinema. My brother, Rudy, ten years my senior, had been a film buff long before I waltzed onto the scene. I can remember him telling me about the first R-rated horror picture he saw in a theater (for the record, *The Amityville Horror*, when he was eight), and how he had begged our mom to take him. She finally relented, either because she wasn't too concerned about its content or just got tired of hearing him whine about it. Maybe, at the time, she wanted to see it herself. Who knows? The point is, Rudy was terrified of the film about the alleged haunted house on Long Island, and he loved that feeling. I loved it, too, my early youth coinciding with the advent of VCRs and video rental shops.

A child of the 1980s, I was the youngest of three, and by the time I came around my parents weren't so concerned about what I watched as long as I was aware of the difference between reality and the fictional magic of movies (they drew the line at *Silent Night, Deadly Night*, though, which I didn't see until I was nine). Imagine a first-grader choosing to rent *The Texas Chain Saw Massacre* alongside *The Goonies* and *Strawberry Shortcake: Housewarming Surprise*, and that was me. Apparently, the Video Villa clerks got a kick out of me and the wildly disparate films I would giddily walk up to the counter to check out. Even at such a young age, I wasn't particularly scared by the slasher flicks I would watch so much as taken with the filmmaking side of things and the thrill they gave me (Disney's seriously scarring *Return to Oz*, on the other hand, was a different story, what with Dorothy's stormy nighttime escape from a mental institution and Princess Mombi's disembodied gallery of heads). Rudy and I bonded over this shared hobby, and later on as I got a little older he would take me to the movies every Friday night, using the hard-earned money he would make bussing tables to pay for it. In hindsight, now that I'm older and Rudy is no longer with us (he passed away in 2003 at the age of 31), I realize just how truly special and fleeting that time was.

I can still remember the first time I was allowed to see a horror movie on the big screen. It was August of 1988, and my mom took me to see *A Nightmare on Elm Street 4: The Dream Master*. By this time, at the seasoned age of six, I was already intimately familiar with the series, and Freddy Krueger's metamorphosis from being a monster to be feared to a monster who made silly quips as he claimed his teenage victims in their sleep had my mom and I entertained throughout. As my tastes matured, so did my interest in film criticism. I loved reading and learning about movies almost as much as viewing them. *Siskel & Ebert* was a weekly television ritual, and every year I would excitedly await the release of the updated editions of *Roger Ebert's Movie Home Companion* and *Leonard Maltin's Movie Guide*. Just for fun, I started writing capsule reviews on my PC, typing out the cast lists and modeling my critiques after these influential critics. Then, in 1995, I wrote my first full-length reviews for the Pauly Shore comedy, *Jury Duty,* and the animated pic, *The Pebble and the Penguin*. This was the pre-Internet era (or at least it still was for me), and it is probably a good thing those sincere but amateurish critical essays are long lost on the hard drive of a computer currently buried in a landfill.

Beginning in July 1997, my online-based reviewing career kicked off with Robert Zemeckis' *Contact*. I was 16 at the time. Modest at first, posted on a handful of primitive self-made websites and via the *rec.arts.movies.reviews* newsgroup, my writing eventually graduated to syndication and found a brand-new personal outlet with a more sophisticated professional design. Originally called *TheMovieBoy.com* until I decided I was getting a little long in the tooth to go by that moniker, the site was later rebranded to its current permutation, *DustinPutman.com*. Through high school, college and a central career, I have continued to moonlight as a film critic for the last sixteen-plus years. It's what I know. It's one of my great passions in life. And now, finally, I have married my love for movies with that of the holiday nearest and dearest to my heart.

For as long as I can remember, my favorite season has always been autumn. The falling of the temperatures and the chill in the breeze. The radiant golden colors of the foliage. The dwindling daytime hours of sunlight. The fresh pumpkins sitting in yards and on porches. That special, indescribable smell in the air. For me, these characteristics signal only one thing: Halloween is on its way. As much as I live for the fall, I live for the final day in October more. It is a holiday that I find as sacred as Christmas or Thanksgiving, and one that has given me some of my most fond memories from childhood and early adulthood. Because of this, it should be no grand revelation that I have been a fan of the horror genre since the age of four (yes, *four*). Or, perhaps because I love horror, it should be no surprise that I am equally enamored with Halloween. Around the month of October, these two things go hand in hand.

This book is **not** meant to be a comprehensive assessment of scary movies or an all-encompassing "best-in-horror" list. Indeed, some of the films covered aren't strictly considered horror at all. Instead, think of what follows as a collection of essays highlighting 150 motion pictures—some well-loved, some underrated, and some you might not have heard of—that, for me, represent ideal viewing selections to celebrate the coming of All Hallows' Eve. Maybe you will not agree with every single choice, but that is par for the course when it comes to varying opinions and viewpoints. At the least, I hope you will understand after reading each entry why that particular film holds value in my eyes. Many of the compositions herein have been gathered from my years of film criticism, some have been extensively rewritten and fine-tuned for the purposes of publication, and others are completely new and previously unprinted. Because no worthwhile film goes out of style, do not think of this book as a resource only valid during the months of September and October, either. With 364 days per year technically falling before Halloween, it is never too early to get a jump on all things creepy, kooky and spooky.

Happy viewing!

Little me and my big brother, Rudy, in 1988.

All the Boys Love Mandy Lane

2008 - Directed by Jonathan Levine

The provocatively titled *All the Boys Love Mandy Lane* premiered to much acclaim and fanfare at the 2006 Toronto International Film Festival. A $750,000-budgeted teen horror picture that excelled at its multiple genres and seemed destined for wide appeal, it was quickly snatched up by The Weinstein Company, who paid an exorbitant $3-million-plus for distribution rights in the U.S. As is characteristic of TWC, the studio began shuffling the release date, scheduling it for July 20, 2007, following a couple winter and spring delays. Mere days before this Friday opening, the release was canceled again.

Senator Entertainment, a new up-and-coming company, bought *All the Boys Love Mandy Lane* from the Weinsteins shortly thereafter, promising an early-2008 berth on no less than 1,000 screens. As the film began to open theatrically in overseas territories in 2008, the early months of the new year came and went with no North American start. Rumors of an April 2008 release never materialized, with Senator throwing out some cockamamie story about how they wanted to sit on the film until director Jonathan Levine's sophomore effort, Sundance favorite *The Wackness*, opened in the summer and gained the filmmaker some wider cred. Sure enough, *The Wackness* came out in July, but its mediocre box office in limited release didn't exactly set the world on fire as Senator had assumed. An incredible five more years passed with *All the Boys Love Mandy Lane* stuck in limbo. In that time, the Stateside distribution rights had reverted to the Weinstein's On-Demand/theatrical shingle RADiUS-TWC. The film finally saw the light of day in the autumn of 2013, but how does one accurately sell a movie to audiences that has been widely available on DVD/Blu-ray in most foreign territories for over half a decade?

One can only hope *All the Boys Love Mandy Lane* finds its rightful audience after the unfair abuse it has taken from the clueless Hollywood studio system. The film, twisting in fresh ways that set it apart from the usual paint-by-numbers slasher flick—in this regard, it is reminiscent of 2003's expertly conceived French chiller *High Tension*—has been made with an unusual love and care for detail. This becomes exceedingly apparent from the prologue, a journey through a typical high school hallway scored to Bedroom Walls' gorgeous song "In Anticipation of Your Suicide" that leads to a back-to-school party embodying the insecurity, fun, and foolish sense of immortality that comes with being a teenager.

Mandy Lane (Amber Heard) used to be a wallflower—someone only paid attention to by best friend Emmet (Michael Welch)—but after a prosperous summer she returns to high school a blossomed beauty. Every boy wants her, and every girl secretly wishes she could be her. Nine months following a classmate's tragic accidental death at a pool party, pothead Red (Aaron Himelstein) plans a weekend trip with friends—lustful buddies Bird (Edwin Hodge) and Jake (Luke Grimes), and argumentative gal pals Chloe (Whitney Able) and Marlin (Melissa Price)—to his family's secluded ranch. He invites Mandy along, and she accepts, eager to branch out of her shell even if she's not the type to partake in much of their brand of fun. Frivolity, drinking, recreational drug-taking and relationship tensions lead to confusion and fear when the attendees begin falling victim to a sociopath on the property.

It is tempting to say that *All the Boys Love Mandy Lane* is actually better in the first half, before the more horrific plot elements emerge, but that is because Levine does such an extraordinary job of setting up his characters and the milieu they live within. A scene set on the school's outside track and bleachers, The Go-Go's "Our Lips Are Sealed" blasting on the soundtrack, is like a great 1980s teen movie sprung to life. A little later, a montage using Juliette Commagere's wistful cover of America's "Sister Golden Hair" proves how powerful the mixture of music, image and editing can be on film when a true artist is at the reins.

Levine takes the valuable time to set up his characters and develop them free of stereotypes so that when a hooded killer enters the equation, first frighteningly glimpsed so subtly in the background that the viewer questions if he or she really saw anything at all, their demises mean more than if they were just one-note caricatures. Before this, suspense is ratcheted with notable skill, as in a scene where a water snake slithering perilously close to Mandy as she swims in a pond turns out to only be an example of intentional misdirection. When the killing spree takes off in the picture's second half, the reveal of the murderer's identity comes a little too early and lessens the potential to outright scare. Still, by the end, the reason for why this occurs is uncovered, leading to a surprise in the finale that totally alters the story's trajectory and adds newfound relevance to our current times.

If a motion picture is going to be so bold as to use a title like *All the Boys Love Mandy Lane*, it is imperative that viewers understand what makes Mandy so desirable. The casting directors did their job splendidly by casting Amber Heard in the role. Heard is strikingly beautiful, but, in portraying Mandy Lane, she also seems so personable, down to earth, and pure of heart that it is easy to see why others would be so drawn to here. More than that, though, Heard develops Mandy into a three-dimensional person, still confronting the effects that the deaths of her parents have had on her, and rather touching as she navigates through a sea of drooling peers who often treat her as nothing more than a prize to be won. The rest of the performances are strong—Anson Mount, as the polite, slightly older farmhand on the ranch property, Garth, and Whitney Able, as the ignorantly self-involved Chloe, are especially characterized with more than one shade—but this is Amber Heard's showcase to steal.

Shot on location outside of Austin, Texas, reportedly only miles away from where 1974's *The Texas Chain Saw Massacre* was filmed, *All the Boys Love Mandy Lane* is fitfully foreboding in its sun-dappled aura of isolation. As much a comment on the objectification of women—and, more specifically, teenage girls—as it is a grimy, violent, enthralling slasher pic, director Jonathan Levine and first-time screenwriter Jacob Forman have crafted one of the more memorable teen-oriented horror movies of the twenty-first century. Were the death toll to be stripped from the film, there would still be enough layers to delve into for it to still work, and that is the key to a solid script. With distaff remakes overwhelming the genre as of late, it is a shame that something original and demographically relatable like *All the Boys Love Mandy Lane* has had such a difficult time reaching the big screen. Its moment in the spotlight is long overdue.

Antichrist

2009 - Directed by Lars von Trier

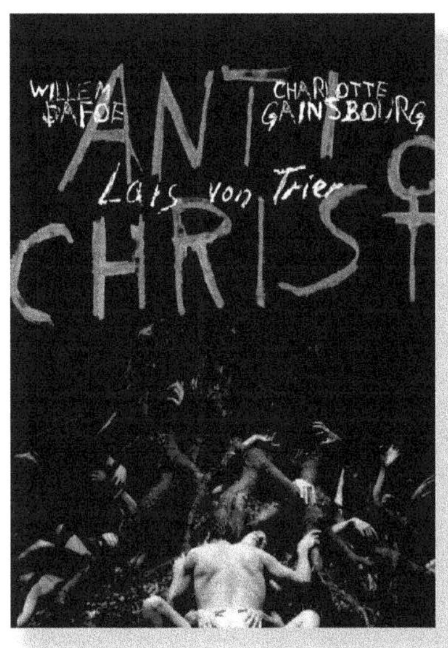

The universal eventuality of death is at the darkened heart of *Antichrist*, a wounding, psychologically complex piece of work written and directed by Lars von Trier. The picture, sharply dividing critics and audiences at the Cannes Film Festival for its unflinching blend of graphic sexuality and violence, has been widely touted as von Trier's first true foray into the horror genre. Anyone who is familiar with the Danish filmmaker's work, however, will know not to expect conventional genre fare with all the usual scare tactics. No, his aims are much more encompassing and auspicious than that, turning a tale of grief and despair into one that pulls those very emotions from the viewer, as if he or she were living it. *Antichrist* is as difficult as it is mesmerizing, an open invitation for personal interpretation made all the more fascinating for its heavy coating of symbolism. It also wouldn't be a bad idea for theaters showing the picture to hang signs at the door reading, "Abandon all hope ye who enter here."

When their toddler son, Nic (Storm Acheche Sahlstrøm), falls out a window to his death while they make love one room away, a married couple (Willem Dafoe and Charlotte Gainsbourg) are left shattered by the tragedy. He is a therapist—and a cocky one at that—under the belief that he can check his wife out of the hospital and better treat her bereavement than they can. "Where are you most afraid?" he asks her. "The woods," she replies, and more specifically Eden, a secluded location in the wilderness of Washington State where they keep a summer cabin. It is here that he works with his spouse day and night, hoping to ease her through the painful stages of mourning so that they may eventually be able to move on with their lives. What they find, though, is anything but peace, either spelling the end of their sanity, or, quite possibly, the end of days.

The troubled man and woman in *Antichrist* pass through the film unnamed, credited as only He and She. If the biblical Eden was the garden of God where Adam and Eve were ultimately cast out, then the Eden in *Antichrist* is no less than the garden of Satan, and He and She are staying put until their own destruction. He and She exchange precious few faith-based conversations, but from the title, to the ironic location name, to the horrific events that guide us to their bitter culmination, it is very clear that Lars von Trier has devised a mirror image of all that is good and light. The results are powerful enough to haunt a person's conscience, perhaps no line more shattering and frighteningly true than the wife's proclamation that the sounds of nature are like "the cry of all the things that are to die." Death for humans, for animals, for plants, for minerals and everything else is imminent and unavoidable, and it is this notion that weighs down all the heavier on her as acorns ceaselessly pelt their cabin roof and she mentally deteriorates.

Or, could it be that she is actually reaching newfound clarity? Without giving away all of the revelations and turns within the story, it can at least be noted that not everything is as it seems, both in the past and in the present that she has made for herself. As the various pieces of the puzzle assemble—e.g., he finds her abandoned thesis on genocide in the attic of the cabin, her writings from the previous summer when she stayed there with Nic increasingly erratic; his son's autopsy results report a slight bone abnormality in his feet that he thinks nothing of until he comes upon photographs that may explain the cause—she begins to confuse her original study of the evil done against women with the evil *of* women. She has her reasons.

Carnal and surreal, *Antichrist* is a dream-turned-nightmare (the turn, for those keeping track, arrives in the prologue, a slow-motion montage of He and She in the throes of ecstasy while Nic innocently and unsuspectingly moves toward his own doom, scored to the aria "Lascia ch'io pianga" from Georg Friedrich Händel's opera *Rinaldo*). From there, things only grow more dire, a filmic warning of the seismic injustices done to the living and the twisted fate that higher powers—if, for that matter, there *are* higher powers—have in store for us all. As the struggle between He and She intensifies, ominous prophetic run-ins with a deer and its stillborn calf, a self-cannibalizing fox, and a buried black crow that won't die—"The Three Beggars," only devious—hint at the grim destiny hovering upon the horizon.

In fearless performances that must have taken a physical and emotional toll on them, Willem Dafoe and Charlotte Gainsbourg delve into raw, charcoal-black areas of the human condition as He and She. Dafoe, playing the more logic-driven of the two, hopes to help his wife as a means of not directly dealing himself with the emotions he feels about losing a child he was not as close to as he knows he should have been. For her part, Gainsbourg bares her soul and her body in a way that only an actress without vanity could. Watching the film, the viewer thinks he or she knows where this guilt-stricken woman is coming from. That there is far more to her than meets the eye requires that Gainsbourg be constantly playing two levels at once. She is nothing short of exquisite.

Is *Antichrist* misogynistic? That the end credits tell us there was a "misogyny researcher" on the production points to no, that director Lars von Trier's view of the female persuasion is not consenting to his genocidal themes, but a critical comment on the persecution of women throughout the centuries for being, in certain chauvinistic views, less than a man. Nevertheless, von Trier does acknowledge that anyone is capable of evil ways and refuses to back pedal as he steers toward a climax just about as bleak as the very sun burning out. Filmed in Westphalia, Germany, filling in for the Pacific Northwest, cinematographer Anthony Dod Mantle captures Eden and the surrounding forests as a fairy tale gone fatalistically wrong, the stark opposite of happily ever after. A catharsis never comes—von Trier leaves his audience dangling on the cliff of the abyss—nor is one intended. As such, *Antichrist* does not satisfy so much as it impresses with its sheer dauntless, sobering nerve. Love it or hate it, you cannot ignore it.

April Fool's Day

1986 - Directed by Fred Walton

Mischievously turning the conventions of the slasher film on their head a full decade before *Scream* did it, *April Fool's Day* is a smartly written, too often overlooked slice of postmodern fun. When it was released in 1986, the stalk-and-slash genre was nearing the end of its popularity within the era. Since the film was produced by Frank Mancuso Jr. and distributed by Paramount Pictures (both responsible for the *Friday the 13th* franchise), audiences naturally expected more of the same. What they got, instead, skewered the very rules they anticipated would be strictly followed, and the picture ended up being a box-office disappointment because of it. Watching *April Fool's Day* from a contemporary perspective, it reveals itself to clearly be ahead of its time in much the same way that 1994's brazenly imaginative, unsuspectingly groundbreaking *Wes Craven's New Nightmare* was.

The opening titles sequence is a memorable one. As Muffy St. John (Deborah Foreman) is cleaning up the basement of her father's island estate in preparation for a weekend get-together with her college friends, she stumbles upon a jack-in-the-box from her childhood. As the credits roll, the film flashes back to the birthday when she received the toy, and to a dirty prank her parents pulled on her that could very well have shaped who she has become as an adult. The weekend begins roughly when Buck (Mike Nomad) is involved in a ferry accident and must be rushed back to the mainland, but soon things have settled down as frivolity and some harmless April Fool's Day pranks take over.

The fun gradually dissipates when Muffy seemingly changes overnight (her cheerful personality and stylish clothing are traded in for sheer morbidity and a schoolmarm get-up), and her friends—first Muffy's cousin, Skip (Griffin O'Neal), and then the outspoken Arch (Thomas F. Wilson)—mysteriously start disappearing. By the time girl-next-door Kit (Amy Steel) spots a dead body floating under the docks and charming vixen Nikki (Deborah Goodrich) falls into a well populated by waterlogged corpses, it is safe to say that the games are over and a killer is among them.

Taking inspiration from the setup of Agatha Christie's *And Then There Were*

None, April Fool's Day places nine characters in an isolated setting and then follows them as the group quickly dwindles. Whereas the *Friday the 13th* films have always been about lining up paper-thin, albeit usually attractive, teens and then knocking them off by a masked killer, the people onscreen here are given a bit more time to develop and grow, helped in no small part by snappy dialogue from Danilo Bach's auspicious screenplay. A sequence in which Skip confides in Nan (Leah King Pinsent) about feeling like the black sheep of the St. John family is quietly effective, and another between Muffy, Kit and Nikki as they take a magazine sex quiz is funny and naturalistic through the behavior of the characters.

The viewer does not necessarily learn a great deal about everyone's background, but there is enough touched upon for them to become likable individuals. It helps, too, that they are not high schoolers, but upscale college students nearing graduation who, when asked by Arch what they plan to do with the rest of their lives, admit to having no idea what their futures hold. Furthermore, a scene in which the quiet, intellectual Nan discovers the sound of a baby crying in her bedroom via a tape recorder at first seems to just be another silly April Fool's joke, but garners further weight when it is revealed that she recently has had an abortion.

Lest it seem like *April Fool's Day* is but a talky, introspective bore, the film does a solid job of intermixing the character work with a well-paced horror plot that grows creepier and more involving once the ensemble has been whittled down to only a few. The climax, wherein Kit and boyfriend Rob (Ken Olandt) piece together the dark secrets from Muffy's past as they sense an immediate danger lurking around them, generates slick suspense, several indelible images (murdered baby dolls and eyes behind a painting spring to mind), and a whopper of a twist ending that lifts the picture above and beyond the typical, standard-issue slasher fare. It should be said that this surprise conclusion tends to leave some viewers feeling cheated, a claim that doesn't hold water since it is so very original and, save for maybe one or two minor story contrivances, completely logical.

Performances are above-average for what, in essence, is a modestly budgeted horror flick. The actresses, however, largely have more to work with than their male counterparts. Deborah Foreman (a temporary starlet of the 1980s whose biggest claim to fame was 1983's *Valley Girl*) is a quirky delight as Muffy St. John, warm at the onset before transforming into someone you wouldn't want to be alone with. Amy Steel (known best for her lead role in 1981's *Friday the 13th Part 2*) is an earthy beauty with real presence as protagonist Kit. And Deborah Goodrich (another actress who slipped into obscurity once the big, bad '90s rolled around) is a ball of energy and sass as Nikki, a character treated with more respect and layers than the one-note sex kitten she could have turned into.

Directed by Fred Walton and with an unconventionally eerie music score by Charles Bernstein (himself the composer of 1984's *A Nightmare on Elm Street*), *April Fool's Day* regrettably slipped through the cracks when it came to theaters, but has found a deserved cult following in the years since. A loose 2008 remake of the same name went straight-to-DVD, its only worth being that it proved how superior the original was, and still is. *April Fool's Day* isn't completely reinventive, but it deserves its share of accolades for taking a sharp U-turn away from the same old thing and into fresh territory that hadn't been mined nearly as often in horror films of this ilk. Even today, it holds up as a spooky, flirty entertainment, doing justice to the folly and mirth of its namesake holiday.

Baghead

2008 - Directed by Jay Duplass and Mark Duplass

Baghead takes two disparate genres—a relationship comedy in the mumblecore mode and an eerie thriller one stab wound away from being a slasher film—and juggles them together, creating a refreshingly drastic change of pace from what moviegoers have grown accustomed to expect in today's cinematic landscape of formulaic predictability. Shot lucidly with handheld cameras and styled with a *cinéma vérité* approach that drops the viewer off in the midst of lives authentically being lived, writer-director brothers Jay and Mark Duplass have the beats, rhythms, and meaningful silence of everyday human interaction down to a science. When they finally introduce the film's darker potential as a horror movie, their subdued aim for scares is effective precisely because enough unhurried time has been spent with their characters to genuinely care about them as real people.

Beyond all of that, *Baghead* is a motion picture about the natural desire to create art and find meaning in one's existence. In the case of struggling actor friends Matt (Ross Partridge), Chad (Steve Zissis), Catherine (Elise Muller) and Michelle (Greta Gerwig), the former three know full-well that they are aging fast and have but a limited window in which to hit it big in their careers. By comparison, Michelle is younger and more impressionable, just starting out in the business and still without an agent. She also, evidently, has not made it clear that her relationship with the chunky, less-assured Chad is one that she sees as strictly platonic. Carnally, Michelle is more interested in Matt—the one with the "Elvis hair," as Chad enviously tells him—despite his romantic history with Catherine.

Following their attendance at a film festival screening of dreadfully pretentious indie flick *We Are Naked*, the four of them are convinced that they could make something better (and create great parts for themselves while they're at it). Traveling up to a remote house in woodsy Big Bear, California, they set out to tackle writing a screenplay over a long weekend. Their first problem is that they have no idea what their film should be about, and their second is that someone with a paper bag over his or her head is lurking outside. Is it one of them playing a trick on the others, or is there a more immediate threat?

Baghead is original and unassumingly earnest, a fascinating slice-of-life impeded upon by the addition of a faceless, possibly dangerous figure into the equation. The filmmaking talent that Jay and Mark Duplass possess is their ability to pull so much from their actors without even needing them to say a word. Matt, Chad, Michelle and Catherine could be developed more fully—their individual backgrounds are skimmed over—but an inordinate amount is gauged about who they are and what they want through the way they carry themselves, the way they stumble awkwardly over their intentions, and the way that they always seem to be thinking and taking in information even in their moments of quiet.

Matt and Chad, in their early thirties, have yet to win the kind of acting role that will get them noticed, while Catherine, roughly the same age, seems well aware of the sell-by date on actresses in Hollywood. That they and Michelle endeavor to write themselves a film is well and good, but, as Matt asks Catherine in one scene, "How many times have we started something and never finished it?" For Chad, his self-consciousness in his profession—he never seems to be good enough, smart enough, or handsome enough—wins out in a painfully funny sequence where he tries to make a move on Michelle, only for her to cheerily rebuff his advances and compare him to her brother. To make the humiliation worse, Michelle, not out of spite but simply out of cluelessness, starts putting little hairclips all over his head.

When Michelle drinks too much on the first night and falls asleep, she experiences a frightening dream about a person with a bag over his or her head standing outside amidst the underbrush. It's so vivid the next morning, in fact, that her description wins over Matt on what the premise of their script should be. Idea sessions follow, and so does an ominous occurrence where Michelle comes face to face in her bedroom with the mysterious stranger from her dream. She naturally assumes it is Matt who has shown up to scare her, but it turns out not to be. Could the culprit be Catherine or Chad playing a trick on her, angry about her attraction to Matt and out to give her a fright? They deny the accusations, but then, how well can someone really trust the word of actors? This subplot, for the most part taking a backseat to the relaxed interplay between friends, slowly rises to the forefront in the third act. It leads to a scene involving the discovery of an obscured car in the woods that is armrest-clenching in its tension, and a final revelation that is fairly predictable, but also credible and fitting.

Beautifully acted by a leading foursome who never seem to be acting at all—their total embodiment of their characters is the ultimate compliment that can be given to them—*Baghead* carries a loose, conversational quality that allows the audience to feel as if they are right there with them, spending some time with good friends. As the sweetly dippy Michelle, Greta Gerwig (who has since gone on to much acclaim in films such as 2010's *Greenberg*, 2011's *Arthur*, 2012's *Lola Versus*, and 2013's *Frances Ha*) is an extraordinary find, her slow-mannered speech either at odds with her brain processes or in perfect step. Gerwig's adorable quirkiness is offset by her unaffected beauty, and she is never less than delightful to watch onscreen. Alternately hilarious, subtly sinister, and finally poignant, *Baghead* is not quite like any other film in memory. The concluding moments are just right, suggesting that the quartet may creatively be onto something that could find them the accolades they've been hungering for. As is typical of Hollywood, though, their success is not a definite, and where they go next has yet to be discovered.

Behind the Mask:
The Rise of Leslie Vernon
2007 - Directed by Scott Glosserman

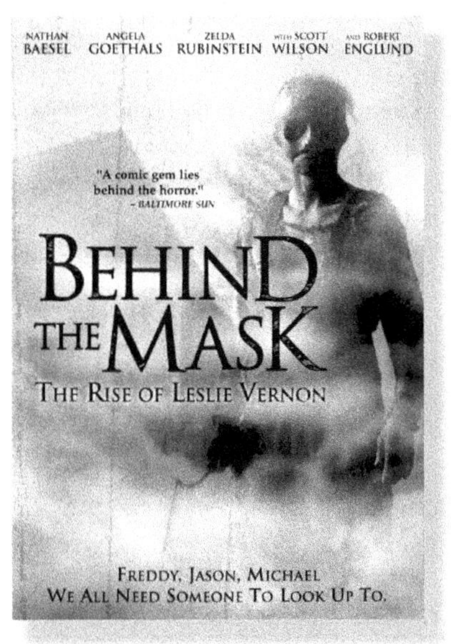

An ingenious modern take on the stalk-and-slash genre, *Behind the Mask: The Rise of Leslie Vernon* is a satiric version of *The Blair Witch Project*, a mockumentary on the order of Christopher Guest, and an old-school, late-'70s/early-'80s mad-slasher flick all rolled into one. One of those rare indie horror efforts that deserved to see a wide theatrical release with a major distributor (Anchor Bay ultimately released it), the film marks an auspicious debut for writer-director Scott Glosserman.

Along with co-screenwriter David J. Stieve, Glosserman has reimagined a world in which Jason Voorhees, Freddy Krueger, Michael Myers and the rest of the top cinematic killers of horny teens have resided. Hoping to follow in their bloody paths and make an infamous name for himself is Leslie Vernon (Nathan Baesel), who has agreed to be the centerpiece of a documentary being made by aspiring grad school film major Taylor Gentry (Angela Goethals). Following brief trips to Camp Crystal Lake, Springwood and Haddonfield for a little background on the serial killers of the past, Taylor narrows her gaze on Leslie.

Something of a myth in the sleepy Maryland town of Glen Echo—he is thought to have been killed by local residents years ago—Leslie is in the middle of serious preparations for his planned reign of teen slaughter. As she follows his day-to-day actions—lots of cardio training to get himself into shape, and the stalking of virginal 17-year-old high schooler Kelly (Kate Lang Johnson), who he has labeled "Survivor Girl"—Taylor has no idea what she has gotten herself into until Leslie's systematic plans of murder become all too real. Will Taylor be able to stand by and let Leslie pick off the clan of teen victims one at a time, or does she have it in her to try and stop him?

Behind the Mask: The Rise of Leslie Vernon works on several different levels, sometimes all at once. For a long time, the film is a very funny comedy (not on the broad order of a *Scary Movie* entry, but as a sly comment on the tried-and-true conventions of the classic slasher blueprint). Somewhere toward the middle of the second act, Leslie—who until now has portrayed himself as an affable, well-mannered fellow—snaps at Taylor and shoves her against the side of her production van. She has begun to get in his way and pass judgments where they aren't wanted, and in that crucial moment the viewer sees a more dangerous and demented side of Leslie's psyche that accurately sets up the dark-toned climax. The film isn't as frightening as it could have been—the chosen teen victims are never more than one-dimensional walking clichés even when things turn serious; the violence and viscera are a little too reserved to reach the level of inspiration that surrounds them, and the jokiness in the first half marginally lessens the scare potential of the third act—but the picture remains an enthralling experience that refuses to shortchange its own imagination.

More than anything, *Behind the Mask: The Rise of Leslie Vernon* will be a treat for anyone who reads *Fangoria* or has seen his or her fair share of "Dead Teenager" movies. Giddy in its use of self-referencing (think of the *Scream* series, but skewered an extra notch), the number of throwbacks to movies of old are, indeed, so plentiful and encompassing that it would take many viewings to catch them all. On first glance, some of the most clever homages include the returns to the fictional settings of Springwood and Haddonfield (filmed at the actual houses used in Wes Craven's *A Nightmare on Elm Street* and John Carpenter's *Halloween*), a brief appearance of the jump-roping children from *A Nightmare on Elm Street*, a classical song cue from *The Shining*, and the best use of a barn in a horror film since *Friday the 13th Part 3-D*. There is also a Captain Ahab character (much reminiscent of the late Donald Pleasence's Dr. Loomis) in the form of Doc Halloran (Robert Englund), Leslie's determined arch-nemesis, and a hilarious cameo from *Poltergeist* veteran Zelda Rubinstein as a helpful librarian with a penchant for over-detailing expository information. Rubinstein (who passed away in 2010) gets the biggest laughs with her pricelessly overzealous line deliveries of some purposefully exaggerated dialogue.

Save for an always-welcome Robert Englund, this time playing quirky good guy Doc Halloran, and Scott Wilson, as Leslie's offbeat mentor, Eugene, the picture belongs to the outstanding work of Angela Goethals and Nathan Baesel. While the rest of the supporting players commit to their roles and do a nice job, they are fairly peripheral to the main storyline. Goethals, an underutilized actress who has been around for years (she played one of Macaulay Culkin's sisters in 1990's *Home Alone*) but not gotten the recognition she deserves, is naturalistic, always convincing, and ultimately sympathetic as documentary maker Taylor Gentry, who slowly comes to realize how in over her head she has gotten. Goethals is also an ace at reactionary facial expressions that sell the unlikely premise of an even-keeled filmmaker following a psychopath around as he prepares for his killing spree. In his first feature film lead, Baesel is superbly funny—and then creepy—as Leslie Vernon, having a blast as he puts a spin on what Jason Voorhees or Michael Myers might be like during their off-time. When it's time to get down to business, however, Leslie isn't fooling around, and it's a testament to Baesel that he is able to plausibly make that haunting switch between seeming harmless and threatening.

In bringing *Behind the Mask: The Rise of Leslie Vernon* to the screen, director

Scott Glosserman delights in juggling different tones, both light and dramatic, as well as his audience's expectations. It isn't that Glosserman surprises in his plot developments—most of them are admittedly predictable—but that he uses those very archaic slasher film conventions in a way that wryly comments on their silliness while simultaneously revitalizing the formula because of them. Special kudos also for the inclusion of The Talking Heads' atmospheric song, "Psycho Killer," during the brilliantly realized end-credits sequence. Big fun that mixes well its comic aspirations with gritty, down-and-dirty suspense, *Behind the Mask: The Rise of Leslie Vernon* doesn't just document the title madman's trek toward gruesome infamy, but also the introduction of an original and invigorating new filmmaking talent. Having earned a small but passionate cult following since its release, the picture should deservedly position Glosserman next to Eli Roth and Alexandre Aja as a modern connoisseur of the genre.

Beyond the Black Rainbow

2012 - Directed by Panos Cosmatos

A psychedelic study in free will. A freaky-deaky meditation on the brevity of life. A fantastical crescendo of the futuristic present as seen through 1983 aesthetics. A collection of imagery and sound that doesn't pay homage so much as it seriously equates itself to the calling-card work of yesteryear by the likes of Argento, Carpenter, Kubrick, Cronenberg, Lynch and Hooper. In *Beyond the Black Rainbow*, which holds a rhythm, feel and moody intuition all its own, writer-director Panos Cosmatos displays a reverence for these aforementioned artists, but sees no use for mimicry when his own vision is so startlingly unique. An uncategorical corkscrew of genres—sci-fi, horror, tragedy, mystery and exploratory razzmatazz all have their moment in the spotlight—the film demands a lot of the viewer, but also gives a lot in return. Strictly mainstream-minded audiences might as well take their business elsewhere. The adventurous, meanwhile, will probably long for multiple viewings. Like *2001: A Space Odyssey* crossed with *Vanilla Sky*, *Poltergeist*, *Halloween* and *Inland Empire*, it's the kind of special, remarkably rare motion picture that should keep on giving through the ensuing decades, so overflowing with lofty ideas, bizarre head trips, and out-there flights of nightmarish fancy that one could see it fifty times and probably get something new out of it in each sitting.

At the sterile, labyrinthine, neon-infused Arboria Institute, scientist Barry Nye (Michael Rogers) has taken up where his predecessor, the now-elderly Dr. Mercurio Arboria (Scott Hylands), left off. Following neuropsychological practices that incorporate heavy doses of pharmacology and energy sculpting to achieve a state of happiness in his patients—"Serenity Through Technology" is the company's tagline and way of life—all that the good doctor has really done is left the young, fair Elena (Eva Allan) borderline-catatonic as she longs deep down inside her drugged exterior for a way to escape. When he manages to bring tears to her eyes after one session together, Barry remarks with a silky slither, "This is always the highlight of my day." One can almost see why. Save for a wife (Marilyn Norry) at home who seems to be perpetually distant, Barry's life outside of the desolate chambers of Arboria is lonesome and miserable, his respective search for contentment coming in the form of five blue pills he swallows down in the bathroom each night. Were the company not such a secret, built beneath a handsome domed garden, the FDA would have shut it down years ago and sent all the workers to the loony bin. Darker forces are at work, however, paving a path all the way back to 1966 when the start of the facility, the birth of Mercurio's child, and an inky dip into a hellish portal all came together in one fateful moment.

Beyond the Black Rainbow is close to impossible to mold down into a tidy synopsis, and even more difficult to accurately explain the experience of watching it. That's part of the thrill, though. Shot for very little money but so propulsive in its look and ambition that it could just as easily have cost many millions, the film's either reminiscent of a fever dream, or a bout of hypnosis, or both. Cosmatos, who might be some kind of genius behind his willowy veil of novice pretensions, has made an unforgettable art piece as much as he has a creepy fright pic. The root to his madness, he has explained in interviews, is simple. As a child, he was not allowed to watch violent horror movies, but while at the video store he would constantly see the vivid VHS boxes to these very films and try to imagine what they were like. Naturally, his imagination ran rampant, and *Beyond the Black Rainbow* is his attempt to put those thoughts into something of a cohesive whole. Whether he's entirely successful or not is up for debate—some of the ideas and content is more mature and complex than what a kid could accurately form in his mind—but it's a fascinating experiment all the same. For all of its loopy tangents—telepathy and mind-control; a mysterious garbled call from a phone not plugged in; a flashback told through ominous plumes of cloud and smoke and intentionally overexposed film stock, and the transformation of one character into a demonic, knife-wielding psychopath all play a part in the proceedings—it is a miracle how most of the narrative threads come together for those paying attention.

With his slow, measured, monotone deliveries, Michael Rogers, as Barry Nye, very nearly works the viewer into the same submission that he does poor Elena. A willing sacrificial lamb who will do anything for the Arboria Institute, he finds himself at a loss how to carry on when he's at home. For a man taking wrongheaded but earnest steps to achieve happiness in his patients, his is a spectacularly depressing existence. In playing things so straight, Rogers is able to subtly unleash the malevolence laying in wait underneath. One must remember that, for all intents and purposes, he is also a psychologically punishing kidnapper, and maybe something even more sinister than that. As founder Mercurio Arboria, Scott Hylands is seen as a younger man in a grainy advertisement for the company, and then later as a withered old soul on the edge of dying. From his bed, he watches a promotional tape about a beautiful island resort, haunting in its implications as his life slips away from him. "Paradise comes and goes," the narrator on the video says. "Aloha, and, far too quickly, farewell."

Very deliberate in its pacing, *Beyond the Black Rainbow* is the epitome of a slow burn. Some may be frustrated by the way Cosmatos edits each scene—

indeed, since she's still fighting a drugged haze, even Elena's third-act attempt to escape never rises above a feet-dragging walk—but pulled together, there's an entrancing poetry to it all. Jeremy Schmidt's synthesizer theme music is outstanding, like John Carpenter by way of Goblin, while the cinematography by Norm Li outdoes itself, each shot taking on the appearance of a vibrant-colored painting as seen through the eyes of a hallucinating, time-traveling hippie from the 1960s whose just stepped foot into 1983 after a quick trip to 2075. The conclusion, paying off elements mentioned all the way back in the first scene, sees Elena taking a ghastly elevator ride (memories of 2012's *The Cabin in the Woods* are unmistakable) and coming into contact with the facility's front as a majestic domed greenhouse before literally rising from a grate in the ground. In taking what could be her first steps outside, she is rendered a newborn once more, her attempts to get away alternating with an in-pursuit Barry's journey down a nighttime dirt road, the seemingly endless farmland on both sides illuminated by his headlights. Evocatively, a final image of a glowing TV in the window of a suburban house reminds of an earlier scene where Ronald Reagan is seen making a speech about the Soviet threat. Elena may be away from immediate harm, but her newfound innocence won't last for long amidst the harsh realities of the real world. At the very least, her life will now be her own to live. *Beyond the Black Rainbow* is imperfect, but gloriously so, creating, in its own way, a new, exciting, disorienting, unsettling and long-overdue filmic language. It confidently stands apart as a motion picture not quite like any other.

Black Swan

2010 - Directed by Darren Aronofsky

What director Darren Aronofsky did for Mickey Rourke and wrestling in 2008's *The Wrestler*, he does for Natalie Portman and ballet—with a macabre bent—in *Black Swan*, an enrapturingly inventive psychological drama that dabbles in several different genres and defies easy categorization. On the one hand, it's a vividly conceived character study about a young woman's overwhelming drive to succeed at the prestigious, but ultimately fleeting, profession she has chosen. The often handheld camerawork by cinematographer Matthew Libatique never stops following the protagonist, frequently from behind like an invisible guardian angel, almost disappearing within her shoes. What she goes through, the viewer goes through, her accomplishments and downfalls meaning all the more because of Aronofsky's blistering human snapshot. Not stopping there, the picture also works as a mystery, as a candid glimpse into the disciplined, physically grueling, sacrificial world of ballet dancing, and as a colorfully artsy horror film of the sort Dario Argento might have made decades ago (echoes of 1977's *Suspiria* cannot be a total coincidence).

As a member of a distinguished New York City Ballet company, Nina Sayers (Natalie Portman) is well into her twenties and sensing that if she ever hopes to rise to the top of the ranks among her colleagues, she'd better do it soon. She is a splendid dancer whose sharp technique gets in the way of her outward passion, and creative director Thomas Leroy (Vincent Cassel) is unsure she has what it takes to play the dual lead roles of the White Swan and Black Swan in an upcoming production of Tchaikovsky's *Swan Lake*. Through a little luck and a fateful private encounter with Thomas, Nina nabs the part, leaving longtime, over-the-hill prima ballerina Beth MacIntyre (Winona Ryder) out in the cold. Nina is thrilled to finally have the star turn, and so is her domineering mother, Erica (Barbara Hershey), but the rigors of rehearsal slowly begin to get the best of her. Overworked and increasingly paranoid that new fellow dancer Lily (Mila Kunis) is conniving to steal the role from under her, Nina's mental state unhinges with grisly results as opening night draws near.

Physically and dramatically, Natalie Portman is nothing short of stunning as Nina Sayers (there is a reason she earned an Academy Award for this performance). Having trained for six months prior to shooting, a lithe but fittingly muscular Portman looks every bit like the ballerina she's playing, and the lack of cutaways for stunt performers and stand-ins ensure that she does nearly all the dancing herself. It's an amazing transformation, one that Portman has clearly given her full body and soul toward. When Nina discovers she has won the coveted lead in *Swan Lake* and drops into a bathroom stall to call her mother and give her the good news, her utter elation is so infectious it's impossible not to smile. Alas, that happiness is short-lived as Nina gets down to business and starts struggling to capture the sexual ferocity of the Black Swan. All the while, Aronofsky paints a visually foreboding, off-kilter canvas mirroring both the plot of *Swan Lake* and Nina's descent into what may very well be madness.

Black Swan is fascinating it its uncompromising depiction of what goes into ballet dancing (busted toenails and cracking bones are just the tip of the iceberg). Likewise, its cutthroat competitive nature bristles with a claustrophobic coldness that takes the fun out of training, but makes watching it all the more riveting. Screenwriters Mark Heyman, Andres Heinz and John McLaughlin effectively weave a creepy atmosphere into the proceedings, first subtly (Nina swears that she keeps seeing a doppelgänger of herself around the city, and also spots out of the corner of her eye one of her mother's paintings move) and then with violent force. By the final third, grim surrealism takes over, leading to a conclusion that dare not be discussed except to say that it's as wickedly conceived as it is unforgettably original. Even so, there does come the feeling that Aronofsky does not push things as far as he could have. One sees how the creep factor could have become downright terrifying with a few uninhibited tweaks, its aura of unhinged determination a kaleidoscopic nightmare were the filmmaker to have embraced his genre leanings. Because so much of the film is predicated on what happens at the very end, the whole comes off as more of a crafty exercise than the more down-to-earth human story it begins as.

In a stripped-down cast of supporting characters, all the actors indelibly leave an imprint. Vincent Cassel perfectly embodies that of tough, unsentimental ballet director Thomas Leroy, talented as an instructor but also just as willing to spit out his students if they are getting a little long in the tooth or don't provide what he's looking for. Mila Kunis is alluring and appropriately shady as fellow dancer Lily, her intentions left open for interpretation. As the dark swan to Nina's good one, does Lily really care about being friends with Nina, or is it all an elaborate means of stealing ahead herself? As Nina's mother, Erica, Barbara Hershey is a frightful villainess, deceptively caring at the onset before her cheery veneer cracks to reveal a horrid, possibly psychotic shrew whose only means of living is through her daughter. Finally, Winona Ryder bitterly stands on the fringe as Beth MacIntyre, cast aside by a younger, fresher face and sickened by the thought of having to go through the formalities of handing down the gauntlet to a person who basically has stolen her job. Ryder isn't on screen for long, but her tragic character haunts the company even after she's gone.

In a narrative that grows in abstraction the further it presses on, it is difficult to consistently tell reality from mind games. *Black Swan* toys with this confusion so that what might be considered a plot hole in a more straightforward tale instead just comes off as another piece of the deceptive puzzle. Intriguing to a fault—if not always on solid ground about what kind of film it wants to be—the picture is enriched not only by Natalie Portman's *tour de force* turn, but also by the classically fueled music score by Clint Mansell and the exquisitely detailed, at times dreamlike, art direction by David Stein. The story of one person's desire to succeed even at the expense of her mental health and everything else she holds dear, *Black Swan* may not sway many viewers toward Nina's career path, but plenty should be flooding theatres afterwards to see the one-of-a-kind art form up close and personal.

The Blair Witch Project

1999 - Directed by Eduardo Sánchez and Daniel Myrick

"In October of 1994, three student filmmakers disappeared in the woods near Burkittsville, Maryland while shooting a documentary. A year later their footage was found."

With this foreboding opening text, so begins *The Blair Witch Project*, a microscopically budgeted, largely improvised faux-documentary made by first-time directors Eduardo Sánchez and Daniel Myrick. Its mark on cinema history should not be marginalized. Originally billed as actual found footage documenting the days before three college students disappeared—"missing" flyers were even posted around the Maryland-DC-Virginia area—the film sent audiences at the 1999 Sundance Film Festival into a frenzy, its authenticity causing some to think they had just witnessed a virtual snuff movie. As the buzz grew, the Orlando-based Haxan Films production company carved out a viral campaign—really, one of the first of its kind—in the days when Internet-based film promotion was still in its infancy. By the time the picture came to theaters nationwide in the summer of '99 and grossed a staggering $248-million worldwide, its self-made mythology had become practically legendary. People had to see the movie for themselves, and, until its actors began showing up on talk shows soon after, some viewers continued to believe there was nothing fictional about it. Beyond that, the film is responsible for starting the trend of first-person POV flicks that are still, to this day, getting made. There have been some great ones—2007's *[REC]* and 2008's *Cloverfield* spring to mind—but *The Blair Witch Project* remains the best of the bunch.

Supposedly culled from 16mm and video footage found in the woods of Burkittsville, Maryland, the story kicks off with a trio of Montgomery College students preparing for their trip to the sleepy town in question. Home of the infamous local legend known as the Blair Witch who, as the residents they interview tell it, lurks within the Black Hills Forest, Burkittsville's lore grows shadier the more the filmmakers learn about it. With a string of child murders in the 1940s committed by a man named Rustin Parr perhaps its most shameful stain, Burkittsville's Blair Witch looms mysteriously over the stories of the past and present. Playfully shrugging off such horrific tales, the headstrong Heather

(Heather Donahue), constantly with a Hi-8 video camera in her hand, leads Josh (Joshua Leonard), shooting with a grainy black-and-white 16mm camera, and Michael (Michael Williams), the sound technician, deep into the woods for what is supposed to be a simple two-day excursion. It doesn't turn out that way, however, as they ultimately never make it back to their car on the second day and are forced to set up camp another night. Faint footsteps are heard in the distance and stick figures and eerie symbols are found hanging from the trees. With their map and compass lost, the days tick by, their food dwindling and the freezing, pitch-black nights punctuated by increasingly threatening cackling noises and screams surrounding them. Hopelessly lost within the mouth of the forest, the three students have no choice but to come to terms with the stark gravity of their situation as they begin to reconstruct their personal visions of what raw, unadulterated horror really is.

Shortly after *The Blair Witch Project* premiered at Sundance but several months before it came to multiplexes, an unlabeled VHS cassette ended up in my possession. How and why, I do not recall, but the copy on the tape was of poor quality, shaky and heavily grainy with audio that clearly had not received its final release-ready sound mix. Normally, this would not be an attractive viewing situation, but, for *The Blair Witch Project*, it was entirely ideal, magnifying the film's plausibility and rustic aesthetic tenfold while making the whole thing all the more petrifying. That the publicity machine had not yet shifted into overdrive was another positive. I was savvy enough to know the film wasn't a documentary, but that didn't keep it from working its unforgettable spell upon my widened eyes. Choosing to watch the picture for the first time alone in a darkened house was either a smart decision, or a very dumb one. By the end, I was curled up in my chair, literally shaking, filled with so many strong, passionate emotions that it was difficult to decipher them all. Afterward, every opened doorway in my house became another opportunity for the Blair Witch to leap out.

Years later, *The Blair Witch Project* has been the subject of frequent lampoonery and a public backlash from viewers who were either disappointed it did not live up to their heightened expectations, affected by the audience they first saw it with, or are too young to remember just how novel its premise and style were back in 1999. Taken in its proper context, it endures as a landmark of the horror genre, breaking ground in every way while proving talent and ingenuity are much more important than budget when it comes to making a good motion picture. The antithesis of the post-*Scream*, pre-manufactured slasher era, the film is drenched in such a thick, smothering veil of hopeless dread and utter realism that it finally ceases to merely be a "movie" and is transformed into something that means and says more—about dreams, about responsibility, about life and death.

Unlike very few features that had been seen up to this point, *The Blair Witch Project* is shot from the point of view of the characters' cameras. This *cinéma vérité* style adds to the constant feeling that what is being watched is genuine, dropping one smack dab in the middle of an absolute nightmare. Jittery, shaky and hand-held, the lens ultimately takes on a life all its own, used as a thematically loaded metaphor for the off-kilter frame of mind the characters are forced to obtain as their spirits diminish and they start to question whether they will survive their dire, inexplicable ordeal.

To put it bluntly, there is no acting in *The Blair Witch Project*. There *is* in the strictest sense, since Heather Donahue, Michael Williams and Joshua Leonard are playing characters (despite having the same names), but there isn't a minute, a second, or even a frame where one can catch the performers "acting." Their committed, entirely unaffected performances often do not get the proper credit; without them, the film's perilous balance would be thrown off. Starting as a confident young woman and the leader of the group, Heather gradually finds that her need to always be right is only a façade to hide her own weaknesses and fears for the future. Vulnerable and beyond frightened, their communication breaking down, she, Michael and Joshua eventually have nothing to do but pray that they will make their way out of the seemingly endless wilderness before whatever really is out there gets them. In a late scene filled with unquenchably raw power and honesty, Heather films her last rites, the camera framed on her right eye and nose as she devastatingly pours all of her emotions out, confessing to the faults in her own life, apologizing to her family and friends, and, finally, making peace with her destiny.

To see *The Blair Witch Project* is not to simply watch it, but to experience it. In the annals of films that can intoxicate, terrify, and leave one's spirits distinctly rattled, only the best of the best can match it. *The Blair Witch Project* isn't simply a masterpiece of the medium, but had the ability to reaffirm my dedication to the art form and my desire to write about cinema during a formidable time when adulthood and future plans were just a breath away. Writer-directors Sánchez and Myrick have never been able to replicate the one-of-a-kind success they had with this, their debut effort, but their legacy within horror's storied past is forever.

The Burning

1981 - Directed by Tony Maylam

The first movie to be distributed by Miramax Films—former head honchos Harvey and Bob Weinstein receive story and screenplay credits—*The Burning* was released in May 1981, a time when the marketplace was being inundated with knockoffs of *Halloween* and *Friday the 13th.* Though it didn't reach the success hoped for and a planned sequel was never shot, *The Burning* stands up today, over three decades later, as one of the more inspired early-'80s slasher pics. It also holds the prestige of marking the first screen appearances of a number of well-known faces, including a pre-bald Jason Alexander, Holly Hunter, and Fisher Stevens.

When a cruel but seemingly harmless prank at Camp Blackfoot goes awry, mean groundskeeper Cropsy (Lou David) is left horribly burned and an inch from death. Five years later, healed but horribly disfigured—"Sorry, the skin grafts just didn't take," the doctor tells him—Cropsy is released from St. Catherine's Hospital and heads back to his old stomping ground. Though Camp Blackfoot has since been closed down, Camp Stonewater is located on the other side of the lake, filled with playful teen girls and oversexed boys ripe for the picking. When a group of the campers, headed by counselors Todd (Brian Matthews) and Michelle (Leah Ayres), head out on an overnight canoeing trip, they become the prime targets for Cropsy's maniacal act of revenge.

It's hard to imagine *The Burning* existing without the inspiration of *Friday the 13th*. Both films are set at a summer camp, both involve killers out for vengeance over a tragedy that occurred years before, and both incorporate memorably nasty splatter and make-up effects by Tom Savini the likes of which just don't seem to get used anymore in current films of this ilk. Unlike in *Friday the 13th*, though, director Tony Maylam isn't concerned with picking off his entire cast in a race to see how high the body count can go. Oh, there's plenty of deaths at the hands of Cropsy's garden sheers, but Maylam bravely chooses to spare half of the principle cast and treat the story with a modicum of realism. Before he gets to the mayhem, he also takes the time to distinguish the summer camp atmosphere of dinner halls, softball games, outside shower stalls, and gossip sessions in the bunks. Though not everyone is developed as well as they could be, they at least are written as intelligent people. Counselors Todd and Michelle are displayed as responsible in-charge types who still treat their charges as friends and do the sensible thing when disaster strikes.

The Burning fulfills most of the requirements of the commonplace slasher film, but also bucks the trend when it comes to the cornerstone belief that sex equals death. Interestingly, one of the first victims is Karen (Carolyn Houlihan), attacked moments after denying the sexual advances of pushy sort-of boyfriend Eddy (Ned Eisenberg). Perhaps it is her nakedness—she has just gone skinny-dipping—that seals her fate. The most memorable setpiece of the picture is a doozy. When their canoes turn up missing, some of the kids agree to row back to camp on a raft to bring assistance. When they spot one of the canoes floating desolately in the distance, they slowly make their way over to it, their laughs and goofing around not preparing them for Cropsy's sudden brutal attack. It's a stylish and frightening sequence, boldly edited and appropriately catching the viewer off-guard.

The performers are well-chosen and diverse—well, as diverse as a group of strictly white kids can be—and their unforced turns are ideal in setting up the raucous milieu of teenagers away from home and attending summer camp. Leah Ayres, who would go on to rack up a load of television credits, is fresh and eye-catching as counselor Michelle. Larry Joshua is too old for the role of Glazer, but he's got a great look and the macho bonehead act down pat. Jason Alexander (who, of course, would go on to star in TV's *Seinfeld*) stands out even with little to do as wisecracking Dave, an obvious natural even this early on. And, as Tiger, Shelley Bruce (just coming off of the title part in Broadway's *Annie*) is a red-haired bottle of peppiness.

As is a customary downfall of low-budgeters of the era, *The Burning* has a few awkward filmmaking moments, including some unfashionable fade-outs between scenes and a few parts where it looks to change from day to night and back again. In a way, this gives it a certain charm. The third act does admittedly drag out a bit too much, but the climactic confrontation with Cropsy in an old mine shaft holds two jump-out-your-seat moments that work like gangbusters. The wrap-up, bringing the legend of Cropsy around full-circle for a new set of campers, sends things out on a satisfying note. *The Burning* has never received the respect or fame of *Friday the 13th*, but it is as good as, and maybe a little smarter than, that Sean S. Cunningham original.

Cabin Fever

2003 - Directed by Eli Roth

Following a year of hype after it took the 2002 Toronto International Film Festival by storm, director Eli Roth's low-budget *Cabin Fever* was blessed with a sizable marketing campaign and a 2,000+ screen count that matched, if not surpassed, most studio horror films of the day. While hype is a dangerous thing (look no further than the backlash for 1999's *The Blair Witch Project* for proof) and *Cabin Fever* ultimately does not match it, the film was as faithful (at the time of its release) as any twenty-first century effort had come to matching the look and feel of a 1970s "backwoods" splatter flick. The superior *House of 1000 Corpses* came close, and *Wrong Turn* trailed right behind in inspiration, but *Cabin Fever* gets it just right. In fact, a close knowledge of that era's horror genre (think *The Last House on the Left*, *The Hills Have Eyes* and *The Evil Dead*) is almost a necessity in fully appreciating what *Cabin Fever* has to offer, and Roth makes no bones about it from the unsettling opening credits to the outrageous, borderline-inappropriate final scenes.

The catch is that, instead of a masked psychopath or demonic forces or inbred rednecks as the villain, the slasher here is a flesh-eating virus to which, once infected, there is no escape. To celebrate the end of their college careers, five happy-go-lucky friends—platonic pals Paul (Rider Strong) and Karen (Jordan Ladd), horny couple Jeff (Joey Kern) and Marcy (Cerina Vincent), and solo doofus Bert (James DeBello)—travel to a middle-of-nowhere cabin in the woods for a week of partying. Their fun is cut short when they come into contact with a hermit with a very serious, highly contagious virus that has him coughing up blood and his skin falling off. Once dispatching of him, the five buddies turn against each other as paranoia sets in and they start exhibiting some gruesome symptoms of their own.

Cabin Fever is a stomach-churning, blood-drenched romp that deserves points simply for being worthy of these adjectives in today's times. Too often, horror films are forced to play it safe, either falling victim to the MPAA's asinine rampage or getting watered down to a PG-13 by their studio. With enough sex and Karo syrup to make Wes Craven blush and Sam Raimi stand up and take notice, *Cabin Fever* is a gory (this goes without saying) and grim experience. It's definitely not the type of horror movie your grandma used to know.

Had *Cabin Fever* remained a straight scare picture, it might have been a masterpiece, as unrelenting and genuinely disturbing as any in the recent years leading up to its release. In his quest to remain truthful to the '70s, however, writer-director Eli Roth has also seen fit to include the kind of off-the-wall black humor prevalent of the time period. It works for the majority of the running time (such as a party-animal cop the kids run into, joyously played by Giuseppe Andrews), because off-weighing the comedy is a story that becomes exceedingly more nerve-racking and horrific by the minute. As we meet and initially get to know the five protagonists, we are charmed by their camaraderie, which is laid-back and accurate to the way real friends act around each other. And then, as they become infected by the virus one by one and suddenly see their hopes and dreams (and lives) cut short, the result is not only terrifying, but also sort of poignant.

The leads, including Rider Strong and Cerina Vincent, ably fulfill the requirements of their roles, looking scared on command and digging into the dark reality of the situation. Deserving special note is James DeBello, stealing every scene as simultaneously lovable and frustrating jokester Bert. We all inevitably know someone like Bert, and DeBello takes the role to the limit.

Astute to the conventions of the genre, Eli Roth (in an admittedly quite impressive directorial debut) successfully creates a rising tension and palpably alarming atmosphere that becomes nearly suffocating in the final half-hour. Regrettably, because the villain is not a human or supernatural force and there is no way to stop the virus, Roth paints himself into a corner that he seems unsure how to get out of. The final ten minutes are at a loss for where to go, and the horror that had been so effective is replaced in favor of oddball, jokey plot developments and an irony-filled final scene that is just a little too cute by a half. Instead of walking out of the theater with chills running down one's spine at the end, Roth sends his viewers out laughing and, undoubtedly for some, unsure of what to make of it all.

This, then, returns us full-circle to the original point. Casual moviegoers who are fans of *Scream* and *I Know What You Did Last Summer* but have no idea who lived on *The Last House on the Left* will be bewildered by the final segment of *Cabin Fever*. However, those who are well-versed on '70s gore flicks will know exactly what Eli Roth has done, and what he has achieved, giggling in acknowledgment afterwards for an entirely different set of reasons than why a casual teenybopper might. Even when *Cabin Fever* first came out, it was nigh impossible not to smell a cult following in the making.

The Cabin in the Woods

2012 - Directed by Drew Goddard

The Cabin in the Woods may have been the most difficult film to review in 2012. Every angle one wishes to discuss is an instant invitation for providing spoilers, even of the inadvertent variety, and yet this is one special cinematic experience that viewers would be wise to know as little about as possible walking in. The smashing directorial debut of Drew Goddard (writer of 2008's *Cloverfield* and TV's *Lost*) and respective brainchild of he and co-scribe Joss Whedon (TV's *Buffy the Vampire Slayer*), the film audaciously, at times awe-inspiringly, subverts, toys with and tramples upon every cliché and expectation that typically comes with a genre pic set in this one's foreboding title locale. Like a post-modern update of 1987's *Evil Dead II: Dead by Dawn* as masterminded by a Lovecraft-obsessed existentialist who has set out to make the ultimate horror movie to end all horror movies, *The Cabin in the Woods* is blackly comic, thrillingly creepy, and then something wholly transcendent.

In order to not give anything major away plot-wise, all that can be described is what happens in the first act. Following that, all bets are off for anyone who thinks they know where things are headed. Five college friends—semi-virginal good girl Dana (Kristen Connolly), intellectual Holden (Jesse Williams), jock Curt (Chris Hemsworth), newly blonde sexpot Jules (Anna Hutchison), and faithful stoner Marty (Fran Kranz)—set out for a weekend getaway to Curt's cousin's rustic, secluded cabin, without a clue that they are being tracked by shady men in business attire who are keeping surveillance on them. On their way, the kids stop for gas, ignoring the harbingers of doom spouted off by the kooky attendant (Tim De Zarn) before continuing to their middle-of-nowhere destination. The cabin has its eccentricities—there are violent old paintings on the wall and a one-way mirror separating two bedrooms—but they're not about to let this ruin their fun. The deadly forces they've just released from reading a Latin incantation in a diary they've found in the cellar will do that for them.

The pleasure of each new surprise and ingenious discovery in *The Cabin in the Woods* was one of the biggest treats of its release year's cinematic landscape. The film was undoubtedly 2012's most giddily imaginative, so fresh and different as to not only be groundbreaking, but also transformative. If 1996's *Scream* made audiences self-aware of slasher tropes, commenting upon them even as they were carried out, *The Cabin in the Woods* does something very similar, then goes another step toward true meta-toppling clarity. To not be able to talk about the film but in general terms is to give those possible viewers on the fence about seeing it the wrong impression. This is not your ordinary, everyday splatter flick about stupid young people going into the woods and getting killed. Well, yeah, there is a little of that, but the characters are attractively defined, likable as they move beyond archetypes, and the places the movie goes are unlike anywhere a picture of this sort has dared go, or been smart enough to think about going, before.

The screenplay, expertly weaving together interconnected tales—that of the imperiled friends at the cabin, and two veteran colleagues, Sitterson (Richard Jenkins) and Hadley (Bradley Whitford), manning a mysterious control center—is superb in the way that it does not try to fool the viewer, or stack all its cards on a single twist of some kind. Instead, it lays the players out on the table by the five-minute mark and then gradually but surely builds and builds throughout as mounting revelations lead to a phantasmagoric climax powerful and savvy enough to turn everyone watching it into a kid again. The very act of seeing it unfold might have some viewers in disbelief. Before this final twenty minutes of immeasurable creepy-crawly fun—leading, it should be noted, to an unexpectedly poignant ending that considers the fleeting state of one's mortality—director Drew Goddard has a field day mounting tension in the face of perverse laughs, and vice versa. A scene where Jules is dared to make out with the head of a wolf mounted on the wall is one of the film's scariest, most cringe-inducing moments, regardless if the sharp-toothed creature comes to life to bite her head off or not. It's the anticipation of wicked things this way coming that are sometimes more effective than the payoff, anyway. P.S. The zinger is that Goddard knows his payoff is a one hundred percent bull's-eye.

The Cabin the Woods was a long time coming. Shot in early 2009 and originally scheduled for theaters in February 2010, distributor MGM ultimately had no choice but to sell off their unreleased titles after filing for bankruptcy. Then there was the flirtation with needlessly converting it into 3-D, an idea that Goddard and Whedon smartly fought against. At long last, the film was eventually bought by Lionsgate. Not only that, but the studio believed in the project so much that they backed its wide theatrical release three years later with a full marketing and promotional push behind it—and not a single frame of footage being altered from the original version. The wait was worth it and, one has to think, kind of serendipitous. Unabashedly unique and terrifically acted—Kristen Connolly and newcomer Anna Hutchison are equally eye-catching as Dana and Jules, while Chris Hemsworth has famously gone on to make a mark in 2011's Marvel franchise-starter *Thor*—*The Cabin in the Woods* is an outright blast while still having more on its mind than just a body count. A motion picture about the endurance of horror as a historical watermark, where it has been, and where it might be able to go from here, it's no less than an all-encompassing celebration of a too often spit-upon genre. Fans will be savoring this one for decades to come.

Carnival of Souls

1962 - Directed by Herk Harvey

Made in 1962 on a shoestring budget of only $15,000, Herk Harvey's *Carnival of Souls* is not a perfect film by any stretch of the imagination, but when considering its low budget and amateur actors, it turned out about as good as could possibly be expected. The film is like a nightmarish puzzle, one that you think you've figured out, but really haven't until the final twist arrives in the last scene.

The film begins abruptly, as a carload of young women are challenged to a drag-race by some lead-footed male joyriders. While passing over a narrow bridge, the ladies' car accidentally loses control and plunges into a deep river. Hours later, as the police have arrived and are attempting to find the car in its dark watery grave, one of the passengers of the ill-fated accident, Mary Henry (Candace Hilligoss), miraculously appears climbing out of the river. Not remembering anything about the accident and looked upon by everyone as a miracle, Mary immediately moves to a small town in Utah to play as the church organist. She rents out a room from a kind, elderly landlady (Frances Feist), meets and is somewhat charmed by the other resident of the home, John Linden (Sidney Berger), and attempts to begin putting the pieces of her life back together. Everything is not perfect, however, as Mary begins to frequently see a ghoulish, frightening phantom figure everywhere she goes—one that no one else claims to see. Is it simply a hallucination, sparked from the trauma of the car crash? If that weren't enough, Mary also begins to sense a sort of mysterious connection to an adjacent, closed-down, desolate amusement park.

At a decidedly too-brisk 75-minute running time, *Carnival of Souls* moves at a gradual, dreamlike pace that makes it almost impossible to not get caught up in the proceedings. And although only with a miniscule budget, since its release, the film has quickly become a cult classic for all horror aficionados. Even George Romero has mentioned, in fact, that he got his idea for 1968's *Night of the Living Dead* from *Carnival of Souls*, and it is obvious that so did David Lynch when he made *Blue Velvet*, *Lost Highway*, and TV's *Twin Peaks*. That these filmmakers were influenced by such a "petty" movie from the early

'60s proves of the extraordinary power that the film ultimately holds, both in its storytelling techniques and glorious style.

Candace Hilligoss, an unknown who was cast in the lead role, contains just the right amounts of vulnerability and strong will to bring Mary to life as a sympathetic character. One of the major highlights of *Carnival of Souls* is Maurice Prather's magnificently atmospheric and brooding black-and-white cinematography that paints the settings, including the unforgettable images of the somehow off-kilter amusement park, as major characters themselves. The sequences of Mary simply walking around the eerie park, which is out on the dock of a bay, are some of those rare moments in motion picture history that, once seen, will be forever ingrained in one's long-term memory.

The story goes that director Herk Harvey scratched together the money to make *Carnival of Souls*, and has never made another film since. That's really too bad, since he obviously was a major filmmaking talent with a knack for haunting visuals and abstract, ahead-of-its-time storytelling. Ultimately, Harvey died in 1996, but left in his memory his one and only film, a movie that affected, and inspired, a generation of moviegoers who had never seen anything quite like what he had achieved.

Special Note: It was an appalling wake-up call to view this motion picture right before its direct-to-video 1999 remake, the updated version all but completely trashing the legacy of this classic. By complicating the story from its originally simple premise, the makers of the '99 edition simply made everything feel contrived, as well as frustrating and confusing. And, tellingly enough, the original *Carnival of Souls* is also infinitely more disturbing, even though it was made over half a century ago. It has aged very well.

Case 39

2009 - Directed by Christian Alvart

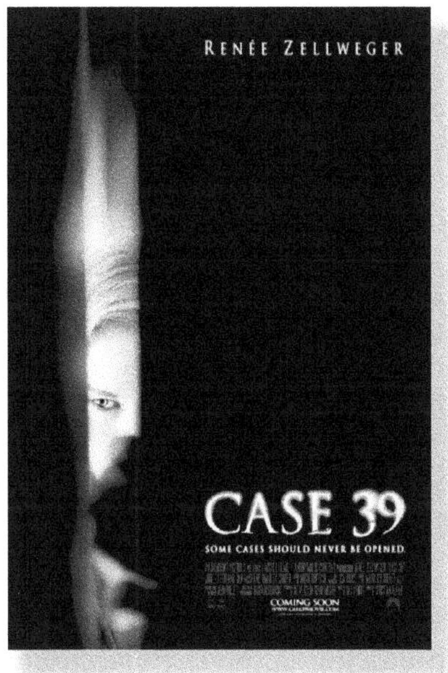

Case 39 traveled a long, winding and unfortunate road to U.S. theater screens. Shot in the autumn of 2006, the film was originally scheduled for release by distributor Paramount Pictures in February 2008, then was pushed to April 2009, then January 2010, until finally, at long last, coming out in October 2010. In that time, director Christian Alvart made and released a follow-up effort (2009's *Pandorum*), star Renée Zellweger's career cooled considerably after a couple box-office bombs (e.g., 2009's *New in Town*), then-unknown supporting cast member Bradley Cooper's status blew up following the success of 2009's *The Hangover*, and the picture came to virtually every other international territory across the globe that same year. Usually when movies are delayed like this, it's a tell-tale sign that they are of the awful persuasion. In the case of *Case 39*, however, it has simply become the victim of a studio that changed heads soon after filming, got rid of the execs that greenlit the project to begin with, and placed it as low priority on the schedule. The shame of it all is that the film deserved a whole lot better. As far as major studio supernatural thrillers are concerned, this one is pretty darn good, smarter and certainly more classically compelling than predated turkeys like 2007's *The Reaping*, 2009's *The Unborn*, and 2009's *The Haunting in Connecticut*. Thematically and quality-wise, *Case 39* is more in step with 2005's *Dark Water* and 2009's *Orphan*.

Overextended social worker Emily Jenkins (Renée Zellweger) has too much on her plate to take on an additional case—her thirty-ninth—but she has no choice after boss Wayne (Adrian Lester) drops it on her desk. Her investigation into the welfare of 10-year-old Lilith Sullivan (Jodelle Ferland) leads her to the little girl's home and to ominous, wild-eyed parents Edward (Callum Keith Rennie) and Margaret (Kerry O'Malley). Emily is convinced Lilith is in danger—Lilith confides that her parents hate her and regularly tell her she's going to hell—and her fears are all the more confirmed when she and cop friend Detective Barron (Ian McShane) barge in just as Lilith is about to be burned alive in her family's kitchen oven. Single and living alone, having bonded already with the little girl, Emily petitions to the court that she get custody until a loving foster family is found. Lilith's parents may have seemed insane, but there was a very good reason why they were trying to kill her. Emily is about to find out.

A horror-thriller that touches upon several tropes of the genre—supernatural and religious threats, creepy kids—and appears at least partially influenced by the Japanese (several shots could have been pulled straight out of *Ringu* or *The Grudge*), the film is atmospherically directed by Christian Alvart with an almost casual layer of portent. The script by Ray Wright, meanwhile, is sturdily conceived, unhurried and engrossing. Side characters, such as Detective Barron, whom Emily confides in, and Emily's sort-of boyfriend, child counselor Doug (Bradley Cooper), are familiar types, but written with specificity. At its center is Emily Jenkins, a woman who surprises herself by actively seeking to care for Lilith even as she has never appropriately gotten over her haunting childhood and the reverberations of an absent father and clinically unwell mother. As Lilith's personality and demeanor curve downward and mysterious deaths connected to them both start occurring, Emily's ostensibly indomitable conflict is split in two. There doesn't seem to be an escape from Lilith—in one devious scene, she calmly demands that Emily do whatever she says, or else—but if there is, Emily's only hope comes in not only facing her present-day nightmare, but simultaneously the demons from her past.

At the time of this movie's release, Renée Zellweger had been recently criticized for everything from her project choices to her physical appearance. When things aren't going an actor's way in Hollywood, it is far too easy for people to suddenly lose their long-term memory as a means of forgetting just how talented certain actors are and what they're capable of. Indeed, Zellweger was nominated for an Academy Award two years in a row (for 2002's *Chicago* and 2003's *Cold Mountain*) and won for the latter, but none of that seems to matter if she's got a couple of duds since then under her belt. Because of its rocky history, *Case 39* was most definitely lopped in as just one more sign that her career had lost its way. The sad truth is that this negativity was based purely upon the film's belated release and not on her performance, which is strong, likable and fully committed. Zellweger fully anchors the potentially ridiculous story in a reality that the audience can believe in. She's a kind, professional, identifiable protagonist who's worth following for nearly two hours. As Emily loses control, begins to fear for her life, and struggles to find someone else who will believe her about Lilith's devious true identity, we are placed in her shoes, wondering what we'd do in the same situation.

As Lilith, Jodelle Ferland is scarily confident in her deceptive, multilayered role. Meek and sensitive at the onset, Lilith appears every bit the victim until a switch is flipped midway through and she transforms into an entirely different person who just happens to look the same. Now the victimizer—and a passive-aggressive one, at that—Ferland is exceptional at getting under one's skin without so much as having to raise her voice. Lending fine support are Ian McShane as Det. Barron, a religious man who Emily succinctly points out has trouble believing in his own life the same things he's taught to believe in church; Bradley Cooper as Doug, whose phobia of bees comes back to terrorize him in a big way, and Alexander Conti as Diego, another one of Emily's young subjects led to commit an unthinkable crime.

Looping around to where it began before diverging on a game-changing tangent, *Case 39* makes an argument for how easy it is to repeat the past, and also how possible it is to knowingly change it. Stylishly shot in brooding gray and blue hues by cinematographer Hagen Bogdanski, the sky consistently overcast and the anonymous city in which it's set (is it New York, Seattle, Vancouver, or somewhere else?) lending an added air of mystery to the happenings, the film looks stupendously sleek. With tension mounting but the ending seemingly written in stone, director Christian Alvart cunningly dodges expectations during the climax. At once satisfyingly finite and frustratingly open-ended, the movie ends on a note of catharsis for Emily, but also one that doesn't bother to suggest what the ramifications will be for what she's just done. A moment's thought reveals a grimness to the end that Alvart overlooks, or simply chooses not to deal with. Either way, it's the one element that doesn't quite sit well in a nimbly crafted, aesthetically artful suspenser that looks and feels awfully good in spite of its conventional plot.

Chernobyl Diaries

2012 - Directed by Brad Parker

A stock horror movie setup and a real-life tragedy from the mid-1980s merge in anxiety-inspiring ways in *Chernobyl Diaries*, a thoroughly frightening study in how to do a tried-and-true formula proud. Brad Parker, a special effects supervisor on films such as 2010's *Let Me In*, makes his taut directorial debut under the tutelage of one Mr. Oren Peli, the creator of 2009's *Paranormal Activity* who produces and, along with Carey Van Dyke & Shane Van Dyke, writes here. Favoring old-fashioned suspense and a creeping sense of danger that finally bubbles over in the home stretch, Parker crafts a genre piece that is only graphically violent when the narrative calls for it (not often), and willing to leave the major threat in the obscure shadows. Indeed, what the viewer's imagination ratchets up is probably far scarier than what the makers could actualize on the screen.

During their travels across Europe, the responsible Chris (Jesse McCartney), his longtime girlfriend, Natalie (Olivia Taylor Dudley), and her recently dumped best friend, Amanda (Devin Kelly), stop in Kiev to visit Chris' fly-by-night older brother, Paul (Jonathan Sandowski). He moved out of the States a while back, much to the protestations of their parents, and now Paul wants to show Chris and his buddies a good time. His plan: take them on an "extreme tour" hosted by Uri (Dimitri Diatchenko) to the abandoned city of Pripyat, once home to the workers and families of the 1986 Chernobyl power plant meltdown. With backpackers Michael (Nathan Phillips) and Zoe (Ingrid Bolsø Berdal) also along for the tour, the group set out on the two-hour trek to their destination. They are assured that radiation levels are low enough to be safe for the short amount of time they'll be there, and so the sightseeing and walks through the desolate buildings are at first fun and intriguing. Once the truck won't start—it's been tampered with—and night falls, however, circumstances quickly spiral downward. Separated from the outside world, it becomes exceedingly probable that they are not really alone.

The idea of whole neighborhoods and towns getting abruptly deserted and largely forgotten about is unsettling to think about, said places frozen in time and haunted by those that are no more. Such is the very authentic case of

Pripyat, within seeing distance of the Chernobyl reactors. It's such a humdinger of a location for a horror movie that it's surprising it hasn't been more often used as fodder for things going bump in the night. That *Chernobyl Diaries* was filmed at least partially on location there lends it an uncommon authenticity. The production values of its natural, broken-down, dilapidated state can't be bought or convincingly replicated. What they do achieve is bless the proceedings with a decidedly consistent lurking foreboding. Although Parker takes his time in revealing the whos and whats that the protagonists face, it is readily apparent that lives are in danger. That's all that truly needs to be known for Parker to work his blackly magical spell.

It is a given in this kind of movie that characters will occasionally do things that place them more in harm's way than not. Credit this one, at least, for masterminding legitimate reasons why the people go into dank structures or out into the pitch-dark woods when they know better. Likewise, though there are a few leaps in logistics, a couple of them having to do with their super-charged but presumably signal-free cell phones, the bulk of what occurs does so through the unavoidable hands of fate and not for a lack of trying. As for the aforementioned ensemble, they are fairly cut-and-paste as multidimensional figures, but sympathetic and raw enough to put rooting stakes in. Placed in a heightened life-or-death struggle like this, anyway, there probably wouldn't be a whole lot of time for getting-to-know-you chit-chat. All the actors do their jobs very well in that they act natural and scared out of their wits. Of them, recording artist Jesse McCartney is the best-known and most charismatic. Watching him here and remembering how very good he was on the 2004-2006 CW drama, *Summerland*, there's no reason for him not to have the same level of career as someone like Zac Efron.

Chernobyl Diaries will have all but the most stoic of audience members jumping and squirming in their seats. It's an enthralling experience, methodic but solid in its editing as things get ever hairier. Scenes involving a very big something (we'll keep it on the down-low) barreling through an empty apartment building, another involving a pack of wild dogs and a rickety bridge, a run-in with a child-sized figure standing motionless in the moonlight, and a cat-and-mouse game in a kitchen reminding of the velociraptor sequence in 1993's *Jurassic Park* are just a few memorable setpieces of many. As for the finale, a breathless chase up and down and through a steely industrial landscape culminating in the discovery that they've wandered perilously outside of the safety zone, it lives up to expectations while remaining relentlessly uncompromising. Not everything is answered at the end of *Chernobyl Diaries*, and that's precisely as it should be. The unknown genuinely is the scariest thing of all.

Cloverfield

2008 - Directed by Matt Reeves

One of the most treasured capabilities of cinema—a power too seldom achieved—is to so thoroughly engulf audiences that they are made to believe the unthinkable. An even better film is one able to seemingly plant the viewer in the bodies of the characters onscreen, enmeshed in their lives and the circumstances that have led them to the position they are in. The rabidly anticipated *Cloverfield* pulls off both of these remarkable feats. After six months of growing hype, begun with the release in July 2007 of a frightening, purposefully obscure, title-free teaser trailer, there was the initial sense prior to the screening that the picture wouldn't possibly be able to live up to the impossible standards set by a complex and stunningly imaginative viral marketing campaign. Those fears, thankfully, are snuffed out in the hauntingly tranquil, early-morning opening scene—a quiet respite to the almost unimaginable horrors about to take place.

Director Matt Reeves, screenwriter Drew Goddard, and producer J.J. Abrams deserve all the accolades heaped upon them for bringing *Cloverfield* to such stark, nightmarish light. In the way that the story is told solely from the lens of a spectator's video camera, the film could have felt derivative of 1999's *The Blair Witch Project*, a groundbreaking motion picture of its time, but does not. The naturalistic approach, aided by unaffected performances and the kind of overlapping dialogue and chaos that come from a person's home movies, works brilliantly for what, in essence, is a grand-scale monster bonanza spun out of a single person's small-scale vantage point. There has never been anything quite like it—a breathlessly horrifying sci-fi/horror/disaster film that narrows its gaze not on the giant otherworldly attacker and the destruction left in its wake, but on the vulnerable human souls who, faced against insurmountable odds, find a strength and compassion inside of themselves that they could have never guessed they were endowed with.

The premise, as it were, is whittled down to the bare essentials and then goes about surpassing the viewer's expectations with the level of artistry, innovation and intimacy brought to the material. On an introductory title card, it is established that the following recording was recovered from incident site

'U.S. 447' ('area formerly known as Central Park'). What begins as a farewell tape commemorating a going-away party for Rob Hawkins (Michael Stahl-David), about to leave for Japan on business, turns into something entirely different when an enormous creature emerges from the New York City harbor. As Rob, brother Jason (Mike Vogel), Jason's girlfriend, Lily (Jessica Lucas), and Lily's friend, Marlena (Lizzy Caplan), attempt to survive amidst a catastrophic event unlike anything the world has seen before, appointed videographer Hud (T.J. Miller) clings to the camera, saying, "People are gonna want to see how it all went down."

Born from an idea producer J.J. Abrams got while visiting Japan with his son and realizing that America never really had an iconic monster movie to call its own like that country's *Godzilla*, *Cloverfield* is just about as authentic and large in scale as the genre has seen. That the film was made for a reported $25-million is frankly amazing and proves that a budget of hundreds of millions is unnecessary. The visual effects in bringing the monster(s) and the disaster itself to life are close to seamless; for an hour and a half, the viewer is led to wholly buy into the idea that Manhattan has become an apocalyptic landscape. Images recalling those seen on 9/11 are unmistakable and unavoidable, from the sight of buildings erupting into balls of flames, to the onlookers' use of their cell phones to record the events, to people seeking shelter from the smoky debris closing in on the streets around them, to disquieting television news coverage by reporters who scarcely know how to keep their composure and handle what is unfolding before them. The results are alarming and nothing short of terrifying.

Cloverfield is filled with visions destined to seep into the viewer's memory and not let go, some of them involving the encroaching monster, seen at first in brief, scary flashes and later in all of its awe-inspiring glory, and others not—Rob's call to his mother as he and his friends seek safety in the underground subway is heartbreaking. Barely letting up except for in moments where the characters catch their breath or passingly connect as only human beings can in times of tragedy, the film pushes forward like a juggernaut, always prepared to pull something else out of its sleeve just when the audience thinks they can rest easy. Some might scoff at first when Rob insists on going deeper into the city to try and rescue his sort-of girlfriend, Beth (Odette Yustman), who is trapped and injured in her apartment and may or may not still be alive, but it is presented in a plausible manner and allows for the viewer to question what he or she would do. If your own loved one was in the same predicament, most people, I suspect, would do what Rob does, the knowledge of uncertain death a non-issue.

For any picture relying on captured realism to such a heavy degree, it is imperative that the writing and acting are strong enough to not show the threads of what is, indeed, fiction. *Cloverfield* gets these things right, too. The dialogue is palpably felt and never contrived, director Matt Reeves confident enough to let the emotion of each situation speak for itself. As unfair as it is, none of the characters are safe; some die in an uncompromising instant, as it would actually occur. The performances from a cast of then-little-known or unknown actors, are first-rate, all of them superbly realized and empathetic without calling attention to themselves.

The conceptual design of the monster and its fruition via masterful special effects is better than one could imagine, a staggeringly eerie, full-blown original that is nothing, it turns out, like Godzilla. Save for a few on-the-fly theories that Hud throws out, its origins and motives are thankfully never explored. By retaining a complete air of mystery about what it is and where it comes from—which is how it would be if something like this ever suddenly occurred—the creature's threat is further heightened. As a tried-and-true genre piece, the film is drenched in atmosphere and the sort of tension you could cut with a knife.

Where *Cloverfield* goes one step further, however, becoming more than just a horror show, is in the scenes between Rob and Beth, shot a few weeks before, that bookend the mayhem. That the opening and closing moments, depicting the idyllic morning of and late afternoon that he took her to Coney Island, are in such sharp contrast to where these two characters' approaching fates ultimately end up is devastating. Their final recorded moments at the amusement park, the last images before the end credits, transform the film from a marvelously rendered monster-invasion pic into something so much more—an existential rumination on humanity in general, and the unforeseen and not always blessed turns life throws at all of us. *Cloverfield* is an unadulterated masterpiece.

Clownhouse

1990 - Directed by Victor Salva

Financed in part by Francis Ford Coppola and premiering at the 1989 Sundance Film Festival, where it competed for the Grand Jury Prize in the Dramatic Competition category, *Clownhouse* has a prestigious background far outweighing most low-budget horror fare from the late-'80s/early-'90s. Laden in methodical foreboding and surely rising tension that places it much closer in spirit to 1978's classic *Halloween* than it does to the proceeding slasher imitators, the film's worth as a motion picture has unfortunately been overshadowed by its checkered behind-the-scenes history. Shortly after the film was completed, writer-director Victor Salva (who later would helm 2001's *Jeepers Creepers*) was arrested on five felony counts of sexual misconduct with a minor, the victim being Nathan Forrest Winters, the then-12-year-old star of *Clownhouse*. Sentenced to three years in prison, Salva was ultimately released after serving fifteen months.

While this ugly crime should in no way be downplayed or marginalized, it has unfairly formed a stigma around *Clownhouse* that few people can get past when discussing the movie. Viewed solely on its own cinematic merits, the film is a skillfully crafted thriller, cunningly envisioned and brought to life. For sufferers of coulrophobia (the fear of clowns), watching it will either be a traumatic or therapeutic experience. And, for those who wonder what the big deal is with those face-painted circus performers, the picture might make them think twice before visiting the big top again.

Left home alone on a Friday night, 11-year-old Casey Collins (Nathan Forrest Winters), supportive middle brother Geoffrey (Brian McHugh), and passive-aggressive eldest sibling Randy (Sam Rockwell) visit the traveling circus in town. Following a portentous session with a fortune teller and an embarrassing moment with one of the performing clowns that confirms Casey's uncontrollable phobia, they return home for an evening of storytelling and movie-watching. What they don't yet know is that three escaped lunatics from the local mental hospital have crashed the circus, killed the three clown talents, and stolen their costumes and make-up. Lurking outside the boys' house, the trio of psychopaths patiently await their chance to pounce, in turn making every hang-up Casey has about clowns a reality.

Clownhouse is rated R for language and some decidedly tame violence, and would be ideal for younger teenagers at a sleepover in search of a scary film to watch. Adults, of course, will also be able to appreciate it for its compressing mood, thematic truth, and penchant for mounting apprehension over straightforward explicitness. Salva cleverly plays with the viewer's expectations as the threat level rises and the clowns, each one with their individual personage, close in. A noose swaying from a tree in the front yard, for example—a decoration for the approaching October holiday—is used several times when a character's fate is in question and the dummy hanging from it is established to quite possibly be no dummy at all.

Also memorable are a number of stylistic tricks that work splendidly, signaling the care and attention to detail of the project. When the power goes out, Randy ventures into the gloomy attic to check the fuse box. As the lights flicker, creating a strobe effect, one of the clowns can be seen darting behind a large object in the background. In another sequence, Randy walks by a sliding door, the clown on the other side of the glass mimicking his movements. The body count is low for this type of film, relying on the possibility of what could potentially occur instead. Still, the few murder setpieces are far from throwaways, with one unfortunate victim being turned into a human balloon animal.

Upon first viewing, *Clownhouse* was like a dream to watch for my 11-year-old self with a fascination for the subject matter. Seeing it years later as an older audience member, the film still works just as it should, but its handful of flaws also jump out. The acting ranges from solid—Nathan Forrest Winters (in his one and only feature) is sympathetic and real as Casey—to unpolished—Brian McHugh (also in his only screen credit) fails to sell his bigger moments as Geoffrey—to annoying—Sam Rockwell, now a talented big Hollywood star, overplays his role as the obnoxious Randy. The bickering between brothers, while authentic to some siblings' relationships, also gets to be too much by the second half. Fortunately, Salva does make an attempt to round out these characters and their underlying protectiveness of each other, and it comes as a pleasantly affecting moment when Casey gets scared walking down a desolate lane in one scene and Randy allows him to hold his hand.

When the three deranged clowns let their attack on the house be known in the final twenty minutes, the action barely takes a breather as it sprints to the finish. The chase scenes, with danger hiding around every corner, are tautly shot, and the personal arc that Casey goes through as he finally must face his fears up front should be identifiable for anyone who has ever been trepidatious of something in their own life. The closing onscreen text reads, "No man can hide from his fears; as they are a part of him, they will always know where he is hiding." Concluding a film of this nature on a moralistic note might have come off as cornball in lesser hands, but here it has a lingering impact, turning a fairly conventional horror flick into one with a valuable point to make. That the unhinged clowns show up at Casey's house isn't merely an unfortunate coincidence, but a provocative part of his very fate in the process of his own coming of age. For that, *Clownhouse* holds a certain relevance and universality, besides being a spookily good time.

The Conjuring

2013 - Directed by James Wan

In my 2011 review of *Insidious*, it was suggested that director James Wan had a tendency of being overly self-congratulatory, his onscreen credit so large and bold and lingering during both the opening and ending titles that it would make even someone as allegedly egotistic as M. Night Shyamalan blush. With an uneven résumé up to that point consisting of 2004's *Saw*, 2007's *Dead Silence*, and 2007's *Death Sentence*, it was concluded that Wan had not quite proven what the credits slyly suggested: that a master filmmaker of noted importance was in charge. With time comes perspective, however, and in the years and multiple viewings since that original review of *Insidious*, the film has only grown in impact. It's just as leap-out-of-your-seat chilling as it was the first time, and Wan's skill deconstructing the family unit while delving into supernatural subject matter that bypasses obvious frights while getting to the true heart of darkness and the unknown is virtually second to none. If *The Conjuring* is perhaps a fraction less rattlingly scary than *Insidious*, that's still far creepier than the average studio-released horror films that come out these days. Credit must go to Wan for also not merely repeating himself; while it must have been tempting since both pictures are basically "haunted house" movies, this one never feels derivative. With a sure-footed elegiac pace and a keen understanding that anticipation and what we don't see is sometimes more affecting than the payoff, *The Conjuring* plays like a loving throwback to cinema of the '70s, the director comfortably joining company as reputable and varied as Alfred Hitchcock, John Carpenter, William Friedkin and Roman Polanski.

Based on the true accounts of married paranormal investigators Ed (Patrick Wilson) and Lorraine Warren (Vera Farmiga), the film centers upon one of the most difficult and daunting cases of their careers. The year is 1971, and the Perron family—Carolyn (Lili Taylor) and Roger (Ron Livingston), along with their five daughters—are excited about their fresh start as they move into an old Harrisville, Rhode Island, farmhouse that they bought at auction. Carolyn notices that the clocks keep stopping every night at 3:07 a.m., a rank smell of rotting meat seems to permeate certain rooms before vanishing in the morning, and on only the second day in the house the family dog is found dead outside. Then things get seriously strange, with middle daughter Christine (Joey King) terrorized in the night and youngest April (Kyla Deaver) gaining an imaginary friend named Rory who allegedly appears in the reflection of a music box mirror every time the lullaby stops. Worried first and foremost about the safety of her family, Carolyn seeks out the Warrens, noted clairvoyant Lorraine and demonologist expert Ed. Immediately, Lorraine senses a terrible energy that has latched onto the Perrons, unwilling to let go. As their investigation continues, Lorraine's research into the previous owners reveals a grisly tale of madness, satanic rituals, child murder and suicide.

Imbued with a crisp autumnal atmosphere and elegant period flavor—costumes and production design are authentic without becoming overly tacky, while soundtrack cues (e.g., "Time of the Season" by The Zombies; "Sleep Walk" by Betsy Brye, and "In the Room Where You Sleep" by Dead Man's Bones) bring shading and color to the proceedings—*The Conjuring* might as well have been shot back in 1971. Relying almost entirely on technical effects and camera trickery over CGI and concentrating on the reality of characters as much as the heightened situations they find themselves faced with, director James Wan and screenwriters Chad Hayes and Carey W. Hayes get off to an indelibly ominous start with a prologue introducing the Warrens through their 1968 case of an otherworldly presence haunting two college roommates through their Annabelle doll. The face of the doll alone could put a shiver up the sturdiest of spines, and, indeed, when Annabelle appears in the home of the Warrens behind a glass casing surrounded by all of the past artifacts and objects from their cases, it's only a matter of time before Wan takes that porcelain nightmare to the next level. Other humdinger moments, from a game of hide-and-clap gone awry, to a startling run-in with a spectral maid, to Christine's nighttime bedroom terrors, play terrifically into the threatening pall of doom cornering the Perrons.

Vera Farmiga and Patrick Wilson should be commended in the way they shatter expectations to find the core love, respect and normalcy of Lorraine and Ed Warren, a couple who happen to specialize in the paranormal without letting that define them as people. These two don't superstitiously wander about with crosses and Bibles while speaking in hushed tones. Instead, they're loving parents themselves to daughter Judy (Sterling Jerins) and forthright and empathetic to their hosts, able to figure out fairly quickly whether a place is genuinely haunted or if there are simple explanations for the suspicious goings-on. Farmiga is particularly fascinating as Lorraine, gifted with strong intuitions that help her in her job, but also force her to feel and identify with things more strongly. As the heads of the imperiled Perron clan, Ron Livingston's role is underserved and mostly reactionary, but Lili Taylor more than makes up for it with a committed, multilayered turn as Carolyn. The film forces her to go through a lot, and Taylor is convincing without fail.

On its way toward a conclusion that manages to recall 1973's *The Exorcist* while taking the treatment of a real-life exorcism in a whole different direction, *The Conjuring* doesn't quite explore the tragic, malevolent backstory of the

Perron farmhouse with the level of detail hoped for. Likewise, there is the sense that Wan missed an opportunity or two in taking things to the next level—a level that *Insidious* managed to get to on several occasions. With that said, *The Conjuring* is a graceful, suspense-laden thriller in the classical mode, violence kept to a minimum in favor of the power of apprehension. Stunningly shot by cinematographer John R. Leonetti, taking full advantage of the space within his frame, the picture proves to be a solid dispute to the claim that they don't make horror movies like this one anymore. As a matter of fact, they do, and James Wan does nothing if not play his audience like a master's concerto.

Creepshow

1982 - Directed by George A. Romero

When I think of *Creepshow*, I think fondly of my childhood. I think of renting the videotape, and being scared out of my wits just at the early-'80s Warner Bros. logo, knowing full-well (because I'd seen it so many times) what was about to come. I think of the opening scene, thick in atmosphere and spooky as anything. I think of the jack-o'-lantern glowing in the window of a suburban home. I think of Tom Atkins' spiteful portrayal of an abusive father who thinks he knows better and snatches away his young son's comic book. I think of the father throwing the comic in the garbage can, the night brightening in a flash of lightning and the sound of a demonic cackle faintly heard in the distance. And, I think of the son (played by Stephen King's real-life son, Joe), smiling as he sees the corpse-like Creep standing outside his bedroom window, silently assuring the boy that his father will live only to regret the way he's mistreated him all his life.

A gloriously faithful ode to the E.C. Comics of the 1950s, *Creepshow* ranks as one of the very best horror anthology films (none better instantly come to mind). The collaboration between director George A. Romero (one-upping his 1968 classic *Night of the Living Dead*) and screenwriter Stephen King is something special, indeed, eliciting an unmistakable comic book tone and an irresistible blend of lighthearted darkness and darkhearted lightness. When most horror movies of the 1980s were either exploitative, depressing, or both, *Creepshow* reintroduced a sense of fun back into the genre. It was okay to be scared—and make no mistake, viewers would be—but it was also okay to be completely entertained and cheering the entire time.

Beyond the wraparound sequences, the picture is comprised of five short stories, each one beginning and ending with a segue from the animated comic drawing to live-action, or vice versa. There isn't a weak one in the bunch. The party starts with "Father's Day" (my personal favorite as a kid of about seven or eight), wherein an annual family get-together on the anniversary of the patriarch's death (which also happened to be the title holiday) is interrupted by his return from the grave and a mission to finally get his Father's Day cake. Viveca Lindfors is comic dynamite as the booze-swilling Aunt Bedelia ("Screeches to a halt, as they say!"), as is Carrie Nye as tell-it-like-it-is family member Sylvia Grantham ("Turn that music down! Turn it down, and turn it down right now!"). The clever ending of the tale, set in the murky kitchen of the estate, the dinner boiling on the stove, is perfection.

Next up is "The Lonesome Death of Jordy Verrill," wherein a lunkheaded farmer (Stephen King) witnesses a meteorite crash to Earth and makes the wrong decision in touching it. As green moss spouts over his entire body and an infestation of fern grows outside, Jordy has no choice but to make amends with the crummy life that is about to end. In his most prominent acting role to date, Stephen King is terrific as Jordy Verrill ("I'll be dipped in shit if that ain't a meteor!"), mixing humor with pathos as if he were a professional actor. Jordy is a born loser, and he knows it, but he's also so gosh-darn likable that you hate to see him reach for that shotgun at the end.

The third macabre offering is "Something to Tide You Over," starring Leslie Nielsen as Richard, a wealthy husband who seeks revenge on his cheating wife (Gaylen Ross) and her boyfriend (Ted Danson) by burying them alive on the beach. The couple die, drowned by the sea, but return as waterlogged corpses to haunt Richard. Leslie Nielsen is delicious at playing cold-blooded ("I can hold my breath for a looooooong time!"), a far cry from the spoof movies he became most known for, and the climax where he receives his just desserts is fittingly suspenseful and, finally, amusing.

The fourth story is also the longest, clocking in at almost forty-five minutes. "The Crate" stars Hal Holbrook as Henry Northrop, a henpecked college professor husband who discovers a crate concealing an insatiable monster and uses it to get back at the people who have wronged him. Adrienne Barbeau is hilarious as wife Wilma ("Just call me Billie, everyone does!"), a loudmouthed, obnoxious sort who annoys everyone around her and hasn't a clue that they hate her. "The Crate" could have probably been trimmed a little in its midsection, but the characters are enjoyable and well-developed and the creature, when revealed, is as chilling as one could hope.

Finally, "They're Creeping Up on You" is a gross-out satire in which terminally clean grouch Upson Pratt (E.G. Marshall) finds his sterile, all-white apartment invaded by cockroaches. When a blackout hits, the insects prepare to make their attack. E.G. Marshall chews up the scenery as the insufferable, bigoted Upson Pratt ("Now, if you'll excuse me, I have this bug problem..."), and the ending of the tale shows off some mischievously gruesome effects work. For anyone who hates bugs, this segment will have you wriggling in your seat, and for anyone who doesn't mind them, it may make you reconsider your stance.

Intricately and eye-poppingly photographed by Michael Gornick, taking on the stylized look and feel of a vintage horror comic, *Creepshow* is a feast for anyone who enjoys a case of the heebie-jeebies and wants to have a grand time in the process. The brilliantly malevolent, piano-tinged music score by John Harrison keeps the pace moving, each story seamlessly gliding into the next. It's too bad George A. Romero and Stephen King have not worked together more often; they fit each other like a snug, bloodily battered glove. All of the pieces of *Creepshow* come together in a smorgasbord of ghastly images, welcome humor, and solid, old-fashioned storytelling. This film, horror and comic book fans, is a very special treat, ideal for the Halloween season or any time at all.

Cthulhu

2008 - Directed by Dan Gildark

A revisionist take on the works of H.P. Lovecraft (most notably novella *The Shadow Over Innsmouth*), *Cthulhu* is breathtaking insomuch that a hallucinatory nightmare involving a small-town cult, the oncoming apocalypse, and a plot involving humankind's return to the seas can be. The production was troubled, with principal photography taking a year and a half to complete due to financial issues, but the finished product is more than enough proof that a little passion, talent and perseverance can go a long way. As far as moody melodramas dipped equally in the revered lakes of David Lynch and 1971's cult classic *The Wicker Man* go, *Cthulhu* is a trippy, unsettling experience with a clear eye for mesmerizing visuals.

Russ March (Jason Cottle) is a respected college history professor living in Seattle who receives word that his mother has died. On his trip back to his coastal hometown of Rivermouth, Oregon—a place he has had good reason not to return to in many years—Russ witnesses the aftermath of a fatal auto accident and watches as the victim passes away before help arrives. It's a harbinger of doom to come, as are the flurry of radio news reports on dire world happenings, ecological and otherwise, that intermittently underscore the action.

The reunion between Russ and his father, Reverend Marsh (Dennis Kleinsmith), recaptures just how tumultuous they used to be—patriarch Marsh questions his son constantly on his homosexuality, deriding it every step of the way—while younger sister Danni (Cara Buono) struggles to hold it together and play both sides of the fence. As for Russ himself, he is torn between fleeing back to Washington and sticking around to see how his relationship with former best-friend-with-benefits Mike (Scott Green) develops. As Russ goes about his everyday business, he is inundated with freakish delusions that could be real and ghastly experiences that must be true. Something very, very strange is occurring in Rivermouth, and something even more unimaginable is fast approaching.

A whopping mood piece as much as a horror film, and a poignant, nostalgia-layered story about tentative love and desire as much as a mood piece, *Cthulhu* covers multiple genres without losing sight of any of them. Introducing a gay slant to a premise that otherwise remains truthful to H.P. Lovecraft's sensibilities has led to some controversy, but these worries are much ado about nothing. In actuality, Russ' orientation adds a new, excitingly provocative layer to the story, finally leading toward a devastating, intentionally open-ended climax that says a great deal about the twenty-first century's continued archaic tendencies toward sexual repression of those different than oneself. Thus, when Russ is breathlessly traveling across town, stalked by otherworldly forces, brainwashed townspeople, briefly glimpsed creatures, and a collapsing society, he is not only trying to save his own life, but also the very fabric that makes him the individual, free-thinking person that he is.

The $750,000 budget is frankly awe-inspiring for what *Cthulhu* accomplishes. With the exception of the occasional underlit moment, the film is a stunning achievement in cinematography and art direction. Location shooting along the coasts of Oregon and Washington is ravishingly haunting, complete with swooping aerial shots of the beaches, fields and rocky seaside cliffs, and a real knowledge for portraying the off-balance setting of the fictional Rivermouth. Color hues are prevalent in deep blues, equating to the blustery, overcast feel of the Pacific Northwest.

Additionally, director of photography Sean Kirby's shot compositions and camera movements couldn't be better, giving the picture an invaluable, almost free-floating dreamlike quality. A scene in which Russ escapes by boat directly below a line of robed strangers crossing a bridge at dusk is atmospheric and classy, as is another one where Russ and childhood acquaintance Susan (Tori Spelling) visit a polar bear aquarium. This same kind of ingenuity continues throughout, with suspenseful setpieces that impact because of their enthralling minimalism. A sequence set in an underground tunnel, lit only by camera flashes, reveals just enough to seriously scare, and the taut climax detailing civilization's last gasp before the end of days has the scope and disquieting imagery of a big-budget studio release.

The cast, filled mostly by unknowns, is a tad uneven. As Russ, Jason Cottle is outshone in the first half by an unfortunate wig, but seems to improve the moment he shaves his hair off. His strongest work comes when he shares the screen with Scott Green, exuding charisma as Mike. Memories of their unorthodox friendship and sexual experimentation as teens return once they come back into contact with each other. While Russ has embraced who he is, Mike has had a child in the interim and attempted to settle down. When the two encounter each other again after years of being out of touch, neither can deny that a flame still burns between them. As Russ' overbearing, devious father, Dennis Kleinsmith is the epitome of a man set in his ways who does not understand his son, and never will. Finally, the biggest name in the ensemble is Tori Spelling, playing against-type and failing to impress as a woman from Russ' past with an ulterior motive.

Cthulhu doesn't hedge its bets on acting, but on tone, ambiance, and timely thematic relevance. It is at these levels that the film is something quite special, journeying to the heart of darkness with little hope waiting on the other side.

Mischievously discombobulating, leaving the viewer disturbed and on edge as Russ is confronted by any sane person's worst fears, *Cthulhu* does H.P. Lovecraft proud while blessing his ideas with a modern-in-spirit facelift. Genre fans grown weary by today's mainstream spate owe it to themselves to seek out this grim, creatively sumptuous, unapologetically chilling indie effort.

Curtains

1983 - Directed by Richard Ciupka

Arriving near the end of a late-'70s/early-'80s slasher-palooza that was put into overdrive following the success of John Carpenter's seminal *Halloween*—the most profitable indie of its time—*Curtains* didn't create much of a stir in 1983, yet has built a passionate cult following in the years since. There are several reasons why, all of them valid. In lieu of a straightforward plot pitting dopey teens against a psychopath picking them off one at a time, *Curtains* has an entirely adult cast and a layered narrative that embraces its eccentricities. The central goal is not to merely slice through the ensemble—though this does happen, as well—but to explore the seedier cutthroat politics of moviemaking and the desperation that often comes when reality does not match up to one's aspirations. Beyond that, the film features a truly disconcerting killer cloaked in an old hag's mask, and a round-up of outstanding horror setpieces, two in particular saturated with an eerie mood and theatrical ingenuity.

Smarmy film director Jonathan Stryker (John Vernon) is preparing his new project, titled *Audra*, and has promised veteran actress Samantha Sherwood (Samantha Eggar) the juicy title role. When she takes her method preparation to the next level, convincing doctors that she is crazy as a ploy to getting admitted into a mental hospital, Stryker cruelly leaves her there and sends out invitations to six young hopefuls for a weekend casting call at his secluded mansion. With a wintry snowfall fast approaching, the actresses convene at his woodsy abode. Well, five of them do; the sixth, the role-playing Amanda Teuther (Deborah Burgess), is stabbed to death before she has time to leave her own house. As the women vie for the part in their own tactical ways, they are accosted by a disguised lunatic out to cut the competition. Adding to the sordid mystery, Samantha makes a surprise reappearance, having escaped from the institution and determined to convince Stryker she is the right person—the only person—to play Audra.

Like other genre pics such as 1980's *Prom Night* and 1981's *My Bloody Valentine* that were filmed around the same time, *Curtains* was made under a Canadian Tax Shelter which helped to minimize up-front costs in exchange for employing a crew largely made up of citizens from U.S.'s neighbor up north. The production was a bumpy one, to say the least, with at least one major casting change and a one-year hiatus during filming that led to rewrites and reshoots. Director Richard Ciupka, unsatisfied with the final edit, replaced his opening name credit with the onscreen director's own, Jonathan Stryker. While it is probably immensely disappointing for a filmmaker to see his original vision not come to fruition, Ciupka should have taken a closer look at the finished film and realized that what was there was still pretty darn good. Is it a little rough around the edges? Could a fuller, more developed director's cut have led to an even better finished product? Yes and yes. Sadly, there have been reports that the sole remaining film elements of said uncut version, running over fifteen minutes longer, were outrageously ordered destroyed in 2009. What a shame.

There is something to be said, however, for the fevered mystique that *Curtains* has acquired in the decades since its release. The picture doesn't always play by conventional slasher rules and its more surrealistic aspects render it all the more fascinatingly esoteric. A curtain swishes open and closed to signal sporadic scene transitions. A toddler-sized doll, its arms outstretched and a frown on its face, is used as an emblem of doom, in one haunting moment showing up during a rainstorm on a winding mountain road. For fans who know *Curtains* well—and for those who remember very little—there is often one particular sequence that none of the above forget. Professional ice skater Christie Burns (Lesleh Donaldson), who is hoping this unorthodox casting weekend will help her to make the leap into acting, heads out for an early-morning skate on a nearby frozen pond. As she swoops and glides to the sounds of Burton Cummings' "You Saved My Soul" on her boombox, she is alarmed when the cassette tape is abruptly stopped by someone while her back is turned. Going over to check it out, Christie doesn't realize that the masked hag killer is in her midst, skating toward her as a razor-sharp sickle is revealed from behind his or her back. That this scene is set in the bright light of day, further illuminated by the whiteness of the snow surrounding them, injects the dire circumstance all the more with a shuddersome menace.

"Have you ever wanted something so badly you would do anything for it?" asks stand-up comic Patti O'Connor (Lynne Griffin) during one of her acts. It may be the setup to a punchline, but it also rings true for Patti and all of the young women hoping the role of Audra could be their big chance to be taken seriously. In *Curtains*, Richard Ciupka and screenwriter Robert Guza Jr. provide novel misdirection as director of photography Robert Paynter casts a purposefully off-balance theatricality to his imagery, finding beauty in terror and vice versa. The climactic chase between the murderer and Tara DeMillo (Sandee Currie) through a backstage prop shed, the darkness of the space lit by a large "applause" sign in the background, cooks up crafty tension and a quirky visual spark. In their search for recognition—the applause, so to speak—these ladies are about to pay an irrevocably large price. The closer one peers into the weird and macabre pleasures of *Curtains*, the more its technical mastery and subtextual implications reveal themselves.

Dark Shadows

2012 - Directed by Tim Burton

Dark Shadows may be something of a mess, its narrative strands scattered and character interactions never quite congealing the way a familial unit should, but at least it's a deliriously macabre, deliciously off-kilter mess. Save for his magnum opus of the new millennium, 2007's marvelously ghastly musical *Sweeney Todd: The Demon Barber of Fleet Street*, this is director Tim Burton's most inspired effort in years, more genuinely recollective of the originality and entertaining quirkiness of 1988's *Beetlejuice* and 1990's *Edward Scissorhands* rather than more recent plasticized efforts like 2005's *Charlie and the Chocolate Factory* and 2010's *Alice in Wonderland*. Based on the 1966-1971 soap opera by Dan Curtis, this long-in-the-works big-screen adaptation is fittingly lavish and tongue-in-cheek without, as the misleading trailers would have a viewer believe, turning the material into a joke. Mixing vampires, werewolves, witches, spooky mansions, pot-smoking hippies, Alice Cooper, and a particular affection for '70s fashion and music, the finished film is offbeat in the best way and should have more than a few audience members scratching their heads. If they didn't already know to expect just as much from Tim Burton and first-time screenwriter Seth Grahame-Smith (author of *Pride and Prejudice and Zombies*), then they're probably not cinematically hip enough to understand *Dark Shadows* in the first place.

In 1760, the Collins clan left Liverpool and settled in Maine, establishing a lucrative seaside fishing business that led to the naming of the town Collinsport. When the son, Barnabas (Johnny Depp), grew into a man, his true love for the fair Josette (Bella Heathcote) and subsequent rebuffing of beautiful sorceress Angelique Bouchard (Eva Green) brought about a curse that left Josette dead and Barnabas an unwitting bloodsucker buried alive by the pitchfork-waving community. Over two hundred years later, Barnabas' unearthing in the year 1972 coincides with the arrival of Victoria Winters (Bella Heathcote, in a dual role) to Collinwood Manor. An innocent-looking, soft-spoken transplant from New York, Victoria hopes to nab the open position as governess. The family living there—descendants of Barnabas, whose painted portrait hangs prominently on the wall—are a decidedly dysfunctional lot: matriarch Elizabeth Collins Stoddard (Michelle Pfeiffer) and her sullen 15-year-old daughter, Carolyn (Chloë Grace Moretz), along with Elizabeth's widowed brother, Roger (Jonny Lee Miller), his introverted young son, David (Gully McGrath), and live-in psychologist Dr. Julia Hoffman (Helena Bonham Carter). An eerily pale-skinned man showing up to their door looking like one of their ancestors raises eyebrows, but before long Barnabas has been welcomed into their home. What he does not yet know is that the equally immortal Angelique still lives herself. When she discovers the man she's been infatuated with for several centuries is above ground and kicking, she vows to either have him once and for all, or destroy him for good.

Dark Shadows is a curious motion picture, fascinating for being so unusual as it melds together gothic supernatural horror and Vietnam/Watergate/ Woodstock-era satire. The vast majority of the overt comedy has already been glimpsed in a marketing campaign that has seemingly pulled together every "funny" line in the film for a two-and-a-half-minute trailer spot. The rest is more clever and also more serious, beginning with a sweeping, sorrowful prologue that details the history of the Collins family and, especially, Barnabas' tragic fate at the malevolent, magic-weaving hands of a spurned Angelique. With Danny Elfman's characteristically catchy, soaring, atmospheric music score put to its first good use against the backdrop of rocky nighttime cliffs, restless shores, and period-set costumes of extravagance, the picture effectively segues to 1972 with an opening titles sequence hauntingly complemented by The Moody Blues' "Nights in White Satin." It's a great start to a film that simultaneously never quite becomes what it could and, oddly enough, surpasses most expectations.

As fans of the old television series (over a five-year span, some 1,225 episodes were produced), Tim Burton, producer-star Johnny Depp, and writer Seth Grahame-Smith have taken the essence of *Dark Shadows* and transformed it into what the low-budget show might have been able to do with an uptick in talent and $100-million at its disposal. No longer nearly as sudsy but certainly sordid, the film dares to go over-the-top while relaxing with laid-back flower-power vibes. The Collins family members are a disaffected bunch—or they at least put on an air of such—which ultimately places walls between the characters. This is partially the point of who these people are, their dynasty rotting away even as their cannery has continued to provide them with financial wealth, but the disconnect between Elizabeth, Carolyn, Roger and David leaves things emotionally standoffish. Extending to new housekeeper/teacher Victoria, groundskeeper Willie Loomis (Jackie Earle Haley), and the boozy, lonely Dr. Julia Hoffman, there simply aren't enough scenes where the characters associate with each other in order to build relationships. Instead, they often are in their own worlds—again, maybe the point, but not exactly helpful in getting to intimately care about them as people. When they finally do stand up for each other in the third act, it's too little, too late to leave an impression.

And yet, *Dark Shadows* makes countless other positive impressions. As only Tim Burton can swing it, his visual strokes are stunning, every frame like a picture and every set so ornately designed that very few of them feel like studio backlots at all. The location work in actual exteriors brings an evocative reality and impressive scope to the proceedings, while the rest gets away with looking and seeming just as authentic through sheer artistry and craftsmanship. The use of the 1970s as a vast counterpoint to Barnabas' old life in the eighteenth century is smartly handled, the texture of the decade (along with an outstanding soundtrack featuring everyone from Donovan to The Carpenters to Elton John to T. Rex to Iggy Pop to the aforementioned Alice Cooper, appearing in a memorable cameo) giving color and funk to the *mise-en-scène*. There is some humor from this fish-out-of-water scenario—a run-in Barnabas has with a van full of peace-loving hippies goes from amusingly uncomfortable to frightful in seconds—but the time period is used as background shading rather than an easy punchline.

In his eighth collaboration with Burton, Johnny Depp is dead-on as the slightly inscrutable Barnabas Collins, a good guy who has uncontrollably become an antagonist (to people outside the Collins family, at least) thanks to his vampiric curse. The dynamic is especially interesting because he's a character to root for who nevertheless leaves a string of bodies in his wake. If he's evil, though, it's out of his true self's control. Angelique, on the other hand, is a psychotic menace, a lethal siren who cannot accept that Barnabas does not, and never will, love her. Eva Green plays a fantastic *femme fatale*, one who cracks and crumbles like a particularly tough porcelain doll in one of the movie's most noteworthy special effects. While Jonny Lee Miller and newcomer Gully McGrath barely get a chance to register as father and son Roger and David, relegated too often into the title shadows, Michelle Pfeiffer and Chloë Grace Moretz dig into mother and daughter Elizabeth and Carolyn with fetching, self-deprecating twinkles in their eyes. As Dr. Julia Hoffman, Helena Bonham Carter's part is very much a supporting one, but she makes the most of her screen time as a woman yearning for her fading youth and drawn to Barnabas. Though she's more or less a shrink who lives with the Collins', there's ironically no actual sign that she's helping any of them. As for the roles of both the doomed Josette and the evasive Victoria, Bella Heathcote is an eye-catching find, ethereal in her beauty but just unconventional enough that one could see her becoming a go-to performer in Burton's future endeavors. She holds the camera even when she's not speaking.

Handsomely photographed by Bruno Delbonnel and dripping with meticulous, Oscar-worthy art direction—the sight of the rustic Victorian manor looming on the hill above Collinsport is reminiscent of Edward Scissorhands' own lonesome hideaway—*Dark Shadows* is a phantasmagoric experience with cookie-cutter Hollywoodization kept to a minimum. Because Tim Burton has earned the trust of studios in recent years, he has been left to his own devices here and has come up with a weird horror-fantasy hybrid of the anything-goes variety. Nothing and no one is safe as the climactic showdown kicks into high gear, Angelique finally barking up a tree called Collins that bites back. Though the viewer's wish that he or she had gotten to know all of them a little better will likely never be fulfilled—the chance for a return engagement pretty much went out the window following disappointing box-office returns—that's okay, too. Hodgepodge or not, the nostalgia-laced *Dark Shadows* is as imaginatively eccentric as it is blithely ghoulish. To see it is to view something that feels different right to its core. How often can that be said in today's studio system?

Dark Skies

2013 - Directed by Scott Stewart

Leading up to the theatrical release of *Dark Skies*, distributor Dimension Films did not exactly inspire optimism in impending viewers. Not only did the picture not screen in advance for press—nearly always a stark sign of a studio's lack of faith in the quality of their product—but memos were sent out to theater chains forbidding them to run the film at late-Thursday midnight showings. This latter occurrence was then, at the last minute, retracted, but by then feelings of doubt had already materialized. Having now seen *Dark Skies*, one can only question and scoff at Dimension's gross negligence in supporting what proved to be one of 2013's early sleeper surprises, an intensely evocative, absolutely spine-tingling thriller that paints an empathetic portrait of realistically strained modern-day suburban domesticity before little by little introducing a rasping pall of doom decidedly a bit more troubling than some missed mortgage payments. It is a terrible shame that the movie now must carry with it a negative stigma because it's a whole lot better than that, earning the right through its very intelligence and airtight grasp of informed genre filmmaking to be uttered in the same breath as 1993's *Fire in the Sky* and 2002's *Signs*.

The Barrett family live in a peaceful, well-to-do community, sharing barbecues with friends and neighbors and putting on carefree airs. Behind closed doors, however, they are struggling with mounting stress and a pile-up of bills. Mother Lacy (Keri Russell), a real estate agent, heaps pressure on herself to sell fixer-uppers to prospective buyers. Father Daniel (Josh Hamilton) has been laid off for too long and desperately needs a job. 13-year-old son Jesse (Dakota Goyo) has begun hanging out with an older boy down the street who Lacy and Daniel are correct in believing is a bad influence, while their youngest, Sam (Kadan Rockett), can't get enough of his big brother's scary stories. Literally overnight, strange things begin to take place, from their security system being simultaneously breached at all eight entry points, to photos vanishing from frames, to an array of cans and dishes seemingly manifesting in ornate stacked configurations on the kitchen table. Confusion and skepticism is eventually replaced by outright fear when Lacy is convinced she sees a figure hovering over Sam's bed. Bruises and mysterious branding marks show up on the kids' bodies, and all four of them begin to sleepwalk and lose track of time. What, exactly, is happening to them, and why are they being targeted? Long before Lacy and Daniel decide to visit extraterrestrial expert Edwin Pollard (J.K. Simmons), they've pretty much already come to the conclusion that what troubles them is not of this world.

At a time when studio-produced horror films too often are destroyed by needless higher-up interference, *Dark Skies* thrives on the singular vision of writer-director Scott Stewart, a man who knows very well from past projects like 2010's *Legion* what it's like when an overabundance of cooks start stirring the same pot. Fortunately, that hasn't befell him this time, the results all the better for sticking to the riveting story at hand without losing sight of the key component in caring at all about what happens: dynamically written, three-dimensional protagonists. Initial conventions—the discovery of a ransacked refrigerator from an incorrectly presumed wild animal, followed by the aforementioned stacked objects in the kitchen—are broadly reminiscent of *E.T. The Extra-Terrestrial* and *Poltergeist*. From there, the experience grows exceedingly more absorbing and sinister, a dark cloud settling over the Barretts that none of them can escape. Paced with a methodical deliberateness that expertly draws its audience in, the film needs not fall into the trap of hoary jump scares and the like (by my count, there is only one, the rest of the time the frights and seat-jolting coming from one's deep involvement in the onscreen goings-on rather than false alarms popping out at random). Stewart trusts in the power of his committed actors, his tautly woven script which vividly pays attention to the psychology of his four-person family dynamic, and the sort of super-classy lensing from cinematographer David Boyd which confidently—and creepily—turns a vision of middle-class normalcy on its malevolently dysfunctional head.

Keri Russell and Josh Hamilton transcend all expectations of the kind of performances that normally come from films where scary things stir in the night. As married couple Lacy and Daniel, Russell and Hamilton are not merely conduits for spooky stuff happening to them, but are given plausible, layered people to play, the struggles in their marriage running parallel to inexplicable events they cannot decipher. Sure, it takes about a scene too long for Daniel's skepticism to subside, but then again he's playing a stubborn guy with a relatively short fuse. As sons Jesse and Sam, Dakota Goyo and newcomer Kadan Rockett are unaffected naturals, with Goyo especially memorable as a young teenager whose raging hormones coincide with something much larger that he also cannot understand. In a supporting role treated with an appreciable seriousness, J.K. Simmons all but wholly disappears into the role of Edwin Pollard, a man who identifies with the Barretts because he knows what they are going through.

For long stretches, *Dark Skies* works like gangbusters, courageously delving into bleak subject matter colliding with some money shots that just may have audiences searching for a pillow to cower behind. Rarely straying into an over-the-top zone, Stewart plays by his own rules while coming up with a last few scenes that are at once baffling, thought-provokingly symbolic, and incalculably sorrowful. If the Barretts are left with frustratingly more questions than answers, that's the point and the damn of it all. Indeed, they may never be able to grasp all that they've faced and what it means, but they do know firsthand that yes, being aware of a universe in which we are not alone is every bit as terrifying as one in which we are.

Dark Water

2005 - Directed by Walter Salles

One link in a chain of major American remakes of supernatural Japanese horror titles, the aptly named *Dark Water*, while sharing some narrative and technical similarities with 2002's *The Ring* and 2004's *The Grudge*, sets itself apart by emphasizing psychological horror over more traditional thrills. In a way, the cumulative impact on the viewer is more effective even with a subtler hand, building slowly, minute by minute, scene by scene, an uncompromising shroud of quaking dread. Indeed, the masterfully moody, genuinely chilling *Dark Water* is so concentrated on excellent character work and thematic complexity over cheap jump scares and dumbed-down excess that, yes, favorable comparisons to classics of the genre such as 1968's *Rosemary's Baby*, 1973's *Don't Look Now,* and 1991's *The Silence of the Lambs* are fully warranted.

Filmed on location on Roosevelt Island, a deteriorating, practically forgotten town connected to Manhattan via tram, the novel, unfamiliar setting of *Dark Water*, complete with requisite downpours, ominous skies, and intimidating, looming, dilapidating buildings, adds the perfect aesthetic sheen to support the characters' feelings of being adrift in a new lifestyle and foreign surroundings. Going through a divorce and dealing with a nasty custody battle has left newly single mother Dahlia (Jennifer Connelly) stressed out and ruminative of her own unhappy childhood. Without the funds to afford anywhere else, Dahlia and bright young daughter Ceci (Ariel Gade) decide to move into a ramshackle apartment complex on the aforementioned Roosevelt Island, partially out of desperation and partially in Dahlia's desire to make a positive fresh start of their lives. The longer they live there, however, the more obvious it becomes that something is not right. A nasty dark leak from the ceiling refuses to go away. Footsteps are heard in the apartment above despite no one living there. Ceci begins talking of a new friend named Natasha, presumed imaginary, who is affecting her behavior in class. And all the while, the question arises whether Dahlia is or isn't merely self-destructing altogether, haunted by an abusive, neglectful past and a fear of failure at parenting and life in general.

Scrupulously directed by Walter Salles and maturely written by Rafael Yglesias, *Dark Water* is just about as classy and smart as psychological thrillers—and supernatural chillers—get in the land of Hollywood. Of course, it doesn't hurt to be faithfully based on a novel by Kôji Suzuki and a Japanese feature film from Hideo Nakata (writer of the original *Ringu* and directing casualty of 2005's dim-witted American sequel, *The Ring Two*), be blessed with an A-list cast of brilliant character performers headed by Jennifer Connelly, and be helmed by an up-and-coming Brazilian filmmaker in his auspicious English-language debut.

No question, Salles' gift is in portraying the stark, ever-vivid drama of people going through real-life dilemmas and dealing with them in as authentic a fashion as possible. By taking the time to depict the lives and conflicts of Dahlia and daughter Ceci in a three-dimensional way before the paranormal elements come into play, the film's unblinking reality is given an extra jolt of apprehension by meshing so seamlessly with the eventual otherworldly happenings. Instead of firing out one rapidly edited scare scene and phony make-up effect after the next, Salles works his audience with the graceful skill of a cinematic craftsman, deliberately building the kind of unshakable details of both internal and external horror that stick with and fester in the mind of the viewer for much longer than something along the lines of a cat suddenly springing out of a closet or an axe-wielding maniac stalking scantily clad bimbos.

Dark Water works under one's skin within the first frames and stays there for the duration thanks to an exemplary collaboration of first-rate acting, methodically strong pacing, sumptuously distinct cinematography by Affonso Beato, elegant music from David Lynch regular Angelo Badalamenti, and a narrative that makes concise sense within the framework of its plotting and characters. As the picture moves assuredly into its second and third acts, there is an intentionally progressive schizophrenic feel to the editing and scene placements that further add psychological depth to the unraveling of Dahlia's world. For those unfamiliar with the Japanese original, the climactic developments, abrupt in the way life and death really is and poetic in its thematic resonance, are nearly impossible to predict.

Jennifer Connelly is mesmerizing in what could well be the best performance of her career, no small words for a smart actress who has been great many times before, all the way back to her days in 1986's *Labyrinth*. Watching her blossom on screen though the years into a formidable adult talent to be reckoned with has been a treat and here, made to carry a film almost entirely on her own back, she does not disappoint in the least. As Dahlia, Connelly has created a multilayered character woven with pain, heart-wrenching vulnerability, desperation, warmth, and underlying strength, and she does it without a single false moment. It was one of the standout leading performances of its decade. Also stronger than the average child actor, Ariel Gade is ideally cast and unaffected as daughter Ceci. The memorable supporting work from John C. Reilly, as wheeler-dealer real estate agent Mr. Murray; Tim Roth, as Dahlia's lawyer, Jeff Platzer; Dougray Scott, as her non-stereotypical ex-husband, Kyle; Pete Postlethwaite, as the apartment's not always forthcoming super, and Camryn Manheim, as Ceci's concerned school teacher, couldn't be better.

When *Dark Water* was released in the summer of 2005, the packed opening-night audience I saw the film with did not know how to react to its surprising thoughtfulness, the ruminative tone lost upon a theater full of loudmouthed, ill-behaving teenagers expecting a low-rent ghost movie with lots of "boo!" moments, flash cuts, and requiring a minimum of contemplation and introspection. *Dark Water*, a more durable, classically constructed adult horror-drama that rarely gets made in today's studio system, couldn't be further from this. Excelling in its intellectual study of the disintegration of a family—a loving mother and daughter simultaneously torn apart by the pitfalls in their natural life and coming undone by the dark secrets living with them in their apartment building—*Dark Water* proves that the horrors of the human condition are just as frightening, if not more so, than all things that go drip in the night.

Dawn of the Dead

2004 - Directed by Zack Snyder

Call me a blasphemer, but George A. Romero's original cult classic zombie trilogy—1968's *Night of the Living Dead*, 1979's *Dawn of the Dead*, and 1985's *Day of the Dead*—never impressed me in the way that it did most other horror fans. Maybe my lack of interest is linked to the speed of the undead. In Romero's world, the villains lumbered along weakly, daft looks plastered on their faces, and never seemed to pose much of a serious threat. And while *Night of the Living Dead* does hold some worth in that, when it was released in the late '60s, it was considered a groundbreaking story idea, *Dawn of the Dead* always struck me as a curiously outdated product of its times, filled with cheesy make-up effects, groan-inducing humor, mostly amateurish acting, and an overblown music score by Dario Argento and The Goblins that was just asking to be ridiculed. Watching it just one day before the release of its remake, the earlier *Dawn of the Dead* did not scare me, did not make me laugh, and dragged itself out to an interminable 127 minutes. Indeed, the film's one notably strong point is its sharp satire on consumerism.

A reimagining more than a direct update, 2004's *Dawn of the Dead* misses that potential satire altogether, but gets just about everything else, including all the glaring faults of the original, exactly right. In the world according to screenwriter James Gunn and director Zack Snyder (in his auspicious debut), the undead are fast and powerful, perhaps more so than live humans, and so the threat that they bring to the proceedings is very real and exceedingly palpable. Aided by stylishly saturated cinematography by Matthew F. Leonetti, who lends the picture a wide scope, and urgency-drenched editing by Niven Howie, the speed and rabid nature of the zombies raise this *Dawn of the Dead* to an unexpectedly high plateau in the annals of modern horror movies. It also achieves the unthinkable, greatly improving upon the original in a way that 2003's remake of *The Texas Chain Saw Massacre* failed to.

The ten-minute pre-credits sequence is a showstopper, an adrenaline-fueled nightmare come to life as downright horrifying as any movie opener since 1996's *Scream*. Young nurse Ana (Sarah Polley) leaves the hospital she works at and drives to her home in the middle of Milwaukee's idyllic suburbs. She makes out with her boyfriend in the shower and goes to bed, missing all of the signs around her, including a news report, that something dire is afoot. When Ana awakes to find her boyfriend mortally wounded (a neighbor child has ruthlessly bitten him on the neck), she narrowly escapes when he suddenly attacks her after his heart has stopped. Pure chaos has rang out on the streets, leaving Ana fearful and perplexed as to what is happening in the world. Cue Johnny Cash's haunting "The Man Comes Around" and a marvelously innovative and atmospheric opening credits scene, and you have a flawlessly rendered setup to a superior, graphically violent horror picture.

The pulse-pounding pace at the onset slows down soon after so the rest of the premise and characters can fall into place. After totaling her car in an accident, Ana finds herself hiding out in the Crossroad Mall with police officer Kenneth (Ving Rhames), Michael (Jake Weber), and Andre (Mekhi Phifer) and his pregnant wife, Luda (Inna Korobkina). "When there is no more room in Hell, the dead will walk the Earth," a television evangelist says before the broadcast suddenly ends. That is, until it becomes clear the real culprit is a fast-acting virus spread through bites that will reanimate the carrier into a bloodthirsty zombie once he or she has died. Soon joined by some more humans, including three security guards and several other refugees, Ana watches as the days tick by and the number of zombies increase at the mall entrances. In lieu of waiting for their own doom, the group devise a plan to escape to the nearby marina and sail to a hopefully deserted island. First, however, they will have to get past the hordes of dangerous, angry undead clustering the streets.

This new *Dawn of the Dead*, even more so than its late-'70s predecessor, is an unremittingly bleak motion picture, a gory, frightening portrait of what is, in essence, the end of the world. As much as these characters, including resourceful heroine Ana and tough nice guys Kenneth and Michael, try, there is ultimately no true escape from the inevitable. And while there are a handful of genuinely funny moments that naturally come out of the dialogue, things are more or less played relatively straight. Romero's *Dawn* used broad, corny comic strokes in the midst of its carnage, while Snyder's *Dawn* more appropriately deals with the reality of the situation. The latter effort, no surprise, enormously holds more scares and effectiveness. Speaking of the dark and hopeless conclusion, do not dare leave before the end credits are over. Walking away after the sight of the first end credit will cause one to miss the entire conclusion of the film, including the ultimate fate of the characters.

Sarah Polley, a Canadian-born indie staple who rarely ventures into the mainstream, is exceptional as Ana, a young woman devastated by what is happening around her, but who refuses to give up hope. Polley brings to her lead role the stark, honest emotions and no-holds-barred reality that goes along with the situation. In the process, she elevates what could have been a standard-issue horror heroine part to one with three dimensions and worth rooting for. All other performances, save for the grating Michael Kelly as stubborn security guard CJ, are concentrated and unfailing. Nonetheless, most of the characters could have afforded the depth and care brought to Ana, who is the only one we see with a life before things literally go to Hell.

Amidst the heightened suspense and skillfully created terror, Snyder does make a few key errors that keep the film from being the masterpiece it often flirts with becoming. For one, it is suggested that what is occurring is strictly virus-based, but if this is the case, then it is implausible that the entire town would fall apart overnight. Where did the virus come from to begin with? And if he wants us to believe that the long-since dead have risen from their graves, then the film is missing any such clarification (a brief scene where Ana drives by a cemetery and witnesses the dead rising would have cleared this up, but is nowhere to be found). Any way you look at it, it is an unavoidable and clumsy plot hole. Likewise, a stronger sense of the interior mall setting should have been rendered, instead of the majority happening in front of the same store over and over. If anything, the Romero-helmed *Dawn of the Dead* did do a more satisfying job of this.

Nitpicks notwithstanding, *Dawn of the Dead* is creepy, smart, classy moviemaking. The film takes no prisoners in its sole goal to scare a person silly. And what the viewer is left with by the end is an unshakable sense of both pure despair (at the narrative's outcome) and adulation (at the film's well-made nature). If the vintage *Dawn of the Dead* remains a classic of zombie cinema, then Zack Snyder's version deserves the same label. Despite what prerelease naysayers and skeptics might have thought, it defies lowered expectations. Superior in almost every way, *Dawn of the Dead* is an unforgettable, nerve-tingling ride through the American Dream gone hideously, gruesomely wrong.

The Descent

2005 - Directed by Neil Marshall

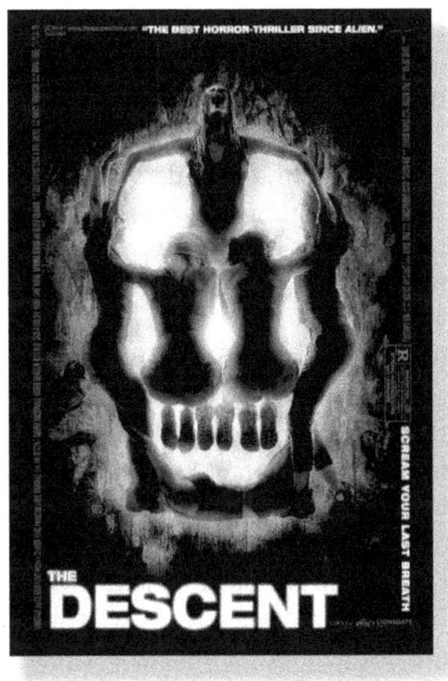

The Descent does just about everything right that *The Cave* did wrong, and hallelujah for that. There are plot similarities between the two—both detail a cave expedition that goes horribly awry when the spelunkers get lost and are subsequently stalked by ghoulish underground dwellers—but it is in the all-important area of filmmaking craftsmanship that makes them as different as night and day. *The Cave* was one of 2005's worst, the type of incoherent, tension-free dud that takes the wind out of the sails of horror lovers and makes the viewer wonder if newborn apes rather than human beings were handed a camera to make it. *The Descent* is a claustrophobic nightmare come to life, driven by a stark realism made increasingly unsettling when even its otherworldly elements turn out to be freakishly plausible.

It has been one year since Sarah (Shauna Macdonald) lost her husband and daughter in a tragic auto accident. In an attempt to try and move on, she agrees to a weekend getaway deep in the Appalachian Mountains with five friends and acquaintances. What starts off as a fun, physical day trip to explore a well-documented cave takes a turn for the worst when one of their passageways collapses and they become trapped. Worse still, daredevil caving know-it-all Juno (Natalie Mendoza) confesses that they aren't even in their intended tourist-attraction cavern, but one that, to her knowledge, has never been stepped foot in before. Unsure if there is even another way out, Sarah, Juno, the faithful Beth (Alex Reid), stepsisters Rebecca (Saskia Mulder) and Sam (MyAnna Buring), and wild-child videographer Holly (Nora-Jane Noone) have no other choice but to press forward. As fear and paranoia take over for the girlfriends, Sarah catches a glimpse of someone or something in the distance. Juno insists it's her mind playing tricks on her, but Sarah knows what she saw. Soon, their survival will hinge on a lot more than reaching the surface.

Written and directed by Neil Marshall, *The Descent* becomes so enthralling and intense that perspective viewers shouldn't be surprised if they forget to breathe for minutes at a time. A perfect world would have had this UK export being advertised in U.S. television ads and trailers without even a hint that bloodthirsty creatures fall into the equation. They don't make their first appearance until the halfway point, which would have been one of the most chilling plot surprises in recent years. Alas, they are all over the marketing campaign and anyone choosing to see *The Descent* will know basically what to expect. What these same audiences can't expect is that the creatures—actually billed as Crawlers and suggested to be humans that have evolved into blind underground cannibals who hunt through their sense of sound—aren't even the scariest part.

No, what is most frightening is the feeling of hopeless isolation Marshall evokes from the quandary of being lost in a dark, foreign place, and the effect this has on human behavior and relationships. The first act inside the cave is the film's strongest section, as the girls climb and crawl deeper and deeper. Before anything has even really happened, writer-director Neil Marshall, aided invaluably by Sam McCurdy's moodily suffocating cinematography and Simon Bowles' eerie and believable production design, suggests through camerawork, unhurried editing and the power of silences the possibilities of grave danger these six friends are bringing upon themselves. The same is true after their fates take a downward spiral and they must hang on to the belief that the cave has more than one exit.

Bringing the added threat of murderous living beings into the fold certainly ratchets up the stakes again, provocatively affecting each of the characters in highly diverse ways. As their fight-or-flight response takes over and friendships are tested under unthinkable circumstances, the already-fragile Sarah's psyche begins to crack, Juno must carry a terrible secret with her, and Rebecca and Sam will do whatever is necessary to stay alive. In Sarah's case, who senses death is imminent, she begins hearing the presence of her deceased daughter over her shoulder. Whether there is really anything there or it is simply another part of her fractured mindset is left to interpretation. For what is essentially a down-and-dirty genre pic, Marshall thoughtfully places just as much emphasis on the internal drama of the characters as the external, invigorating the proceedings with a layer of weight it wouldn't have had if the makers of *The Cave* had been in charge. It also helps to have a cast of six able and willing female actors, all of them more or less unknowns, to bring their characters' individual turmoil to life. They look like real people rather than models, and their earthy qualities make them largely accessible and sympathetic.

On the basis of the story's supernatural currents, the film's most indelibly bloodcurdling moment has no gore or violence at all. Instead, Marshall relies on the ultimate powers of suggestion, subtlety and simplicity when Sarah spots for the first time one of the Crawlers, hunched over and gnawing on something at the end of one of the cave's tunnels. It is one of the most haunting cinematic images in memory—the stuff bad dreams are made of—but a little bit of its created apprehension softens once the Crawlers take a bigger role and are seen more often. The basic stalk-and-slash (or in this case, bite) sequences grow repetitive after a while, and the villains might have been better to stay off-camera for longer periods so that they remained mysterious. No matter, jittery suspense is consistently prevalent and certain shots and ideas owe a debt of gratitude to 1979's Ridley Scott opus *Alien*, which Marshall pays fond homage to.

If the distinctly accurate portrayals of human nature—its bleak side as well as its resilient and empathetic—is the highlight over the conventional monster movie-inspired horrors, then that is but another testament to the tightness of Neil Marshall's straightforward script. Serious and smart about its high-voltage scares and oppressive atmosphere, *The Descent* is a harrowing experience. This one knows how to get the job done, and it isn't afraid to tear up bodies, shove spikes in people's necks, and crack some bones to do it.

Detention

2012 - Directed by Joseph Kahn

A labyrinthine but not impenetrable bubble gum pop explosion, *Detention* should earn major cult-hit status if for no other reason than for its fierce, unflinching juggling of genres and conventions. Is it a straight-up slasher pic, or a send-up of bloody slice-and-dicers? Is it a reference-heavy teen satire or a sobering coming-of-age wake-up call to today's technologically advanced but increasingly impersonal "newer-faster-now" culture? Or maybe it's simply a corkscrew-laden time-travel comedy wrapped up in a lot of flash, pizzazz, and a murderous horror movie villain by the name of Cinderhella who has come fatally to life. Indeed, the film does not fit into any easily defined boxes and plays squarely by its own rules. Quick-witted enough to cause whiplash in the unprepared and infirm, writer-director Joseph Kahn and co-writer Mark Palermo ensure that a single viewing won't do; to really get a handle on all that *Detention* lobs at you, this is one case that practically screams out for a second visit. Whether a return trip to the ADD-riddled town of Grizzly Lake will improve one's opinion or call attention to said film's ambitious failings is another matter altogether, up to everyone to decide.

When popular, well-liked (read: stuck-up, envied and hated) classmate Taylor Fisher (Alison Woods) is brutally murdered, rumor has it that a psychopath is on the loose around Grizzly Lake High School. Most of the student body are too involved in themselves to notice, but suicidal outcast Riley Jones (Shanley Caswell) suddenly finds a couple reasons to live when she becomes the killer's next target and simultaneously catches the eye of soulful, skateboarding, oh-so-cool Clapton Davis (Josh Hutcherson). With all of the possible suspects placed in weekend detention on the same day as prom night, Riley, Clapton, '90s-obsessed cheerleader Ione (Spencer Locke), loner-with-a-crush Sander Sanderson (Aaron David Johnson), and the rest of the rag-tag group are faced with fingering the culprit and righting the wrongs of the past as a means of stopping no less than the impending end of the world.

Detention gives new meaning to the "everything-but-the-kitchen-sink" adage, intermixing all of the above with the coinciding theatrical release of

Cinderhella II, reported UFO sightings, the occasional breaking of the fourth wall, and the school's mascot, a taxidermic grizzly bear who can transport students back in time in its hollow stomach. It's an overstuffed but ridiculously fun and gleefully original concoction. If it spends so much time being clever that it never quite lives up to the meaningful emotional core it's aiming for, that's the one notable shortcoming in a film that races a mile a minute to keep up with the twenty-first century's populist culture of spoiled, instantaneous satisfaction. From the knock-out first-scene murder of Hoobastank fangirl Taylor Fisher leading right into the crafty opening credits that appear on walls, shoes, even urinal cakes as cinematographer Christopher Probst introduces all the central characters passing through the lockered hallways of GLHS, *Detention* refuses to settle down.

Encyclopedic references spanning from present day all the way back through the '80s (with a particular fascination with 1992 for good reasons yet to be uncovered) come fast and furious—hey, is that an instrumental version of Hanson's "mmmBOP?"—in a whirlwind of pop-culture history. "You're as funny as Bronson Pinchot!" the time-warped Ione tells her gym coach, Mr. Cooper (James Black). Forever stuck in a '90s frame of mind, she describes Clapton as "all that and a bag of chips," and compares the moralistic undercurrents of *Cinderhella II* with those found in disaster movie *Volcano*. Meanwhile, Clapton may be physically smaller than bully Billy Nolan (Parker Bagley), but with moves he's learned from studying *Road House*—"the power of Swayze," as he calls them—he just might come out on top. As one can already imagine, there is a lot going on in *Detention*, to the point where some viewers may forget they're watching a horror movie at heart. There is a terrific outdoor chase through Riley's neighbors' backyards when Cinderhella attacks, but by and large the film just isn't focused enough to earn substantial scares. It works better, then, as a comment on teenage life in 2011 shredded with the nostalgia of 1980s John Hughes angst and early-1990s cinematic garishness.

The supporting cast looks more colorful than their underwritten personalities suggest, but the central protagonists are a different story. Josh Hutcherson, also serving as an executive producer for the first time, is an awesome Clapton Davis, the epitome of what's hot as he steadfastly plays to his own drum, has seemingly invented his own neon fashion sense, and still remains sensitive at the end of the day. He and newcomer Shanley Caswell, as lead heroine Riley Jones, make for a cute pair right down to their eclectic and unexpected prom dance. Caswell is immensely likable besides, playing a girl who feels hopelessly downtrodden but also has too much verve for life to go through with her own planned demises. Countering her perfectly is Spencer Locke as the spunky, snobby Ione, her love of eras gone by serving as her most blessed redeeming quality. And, finally, Dane Cook plays things mostly straight as hard-nosed Principal Verge, a former star student of Grizzly Lake harboring a possible grudge.

"It's just high school, it's not the end of the world," someone says at the end of *Detention*, and it rings true. Teenagers, so absorbed in their own here and now, can never seem to look beyond their latest personal crises. In high school, everything feels like the be-all-end-all of existence when, let's get real, it isn't. It's a lesson kids would be wise to learn. The levity that shines through in *Detention* is due to the auspicious density of Joseph Kahn's and Mark Palermo's screenplay, the kids' fight for survival against Cinderhella little more than symbolic of their respective struggles to retain individuality and compassion in a society bred in apathy. Had the rapid pacing been allowed to slow down, however, there might have been further room to make a dramatic impact. As detail-oriented as the picture is, it only scratches the surface of its characters and their immediate plight. What *Detention* is never lacking in is go-for-broke gumption. With every movie more or less a retread of what's come before, here is one that's its own vibrant entity, take it or leave it.

The Devil's Rejects

2005 - Directed by Rob Zombie

A sequel-cum-spin-off of 2003's cult-classic-in-the-making *House of 1000 Corpses*, *The Devil's Rejects* swerves to make a 180-degree turn away from that film's psychedelic funhouse nightmare of horror to something much grittier, pulpier and more realistic in tone. The change is, perhaps, disappointing for a minute or two—gone is all of the freaky intercut stock footage and camera tricks—and then the story becomes so intensely involving that the viewer stops comparing and accepts the film as its own separate entity. With only his second motion picture, writer-director Rob Zombie cemented his place as a new maven of the horror genre, a stylish auteur who paints a bravura canvas of blood, guts, terror and on-target character work, all the while paying an affectionate homage to the low-budget '70s movies (*The Texas Chain Saw Massacre*, *The Hills Have Eyes*, etc.) he grew up with. Though clearly talented, it warrants being mentioned that his command behind the camera has not always paid off, with 2007's misguided *Halloween* remake and 2013's oddly antifeminist, Jean Rollin-inspired *The Lords of Salem* unable to match the heights of his earlier work.

While having previously seen *House of 1000 Corpses* isn't a necessity, it does give this new incarnation a depth and texture that will be lost upon those unfamiliar with the psychopathic Firefly clan. As *The Devil's Rejects* gets underway, the tight-knit family of serial slashers find their house surrounded by a sea of gunfire from the cops outside. Leading the brigade is Sheriff Wydell (William Forsythe), who is dead-set on making them pay for the death of his own brother. Mother Firefly (Leslie Easterbrook) is promptly captured, while siblings Otis (Bill Moseley) and Baby (Sheri Moon Zombie) narrowly escape. With clown father Captain Spaulding (Sid Haig) soon meeting up with them, the trio set out to elude the police hunting for them, leaving a new path of death in their wake.

For aficionados of '70s horror, *The Devil's Rejects* will come as a godsend. Filmed in luscious and grimy 16-millimeter, overflowing with technical conventions of that era—slow-motion, freeze frames, sliding scene transitions, and uncompromisingly brutal violence—and cast from one end to the other with great, all-but-forgotten B-movie actors of the past, the film is, indeed, a treat just for its auspicious vision and scope. For newer audience members not so learned in that decade's underground cinema, the movie plays like a nasty, unapologetic wake-up call against the watered-down PG-13 horror crap they are probably used to having shoved down their throats. *The Devil's Rejects* is mean-spirited, graphic and bubbling over in ultra-realistic viscera, but it isn't without sociological merit—something that will no doubt be lost upon those who already know this type of flick isn't their cup of tea.

By taking on the point of view of the villains, *The Devil's Rejects* walks a fine line between portraying them as both despicable human beings of the lowest, most demented form, and as human beings who, stripped of their heinous crimes, slowly gain our sympathy. In other words, they are humanized enough here that they become more than just psycho stick figures—they are, after all, a fairly loving family besides—but director Rob Zombie does not make excuses for who they are and what they have done. We as viewers are supposed to hate them and rally behind Sheriff Wydell's journey toward vengeance, but the eventual villains-turned-victims have been written with such a clear eye that one cannot help but acknowledge them by the end as people who have taken an awful path in life rather than just irredeemable monsters.

The performances are mesmerizing, right down to the smallest part, and the plethora of emerging actors from years' past fit in effortlessly without a hint of gimmickry. When Zombie mentions in interviews that he cast these thespians for their talent and not for the sole novelty of it, one cannot possibly watch the film and not believe what he is saying is the truth. From Ken Foree (1979's *Dawn of the Dead*) to Geoffrey Lewis (1974's *Macon County Line*) to Priscilla Barnes (TV's *Three's Company*) to Michael Berryman (1977's *The Hills Have Eyes*) to P.J. Soles (1978's *Halloween*) to E.G. Daily (1985's *Pee Wee's Big Adventure*) to Mary Woronov (1982's *Eating Raoul*), the actors are exciting, eclectic, and too often sorely overlooked. Their performances, meanwhile, are superb, with Lewis and Barnes particularly affecting in emotionally demanding roles as an ill-fated married couple traveling on the road with their four-person band.

The central cast members are in just as fine a form, slipping back into their previous roles as if they never left. Sid Haig, his part welcomingly increased, is brilliant, plain and simple, as the clown-faced Captain Spaulding, the tell-it-like-it-is patriarch of the Firefly family who is equal parts hilarious and frightening. Interesting, too, how he seems to stand back most of the time and let his kids do the dirty work, as if slaughtering innocents is nothing more than a chosen career choice. As bickering brother and sister Otis and Baby, Bill Moseley and Zombie's real-life wife Sheri Moon Zombie get a chance to really strut their comedic and dramatic stuff. Moon Zombie is especially charismatic, her boisterous laugh and cutesy-pie voice an effectively disturbing counterpoint to the hideous things she does onscreen. And, finally, Leslie Easterbrook takes over for Karen Black as Mother Firefly and is so dementedly plausible that she makes the role completely her own.

That *The Devil's Rejects* isn't so much a straightforward horror movie like *House of 1000 Corpses* as it is a road drama involving merciless serial killers doesn't so much as make it a lesser film as it does simply a very different one. To his credit, Zombie is more assured this time with his expertly crafted script, and knows as well as anyone how to set up sequences of unrelenting dread and no-holds-barred authenticity. The climax, in which Sheriff Wydell transfers the villains' power into his own hands and, in essence, turns them into the hunted, is a fresh, thought-provoking idea that puts a spin on the typical stalk-and-slash scene by making viewers grapple with where their rooting interest lies.

What Zombie does with the *Thelma & Louise*-inspired denouement, brilliantly scored and edited to Lynyrd Skynyrd's classic "Free Bird," is essential to the natural progression of these characters' inevitable fates. If you stop watching before the end credits, you miss almost everything, because what happens in these final moments is necessary. In *The Devil's Rejects*, the antagonists may subtly be treated as the protagonists, but it makes no difference—as it should be, good is ultimately bound to prevail over evil when the road comes to an end, at least in the movies. It's a reassuring notion and the only moment of release in a motion picture drenched with glimpses of human nature at its most hopeless and vulnerable.

Dolls

1987 - Directed by Stuart Gordon

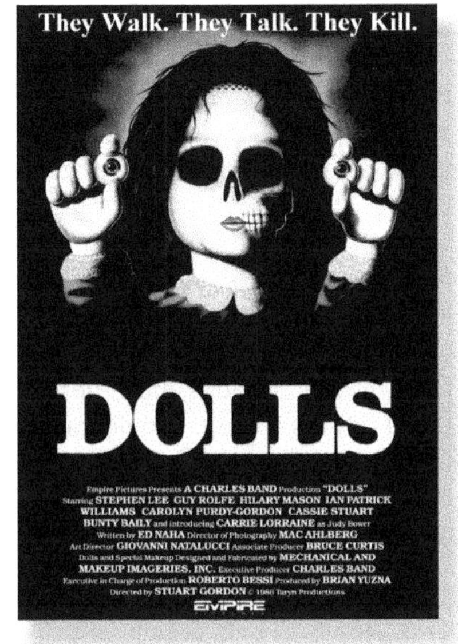

Dolls is an R-rated Grimms' fairy tale, and a surprisingly sweet one at that. Well, as sweet as can be expected for a film about toys killing people, who in turn are shrunk into corpsy, doll-sized versions of themselves. Coming off the *Grand Guignol* double dose that was 1984's *Re-Animator* and 1986's *From Beyond*, director Stuart Gordon changed his pace and broadened the boundaries of what viewers thought he was capable of. *Dolls* is still firmly rooted in horror, but it takes an innocent child's-eye view of a society that has grown up too fast and forgotten too quickly what it is like to believe anything is possible.

6-year-old Judy Bower (the adorable Carrie Lorraine) is a daydreamer at heart, and her temperamental dad, David (Ian Patrick Williams), and wicked stepmother, Rosemary (Carolyn Purdy-Gordon, gnashing her teeth), have no patience for it. While on a road trip, their car gets stuck in the mud and Rosemary cruelly tosses Judy's beloved teddy bear in the bushes. Sad about losing her stuffed animal, Judy cannot help but imagine it growing to human scale and mauling her family to death. With a storm quickly approaching, the three of them seek shelter in a nearby mansion owned by welcoming elderly couple Gabriel (Guy Rolfe) and Hilary Hartwicke (Hilary Mason), the former a dollmaker by trade.

Soon, three more unexpected guests arrive—nice-guy Ralph Morris (Stephen Lee) and the two hitchhikers he picked up, British rocker chicks Isabel (a very funny Bunty Bailey) and Enid (Cassie Stuart). They're all graciously invited to spend the night—"the longest night in the world," Gabriel tells Judy—but as the witching hour approaches and Isabel and Enid scam to steal antiques from the house while everyone sleeps, it becomes clear that the porcelain dolls adorning the shelves and mantles in every room aren't as lifeless as they may seem.

Dolls is whimsical and devilish in equal measures, a spin on the classic haunted house tale and a fable about an underappreciated little girl who finally gets a shot at happiness. Judy's father clearly prefers his snooty, rich wife to his daughter, and Rosemary revels in it. They can't wait for Judy to be out of their lives and back with her real mother in Boston. Judy, meanwhile, keeps a brave face, allowing her gift for imagination to take her away whenever she's feeling low. It is not the inner musings of a child, though, when Judy witnesses Isabel, her face bloodied, being dragged down the hallway by "little people." With her parents no help, she seeks out Ralph, the one grown-up out of all the guests who hasn't lost touch with his childhood and might possibly be able to buy into what she's just seen.

The dolls, in fact, are alive, and, as cute and unassuming as they can be, they don't take kindly to being mistreated or disrespected. As the no-good adult population dwindles, each one of them getting what's coming to them, fast friends Judy and Ralph try to keep their calm as they investigate Gabriel's basement toy shop. Impressive special effects (for 1987) bring the dolls to believable, often malicious life, with Gordon nicely blending stop-motion with animatronics. Violence comes in frequent bursts, and the murder setpieces are inventive without being too graphic or nasty. A sequence involving toy soldiers who blow their horns and sound the drums before popping Enid full of lead is a highlight, as is a vicious, much-deserved attack on Rosemary from all sides. When David returns to bed, cuddling up next to his now-dead spouse as the blood from her wounds leaks through the bedsheet and just out of his eyesight, it is a delightfully twisted moment. The transformation of one of the characters into a Punch doll, who is then given to Judy as a parting gift, is beautifully perverse.

Dolls is as warm and sincere as it is dastardly and spooky. Laced in crimson, its messages—about one's fleeting innocence, about never losing one's sense of wonder, about always keeping the good memories of one's childhood alive—remain well-meaning and pure of heart.

Donnie Darko

2001 - Directed by Richard Kelly

As fascinatingly complex and brazenly original as any movie released in the early years of the twenty-first century, *Donnie Darko* marked the bravura debut feature of then-26-year-old writer-director Richard Kelly. Like a more humane David Lynch, the plot-twisting *Donnie Darko* had been Kelly's dream project for over five years, and his stunning screenplay helped him get his foot in the door of Hollywood and attract the interest of Drew Barrymore, who not only co-stars and executive produces, but also agreed to release it on her own label, Flower Films.

For a relatively independent film, there are also a fair share of mind-bending special effects. The difference between *Donnie Darko* and a big-budget extravaganza, however, is that the effects here serve a definite purpose that aid in furthering the story along, rather than to just be about flashiness. Ultimately, *Donnie Darko* is so multilayered, thought-provoking, and rich with ideas and meaning that it defies a clear-cut definition. Part teen-angst drama, part darkly funny satire, and part science-fiction epic, Kelly has created an unforgettably woven tapestry that covers some pretty heavy topics, including the value of life, the mysteries of death, and the possibility of changing one's past and future, without striking a single false note.

Keenly set in October 1988 during the Bush-Dukakis presidential debates, Donnie Darko (Jake Gyllenhaal) is a far-from-ordinary teenage boy living in Middlesex, Virginia. He is adored by his loving parents (Mary McDonnell, Holmes Osborne) and has close relationships with his two sisters (Maggie Gyllenhaal, Daveigh Chase), but gets in trouble often at school for speaking his mind to the largely clueless administration and sees a psychologist (Katharine Ross) on a regular basis. Lured out of his house in the middle of the night while in a sleepwalking state, he is visited by Frank (James Duval), a human-sized rabbit with an insect mask, who informs him that the world is going to end in twenty-eight days on Halloween Eve. Returning home the next morning after waking up on a golf course, he finds out that a plane engine fell from the sky the night before and landed in his bedroom. The strange thing is, there are no reports of a plane crash nearby, nor knowledge of an aircraft losing its engine.

As Donnie's supposed hallucinations become more prominent and vivid, he starts questioning the feasibility of time travel and the possibility that he may have a gift of seeing into the future. Meanwhile, he is given further tasks by Frank that are getting progressively more hostile, and finds a girlfriend in new-kid-in-town Gretchen (Jena Malone), who thinks Donnie's weirdness is one of his major attributes. Everything seems to be leading to the fateful morning of October 30th (the suspected end of the world), when Donnie is sure to find out, once and for all, whether he is a sane person or a mentally ill young man.

A breakthrough masterwork, *Donnie Darko* is a devastating motion picture as beautiful and innovative as it is structurally offbeat, its twisty pretzel of a plot uncovering the different shades of its characters, their relations and bonds, and the narrative's motifs in a way that brings surprising added depth to all said departments. The ending is appropriately ambiguous, for any neat and tidy resolution would be a cheat to a movie that offers up a great deal to ponder, yet wholly encourages free thinking.

As the title character, Jake Gyllenhaal gives an exceptionally honest performance that proves what a tight grasp he has on understanding the role. He is surrounded by an enormous ensemble of well-known and lesser-known faces, all of which blend seamlessly together and make memorable impressions. Jena Malone nicely plays Gretchen as a conflicted, smart girl who is attracted, rather than turned off, by the eccentricities of Donnie. Mary McDonnell and Holmes Osborne are warm and touching as Donnie's mother and father, whose understanding attitude toward their son refreshingly goes against the grain of typical movie parents and takes on a palpable realism. Drew Barrymore gets a wonderful supporting role as Donnie's English teacher, Ms. Pomeroy, who is grappling with the narrow-minded school board over her teachings of Graham Greene's short story, "The Destructors," while Noah Wyle is strong as his chemistry teacher, Mr. Monnitoff, whom he confides in about the validity of time travel. Maggie Gyllenhaal is superb as Donnie's loving older sister, Elizabeth, and Patrick Swayze is just as good as a smarmy self-help guru whose artificial teachings have taken the town's high school by storm.

Special note should be paid to an overwhelmingly gorgeous, elongated sequence done in just two shots and played to the Tears for Fears song, "Head Over Heels." Using slow-motion, sped-up film, and a swirling camera as it follows nearly the whole cast inside and outside the high school, Kelly creates a flurry of naturalistic activities that act as an unshakably insightful glimpse into the various lives on display. It is three minutes of unadulterated, dizzying brilliance, surrounded by another two hours that are just as extraordinary.

Donnie Darko culminates in a pre-Halloween party thrown by Donnie and Elizabeth while their parents are away, the night before what just may be the end of civilization as they all know it. The morning after, in which everything is concurrently answered and left open to interpretation, makes for a finale that will undoubtedly bewilder and inspire awe in viewers, making way for some fairly complicated post-screening discussions. A story that, at its core, is about a group of people whose fates hang in the balance by the restrictions of time, *Donnie Darko* is a groundbreaking motion picture that not only deserves multiple viewings, but a whole book dedicated to the intricacies of its timely, ruminative themes.

Don't Look Now

1973 - Directed by Nicolas Roeg

Death is one of the great unknowns. Are we predestined to our fate? And is dying really the finite end, or is there something more out there? If so, what happens next? Of course, we can hold out hope, embracing our personal faith to help ease any trepidation we may have on the subject, but no one who is living really, truly knows for sure what exists beyond our current life. Maybe that is why death is so difficult for us to comprehend, even more so in relation to loved ones who have passed on. The tragedy is not simply that we will never see and talk to the deceased again, but that we hold no answers as we grapple with the idea that they are no longer here. It's a disquieting thing to ponder, and precisely the reason why *Don't Look Now* is such an unshakable experience.

Directed with an almost unparalleled sense of control by Nicolas Roeg and based on the short story by Daphne Du Maurier, this is one of the most staggeringly evocative and uncompromisingly honest motion pictures in memory to tackle the mysteries of life and death, grief and love, fear and hope. *Don't Look Now* is categorized as a supernatural horror film, and it is in its own way, but it's also so much more than that. There are no floating specters in sight, no wavery spirits, and the only detectable ghosts are those that exist in our own memories and consciences. Or are there? Roeg, along with screenwriters Alan Scott and Chris Bryant, set up a maze of subtle clues and suggestions to match the foreboding labyrinth of alleyways, streets, bridges and canals populating their Venice setting. The plot's thundering complexity and study in semiotics—e.g., spilled water on a projection slide of a church, a broach, shattered glass, a specifically chosen color motif—lead down innumerable provocative paths, sometimes reaching dead ends, other times wrapping around on themselves in meaningful ways that cannot be fully grasped upon first viewing.

On a lazy Sunday afternoon at their peaceful country home in England, John Baxter (Donald Sutherland) is getting some work done on photographic slides of church architecture and wife Laura (Julie Christie) is researching the answer to a question their daughter has asked her—"If the Earth is round, why are frozen ponds flat?" Outside, son Johnny (Nicholas Salter) runs over broken glass on his bicycle and crashes in the grass, and daughter Christine (Sharon Williams), dressed in black rain boots and a red slicker, tries to retrieve a plastic ball from the edge of a pond. In an instant, John knocks over water on his slide, the liquid turning to the color of blood as it mixes with the image of a mysterious hooded figure sitting in a church pew. He has no time to pay attention to this—the first portentous sign that danger is headed his way—when he senses that something is not quite right. Running outside, John discovers his drowned daughter, unresponsive to his clumsy, desperate attempts at resuscitation.

Switch to an undisclosed amount of time later. John and Laura are staying in the Italian city of Venice while John assists in the renovation of St. Nicholas, a local 16th-century church in disrepair. Their relationship has seemingly withstood the strain of Christine's death as they go about their days in an ominously picturesque location foreign to them. They haven't forgotten, though, with John unable to open up about his internal guilt and Laura feeling empty and sorrowful. When Laura meets two elderly sisters, Heather (Hilary Mason) and Wendy (Clelia Matania), at a restaurant, the former blind and convincingly possessing the power of second sight, she is told that Christine is with John and herself, safe and happy as can be. This information visibly renews Laura's psyche, but John is more than skeptical, refusing to accept his own prefigurative abilities as a clairvoyant, ignoring the omens inundating his everyday life, and disregarding the blind woman's later warning that he is in grave danger as long as he stays in Venice. When word comes that Johnny has been in an accident at his boarding school in London, Laura leaves Italy to be with him and presses her husband on taking a short break from work to follow her lead. The next day, John passes by a boat and glimpses Laura and the two sisters standing at the foot of it, mourners in a funeral procession. But whose funeral is it? And if Laura is in England, how can it be possible that she's in Venice at the same time?

Don't Look Now is intoxicatingly deliberate in its pacing, but never meandering. Each new scene helps to either inform the plot or the characters, broadening the scope of John's and Laura's grief as something even more unimaginable is imminent within their futures. Laura, wanting to grasp onto hope for her daughter's well-being in the afterlife, takes Heather at her word while keeping Christine's red and white ball tucked away in her suitcase as security. She urges John to consider that Heather's foresight might be true, not only about Christine but also about the danger coming to him, but he is in denial, and perhaps not as strong as his wife. In one scene filled with the sort of anguish rarely captured on the screen, John blows up at Laura. "Our daughter is dead!" he yells at her. "Dead! Dead! Dead! Dead! Dead!" And yes, Christine is dead, but how can John explain it away when he and Laura get hopelessly lost one night on their way to dinner, wandering the desolate narrow streets of Venice, and he glimpses a flash of a small figure in a crimson hooded slicker disappear around a corner? That John comments, "I know this place," even though he has no conscionable reason to, is not a mistake on his part.

The cinematography by veteran lenser Anthony Richmond paints the autumnal months in Venice with a spookily drab but realistic palette, the color red popping up throughout to symbolize two very diverse things: memories of the forever innocent Christine, and possible threats toiling in the mundane. Subtle signs of impending menace don't end there. With their hotel about to close for the winter and the prospects of moving to a new nearby location on John and Laura's shoulders, the manager has instructed his staff to pull white sheets over all the furniture in the lobby, their shapes like corpses surrounding them. After Laura has left Venice to care for their injured son in London, John narrowly escapes death or injury himself when the scaffolding he is standing on inside St. Nicholas breaks, leaving him dangling high in the church with only a rope to hold onto. Walking away safely from the incident, John experiences a split-second vision of the past event taking a turn for the worst and himself falling. Moments later, he is witness to the police pulling the scantily clad body of a woman from the canal.

Meanwhile, the aforementioned red figure will show itself several more times, often in the background of shots and not always noticed by the characters. John's choice to follow it in the end is his destiny, and by this time he knows it. Does he truly believe it could be his dearly departed little girl, or is he merely the victim of a fate that cannot be altered? The final ten minutes of *Don't Look Now* are unforgettable, and especially fascinating in the ways that they affect the viewer depending on the number of personal viewings. The first time one sees the ending, it is horrifying—a nightmare happening in the real world. The second time, it is almost as eerie. By the third viewing, the culminating scenes are still creepy, but also emotionally devastating, saying so much so simply about the frailty of life and the brevity with which it comes and goes. The identity of the figure in red isn't important, or the point; the film wisely sticks with John's point of view in these lingeringly stark and beautiful last moments. It is his journey to take.

Don't Look Now is a bravura cinematic masterpiece of a kind Hollywood doesn't seem to make anymore. At once haunting and deeply poignant, richly layered and loaded with underlying tension and gentility, the film only improves the more one sees it. As John and Laura Baxter, Donald Sutherland and Julie Christie have scarcely been as remarkable as they are here, essaying a married couple who never feel less than authentic. A sex scene between them, infamous in some circles for the rumor that the actors, dating at the time, were doing more on camera than simulating the act, is breathtakingly intimate, their love-making interspersed with quiet snapshots of them getting ready to go out to dinner. The viewer almost feels as if he or she shouldn't be watching them in such a private, expressive setting, but it is impossible to take one's eyes off the screen. Wrapped in a pall of substantive dread that mesmerizingly permeates through the proceedings, *Don't Look Now* brilliantly portrays the loves and losses we all experience, our here and now dictated by the fallibility of human nature and the cruelties of time.

Drag Me to Hell

2009 - Directed by Sam Raimi

Deliciously scary and wickedly tongue-in-cheek, *Drag Me to Hell* marked director Sam Raimi's long-awaited, stupendously welcome return to the genre that first made him a household name. Helming big-budget blockbusters—2002's *Spider-Man*, 2004's *Spider-Man 2*, and 2007's *Spider-Man 3*—is well and fine, even impressive, but it is clear while watching his latest old-school ode to demonic spirits and things that go bump in the night that he is having the time of his life. In turn, the goosebump-inducing fun rubs off on the audience, burned many times in the past by wimpy PG-13 supernatural fare that don't have a clue how to tell a story, build characters, and still give the viewer something to scream about. *Drag Me to Hell* succeeds at doing all three of these things while carving out a place for itself in the pantheon of classic modern horror films. It's that good.

Lovely, ambitious Christine Brown (Alison Lohman) is a bottle of hidden insecurities who practices with annunciation tapes to rid herself of her southern drawl and is tempted each morning by, but ultimately bypasses, the shop window of fatty desserts that once were her childhood weakness. Working as a loan officer at California's Wilshire Pacific Bank, she is currently vying for the in-contention assistant manager's position, but is accused by boss Mr. Jacks (David Paymer) of being a pushover not able to make "the tough decisions." When ailing elderly gypsy Mrs. Ganush (Lorna Raver) comes into the bank seeking a third extension on her house's mortgage, Christine spots the lady emptying a jar of candies into her purse and decides on the spot that she will make an example out of her latest customer in order to impress her superior. Believing that she has been shamed, Mrs. Ganush places the curse of the half-goat/half-beast Lamia on Christine, ensuring that after three days of being haunted, she will be dragged straight to Hell. Christine's psychology professor boyfriend, Clay (Justin Long), is skeptical of her claims, but steadfast in his devotion. As the clock ticks down and violent forces inundate her waking hours, an out-of-options Christine seeks the help of spiritual advisor Rham Jas (Dileep Rao), an aficionado of the occult.

Opening with the Universal Studios logo of the early 1980s, *Drag Me to Hell* continues to hearken back to the thriller mainstays of decades' past. The homey art direction and production design, mixing on-location shooting with attractive, atmospheric backlots, reminds of *Psycho*- and *Vertigo*-era Alfred Hitchcock. The sight of a cemetery on a storm-swept night, the tombstones rising over a landscape of hills and valleys, is gorgeous to behold. The cinematography by Peter Deming is buoyed by an imaginative flair, using tilted angles, close-ups, and establishing setups with confidence. Two separate shots of bare tree branches encroaching like demonic fingers upon a car driving down the road leap out with their brooding ingenuity. The string-laden music score by Christopher Young recalls the great Bernard Herrmann and is unmistakably kin to Young's own underrated *Tales from the Hood* effort. At the same time, the classy, off-kilter themes feel totally fresh and never less than inspired. The multilayered sound effects design is also tops, taking the innocuous—creaking gates, tapping fingernails, a buzzing fly—and making them as sinister as can be.

Meanwhile, sly, subtle allusions and winks abound. The séance setpiece, which could have gone the way of 2009's atrocious *The Unborn* and been laughably cornball, instead recalls Robert Wise's elegant *The Haunting* by way of Raimi's own *The Evil Dead*. By the time the human participants and sacrificial goat are possessed by the Lamia and floating through the air screaming for Christine's soul, it has segued effortlessly into *Evil Dead 2: Dead By Dawn* territory. A gross-out scene set in Christine's tool shed approaches *Looney Tunes* lunacy with the incorporation of an anvil into the action. Keen-eyed viewers will also note that Mrs. Ganush drives the very same 1973 Delta 88 Oldsmobile that Ash drove in *The Evil Dead*. The use of a kitten-centric "Hang on, Baby!" wall poster to counter the terror of Christine being hunted in her home by the Lamia is undeniably funny. So, too, is a stop at a psychic's, the cash register prominently looming in the foreground.

Drag Me to Hell has a sense of morbid humor about it, no doubt, but writer-director Sam Raimi and co-writer Ivan Raimi are first and foremost out to rattle the nerves of their audience. This they do in spades, overflowing the screen with rich little details that make it all so much more than it would have been were lesser talents behind the scenes. A sequence set in an underground parking garage, with Mrs. Ganush's parked car and handkerchief spelling impending doom, is horrifying, so suspenseful and macabre that it has to be seen to be believed. The attacks in Christine's house, pushing her to limits she doesn't expect to go, are breathlessly conceived. Onslaughts of various bodily fluids—phlegm, projectile nose-bleeding, and even waterfalls of embalming fluid—add to the stomach-churning quotient while amazingly retaining a PG-13 rating.

Alison Lohman was not the first actress cast in the role of Christine—Ellen Page foolishly dropped out prior to filming—but it is nearly impossible to imagine anyone else playing her. Sympathetic, cute and eager to please, Christine is developed as a three-dimensional character whom the viewer has fallen in love with before the crap hits the fan. Attempting to put the past behind her is easier said than done—Christine not only must deal with the curse, but also the prejudices and judgments of Clay's mother (Molly Cheek), Mrs. Ganush's granddaughter (Bojana Novakovic), and boss Mr. Jacks—and her constant plight to prove that she is better than what her naysayers presume gives the story an additional thematic relevance. The same might be said about the timely portrayal of the picture's modern-day economic woes, and the lengths people will go to better their sometimes make-or-break situations. A fraction of the reason the film is so affecting is due to Lohman's likability and innocence. She could very well rank alongside Jamie Lee Curtis in *Halloween* as one of the top horror heroines in memory. As Clay, Justin Long turns the stock part of supportive boyfriend into someone more textural than that. Long and Lohman are wonderful together, making up a couple one believes truly love each other. And as the catalyst who sets the plot into motion, Lorna Raver is unforgettably chilling as Mrs. Ganush, a woman whose intimidating presence lingers even when she isn't on the screen. Stereotypical or not, Mrs. Ganush exemplifies why gypsies may never be crossed again.

In spite of an ending that logically works but may be a smidge too grim for some, *Drag Me to Hell* remains devilish fun that cinema lovers of all kinds owe themselves to experience. So entertaining it ought to be a crime, the picture proves that not all mainstream, studio-produced horror movies have to be watered-down, insulting, nonsensical, morose, cheap, gore-drenched, predictable, or all of the above. In a day and age when the best genre works are receiving poor theatrical distribution, in some cases being shipped straight-to-DVD, Blu-ray, and for digital download, *Drag Me to Hell* not only was awarded a wide release, but received some much-deserved recognition from critics and audiences alike. That Raimi is a master of the genre goes without saying. We should all be happy to be his puppets.

Dressed to Kill

1980 - Directed by Brian De Palma

Some people vehemently accuse Brian De Palma of being almost plagiaristic in his aping of Alfred Hitchcock's style. Some people favorably note the work he did in the 1970s through the early '90s—e.g., 1976's *Carrie*, 1981's *Blow Out*, 1984's *Body Double*, 1992's *Raising Cain*—as the modern-day equivalent of Hitchcock. Whether one wants to call the so-called "Master of Suspense" merely inspiration for De Palma or something more negative, the fact remains: when De Palma is good, he's usually great. In recent years, he has begun to mysteriously slip with ill-fated films such as 2000's *Mission to Mars* and 2006's *The Black Dahlia* (to be fair, 2013's *Passion* was a sleek, stylish, if surface-heavy return to semi-form), but there was a time when De Palma was able to meticulously zero in on every filmmaking element that, together, formed something breathtakingly intense and seductively beautiful.

Dressed to Kill is perhaps the most outwardly Hitchcockian motion picture that Brian De Palma ever made. It's certainly one of his most successful, at once lurid, sexy, chilling, gruesome, aesthetically eye-popping, and even a little funny. A fan of bait-and-switch storytelling that starts off as one thing and then suddenly twists around, catching the viewer off-guard and feeling unsafe, De Palma used the framework of 1960's *Psycho* for his own splendidly bizarre narrative. Whereas *Psycho* was violent for its time, it is relatively tame today. By comparison, *Dressed to Kill* is very much a product of the 1980 slasher-fueled landscape. The body count is low, but when De Palma strikes a physical blow to his characters he makes it count. The convention of using a POV shot from the killer's perspective, complete with handheld camera and heavy breathing, is also used here near the end, but one gets the impression that the writer-director knows exactly what he's doing, making a comment on the cliché as much as just falling victim to said cliché.

Like Janet Leigh's iconic turn as the ill-fated Marion Crane, Angie Dickinson (most famous then for the 1974-78 TV series *Police Woman*) is the deceptive main character for the opening half-hour. Dickinson plays Kate Miller, a restless middle-aged woman who is secretly unhappy in her marriage and starting to fantasize about something more. She goes to her shrink, the handsome Dr. Robert Elliott (Michael Caine), and questions to him whether or not an affair might be worth it. Then she heads to New York's Museum of Modern Art (interiors were shot in the Philadelphia Museum of Art), where she meets the glances of a mysterious stranger and ends up following him out to his taxi, where they engage in a frank sexual encounter that leads up to his apartment. On a high from the experience, Kate writes her one-night stand a note while he sleeps in the other room and is about to head out when she discovers doctor's papers in his desk diagnosing him with a venereal disease. Kate hurries to the elevator, but must turn back when she realizes she has left her wedding ring on the man's nightstand. This is her fatal mistake, one that costs her her life.

Enter blowsy escort Liz Blake (Nancy Allen), the one witness to have caught a glimpse of the female killer in a circular elevator wall mirror. Through a series of events, Liz is left holding the murder weapon—a bloodied shaving razor—and is immediately placed on Detective Marino's (Dennis Franz) suspect list. As Liz becomes the murderess' next target, she teams up with Kate's whiz-kid teenage son, Peter (Keith Gordon), to find out the identity of the woman and her motive for targeting Kate. They ultimately trace her back to Dr. Elliott, who had been seeing them both as clients.

Dressed to Kill opens with a sensually explicit shower scene that culminates in a man coming up from behind Kate and starting to rape her. This is revealed to only be a fantasy that Kate uses to keep herself interested while she has by-the-numbers sex with her husband. When he's through, he pats her on the cheek like some common whore and heads to the bathroom. Immediately, the viewer understands that Kate's marriage has not been solid for a long time, but she has kept her emotions bottled up, unable to make the first move in talking about their problems. Angie Dickinson is such a humane protagonist and such a force of emotions, many of them locked behind the surface of her levelheaded outward façade, that when she is killed at the end of the first act, the viewer feels it in the gut.

From this point, Liz takes over as the story's heroine, an unapologetic glorified prostitute with a sharply tuned sense of humor and an intelligence that belies her frowned-upon profession. Risking her life to clear her own name, Liz and teenage confidante Peter, himself wanting vengeance for his mom's demise, take on the roles of amateur sleuths. The friendship that forms between Liz and Peter is low-key and unassuming, though some viewers might raise an eyebrow when he invites her to spend the night at his house while his stepfather is out of town, and she accepts. Interesting to consider, if the roles were reversed and an adult man agreed to stay over with an underage girl, it would come off as much more taboo and everyone would have been in an uproar.

Nancy Allen, an early De Palma staple and his former wife, to boot, is terrific fun to watch onscreen. She has can't-miss comedic timing, a great look, and a toughness that doesn't hide her vulnerability. In the complicated role of Dr. Robert Elliott, Michael Caine also makes an impression. The particulars of his part will not be given away here, but Caine tackles Dr. Elliott as a man trying to retain his professionalism even when his female clients come onto him and he receives an ominous answering machine message from Bobbi, a transsexual who could very well be Kate's killer.

What really ups the ante in the effectiveness of *Dressed to Kill* are the long, purposefully drawn-out setpieces. De Palma is a wizard of *mise-en-scène*, building remarkable levels of suspense in the way that he sets up what is about to happen and then edits the material in an intoxicatingly slow fashion that allows for the viewers to be placed in the characters' shoes, imagining all the while what they might do in a similar situation. A ten-minute museum sequence, free of dialogue, is brilliant, with Kate people-watching while making a list of items to pick up at the grocery store. When a dark, devastatingly good-looking man takes a seat next to her, she flirts with him without uttering a syllable. Their ensuing pursuance of each other through the maze of rooms in the museum is shot by cinematographer Ralf Bode with a fluid, dreamlike intrigue and a hint of danger, speaking to the desperation of Kate's character. Other setpieces are gasp-inducingly scary, such as an elevator murder scene, a chase on a subway train that pits Liz against a mounting cavalcade of obstacles, and a climactic sequence that bookends and, to a point, mirrors the opening shower scene.

The use of a transsexual as the villain of the piece is controversial and the very ending is decidedly derivative of De Palma's own *Carrie*. Before this, though, *Dressed to Kill* is a classic thriller as well as a gussied-up, superior horror film that fascinatingly blends sexuality and carnal desire with expert macabre touches. Location shooting in New York City is indelibly interwoven into the action—there is even a late scene set inside the World Trade Center—and De Palma's calling-card split-screen also makes an appearance with apt aplomb. Eerily transcendent, *Dressed to Kill* is a layered machine of on-target character work and the sort of tension that only the best of the best filmmakers can ratchet. Hitchcock would be flattered and proud.

The Eclipse

2010 - Directed by Conor McPherson

Blending romance, drama and supernatural horror into a truly original, thoroughly unforgettable concoction, *The Eclipse* refuses to tip its hand in any one finite direction. Writer-director Conor McPherson is less interested in recognizing genre than he is in telling a multilayered story with beautifully drawn characters, following them wherever their paths may lead. In doing so, he leaves his enraptured audience feeling unbalanced in the best way, unprepared for the unexpected power to come. Poignant, tender and, in a few surprising choice scenes, outright horrifying, *The Eclipse* is best compared to 1999's moody, groundbreaking *The Sixth Sense* and 2005's underrated, richly composed *Dark Water*—fellow tales of a psychological, ghostly nature with similar thematic trajectories. Grieving isn't hard at all, but learning to let go and accept what cannot be changed is.

Set over a life-altering one-week period during the annual Cobh International Literary Festival of Irish seaside community Cork County, widowed woodshop teacher Michael Farr (Ciarán Hinds) has volunteered, as he often does, to be a driver and assistant at the event. A middle-aged man who has long since given up his underlying dream of being a writer, Michael now spends the bulk of his time caring for 10-year-old son Thomas (Eanna Hardwicke) and 14-year-old daughter Sarah (Hannah Lynch) while trying to pick up the shattered pieces left behind in the wake of his wife's death two years earlier. On the night of the festival's opening ceremonies and banquet, Michael is awakened by a noise downstairs and, upon investigation, is faced with the sight of a shadowy figure disappearing into the next room. He believes it may be his father-in-law, Malachy (Jim Norton), but when he calls the nursing home to check on his whereabouts he is reassured that the elderly man is asleep in his room. The next morning, Michael pays him a visit, and Malachy is bitter over not being picked up the night before to attend the banquet. More than that, he's still very much angry about the loss of his daughter—a pain so great, he says, "it almost makes you think there can't be a god."

Over the next few days, Michael will be faced with increasingly alarming visions of the still-alive but unwell Malachy, otherworldly experiences that draw him to renowned writer of the supernatural Lena Morelle (Iben Hjejle), in town for the festival. As she tries to ward off the advances of philandering, egocentric best-selling author Nicholas Holden (Aidan Quinn)—a man she made the mistake of sleeping with once before—Lena finds herself developing a soulful bond with Michael that catches both of them off-guard. Connecting through their respective pasts involving the mysteries of the hereafter, she ultimately plays a pivotal, if fleeting, role in allowing him to realize his potential as a writer and come to terms with a loss too great for him to bear any longer.

Based on "Table Manners" from playwright Billy Roche's short story collection *Tales from Rainwater Pond, The Eclipse* is as fresh as it is immediate. At 88 minutes, the film spares not a moment of screen time, potent with provocative ideas and varied subject matter. The backdrop of the literary festival is a deliciously specific detail that lays the groundwork for themes involving a writer's hope for outside approval and struggle for self-worth. For aspiring literati Michael, he has watched his dreams slip by him and has shoved them so far back in his mind that the mere thought seems like an impossibility. More centrally, McPherson grapples with the concept of death and the impact it has on the living. Michael's spectral encounters are all the more baffling because the spirit haunting him is still intact with its human body—a rare, but not unthinkable, occurrence, Lena tells him. Still, as she confirms in her reading to a room of enthralled attendees, Michael's knowledge of reality as he knows it must be reconfigured due to his sightings—confirmation that there are metaphysical concepts greater than that of life lived from birth to death. In some ways, Mulachy holds Michael responsible for his daughter's passing from cancer—he was supposed to keep her safe—and Michael can't help but feel a similar sense of guilt. Now he must watch his children grow up without a mother as he senses her physical presence drift further away from him. All that he has left are his memories and the pictures that adorn the walls of his home—photographs of people and things that no longer are.

The blossoming relationship between Michael and Lena, traveling from strictly professional to friendly to kindred and possibly romantic, is lovingly developed as counterpoint to Michael's internal struggles. Their time together is only temporary—she will be leaving once the festival is over—which makes their every interaction feel all the more critical and urgent. Lena, who has shut herself off from human companionship—she's not much good at it, anyway, she says—and knows full well she's not interested in Nicholas, sees something different in Michael. There's a humanity and a vulnerability there that she finds disarming. They may not spend the rest of their lives together, but for this moment in time they are exactly what the other needs.

A gifted character actor receiving a rare well-deserved lead role, Ciarán Hinds is outstanding as the tortured Michael Farr, a good man who must face a deeper darkness before he can rise to the light. In his tender scenes with his children, in his quietly emotional showdown with his father-in-law, in his frightened confrontations with the other side, in his comfortable, hesitantly unguarded times with Lena, Hinds paints a full, honest, piercing portrait of a protagonist whose shades go far deeper than black and white. It's easy to see why he won the Best Actor award at the Tribeca Film Festival for this role. As Lena, Iben Hjejle is a radiant, soulful find, her character ripe with a sweetly spontaneous demeanor and a basketful of insecurities. And Aidan Quinn plays against-type as the smarmy, childish Nicholas Holden, an author who can sell books, but hasn't seemed to gain any natural wisdom from his writing. Nicholas verges upon the line of caricature, but Quinn makes sure he never becomes one. For all his belligerence, Nicholas feels authentic, for better or worse.

Because *The Eclipse* appears to be so entrenched in day-to-day realism, its sudden, unforeseen dips into ghostly territory come off as all the more jarringly perverse. To say that the scares are supremely effective is to understate the matter. To say that they are some of the most singularly petrifying, jump-up-and-scream-in-pure-terror moments perhaps in cinema history would not be hyperbole. That they are surrounded by an overall more gentle story about the process of grief and the transcendent turn toward acceptance makes the horror elements all the more special and out of the ordinary. Gifted with handsome cinematography by Ivan McCullough and a sharp eye for both the solitariness of one's private moments and the fortuitous snapshots of human selflessness, *The Eclipse* concludes with an awe-inspiring sign of hope as cathartic as it is oddly soothing. Its ability to take one's breath away—not only in shock, but ultimately in genuine wonder—is irreplaceable.

Elephant

2003 - Directed by Gus Van Sant

Winner of the Palme D'Or and Best Director prizes at the 2003 Cannes Film Festival, *Elephant* is an unshakably disturbing, nerve-rattling paragon from prolific writer-director Gus Van Sant. A fictional, but eerily reminiscent telling of the 1999 Columbine tragedy—at the time, the worst school shooting in American history—*Elephant* manages the difficult feat of finding the profound in the seemingly mundane, beauty in the most unlikely of places, and human complexity in its most naked and raw of forms. It is a film that says so very much—about the frailty and unpredictability of life, the unintentional ignorance of people for what is right under their noses, the impact a single small event or decision can have on another's or their own future—with the unrushed, unblemished, exquisite simplicity that only a master filmmaker can achieve.

Elephant takes an intoxicatingly non-traditional path in unweaving its narrative. Set almost entirely on a single day at an Oregon high school (and, when you stop to think about it, in the same 10-minute period leading up to an unexpected and deadly school massacre), the picture follows one character, or set of characters, as they go about their day, until it changes viewpoints and follows a different person. Sometimes their lives directly intersect, wrapping around a timeline and coming full circle, and sometimes they pass each other without either party noticing. As the leading roles mount, the floor plan and architecture of the school vividly etched, and more information is disclosed, it gradually becomes clear exactly when the shootings are about to take place. The characters, however, have no way of knowing. And when one gossipy teenage girl jokingly tells her two friends, "I just want to survive to see my driver's license," she has no idea just how prophetic and dire her words actually are.

As the film opens, a car weaves down a residential street, knocking off a parked car's side mirror and coming dangerously close to running into a telephone pole. The passenger is John (John Robinson), fed up that his dad (Timothy Bottoms) is drunk again and he's going to be late to school. The event is a distressing omen, and John doesn't yet realize that his father's reckless driving is the least of his impending problems. Once at school, John calls his brother to come pick his dad up, and is then caught by the principal (Matt Malloy) and sentenced to detention. Other characters gradually enter the frames before taking them over. Nathan (Nathan Tyson), a studly jock who doesn't notice a girl's fawning when he passes her in the hallway, leaves gym class and meets up with girlfriend Carrie (Carrie Finklea). Together, they go to the main office to get written out-of-school passes—passes they will not be able to use. Daydreamer Michelle (Kristen Hicks) is cornered by her gym teacher, who asks her why she refuses to wear shorts like the rest of the girls, before heading off to the locker room to get changed. She is late for her volunteer work at the school library during her lunch period. Aspiring photographer Elias (Elias McConnell) takes pictures of two passing classmates before school, promising them copies when he has the roll exposed. He then trudges off to the darkroom to work on his photos. Meanwhile, Jordan (Jordan Taylor), Nicole (Nicole George) and Brittany (Brittany Mountain) chat and gossip as they go to get lunch in the cafeteria before diligently heading to the bathroom to throw it up.

And then there is Alex (Alex Frost) and Eric (Eric Deulen), outsiders who, earlier, ordered a gun online. Alex is seen having spitballs thrown viciously at him in science class. When a classmate notices him taking notes in the cafeteria and asks what he is doing, his response is casual and foreboding: "You'll see." Alex plays Beethoven on the piano while Eric passes the time with a violent computer game. They watch a documentary on Hitler with a lazy detachment. And, on the morning of the shooting, they eat breakfast at Alex's house and his mother's last words to him are, "Don't forget to lock up." Before leaving, his father tells him they might go duck-hunting on the weekend, and Eric rolls his eyes at Alex, whose parents are oblivious to what their son is about to do.

Elephant is a startling, uncompromising motion picture of immense power and poeticism. Van Sant does not take the high and mighty road of even beginning to explain why Alex and Eric do what they do in the third act. He simply doesn't know, and it would be impossible to pinpoint one concrete reason that caused them to snap. For the questions it delicately poses, and for the answers that are never given, Van Sant has constructed one of the most thought-provoking and important films of its decade. The responsibility he offers up with opened arms in getting this story told is telling. The film does not second guess any of its characters, because it hardly has time to; many of their lives are cut short before they have a chance to even think about it. The film does not create false crises and melodrama just to pump up the plot; the people are just going through the motions of their everyday lives at school, unaware of the danger before them.

Further adding to the realism of *Elephant* is the cast Van Sant assembled. All of the teenage characters were real teenagers, high schoolers from Portland, Oregon, with no prior acting experience. The sparse dialogue seems to have been entirely improvised, and the way the teens interact and talk to each other has an unblinking naturalism that one could likely never find with trained professionals. You believe them in their roles because you expect that most of them share distinct characteristics with the people they're playing, and have first-hand knowledge of what their droning, uneventful high school days are really like. Meanwhile, the remarkable cinematography by Harris Savides is in constant motion, taking on a hypnotic quality as the camera smoothly drifts down hallways and dollies behind its characters as they go from one school activity to the next. The music score and subtle sound effects, such as birds chirping in the background and approaching thunder, are deeply evocative, only aiding to raise unbearable tension as one awaits the inevitable to break apart these people's falsely assumed safe existences.

When the shootings erupt during the final twenty minutes, the movie avoids exploitation but still goes for the jugular. The violence is abrupt and depressing when a director with less on his mind might have tried to thrill his audience with blood, guts and action-movie pyrotechnics. Unexpected but truthful, too, in that the late scenes are almost as quiet as the rest of the film. Kids scramble out of the school in silence, unafraid to make a sound and give themselves away. One football player, who makes the mistake of trying to be a hero, is cut short in a blast of cold gunfire. As for Eric and Alex, they are exempt of emotion as they trudge through the empty hallways and hunt down their dwindling prey. By this point, they are on an automatic pilot that is rapidly deflating by the second. For them, they have smacked into a brick wall that they know marks the end of the line. And what, exactly, are they left with?

Elephant, whose intricacies only increase with repeat viewings, is deceptively simple. Not much seems to happen, and yet looking beneath the surface will unveil a contained bubble—the meandering hell that is high school—that, before the day is over, will be cracked wide open forever. The most routine of actions, such as the developing of a picture Elias promised his two subjects earlier in the morning, or the acquiring of a pass to leave school early, will never reach fruition. Unspoken words of truth between friends, lovers and acquaintances will never get to be said. And all that everyone involved is left with is a mind-bogglingly senseless act that, could it not have been stopped, may at least allow those spared to see the world around them a little more clearly, and recognize just how valuable and fleeting every moment of their lives really is.

The unforgettable, heartbreaking cumulative power of *Elephant* is spellbinding long after the end credits have rolled. Gus Van Sant has created a stark, horrifying glimpse into the fallibility of life, consequences and the human condition. When the carnage has subsided, he asks the very question likely to be on his audience's mind: why? Van Sant is at just as much of a loss as the rest of society on the answer. *Elephant* is candid, sumptuously layered, unspeakably authentic, and, finally, devastating.

Enter the Void

2010 - Directed by Gaspar Noé

The word, "masterpiece," is bandied around with a certain frivolousness when it comes to modern film criticism. There are plenty of great pictures, but how many truly deserve their place in the upper echelons of cinema history? *Enter the Void* indisputably earns this distinguished label, reinventing a whole new filmic language with a structure, style and subject matter that are thoroughly and without question unique. Remarkably innovative in form, unshakably haunting in tone, and nothing less than transcendentally devastating—and, ultimately, soothing—in plot and intention, writer-director Gaspar Noé's much-anticipated follow-up to 2003's rule-breaking, highly controversial *Irreversible* is an experience to be treasured, feared and never forgotten. So many movies these days rely on conventions and clichés to tell their stories that it's worth celebrating when one of them defiantly breaks free from the pack and carves out fresh, untrammeled territory. Done almost flawlessly, to boot, and the results are downright miraculous.

Oscar (Nathaniel Brown) is an American living in Tokyo with his younger sister, Linda (Paz de la Huerta), a stripper at a club fittingly named Sex Money Power. In lieu of getting an honest job, he has begun selling drugs—a choice that confidante Alex (Cyril Roy) warns could get him in a lot of trouble one day. As Linda heads out to work for the night, she passingly calls Oscar a junkie. In his mind, he is adamant that he is not even as he starts to trip out after smoking hallucinogenics. Heading to seedy nearby bar The Void for one of his drug deals, he discovers too late that he has been set up by ex-pal Victor (Olly Alexander). Locking himself in the restroom, Oscar is shot dead. His life might be over, cut tragically short by a series of very bad decisions and circumstances, but his journey into the afterlife is only beginning.

Told solely from the point of view of Oscar, the film begins in the young man's skin, the camera seeing what he sees right down to his drug-fueled hallucinations and the blinking of his eyelids. A half-hour later, just as startling and unpredictable as death itself, Oscar is killed. Taking over the perspective of the camera lens, his disembodied spirit rises over his physical corpse and proceeds on a nonlinear, montage-like journey through the memories and snapshots of the troubled life he has led. While freely floating over Tokyo, Oscar's visions soon begin to blend with his eavesdropping on the people he knows and the ripple effect his premature death has had on them. Eventually, he will learn his ultimate fate—not only of his body, but also his soul.

Enter the Void is exquisitely crafted by Noé, never low on visual splendor, thematic resonance and emotional catharses. As much of a character as Oscar and Linda—indeed, it takes on the very otherworldly viewpoint of the lead character—is the stunning cinematography by Benoit Debie, painting Oscar's sight with equal parts kaleidoscopic wonder and nightmarish dread. Tokyo, meanwhile, is portrayed as a neon wonderland of beauty and hedonism, broken dreams and wanton desire. As the ghostly Oscar peers down upon the people he has left behind, he bears witness to beloved sister Linda's discovery that her soul mate and last surviving family member is dead and can do nothing but watch how she unravels in the weeks and months after. He also observes Alex, Victor, Victor's mom, Suzy (Sara Stockbridge), and Linda's club boss, Mario (Masato Tanno). From cityscape to personal homes and apartments to stripping joints to hotels to even an airplane passing overhead, Oscar has no choice but to see it all and go everywhere as he waits for his calling, a course of the afterlife described in detail within *The Tibetan Book of the Dead*.

The heart of the story belongs to the close sibling relationship between Oscar and Linda. Viewed in flashes, Oscar's life happens before his eyes (these scenes are shot from over Oscar's shoulder during all stages of his development, from toddler to adult), helping to inform the person the viewer has already seen he becomes. Their tranquil childhood ripped apart by the deaths of their parents in an awful auto accident, Oscar and Linda survived the ordeal from the backseat but found their ensuing years marked by the trauma and consequences. Forced to live in separate foster homes, they make a promise to reunite and always be there for each other. By the time Oscar is now grown up and able to pay for Linda's airfare to Tokyo, he has already begun down a misbegotten road that tears their plans apart. The joy and heartache of all that life has to offer is mesmerizingly captured by Noé, key moments within Oscar's existence creating a breathtaking tapestry of the fleeting odyssey we as living creatures all must go on. A thrilling scene where brother and sister celebrate being together again and ride a roller-coaster through the nighttime skies of their glittering surroundings is juxtaposed with harsh moments—the car crash; the moment Linda was torn away from Oscar to live with an adoptive family; a young Linda asking her grandmother, now dead, what will happen when she dies—that blisteringly comment on how temporary everything is.

Newcomer Nathaniel Brown is rarely seen but often heard as unknowing tour guide Oscar, his thoughts verbalized alongside his speech during his living moments before being overtaken by the bleak silence of the afterlife. Fearless and uninhibited, Paz de la Huerta turns Linda into a vivid, sad-eyed figure whose attempts at happiness are constantly being met by disappointments. The depression she finds herself in by the end, grieving for a loved one she will never see again while trapped in a foreign place, is shatteringly depicted by de la Huerta. Also worthy of ample praise is the superb work of Emily Alyn Lind as the child version of Linda, pushing herself to the exhaustive limit in difficult scenes where she is faced with the lifeless, bloodied bodies of her parents who just seconds before had no idea their lives were about to come to an abrupt end.

It takes a mighty ambitious film to explore topics as dauntingly colossal as the mysteries of the world and the possibilities of what happens after we die, but *Enter the Void* bravely goes there. Avoiding religion and focusing on the universality of the process of life, the picture horrifies and calms all at once with the personal knowledge that no one knows what happens on the other side until it is our time to go. Director Gaspar Noé does not shed a light on his own beliefs, but offers one version of what could happen. Bathed in drugs, sex and violence, *Enter the Void* avoids sugarcoating the carnality and excesses of humanity—Oscar is no saint, making mistake after mistake as he wanders into a fatal situation—while at the same time making it very clear of the goodness on earth and the complexities within people. In the hectic lives we all lead, we sometimes don't have time to stop and realize what we have until it's gone. Oscar finds this out the hard way, yet also learns by the resplendent last scene that there may be room for a second chance. *Enter the Void* is a big, gorgeous, sprawling, heartbreaking stroke of genius, a motion picture as seminal as it is sublime. Viewers can rest assured that they haven't seen anything like it before.

Entrance

2012 - Directed by Dallas Richard Hallam and Patrick Horvath

Los Angeles. For every dream granted in the City of Angels, how many are snuffed out even before they've begun? As Suzy (Suziey Block) goes about her mundane day-to-day existence, it's difficult not to become disenfranchised by her current lot. Though she shares a cozy house with a great view on the east side of Silver Lake with roommate Karen (Karen Gorham), her job as a barista is going nowhere and her broken-down car has left her increasingly vulnerable as she begins to travel to her destinations by foot. If things don't seem to be going Suzy's way, they only get worse when her dog, Darryl, mysteriously disappears. Owning up to her own realization that she's terribly unhappy and needs a change, Suzy decides that getting away from the city might be her best bet. Leaving, however, is going to be tougher than she thinks.

The banal, ritualistic aspects of our lives creepily beget paranoia and outright terror in *Entrance*, a rapturous display of just how very unforgettably effective a film can be that's been shot in twelve days on a budget of $6,000. Writer-directors Dallas Richard Hallam and Patrick Horvath, along with co-writers Karen Gorham and Michelle Margolis, are major new talents hopefully on the cusp of grand success. What they've crafted here has been described as mumblecore with higher stakes, and that description sounds about right. Staying focused on Suzy for every shot, the picture serves as a poignant, low-key character study of a young woman searching for meaning in a place that appears increasingly hopeless beyond the palm trees and sunshine. Subtly but surely, there arises a threat. Who or what it might be is unknown, but Suzy is aware of her surroundings enough to sense something isn't right. She hears strange sounds of walking while she's in the shower. A car follows her methodically down the street one day, even turning around when she redirects herself, before zooming off. A customer at the coffee shop where she works, Jonathan (Jonathan Margolis), seems uncomfortably infatuated with her and co-worker Flo (Florence Hartigan). Deceptive in its natural beauty, it's almost as if L.A. itself has begun to threateningly close in on her.

For prospective audience members intrigued by the sound of *Entrance*, a few words of advice: avoid all trailers out there, all interviews with the filmmakers, and any potential conversations or message boards that may include spoilers. The intoxicating blend of subtly askew normalcy and dread-induced insecurity is where Hallam and Horvath sell their film as so much more than a whiny slice-of-life about a girl wallowing in self-pity. For one, Suzy is simultaneously identifiable and magnetic, played by relative newcomer Suziey Block with zero affectations and a fearless empathy. The viewer wants to follow her and cannot turn away even when little seems to be happening. Peer closer, though, and everything is happening, the ominous power of suggestion painting a canvas that scene by scene, beat by beat, is fervidly composing tension and atmosphere while undoubtedly leading to a determinate conclusion.

The final fifteen minutes of *Entrance* dare not be given away, but let's just say that one's patience during the first hour is paid off in full during a third act that is as unnerving and sobering as any genre film in years. In an opening scene, Suzy and Karen sit on their balcony overlooking the city and discuss how funny life and mortality are, the way we can often never predict what's coming next. Such existential musings come back to haunt them by the end, played out in extended long cuts that are technically bravura triumphs, the reality of shattered hopes paired with a nightmare scenario sprung from the outer recesses of Suzy's mind. Complex lensing, chilling sound effects (including a song that plays on a record player in one key sequence), and Suziey Block's expertly raw performance all coalesce into the kind of cinematic nirvana that had this viewer exhilarated even while thinking twice about turning all the lights out the night he saw the film for the first time. The key to *Entrance* is that it's never anything less than completely plausible, and possible. As Suzy gazes out at the twinkling lights of La La Land at the end, she's a forever changed person, helpless in the face of cruel luck and broken promises. Proving that small of means does not equate to slight of impact, *Entrance* is a shrewdly distressing knockout.

The Exorcism of Emily Rose

2005 - Directed by Scott Derrickson

One part enthralling courtroom drama, one part scary-as-hell horror tale, and one part thought-provoking rumination on the relationship between one's belief and one's faith, *The Exorcism of Emily Rose* is almost too good to be true. Superlatively written and directed by Scott Derrickson, co-written by Paul Harris Boardman, here is a motion picture—and one distributed by a major studio, no less—that is chock-full of actual ideas to go along with its almost unbearably spine-tingling cathartic pleasures. It is the perfect marriage between intellect and fear, complementing each other without ever becoming intrusive, and also classy proof that not all of today's horror films have to be about nubile hotties getting slaughtered or watered-down, teen-aimed wastes of space. Indeed, *The Exorcism of Emily Rose* manages to squeak by with a PG-13 rating—an initial red flag for a story involving demonic possession—without ever seeming to compromise its vision or its emphatic subject matter.

Derrickson, aided by crackerjack editor Jeff Betancourt, seamlessly interweaves the present with the past through expertly set-up flashbacks to tell the story of 19-year-old college student Emily Rose (Jennifer Carpenter), a studious, kindhearted young woman with a devout Catholic upbringing who was believed to be possessed by six separate demonic entities. As the film opens, she has met an untimely end, and the Rose family's parishioner, Father Moore (Tom Wilkinson), is about to be tried on charges of criminally negligent homicide following a church-blessed exorcism.

Taking the case is underappreciated ace defense attorney Erin Bruner (Laura Linney), a non-religious workaholic who halfheartedly tells Father Moore during their first meeting that she is an agnostic with about the amount of gusto one takes in trying to decide on a drink order. At first skeptical of Father Moore's supernaturally based claims, Erin gradually finds herself opening up to the possibilities of otherworldly forces after she experiences a series of strange occurrences and chance happenings. As the trial presses forward and the many witnesses take to the stand, most siding with the prosecution that the victim suffered from epilepsy and psychosis, Emily's unsettling story, portrayed in flashback, begins to take shape.

Based on the purported true story of Anneliese Michel, a normal college girl whose death followed what many believed to be a real-life case of satanic possession, *The Exorcism of Emily Rose* sticks closely to a believable reality that avoids straining plausibility. The film is never preachy, never promoting any religious agenda, and never one-sided; instead, Derrickson only asks for the viewer to consider what might be possible within our world as it pertains to outside forces many might be apt to immediately write off as rubbish. It makes an increasingly convincing case on just that, no more so than during Erin's powerhouse closing statement, as she surveys the difference between fact, reasonable doubt, and all of the possibilities there might be in between the two. This climactic speech holds all the more weight coming from Erin, a three-dimensional, sharply constructed character who starts defending Father Moore without really buying what he says, and finishes the trial from a completely different place and with a startling, but never less than credible, change in her own belief system.

Lest it seem like the movie is all talk and no action, the most astounding thing about *The Exorcism of Emily Rose* is just how well it juggles the courtroom dealings, Erin's personal journey toward a kind of enlightenment, and the flashback sequences, liberally sprinkled throughout, of Emily's traumatic experiences. Above all, the film is a treasure of psychological horror, building such a heavy feeling of palpable dread and outright terror that it evokes actual goosebumps. Parents taking their pre-teens to a showing of the picture, reassured by the safe PG-13 rating, should probably think again, or risk being up all night with a horrified child afraid to sleep alone. In fact, some adult viewers less prone to the level of intensity Derrickson elicits may experience a similar outcome.

Emily's story is at once touching, inspiring, awful and exceptionally disturbing, with a definite emphasis on the latter. One particular sequence in which she is stalked by hallucinations around her campus, each person she passes transforming into a hideous demon, has to rank as one of the most profoundly scary put to film in a long time. The centerpiece exorcism of the title follows close behind in unadulterated jittery effectiveness, dodging the trappings of being just another clone of 1973's *The Exorcist* and coming up with a wholly fresh way to portray it. Also lending priceless support are the sumptuous, atmosphere-drenched autumnal cinematography by Tom Stern and creepily riveting, imaginatively composed music score by Christopher Young.

Performances are sterling across the board, some even Oscar-worthy, but the film belongs to the three central players. As Attorney Erin Bruner, Laura Linney leads the way with a layered, quietly poignant turn that doesn't step wrong once. It is, in fact, her powerful character arc that the viewer follows most closely, and the role blesses Linney with a bevy of richly diverse emotions to play with. As Father Moore, who faces an uphill battle at being taken seriously but refuses to falter from his faith, Tom Wilkinson brings outstanding command and dignity to his scenes. Finally, Jennifer Carpenter, whose unlikely biggest previous credit was 2004's *White Chicks*, delivers one of 2005's most surprising and harrowing standout examples of acting virtuosity. The role of Emily Rose had to be physically demanding and emotionally draining to say the least, and Carpenter is up to every challenge placed in front of her, appearing sympathetic one minute and evil incarnate the next.

Thoughtful, non-exploitive, engrossing, petrifying, and visually stunning from start to finish (such adjectives are not hyperbole), the film recalls a time when the Hollywood moviemaking system was willing to take chances and make works of cinematic art with more on the brain than just frivolous, throwaway flatulence jokes, explosions, and threadbare jump scares. *The Exorcism of Emily Rose* has more on the brain than that, and pays off with a rare complexity that services the frightening moments to stunning effect. The bravura final shot, subtle and beautifully simple, is the bold last piece of a puzzle that makes all that has come before complete, suggesting that in order to move on in our day-to-day lives, we must be willing to consider, accept and embrace those things that we have no control over. *The Exorcism of Emily Rose* is one of the very best horror films of the twenty-first century.

The Exorcist

1973 - Directed by William Friedkin

William Friedkin's *The Exorcist* has been exhaustively written about and studied since its December 26, 1973, theatrical release. Nothing quite like it had been seen before—there were reported faintings and even a miscarriage at screenings due to its oppressively disturbing subject matter—the film's mature meditation on the unknown and the nature of evil depicted with an uncompromising forthrightness. Adapted by William Peter Blatty from his 1971 novel, itself reportedly inspired by a real-life 1949 case of possession in Cottage City, Maryland, the handsome production went on to receive rapturous acclaim and ten Academy Award nominations. When lists of the all-time best horror movies are made, this title is frequently near, or all the way at the top, of the ranking. Virtually no one who has seen *The Exorcist* can forget where they were and the emotions it provoked upon first viewing. Whether a person has seen the film once or twenty times, however, the experience falters neither in significance nor cathartic potency.

During an archaeological dig in Northern Iraq, Father Merrin (Max von Sydow) stumbles upon an ancient amulet with the uncanny likeness of Pazuzu, a demon he once wrestled years before. His sinking belief that the succubus has returned coincides with unexplained sounds heard in the Georgetown home where actress Chris McNeil (Ellen Burstyn) is staying with 12-year-old daughter Regan (Linda Blair) as she shoots a movie in D.C. Chris thinks there might be rats in the attic, but her concern shifts to Regan's well-being when the young girl's mood and personality start to change soon after she begins playing with a Ouija board. Medical tests and a brain scan detect nothing out of the ordinary, but it soon becomes very apparent that Regan's body has been taken over by a diabolical entity. When Chris' director and new boyfriend Burke Dennings (Jack MacGowran) mysteriously falls to his death, the distressed mother must confront the reality that Regan, who was the only one home at the time of the incident, may have been responsible. Father Merrin and Damian Karras (Jason Miller), the latter a young priest currently facing a crisis of faith after the death of his elderly mother, are called in to investigate and eventually form the opinion that a Catholic exorcism might be necessary. What all involved witness will compel them to rethink everything they thought they knew about God and the sometimes nefarious forces existing beyond life and death.

The Exorcist carries with it either a stigma or a blessing. Frequently regarded as the scariest movie ever made, the film has nonetheless been extensively spoofed in comedies such as 1990's *Repossessed* (which starred Linda Blair alongside Leslie Nielsen) and 2001's *Scary Movie 2*. Much of the profane dialogue that so shocked audiences decades ago has now entered the pop-culture lexicon, as have scenes involving head-spinning and projectile pea soup. This, alas, is the price that films as popular and passionately regarded as this one must sometimes pay. Fortunately, viewed on its own terms, *The Exorcist* has lost precious little of its power to still rattle one's nerves. Those jaded by its lampooning in other movies and media might even be surprised how much it still gets to them. Director William Friedkin lends his filmmaking a level of welcome prestige and intellect while sneaking a slice into one's jugular at precisely the right times.

Ellen Burstyn was nominated for an Oscar for her sterling performance as the embattled Chris McNeil, surrendering to the demands of a role that requires her to fight tooth and nail for the survival of her imperiled daughter. Chris, an atheist, cannot believe it when she turns to a Catholic priest for help, her outlook on religion transforming without her knowing quite how to handle it. She doesn't find God, necessarily, but something far more sinister and equally as unexplainable. A young Linda Blair also received an Academy nod as Regan; though her deviously throaty vocals were dubbed by Mercedes McCambridge in the possession sequences, this was more a technical requirement than a slight against Blair. She is utterly bloodcurdling in her effectiveness in the film's later scenes, standing at staggeringly poignant contrast to the sweet, bubbly preteen she plays in the first act. The rest of the main cast are filled with interesting character actors, each one getting down to the gritty authenticity of their part: Max von Sydow, as Father Merrin; then-stage actor Jason Miller, in his outstanding screen debut as the doubting Father Damian Karras; Lee J. Cobb, as Lieutenant William Kinderman; Jack MacGowran, as the ill-fated Burke Dennings, and Kitty Winn, as Chris' assistant and friend, Sharon Spencer.

A study in faith as much as in possession, *The Exorcist* ponders existential questions far larger than the human figures who desperately want to make sense of all the things they do not—nay, *cannot*—understand. Friedkin approaches the film as if he were capturing real lives in progress as an unearthly energy imposes itself onto them, making its leaps into the fantastically vicious and vile all the more tremulously affecting. Director of photography Owen Roizman breathes a thickly foreboding texture and autumnal specificity to the Georgetown area of Washington, D.C., its exterior locations (including the infamous staircase outside the McNeils' residence) continuing to draw tourists and passersby to this day. Also crucial to the picture's notoriety: the use of Mike Oldfield's atmospheric "Tubular Bells," as in a lovely early scene where Chris walks home from her movie set, the October leaves dancing around her, and Hans Werner Henze's dazzling "Fantasia For Strings" placed over the end credits. With darkness comes the need for hope and the dawn of a new day, and it is this sentiment that the film pitch-perfectly concludes upon (the altered ending of the Director's Cut, released in 2000, is not nearly as strong, trading in a contemplative grace note for something more saccharine and obvious). Without a doubt, *The Exorcist* is a touchstone in horror, seemingly incapable of taking a wrong step. Watching with the lights off is strongly encouraged. Turning them back on immediately afterwards will be a necessity.

The Fog

1980 - Directed by John Carpenter

The Fog oozes atmosphere from its every pore. With 1978's *Halloween* a runaway success, there was a mighty bit of pressure for writer-director John Carpenter and co-writer Debra Hill to come up with a zinger follow-up. While audiences and studio execs probably wanted them to do another slasher film—a virtual knock-off of *Halloween*, no doubt—they instead moved in a different genre direction. Set up as a campfire ghost tale in a prologue delivered by storyteller John Houseman, *The Fog* goes the supernatural route. The characters aren't really the point here. The plot isn't, either. No, this picture is first and foremost a classy, expert study in the creation of mood and the power of locations. For ninety minutes, it truthfully feels as if the mist coming out of the sea and toward Antonio Bay is going to also come through one's television or theater screen. The shameful 2005 remake missed the boat on these key attributes, using inferior sets and replacing practical, more convincing effects with lifeless CGI that never looked like anything other than fake computer-generated images.

In the middle of the night, on the eve of Northern California coastal town Antonio Bay's centennial celebration, a mysterious fog bank rolls off the shore just as strange occurrences plague the sleepy community. Car horns go off. Machines in grocery stores act up. Electricity flickers on and off. Out in the ocean, an anchored trawler of sailors witness glowing in the fog, and then an old ship named the *Elizabeth Dane* sails by. Before everything goes silent and the fog dissipates, the men are dispatched by hook-wielding specters. The next day their bodies are discovered, not the most savory of things to happen on a town's milestone anniversary. With preparations for the evening festivities underway—town council head Kathy Williams (Janet Leigh) and sarcastic assistant Sandy (Nancy Loomis) scurry around trying to make sure everything goes off without a hitch—a host of characters, from fisherman Nick Castle (Tom Atkins) and new hitchhiking bedmate Elizabeth Solley (Jamie Lee Curtis), to soft-talking late-night radio deejay Stevie Wayne (Adrienne Barbeau), to Father Malone (Hal Holbrook), receive ominous signs that something strange is afoot. When the fog returns after dark, blanketing the town as Stevie warns her listeners to stay inside and away from it, the vengeance-seeking founders of the town prepare their attack.

"Is all that we see or seem but a dream within a dream?" asks Edgar Allan Poe, his quote vividly prefacing the opening of the picture. They don't, or rarely, make movies like *The Fog* nowadays. The cinematography by Dean Cundey is intoxicating, putting sumptuous use to the anamorphic 2.35:1 widescreen framing, as well as to the eye-popping locations. Shot in and around Inverness, California, the incorporation of the gorgeous Point Reyes Lighthouse (acting as Stevie Wayne's radio station) of particular note, Cundey takes his time and really soaks up the texture and surroundings of where he points his camera. A scene where Stevie Wayne drives her jeep to the lighthouse and makes her way down the steep stairway leading to the station is a delight, not because anything happens, per se, but because of the heavy, lonesome aura it builds. The same goes for the exterior of Father Malone's church, an unorthodox building of worship that holds a weirdly spooky but unquestionable ambiance. The synthesizer-based music score by John Carpenter is sublime, eerie and hard to forget, ideally matching the film's subject matter and tone just as the score for *Halloween* did.

The pacing is gradual but sure, always building to something, always leading somewhere. Spurts of violence and blood are nonetheless restrained, yet effective. Tensions rise usually from not knowing what could happen—because the villains are spirits, all bets are off—and from Carpenter's terrific mounting of something wicked this way coming. When the fog attacks the town, with Stevie yelling over the radio where it looks to be leading and the rest of the characters trying to outrun it, the viewer believes what he or she is seeing because the effects are not optical. Using fog machines, dry ice and other common tricks, the title villain actually looks far better here than in the 2005 remake, or in 2007's *The Mist*.

Adrienne Barbeau (who would move on to 1982's *Creepshow*) is the quintessential Stevie Wayne, her gentle, smooth voice perfect for the nighttime radio host she is portraying. Save for one scene with her son, Andy (Ty Mitchell), Barbeau is by herself throughout, acting as the other characters' eyes and ears through what she says over the radio, and ultimately commenting on its aftermath. As the male lead, Tom Atkins is handsome and charismatic as Nick Castle, and he ought to be if we are to believe that he bags hitchhiker Elizabeth minutes after meeting her. As Elizabeth (a far cry from Laurie Strode), Jamie Lee Curtis is headstrong and likable, but underwritten; very little is ever learned about her. The standouts of the supporting cast are Janet Leigh and Nancy Loomis (another *Halloween* alumnus), who share an electric chemistry as bickering councilwoman Kathy and assistant Sandy. "Sandy, you're the only person I know who can make 'Yes, Ma'am' sound like 'Screw you'," Kathy tells her caustic helper at one point. "Yes, Ma'am," Sandy replies. Loomis is a hoot, getting most of the film's best lines.

The Fog orchestrates a thick pall of apprehension and good-time suspense as the murderous motives of the ghosts in the fog are uncovered and the climax works itself out. An attack on Stevie at the lighthouse is tautly filmed, as is a setpiece where Andy and his elderly babysitter are accosted in her home by the enveloping stratus clouds. Like any great story to tell around a fire on a chilly night, *The Fog* ends with the portentous notion that it may return. "If this has been anything but a nightmare, and if we don't wake up to find ourselves safe in our beds," Stevie surmises, "it could come again." *The Fog*, like the original *Halloween*, is representative of a time when John Carpenter's name meant something. Once upon a time, before his heart and passion stopped being in it, he really was one of the masters of horror.

1408

2007 - Directed by Mikael Håfström

A classic haunted house tale transplanted into a single hotel room, *1408* is a nifty, chill-inducing thriller that keeps things taut and suspenseful without feeling the need to overcomplicate the narrative. Director Mikael Håfström, along with screenwriters Matt Greenberg and Scott Alexander & Larry Karaszewski, have done a solid job in using Stephen King's short story (from 2003 anthology *Everything's Eventual*) as a jumping-off point to expand, develop and in a few cases reinvent the author's ideas. The finished result is the best big-screen King adaptation since 1995's *Dolores Claiborne*.

Mike Enslin (John Cusack) is an author who travels around the country debunking paranormal activity in allegedly haunted locations. In his work, he has never seen a ghost or experienced supernatural phenomena, and it is this desire to disprove the unknown that leads him to New York City's Dolphin Hotel. Upon arrival, manager Gerald Olin (Samuel L. Jackson) tries to talk Mike out of staying in 1408, a room normally off-limits to guests, revealing that some 56 deaths have occurred there in the hotel's history. "Nobody lasts more than one hour in that room," Gerald ominously tells him. Skeptical as he always is, Mike insists on pressing forward with his research. By the end of the night, Mike will not only believe in the paranormal, but he'll be fighting for his sanity, and maybe his own life.

Ghost stories are a tricky business in the film arena. What reads well on the page often tends to come off as tacky or cheesy when put before a camera. *1408*, like 1999's *The Sixth Sense* and 2001's *The Others* before it, dodges most of these trappings. Instead of relying solely on "boo!" scares to unfold a threadbare plot, Håfström and cinematographer Benoît Delhomme incorporate disconcerting imagery and heightened levels of tension into what is really a universal exploration of loss.

As Mike is accosted by nightmarish happenings in room 1408—in one supremely frightening moment, he tries to get the attention of a man in the building across from him, only to discover it is a skewed mirror image of himself—and all attempts to escape the premises lead to dead ends, his tragic backstory floats into focus. A few years ago, his young daughter died of an incurable illness, a devastating experience that tore his heretofore happy marriage to Lily (Mary McCormack) apart. Mike hasn't been the same since, and when he begins to hear his daughter's voice and see visions of her that he knows aren't actually there, he is forced to confront the torturous memories of his past and ultimately find a way to let them go. A late scene involving Mike and daughter Katie (Jasmine Jessica Anthony) comes out of left field—not because its context is out of place, mind you, but because it blindsides with an unexpected raw power and depth of humanity.

Since his beginning in film in 1983, John Cusack's career has gone unsung. Yes, he has worked on a regular basis and is considered something of a box-office draw, but that doesn't make his long line of diverse performances any less underrated. There is a captivating charm and sincerity in each role he plays that makes him identifiable and wholly believable to the audience. It doesn't matter what the part is; he could be starring as a cold-blooded serial killer, and he would still manage to make the character accessible without once compromising the truth of the person. As Mike Enslin, Cusack is superb, called upon to act for long stretches of time by himself in a single setting. He receives some help in the interest department from the spooky goings-on around him, but the film never loses sight of its focus on Mike. This is his story first and foremost, not the story of an evil hotel room, and that is the reason *1408* works so well. Lending support are Samuel L. Jackson, as manager Gerald Olin, and Mary McCormack, as Mike's estranged wife, Lily. They ably fulfill the requirements of their limited roles, but this is Cusack's movie all the way.

There is a point during the start of the third act where it appears as if the escalating onslaught of special effects are about to negatively impact its conclusion. Fortunately, *1408* reels things back just in time for a denouement that is surprising and even lyrical. The frights come at a clip rate—one setpiece set in an air shaft is almost unspeakably intense, and the use of The Carpenters' wistful love ballad, "We've Only Just Begun," as a means of eliciting shivers is ingenious—but it is the emotional journey Mike goes on that is most memorable and lasting. *1408* is sure to get hearts racing, but that's not all it's about. Underneath the grandeur and pizzazz is an intimate and thoughtful portrait of one man's return from an abyss infinitely more haunting than any old, evil hotel room.

The Fourth Kind

2009 - Directed by Olatunde Osunsanmi

Following the murder of her husband at the hands of a still-unidentified home intruder, psychologist Abigail Tyler (Milla Jovovich) has had a rough time processing the tragedy for herself as she struggles to raise her two children, Ronnie (Raphaël Coleman) and Ashley (Mia McKenna-Bruce), the latter stricken with a bout of blindness since her father's death. Having relocated from North Carolina to the self-contained wilderness town of Nome, Alaska, Abigail has successfully restarted her practice. The more she hears from her patients, however, the more similarities she notes within their experiences, each one sleep-deprived and remembering very little besides a white owl perched outside their bedroom window. Abigail decides to use them for a sleep study, hoping it may help to answer why Nome has been beset by unexplainable occurrences and disappearances dating from the present all the way back to the 1960s. Putting them under hypnosis as a means of recovering memories locked within their subconscious, she discovers, little by little, the terrifying link between these residents and extraterrestrial visitors. Worse yet, they may be coming after her family next, much to the skeptical chagrin of the increasingly suspicious Sheriff August (Will Patton).

The spine-tingling *The Fourth Kind* could do for aliens what *Paranormal Activity* has done for poltergeists. The similarities between the two movies boil down to the restraint with which they have been made, trusting that what you don't see—the power of the unknown—is far more lingeringly frightening than what you do. Whereas *Paranormal Activity* is a fictional film made, like 1999's *The Blair Witch Project*, with home video cameras handled by the actors themselves, *The Fourth Kind* is a super-savvy Hollywood-produced thriller that casts recognizable veteran actors such as Milla Jovovich, Elias Koteas and Will Patton in roles purported to not simply be real, but based on noted conversations and actual recordings of Dr. Abigail Tyler's case studies. Not only that, writer-director Olatunde Osunsanmi uses split screens and expert editing to tell the story alternately—and sometimes simultaneously—through both the conventional acted-out narrative and never-before-seen archival footage of the real people the picture is based upon. Because the script is taken oftentimes straight from the source, the dialogue mirrors the audio and video, as does much of the production design, set decoration, costumes and performances. It is stunning to behold as the viewer is allowed to compare and contrast the dramatizations with reality, and vice versa, lending the storytelling a complementary layer of eerie plausibility with a sense of eavesdropping on aspects of human nature and the paranormal so harrowing one isn't sure whether to turn away or not.

So far, so good. Viewing *The Fourth Kind* as exactly what it claims to be is eye-opening bordering on downright groundbreaking, complete with the sort of sensationalistic—but not too sensationalistic as to stop being believable—archival footage, including therapy sessions and police tapes, that the regular public never expects to see. That the true-life videos offer a fair amount of evidence concerning the existence of aliens and UFOs is like icing on an already bizarre, potentially explosive cake. Because post-viewing online research reveals that the entire case is actually a hoax and a Dr. Abigail Tyler does not appear to exist—the only information that comes up about her and the events surrounding the movie are from fake newspapers and journals in the Northern Pacific area that were created only a couple months before the film's release date—there is undoubtedly a tinge of resulting disappointment. Ponder the picture more closely with this new information, though, and *The Fourth Kind* is reborn as something just as impressive. That Osunsanmi and his unbilled cast of "real" people could so seamlessly pull the wool over an audience's eyes through the rawness and grit of their brilliantly committed performances is astonishing. It also begs to question if there has been any past film quite like this one. In a land of recycled ideas and remakes, *The Fourth Kind* is a valiant original, no matter how deceptive it may ultimately be. The ease with which it fools you is part of the fun.

Upon seeing the film a second time, it works on a new, just as pleasing, level: as a rousing technical and aesthetic achievement where the line between fact and fiction is no longer blurred by what we are told from the start, but through the sheer proficiency of its remarkable cast and production values. Osunsanmi only overplays his cards when the "real" video we are watching would likely be caught up in police files and legal matters, as in the depiction of a murder-suicide of one of Abigail's patients and his family. Nevertheless, the atmosphere of encroaching dread that is mustered is raised high, with scenes of hypnoses, alleged possession, and a worn, disheveled Abigail's 2002 interview with Osunsanmi at Chapman University eliciting a great many goose pimples. Meanwhile, the mere audio recording captured of what could be extraterrestrials speaking in Sumerian ("The Holy Grail of dead languages," one person describes it as) is disturbing in its very inhumanity. Those sounds are, indeed, scarier than any blatant visual manifestation of aliens could have been had the film made the wrong decision to go in that direction. Fortunately, it doesn't.

Attractively lensed in Bulgaria, posing quite well as Alaska, *The Fourth Kind* has got the moodiness of a wooded, isolated, fog-hewn surrounding down pat.

As Dr. Abigail Tyler battles her own demons—including the facts she doesn't want to face in regard to her husband's death—and becomes embroiled in her patients' uncanny otherworldly encounters, she doesn't yet know that danger is irrevocably edging ever closer to her and her children. Milla Jovovich makes for a compassionate, sympathetic Abigail, a more intentionally glamorous version of the "real" Abigail seen in archival video. Free from the constraints of playing a no-nonsense action heroine (as she has in the *Resident Evil* series), Jovovich shows again that she is just as capable of stretching her acting muscles and digging into an eclectic mix of characters. She is ably supported by Elias Koteas, a beacon of support as colleague and friend Dr. Campos; Will Patton, on edge and unwilling to believe what is staring him in the face as Sheriff August, and a long list of uncredited performers (playing the non-fiction subjects recounted in the picture) who deserve a large portion of the credit for making the film so riveting. The existence of intelligent life on other planets and the possibilities of visitation and abduction have been topics widely debated throughout the centuries. With or without the knowledge of its own trickery, *The Fourth Kind* pulls convincing sway for the length of its running time. You will believe.

Freaks

1932 - Directed by Tod Browning

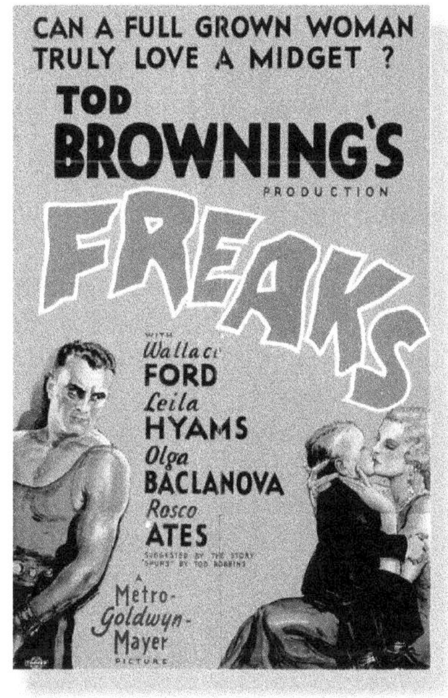

Times, they have a-changed! The story goes that in the very early 1930s, then-MGM production chief Irving Thalberg commissioned Willis Goldbeck to write a screenplay that, as he described, should be "horrible." What Goldbeck ultimately devised, based on the short story by Tod Robbins, "Spurs," was a sordid tale set within the professional milieu of traveling circus performers and sideshow freaks. Tod Browning, who had previously made Universal Pictures' Bela Lugosi-starring *Dracula* the year before, took on directing duties, while real-life circus, carnival and vaudeville talent were cast in many of the major roles. Though *Freaks* was a hit upon release in January 1932, the film was banned from certain states, and, in the UK, didn't see the light of day until well into the 1960s. Many viewers were disgusted and outraged, accusing the filmmakers of being everything from insensitive to shameless in showcasing the physically deformed to the world.

Seeing *Freaks* eighty-plus years removed from its controversy is an eye-opening experience that says quite a lot about the evolution of the general public consciousness and the overall strides that have been made in understanding and accepting people who do not fit the mainstream norm. The film is neither disgusting, nor offensive, nor, as Thalberg saw it, "horrible." Quite the opposite, *Freaks* is a largely respectful and sympathetic portrayal of a close-knit fringe community, people who are often shunned by society but share the same feelings and dreams and vulnerabilities as the rest of us. They might look differently, but they are still very much human beings. Browning's participation in this tender melodrama nearly cost him his career. At the time, he was criticized for having helmed a movie that wallows in exploitation and shock value. The reality, however, is nothing of the sort. The problem was not the film, but those detractors who claimed to be outraged. They didn't like what they were watching, or how it made them react. Indeed, what they truly saw were all of their personal prejudices magnified and reflected back onto them.

On the grounds of a touring big top exists an internal societal microcosm. Trapeze artist Cleopatra (Olga Baclanova), nicknamed "Peacock of the Air," is a beautiful but disingenuous star performer. When she learns of little person Hans' (Harry Earles) inheritance, she schemes with strong-man boyfriend Hercules (Henry Victor) to seduce Hans away from fiancée Frieda (Daisy Earles). Once they are married, Cleo instantly begins poisoning her unsuspecting new husband little by little. When Frieda's compassionate friend, Venus (Leila Hyams), overhears Cleo and Hercules' plot, it paves the way for a stormy finale of ghastly just desserts as the freaks take their revenge on these scheming gold-diggers.

Freaks is a cinematic curiosity both ahead of its time and a product of its era, the film opening with a "special message" to theater patrons meant to prepare them for the "shocking" developmentally challenged sights they are about to witness. Hailed by the circus as "living monstrosities," these entertainers are depicted as outsiders by nature, but treated by Browning with a surprising level of respect. The film's intentions are good-hearted, at least in part, even if its messages are a little on the nose. "They don't realize," says Hans early on, "I'm a man, with the same feelings they have." If viewers miss the movie's point, they aren't paying attention.

By contrast, there is the desire to throw audiences off-guard and, by the climax in which Cleopatra and Hercules are hunted down and terrorized by the freaks, frighten them. A famous scene set at Cleo and Hans' wedding reception alternates between off-puttingly perverse and poignant, the guests' goblet-passing chant, "We accept her! We accept her! One of us...," segueing into a sobering indictment against those that shun them when Cleo angrily makes a scene and calls them a bunch of "dirty, slimy freaks." There is undoubtedly a *Grand Guignol* B-movie flavor to the project and its delivery, but from out of the picture's depiction of supporting players such as conjoined twins Violet (Violet Hilton) and Daisy (Daisy Hilton), affectionate "pinheads" Schlitze, Zip and Pip, and the lovelorn half-man/half-woman (Josephine Joseph), there is also a clear attempt to present these characters as authentic and layered, able to carry on relationships and get their hearts broken just as naturally as anyone else. There is a reason *Freaks* continues to endure and capture attention so long after it was released. Nothing like it had been seen before, and there has been nothing quite like it since.

Friday the 13th

1980 - Directed by Sean S. Cunningham

Some of my earliest memories as a child of four or five were of being taken by my dad to the local video store and renting, over and over, the earlier *Friday the 13th* entries. Even at that young of an age, I was sold on horror films. I also would rent *Strawberry Shortcake* and *The Care Bears*, just to give an idea of how varied my tastes were and how uncorrupted my little mind was. Back in those days in the mid-'80s, *Friday the 13th* was like the Holy Grail of Video Villa's horror section, and it wasn't until I got a little older and more discerning that its flaws began to show. As a nostalgic experience, watching the series many years later brings back fond thoughts of more innocent times. Judged on their respective critical merits, however, they really don't offer much more than any other garden-variety slasher film.

The original *Friday the 13th* is a skillful, if by-the-numbers, stalk-and-slash pic, its very existence resting upon the huge success of the two-years-older *Halloween*. That John Carpenter classic is acclaimed for a reason; it's handsomely mounted and shot, intoxicatingly suspenseful and scary, and almost poetic in its simplicity. In attempting to recreate the same formula, director Sean S. Cunningham adds one element that *Halloween* didn't have, or need: graphic violence. The fact that *Friday the 13th* is bloody and more in-your-face doesn't necessarily lessen its significance in the canon of the genre—with ten sequels and a remake, to date, it has a firm place in the history books—but it also doesn't truly separate itself from the spate of like-minded imitators that came out in the early 1980s.

At rustic, seemingly peaceful Camp Crystal Lake, prospective teen counselors Alice (Adrienne King), Bill (Harry Crosby), Brenda (Laurie Bartram), Marcie (Jeannine Taylor), Jack (Kevin Bacon) and Ned (Mark Nelson) have arrived to get the place into working order for the summer season. Before they have been there twenty-four hours, most of them will be dead, slaughtered at the hands of a psychopath who wants revenge for her son's drowning in 1957. The date: take a guess.

Friday the 13th features a premise about as bare bones as they come, but it is capably made. The murder setpieces are craftily set up and their payoffs (or lack thereof) not always as one expects. A scene in which couple Marcie and Jack make love in the bottom of a bunk bed, blissfully unaware that a mutilated corpse is lying above them, is morbidly clever, while another sequence in a dank bathroom makes stylish use of shadows and shower curtains to generate tension. Likewise, when Brenda is lured out of her cozy bed and into the rain by the mysterious cries of a little boy in the distance, the results are appropriately creepy.

The climax has always been the movie's weak spot. It really shouldn't be giving anything away to say that the kindly looking Mrs. Voorhees (Betsy Palmer) is the perpetrator behind the bloodbath—1996's *Scream* made sure that audiences remembered this tidbit—and that Jason didn't show up until the first sequel a year later. As final girl Alice races around the camp, discovering the bodies of her friends while trying to outsmart and defeat Mrs. Voorhees, the film wavers into campiness. Veteran stage actress Betsy Palmer gives the villainous role her all, but her childlike whispers and repeated remembrances of son Jason slow down the momentum. Fortunately, the culmination of Alice's fight to the death with Mrs. Voorhees is gruesomely satisfying, and the shocker ending, with the tranquility of the soothing, vaguely mournful music score leading into a jump scare, is a doozy.

As heroine Alice, Adrienne King (who later went onto a voice-over career after some troubles with a stalker kept her off the screen for roughly thirty years) is strong-willed, vulnerable and cute. A tomboy who knows how to fix a rain gutter with a hammer and some nails about as well as she knows how to wear a bikini, Alice is an ideal match for a lunatic out to kill her. The rest of the performances are adequate for the material, with Jeannine Taylor, as Marcie, standing out. A story she tells early on about a recurring dream she had as a young girl involving pebbles of rain turning to streams of blood is indelibly and believably brought up, a harbinger of things to come. Also notable is Kevin Bacon in one of his first roles, as pot-smoking, ill-fated beefcake Jack.

Shot primarily in the idyllic rural town of Blairstown, New Jersey, *Friday the 13th* is the first and arguably best in a long-running horror series that got sillier and more far-fetched the further it pressed on (2002's futuristic, space-set *Jason X*, anyone?). The film is no grandstanding work of art and its depth is akin to the shallow end of a swimming pool, but it does the trick as a killer-in-the-woods item that rarely moves outside the realm of clichés. For fans of the genre who have never seen *Friday the 13th* (for shame), it is worth a gander. And for those, like me, whose past with the picture goes all the way back to the age of single-digits, it's close to unforgettable.

Frozen

2010 - Directed by Adam Green

When was the last time a film came along causing such a visceral audience reaction that the viewer sat perched nervously on the edge of his or her seat, wiping away unavoidable tears while aching with a genuine, sustained fear over both the characters' threatened fates and the unthinkable—yet fully plausible—predicament they've found themselves in? It doesn't happen often, and when it does the results are close to miraculous. Watching *Frozen*, written and directed with an uncommonly savvy, airtight assuredness by Adam Green, is akin to swimming in a giant, extra-duty washing machine for 94 minutes. In other words, it puts a person straight through the wringer. While you gasp, the movie mischievously laughs.

In addition to the picture's tightened vise grip over one's emotions, Green goes another step further to explore the human psychology that comes with a person being placed in a life-or-death situation. Terror, anger, blame, hopelessness, acceptance, bargaining—all of these are naturally and astutely explored by a trio of committed actors working with a screenplay that comes to be so much more than just another often-seen survivalist horror-thriller. The plot is a doozy, yes—it has been described in some circles as a snow-set variation on 2004's flawed but effective *Open Water*—but the depth of character and the masterful, unsparing grasp Green and cinematographer Will Barratt have over their *mise-en-scène* are the film's all-important special ingredients.

It's Sunday at Mount Holliston, a dinky, weekends-only New England ski resort where college friends Lynch (Shawn Ashmore) and Dan (Kevin Zegers) have come to shred some powder. Dan's girlfriend, Parker (Emma Bell), has tagged along, too, her novice snowboarding skills only the tip of the iceberg when it comes to the heightened tensions between herself and a feeling-slighted Lynch. Through a series of events best left discovered, the three of them convince the chairlift operator to allow them to get in one last run before the end of the day and are subsequently left stranded halfway up the mountain, nearly 100 feet in the air. Nervous chit-chat leads to outright horror when the lights are turned off and they come to realize they are stranded in the blistering cold and snow for five straight days with little chance of anyone finding them.

A crafty, inventive plot hook only goes so far if there is more style than substance and no one to care about at its center. *Frozen* understands this, turning what might have been an empty exercise overextended to the breaking point into a breathless, poignant, vibrant potboiler where nary a single scene, shot or frame is wasted. The opening twenty minutes are deliberate but absorbing, introducing the three protagonists—Lynch, Dan and Parker—and capturing the tricky, at times tense, dynamic between them. Dan and Parker are in love, making Lynch feel like the odd man out when all he wants to do is hang out with his best friend. Parker, thus, is viewed as the interloper in the equation through no fault of her own but the changing tides of adulthood each of them is currently facing.

Once they become stuck on the chairlift, the film really takes off, and in more ways than one. As Parker freaks out, Lynch tries to keep things light by taking their mind off the situation (e.g., "Name your three favorite types of cereal") and Dan begins plotting a rash move that could either make him the hero or bring him closer to death. Conversations naturally turn far more serious and introspective as the prospect of someone saving them dwindles and frostbite sets in. A discussion about 9/11 and the victims of the World Trade Center who chose to plummet from the building rather than burn to death may sound potentially exploitative, but it feels appropriate and realistic to young people glimpsing their own mortality. Without lessening its taut veracity, the characters little by little form into warm, three-dimensional people, and topics they discuss, from Lynch's story about how he met Dan in the first grade to Parker's heartbreaking empathy for her dog, who will starve to death herself if she never returns, hit home and say quite a lot about the fragility of one's life.

That Parker, Lynch and Dan are reasonably smart people and take advantage of pretty much every chance they have to get out of their ordeal is appreciative, too. Emma Bell, Shawn Ashmore and Kevin Zegers deliver terrific performances equaling the intensity that Green ratchets, embodying specific individuals rather than easy types. As for the tricks up his sleeve, Green does not disappoint. For a motion picture set primarily on a chairlift, it is amazing how potent the pacing and momentum remain. Story points involving wolves circling below, broken bones, and two separate attempts to get from one chair to the next are veritably chilling, almost too uneasy to take. Likewise, the camerawork is dynamite, knowing when to be intimate with the characters and when to back up and bring scope, movement and atmosphere to the proceedings. A sense of haunting isolation is palpable throughout.

One of the producing partners of *Frozen* is A Bigger Boat Productions, a clear reference to 1975's *Jaws*. The two films are not similar from a narrative point of view, but they are on par as expertly devised and conceived thrillers that prefer old-fashioned, incomparable suggestion and restraint over graphic violence and gore galore to tell their story and create suspense. Furthermore, the attention to the human figures pays off handsomely and leaves one actively caring about their outcomes and recognizing themselves within them. It might have done well to add an extra beat or two at the very end, but that is the only possible quibble to give an unremitting film that orchestrates its frightening what-ifs over the viewer with the skill of a prodigy.

The Funhouse

1981 - Directed by Tobe Hooper

Coming after Tobe Hooper's career-making directorial debut, 1974's *The Texas Chain Saw Massacre*, but before 1982's *Poltergeist* (and long before something went terribly wrong and he started making direct-to-video garbage), *The Funhouse* is an underrated gem, a mini-masterpiece of frights and atmosphere. Perhaps the reason more people did not initially discover it was because the print used on VHS was notoriously underlit and murky, nearly impossible to discern half of what was occurring on the screen. With reliable Blu-ray, however, the film is pristine, boasting classy cinematography from Andrew Laszlo that counteracts shadows and darkness with an orgiastic stream of neon colors. With the aesthetics now in tip-top form, the thematically rich, quixotically paced *The Funhouse* is practically begging to be rediscovered.

Despite the warnings of her father to steer clear of the midway, level-headed teen Amy Harper (Elizabeth Berridge) heads out on a first date with hunk Buzz (Cooper Huckabee) and friends Liz (Largo Woodruff) and Richie (Miles Chapin) for a night at the traveling carnival. Harmless fun—they ride the rides, see a fortune teller, attend a magic act—and mild rebellion—they sneak a joint behind one of the tents—leads to an idea so crazy that none of them can refuse. When Richie suggests they spend the whole night in the funhouse, Amy and Liz call their parents and sneakily tell them they'll be sleeping over at each other's houses. Once locked inside the foreboding maze of puppets, pop-up skeletons, and fake spiders, the foursome spy through the floor cracks and, to their shock, witness the murder of prostitute-on-the-side Madame Zena (Sylvia Miles). The culprit is the monstrously deformed grown son of funhouse barker Conrad Straker (Kevin Conway), and, when the four teens accidentally give themselves away, he isn't about to let them get out with their lives.

The Funhouse opens with what can only be described as an intentional loving homage to the first scene in 1978's *Halloween* before changing gears entirely. The deliberate, slow-burn pacing of the film's first forty minutes are utterly enthralling, taking on the appearance and feel of a naturalistic slice-of-life. Amy's date with Buzz starts rockily when he badmouths her father—a man he's never met—but once an apology has been made and the four friends begin enjoying the simple, quirky pleasures of the carnival, the newfound couple hit it off and start bonding.

Every facet of the midway is lovingly explored through Hooper's fixed gaze, a slice of Americana that additionally hides a dark underbelly. Whereas the teens see the carnies, drunks and vagabonds around them as expected presences, Amy's little brother, Joey (Shawn Carson), who has snuck out to attend the carnival by himself, views them as ominous, potentially dangerous beings. Through certain eyes and varied perspectives we see wildly different things, screenwriter Larry Block seems to be saying, and the result adds a surprising layer to the proceedings.

When Amy, Buzz, Liz and Richie enter the funhouse, a sense of expertly achieved claustrophobia takes over. This undeniable dread only deepens once the four of them find themselves running without an exit from a deranged mutant who, with drop-out floors and secret entryways at his disposal, can pop up anywhere at any time. Suddenly, the film transforms into a literal house of horrors, an intensely suspenseful cat-and-mouse game that plays like a cross between a tautly envisioned creature feature and a superior slasher movie.

As the latter, Hooper marvelously toys with the conventions of the genre and leaves no stone unturned when it comes to his ingenious, grittily phantasmagoric surroundings. Refreshingly restrained in its violence, the picture is more suggestive than explicit, and more interested in unsettling the viewer than it is in grossing them out. When Joey is taken in by the carnival manager and his parents are called to come get him, Amy, by chance, spots them across the way. Her screams for help, however, are drowned out by the large fan in front of her, and she's soon left helplessly alone once again.

In her feature debut, Elizabeth Berridge is excellent as Amy, an authentic, unassumingly attractive performer and a born scream queen, to boot. Had she wanted a career in further horror films, there's no doubt she could have been the next Jamie Lee Curtis. Cooper Huckabee is appropriately cast as love interest Buzz; he's got good looks and a seductive personality, which allows the relationship between himself and Berridge to build to more than what is usually seen in this kind of film. And, as Liz, Largo Woodruff has down pat the part of an easygoing free spirit whom the viewer grows to care about.

Menacingly scored by composer John Beal, the booming orchestrations complementing the onscreen action, *The Funhouse* is a scary, fantastical, and most of all intelligent thriller that, like the original *Halloween*, proves slasher films can be sleek and upscale without going for low-rent gore tactics. The climax, rising to a fever pitch within the bowels of the funhouse, is first-rate, while the final scene subtly says a lot without spelling things out. With thoughts of the hellish night she has just had permanently ingrained in her consciousness, Amy stands bedraggled and scuffed up at first morning's light before listlessly stumbling off amidst the rides, tents and attractions of the carnival. Blending in with the heretofore lowlifes and miscreants around her, she has ultimately become one of them, a victim of fate and circumstance. Of all the films attempting to piggyback on the horror bandwagon in the early 1980s, *The Funhouse* confidently stands near the top of the pack.

Funny Games

2008 - Directed by Michael Haneke

Gus Van Sant's underrated 1998 remake of *Psycho* was criticized for being a virtually shot-for-shot copy of the classic 1960 Alfred Hitchcock original, but, even amidst the startling similarities, Van Sant took it upon himself to add his own personal flourishes. That picture's detractors hadn't seen anything yet. *Funny Games*, a U.S. redux of German-born writer-director Michael Haneke's 1997 film of the same name, really, truly is a near duplication, the only differences being a change in cast, a change in spoken language, and a few very minor tweaks to the dialogue. Having the experience of watching both films for the first time only a few days apart is uncanny, and the only apparent reason for this remake's existence is to introduce the story to a wider American audience who probably don't even know the first one exists. If that's what it takes to get people to see it, then so be it. Both films stand amazingly on their own, and neither one loses its raw, unseemly power for having seen the other.

The premise is simple enough to describe, but doesn't quite do justice to its intentionally crushing unpleasantness. A happy-go-lucky family—father George (Tim Roth), mother Anna (Naomi Watts) and son Georgie (Devon Gearhart)—have no sooner settled into their lakeside vacation home when they are paid a visit by two young men, Paul (Michael Pitt) and Peter (Brady Corbet). Their initial well-mannered politeness gradually takes a foreboding turn when they refuse to leave. Before long, the family members are being held hostage, forced into a series of malicious games after being guaranteed that none of them will be alive in twelve hours' time.

Funny Games is tough to take, and will not be palatable for audiences comfortable with only being force-fed conventional, studio-bred horror movie fodder. With almost no onscreen violence, Haneke throttles the viewer over the head, toying and daring them to withstand the kind of deep psychological torture and emotional devastation rarely seen before in cinema. Claustrophobic even when the action intermittently moves to exterior locations, the camera stays on the five central characters, refusing to cut away or release the tension building up throughout. One particular shot—the centerpiece of the film—is approximately ten minutes long; it immediately follows the grisly (again, off-screen) murder of one of the characters, and then leaves the other two alone to try to come to grips with what has unthinkably occurred while also attempting to get out of the situation they are in. The result is equal parts disturbing and breathtaking in its depiction of tragedy and, for a time, the actors cease to exist as the realness of their roles take over.

The very title is almost gleeful in its irony; humor is nonexistent throughout, and the games played on the family are far from funny. What is not immediately known is that Haneke also has another trick up his sleeve, playing a game all along with the viewers who stay put in their seats, interested in how everything is going to turn out. When Paul breaks the fourth wall the first time, looking squarely in the camera and smiling, the effect is at once disconcerting and thoroughly unsettling. *Is he looking at me?* the viewer asks him or herself, and the answer, which slowly becomes apparent, is yes. Paul—or is it Haneke in disguise?—is literally daring the people watching the movie to stay put. Thus, we stop being mere spectators and become willing accomplices in the horrific crimes being committed on this innocent family. Even more fascinating is that Paul and Peter do not so much as raise their voices throughout. Were they not psychopaths who happen to be combing secluded homes in the area and systematically killing the residents, they would be perfectly amiable fellows. That there is a monster hiding under each of their calm, cheerful veneers is what is so scary about them.

Time and again, George, Anna and Georgie are faced with choices in their bid to escape. In retrospect, we realize that if only they had done something differently, they might have been able to get away. These moments, however, are plausible in the direction they go, and not merely an example of typical slasher movie characters doing dumb things. George, Anna and Georgie are written smartly, but even intelligence, they come to find, isn't going to do them any favors against their ceaseless assailants. Haneke's strongest attribute is in his ability to create distinct apprehension in subtle ways—through long, static shots and through dialogue-driven interactions between characters that are just off-center enough to recognize something isn't right. There are no jump scares or sudden bursts of gore or mayhem, and it is in this slow-burn pacing and restrained tone that eventually gets under one's skin.

Naomi Watts, Tim Roth and Devon Gearhart are put through the veritable wringer as Anna, George and Georgie. Their performances, demanding of them to constantly be in states of panic, terror and despair, are powerhouses. Gearhart stands out in that he is much more memorable and naturalistic than the child actor in the original film, while Watts and Roth are equally superb in their portrayal of a married couple whose safe expectations of the world are malevolently pulled out from under them. As the calculating Paul and Peter, Michael Pitt and Brady Corbet are icily terrific in their remorseless homicidal tendencies.

Difficult to like and yet impossible to deny, *Funny Games* is a coldly efficient, spectacularly acted and unremittingly bleak thriller. The audience does not "enjoy" what they see, but that's the point—even though the film is an endurance test, we refuse to turn away from the emotional and physical carnage being laid out before us. It's all just another part of Haneke's barbarous games, and we're the ones left holding the knife.

The Grudge

2004 - Directed by Takashi Shimizu

With the very same director onboard—Takashi Shimizu—and retaining its vivid Tokyo setting, the American remake of the Japanese horror sensation, *Ju-On: The Grudge*, did an accomplished job of staying true to its source material while giving it an added depth all its own. And, in a rare instance where the same filmmaker was given the chance to tackle his original work, this new rendition bypassed many of the mainstream U.S. genre conventions for a fresh and unnerving direct ode to its Asian influences. *The Grudge* genuinely surprises because one is never quite sure where it is headed next, all the while involving the viewer in freakish, unforgettably nightmarish imagery. The chilling cumulative effect the film amplifies is sure to stay with the watcher for much longer than the average studio horror picture tends to these days.

The legend of *The Grudge* goes like this: when a person dies at the hands of a powerful rage, an unstoppable curse is put into motion that goes after anyone who comes into contact with it. When original caregiver Yoko (Yôko Maki) goes missing, American student Karen Davis (Sarah Michelle Gellar), studying abroad in Japan to become a social worker, is asked to take over in tending to an ailing elderly woman (Grace Zabriskie). Once inside the death trap of a house, Karen becomes the latest potential victim of the curse. As she witnesses those who have once entered its doors turn up dead, Karen's countdown to her own fatality begins, her only hope of survival being to unravel the mystery of the so-called grudge before it finds her.

From specter-like children with blackened eyes to frightening videotape footage of one of the ghosts walking toward the camera, the resemblance *The Grudge* holds with *Ringu* (and its 2002 remake, *The Ring*) is not incidental. Although such influences are clear, *The Grudge* finds its own identity through intricately designed nonlinear storytelling and a premise that is cleanly developed, but open-ended enough in its details so that the scary unknown spell it conjures is never broken.

Instead of simply following lead heroine Karen from point-A to point-B throughout the story, *The Grudge* occasionally moves back in time, tracing the history of the house and its inhabitants and the ultimate origin of the supernatural curse. This creative, unconventional approach brings a richness to the proceedings that is progressively all the more intoxicating as more characters briefly move into focus. There is the original family that lived there, a married couple and their young son who suffered a terrible fate. Three years later, an American couple, Jennifer (Clea DuVall) and Matthew (William Mapother), move in with Matthew's mentally unstable mother—the woman Karen eventually comes to work for. Also tagging along to Tokyo is the woman's grown daughter, Susan (KaDee Strickland). And then there is the mysterious man (Bill Pullman) who, in a pre-opening titles sequence, abruptly commits suicide by jumping off his apartment balcony. As these ill-fated souls, and several other people through the years, fall prey to the curse, the film eventually wraps around to Karen's present-day plight.

The cast, headlined by a serious-looking, oft-terrorized Sarah Michelle Gellar, gamely do their jobs with efficiency, seemingly taking on the rhythms and acting approach of their Japanese counterparts. Where *The Grudge* grabs the audience and gets its worth is in a near-succession of taut, jarring setpieces, each one more strange and horrific than the last. Of particular note is a rattlingly elongated sequence that depicts the stalking of Susan, first at her work office and then at her apartment, and a climactic scene involving Karen that should safely have the hairs on one's own arms standing straight up.

Whereas many horror films' plot particulars tend to unravel the more one thinks about them, *The Grudge* has the opposite effect, wholly improving in one's mind as the disturbing scenes and tightly fabricated storytelling play themselves out after the fact. Save for a few too many slow walks down hallways and into rooms—the one clichéd aspect it shares with Stateside horror—*The Grudge* delights in usually defying expectations. Finally, in a welcome addition of profundity that the Japanese version had no way of having, the film almost plays like a genre version of *Lost in Translation*. The leads, almost all American, feel alienated and adrift by their newly foreign and very different surroundings, a nifty aside to the otherworldly horrors they ultimately come face to face with. Instead of wrapping everything up in a neat, tidy bow, the fear that *The Grudge* so expertly exhibits comes squarely from what the characters, and the viewers, do not know.

Halloween

1978 - Directed by John Carpenter

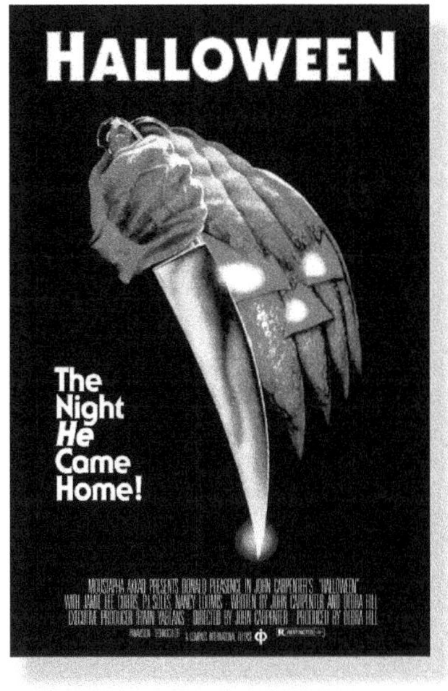

Whenever people find out that I am a film critic, the same question is always asked: "What is your favorite movie?" Time and again, my answer is the same: "*Halloween*." How could I possibly begrudge or ignore its significance in my life? After all, it is the one film, above all others, which I can confidently attribute my lifelong love affair with the cinema to. *Halloween* is the reason I am such an ardent supporter and defender of the horror genre. *Halloween* is the reason I began penning personal capsule reviews on my clunky DOS computer in 1990, still not even ten years old. By God, *Halloween* is the very reason I work a full-time job, and yet still dedicate the majority of my spare waking hours as an online film journalist.

I originally reviewed the picture in 1998. A 16-year-old kid with a lot to still learn about writing, critical deconstruction, and processing his thoughts on the page, I read that archive review now and shudder. To be sure, I feel the same way about *Halloween* as I did then, but there's no denying that the film deserves a more articulate, fully formed discussion on why it is the classic that it has deservedly become, and why it has cemented such a lasting impact.

Made with ambition, enthusiasm and passion in the spring of 1978 on a shoestring budget of $320,000, writer-director John Carpenter and co-writer Debra Hill took a simplistic premise that could have gone the way of trashy exploitation fare—a boogeyman stalks babysitters on Halloween night—and turned it into cinematic gold. Along with 1974's *Black Christmas, Halloween* is the film most responsible for creating the slasher genre and coining the conventions—POV shots of the killer, jump scares, the "Final Girl"—that filmmakers to this day still latch onto. Were the picture not well-made, it would be but a footnote in history, and subsequent copycats (e.g., *Friday the 13th, Prom Night, Silent Night, Deadly Night*), satirical treatments (e.g., HBO's *Tales from the Crypt* and the *Scream* series) and spoofs (e.g., *Student Bodies, Pandemonium*, the *Scary Movie* franchise) would cease to exist. Year after year, generation after generation, *Halloween* endures and garners new fans for one very straightforward reason: no slasher picture before, or since, has been better.

What Carpenter and Hill captured was lightning in a bottle.

The unforgettable prologue deceptively appears to be one unbroken shot (for the uninitiated, see if you can spot the cut). On Halloween night, 1963, an unseen presence lurks outside an idyllic suburban home, spying on a teenage girl and her boyfriend as they head up to her bedroom. Moving inside the house via the backdoor, a butcher knife is pulled from the kitchen drawer. Lingering out of view, the camera watches as the boyfriend says his good nights and exits. Heading up the stairs, the figure picks up a mask lying on the floor and puts it on. The teenage girl, sitting nude at her bureau as she combs her hair and sings quietly to herself, comes into frame. Before she has time to react—"Michael!" is all she gets out—a knife plunges multiple times into her chest before she collapses to the floor. The POV of Michael Myers hurriedly runs down the stairs and out the front door just as a car pulls up. Confused by what they're seeing, a man and woman pull the mask off to reveal their 6-year-old son, staring blankly into the distance as he still grasps the bloodied murder weapon. A crane shot of the parents staring down in shock at their knife-wielding child follows—a chilling tableau frozen in time.

Fifteen years later, on Halloween Eve, Michael escapes from his home at Smith's Grove Sanitarium, much to the chagrin of long-term psychiatrist Dr. Sam Loomis (Donald Pleasence). Returning to his old neighborhood in the bucolic town of Haddonfield, Illinois, he narrows his sights on three high school friends—reserved Laurie Strode (Jamie Lee Curtis), caustic Annie Brackett (Nancy Loomis), and bubbly cheerleader Lynda van der Klok (P.J. Soles). With Laurie and Annie setting off in the evening to babysit across the street from each other, and Lynda and boyfriend Bob (John Michael Graham) arriving later to make good use of an empty bedroom, the girls have no way of knowing how close they are to mortal danger.

Halloween is what happens when every element that goes into the filmmaking process works out beautifully, both separately and collectively. Aesthetically, stylistically, thematically and subjectively, the experience of watching it is mesmerizing and immersive. Atmosphere is painted upon every shot like a work of art. The holiday of the title, rarely, if ever, rendered with such palpable care and dimension as it is here, sumptuously exudes from the frames. Pumpkins, decorations, silly pranks, trick-or-treaters, old scare flicks on television, dead leaves blowing in the chilly breeze—all of these things and more are incorporated into the proceedings to signify the one-of-a-kind mood that comes with October 31st.

The plot, as unpretentious as they come, melds the everyday with the unthinkably horrific. A carefully observed, authentically written teenage slice-of-life wrapped in a threatening box, Laurie, Annie and Lynda are portrayed as average, likable girls, worrying about getting their hair done for the dance and whether or not a classmate they have a crush on likes them back. As they go about their everyday lives, with Annie making popcorn for herself and little Lindsay Wallace (Kyle Richards), Laurie carving jack-o'-lanterns with babysitting charge Tommy Doyle (Brian Andrews), and Lynda gallivanting with Bob, the viewer gets to know and identify with them. Tragically, they are not made privy to what the audience knows: that a psychopathic killer wearing an expressionless white mask is lurking outside their doors or right around the corner, waiting for his moment to pounce and forever change the course of their fates. Meanwhile, Dr. Sam Loomis teams up with Sheriff Brackett (Charles Cyphers) and returns to the scene of the 15-year-old crime. As they wait in the broken-down house where Michael killed sister Judith—a place now known as "the spook house," as Tommy calls it—in the hopes that he will return, Dr. Loomis describes in greater depth who Michael was, and what he has become: "purely and simply evil."

The ensemble cast is effortlessly charismatic and naturalistic, all the performances working on the same level and on the same page. Donald Pleasence, a late veteran actor whose career would have a second life through his recurring turn as Dr. Sam Loomis, brings authority, dignity and vulnerability to his role. He is a man who once cared for Michael, who can't help but feel as if he still shares a bond with him, but who has grown wearisome because he now knows that there is no way of getting through to him. In her very first screen appearance, Jamie Lee Curtis is perfect as Laurie Strode, unaffected and soft-spoken until she demonstrates why she earned the title as reigning "Scream Queen." The fear she exhibits in the breathlessly paced, tautly ingenious climax feels real, mimicking much of the anxiety that the viewer is going through while watching it. As Annie, Nancy Loomis is sarcastic and dryly humorous, ideally keying into the kind of person who always has to have the last word. And, as the energetic, sexually uninhibited Lynda, P.J. Soles is "totally" an utter delight for every second she is onscreen.

The cinematography by Dean Cundey, making brilliant use of the Steadicam and a lush 2.35:1 widescreen format that doesn't waste one inch of the frame, is intoxicating. A character in and of itself, the camera treats the backgrounds of shots with the same care as it does the foregrounds, with Michael Myers imposingly capable of showing up anywhere, at any time. Even in the most innocuous of scenes, Michael's presence eerily looms over the happenings. Also of crucial note is the excitingly creepy, unshakably memorable piano leitmotif found in the score by John Carpenter (billed in the end credits as the Bowling Green Philharmonic Orchestra), as emblematic of the holiday as the film itself. Carpenter exquisitely implements just a few choice piano keys to construct one of moviedom's most perennial compositions. Blue Öyster Cult's "(Don't Fear) The Reaper" adds pitch-perfect flavor to an early scene between Laurie and Annie as they drive to their babysitting jobs, twilight falling upon Haddonfield.

Violent but never gory, *Halloween* is a masterwork of sheer, unadulterated suspense, blanketing low-key, tastefully layered humanity in an identifiably peaceful setting with the kind of darkness that can, and does, exist in the real world. Classy, intimate and exceedingly tense when most of the later derivative slasher releases became low-rent, gruesome-for-gruesome's-sake freakshows, the film has the power and skill to remain as uncompromisingly scary and haunting today as it no doubt was in 1978. To call *Halloween* merely brilliant isn't giving it enough credit. As a horror film and as a historical milestone that single-handedly shaped and altered the future of an entire genre, it's downright transcendent.

Halloween II

1981 - Directed by Rick Rosenthal

When *Halloween* became the highest-grossing independent film of all time upon its release in 1978, it was a given that a sequel wouldn't be far behind. Still, how could another installment even attempt to match the success of its predecessor, a horror masterpiece that aided mightily in the creation of the slasher genre? In short, it couldn't. *Halloween II* is admirable for many things, the most prevalent being its formidable aesthetics, but it's no *Halloween*. Nevertheless, these first two films in the series approximate the same feel, pace, tone, atmosphere and look, which is all the more useful considering they are set on the very same night. Viewers could edit *Halloween* and *Halloween II* into one three-hour epic, the latter picking up immediately where the former left off, and the transition between pictures would be nearly seamless.

With Michael Myers having disappeared after psychiatrist Sam Loomis (Donald Pleasence) shoots him six times off the Doyles' balcony, Dr. Loomis flees the scene to try and stay on the escaped psychopath's trail. As Michael stealthily makes his way through the neighboring houses, stealing a knife from the elderly, sandwich-making Elrods, and claiming a new victim in the home-alone Alice (Anne Bruner), a wounded and distraught Laurie Strode (Jamie Lee Curtis) is transported by ambulance to Haddonfield Memorial Hospital. It isn't long before Myers has reached the medical center himself, determined to find Laurie even as he paints the staff red.

Directing from a screenplay by John Carpenter and Debra Hill, Rick Rosenthal skillfully has tried to replicate the deliberate yet intoxicating pacing and overall mood of *Halloween*. Reportedly, it was Carpenter (not Rosenthal) who helmed post-production reshoots to insert more violence and gore effects into the film. This, of course, is one of the flaws of *Halloween II* that separates it from the original, doing away with restraint and going all out in its depiction of people being scalded alive or getting a syringe full of oxygen injected into their temple. Even as Carpenter misguidedly tried to compete with the most graphic *Friday the 13th*-style movies of the era, he could not destroy the classiness with which Rosenthal mounted the majority of the picture. As for what happened to Rosenthal in the interim is anybody's guess; he returned for 2002's insulting *Halloween: Resurrection*, widely considered the worst entry in the series.

In lieu of a madman randomly setting his sights on three teenage girls, *Halloween II* endeavors to give him a specific motive and a more layered backstory. Thus, as Laurie is knocked out with a sedative and restlessly tosses and turns in her hospital bed, she dreams of a childhood that reveals she is Michael's baby sister, adopted by the Strodes' shortly after the murder of Judith Myers and only knowing him through brief visits to the mental hospital as a little girl. This certainly lends weight to the relationship between Michael and Laurie during the taut climax—a scene where Laurie waits for elevator doors to open as Michael approaches steadily from behind her is especially suspenseful—even as this plot hook was solely created for the sequel. Until this last act, Laurie has little to do but lie in a bed and wake up long enough to pass back out again. Jamie Lee Curtis (by 1981 a full-fledged "Scream Queen" itching to break out into the mainstream) reprises the role and is superb when her character is conscious. There is also a subtly foreboding story point, several times recalled, where head nurse Mrs. Alves (Gloria Gifford) attempts to call Laurie's parents to notify them of what has happened. Mrs. Alves never is able to get through to them—this is increasingly suspicious the later into the night it gets—and at no point in this film or any subsequent sequel is it discussed what happened to them. It is just as well; the act of not knowing and imagining the worst is far creepier than the alternatives.

With Laurie sitting a fair amount of the film out and Dr. Sam Loomis, accompanied by nurse Marion (Nancy Stephens), investigating the links he senses between Michael's behavior and the lore of the holiday, the bulk of the picture centers around the hospital milieu of doctors, nurses and candy-stripers working on Halloween. As they trade barbs, bicker, flirt, take care of patients (there are very few seen, save for a little boy who has become a victim of the old razorblades-in-the-apple trick), and sneak off for a little nookie, Michael Myers lurks through the hallways, picking off his latest prey as he moves closer to Laurie. The palpable air of October 31st is all over these almost observational scenes, with jack-o'-lanterns and decorations throughout, a few scenes in town featuring passersby in costumes—one which involves Ben Tramer, Laurie's noted crush from the original, and another that finds nurse Karen (Pamela Susan Shoop) late for her shift and having to drop friend Darcy (Anne-Marie Martin) off on her way to work—and a synthesizer-heavy music score by Alan Howarth (based on John Carpenter's themes) that practically exudes horror with an autumnal touch.

Halloween II has some sloppy holes in its script that the first movie did not, such as the way the hospital seemingly becomes deserted the further the film presses on, and the fact that the electricity goes out without much mind paid to it (this played a larger part in the television director's cut). If one can overlook these logistical and editorial mishaps, the film is otherwise a well-made thriller, exquisitely photographed by the returning Dean Cundey and mostly respectful to the style of the original. Just because Michael Myers is not in the foreground of a shot does not necessarily mean he isn't there, and Rosenthal is smart in not spelling out these chilling moments by obvious hand-tipping, but allowing viewers to catch on themselves. The elongated third act, wherein Laurie is chased by the Shape and finds herself weak and helpless in the parking lot of the hospital, trying to get Dr. Loomis' attention but unable to scream when the car he is in arrives at the front door, is sensational in its building of apprehension and imminent danger.

Concluding with a three-person face-off between Michael, Laurie and Loomis (the latter, as always, played with stately determination by Donald Pleasence) that would seem to end the Myers saga were it not for money talking, *Halloween II* is a more than solid if admittedly inferior continuation. Even with its added after-the-fact violence, the film still follows the same basic blueprint, with expertly mounted tension the primary goal above just stringing together a body count. For Laurie Strode, her character arc is completed here (well, until 1998's *Halloween: H20*), encapsulated in the part-quixotic, part-eerie ending credits music cue of The Chordettes' "Mr. Sandman." She may have begun Halloween as a meek, mild, somewhat naive teenage girl, but she welcomes the dawning of a new day as a stronger, but also more weary and broken, young woman. In the last shot of *Halloween II*, Michael's body and mask aren't the only things engulfed in flames. So is Laurie's innocence.

Halloween III: Season of the Witch

1982 - Directed by Tommy Lee Wallace

John Carpenter had a valiant idea in how to continue the *Halloween* franchise without Michael Myers. Since the boogeyman of 1978's *Halloween* and 1981's *Halloween II* had been killed off but the name-brand was still profitable, producer Carpenter proposed that a new entry in the series be made each year, every one of them a stand-alone horror story set around the Halloween season. Had it been a success, just imagine all of the different exciting and original genre pictures that could have been made revolving around the namesake holiday by now. Unfortunately, *Halloween III: Season of the Witch* was presumed to be directly correlated with the previous films, and audiences were none too pleased when they walked out of the theater having seen something completely different from what was expected. Ever since, *Halloween III* has been the odd man out, reviled in some circles for having nothing to do with the man in the William Shatner mask.

The hate is unwarranted, based solely around the very notion that Michael Myers is MIA. Who cares? It is precisely because of the story change-up that *Halloween III: Season of the Witch* is so memorable and noteworthy. Viewed as its own separate entity, the film is an imaginative twist on *Invasion of the Body Snatchers* (even the town where that 1956 classic is set, Santa Mira, is the same as it is here) that trades in pod people for robots. It's also pretty terrifying in its own right, based around a diabolical plot to savagely kill the majority of the country's children. Director Tommy Lee Wallace proves adept at setting up a tenebrous ambience while working swimmingly with skilled director of photography Dean Cundey, the latter's anamorphic widescreen lensing comely as ever.

Before novelty store owner Harry Grimbridge (Al Berry) is brutally slain in the hospital by a suited man who promptly blows himself up in the outside parking lot, he forebodingly gasps to Dr. Daniel Challis (Tom Atkins), "They're gonna kill us all," while clinging to a Halloween mask. Haunted by what he might have meant, Daniel accompanies Harry's beautiful daughter, Ellie (Stacey

Nelkin), to the Northern California town of Santa Mira in the hopes of figuring out who is behind his death. Home of the Silver Shamrock factory where the masks are produced, Santa Mira is a strange place, indeed, seemingly run by factory owner Conal Cochran (Dan O'Herlihy) and placed under a strict curfew at nightfall. When Daniel and Ellie, posing as a married couple, get too snoopy, they are put into immediate danger as Halloween draws near and Cochran's plan is set into motion.

"Two more days 'til Halloween, Halloween, Halloween. Two more days 'til Halloween, Silver Shamrock!" Utter that line in a sing-song voice and it's a safe bet that it will sound familiar. This tune, repeated numerous times throughout *Halloween III: Season of the Witch*, is the kind of infectious ditty that gets stuck in your head and stays there. It may be used as an upbeat jingle for radio spots and commercials, but it is also a harbinger of evil, its irresistible catchiness meant to draw children in and latch onto them. As Daniel and Ellie investigate the Silver Shamrock Corporation and later are captured, Cochran's full scope of madness is little by little revealed, culminating in the most unsettling of setpieces. An unsuspecting family—Buddy Kupfer (Ralph Strait), biggest seller of Cochran's masks; wife Betty (Jadeen Barbor), and son Buddy Jr. (Bradley Schachter)—are closed in a testing room. As Buddy and Betty gab away on the couch, they do not instantly realize that Little Buddy, wearing one of the Silver Shamrock masks as he watches the flashing "magic pumpkin" on the TV set, has collapsed to the floor. Suddenly, bugs and snakes escape from the orifices of the mask, subsequently killing the rest of the trapped family members. Grim and squirm-inducing, this no-holds-barred sequence elicits the unadulterated terror of watching an entire innocent family destroyed in a matter of about a minute.

As Daniel attempts to escape from the factory of mechanical horrors around him and rescue imperiled Ellie, the clock ticks down to the moment of truth—"the big giveaway at 9!"—while day turns to dusk and kids across the U.S. are shown picking up last-minute Silver Shamrock masks and trick-or-treating in their neighborhoods. None of them, of course, have any idea of the calamity about to befall them, and Daniel isn't so sure he will be able to stop the airings even if he does get to a telephone in time. Wallace takes advantage of his locations, particularly the dusty, eerie town of Santa Mira and the Silver Shamrock factory, creating a similar but fresh seasonal atmosphere that goes against the usual Haddonfield setting. The music score by John Carpenter and Alan Howarth is deep, rich and layered, while also casting a pall of ominous threat over the proceedings. Its electronic sounds are particularly suitable for the sci-fi plot at hand, as well as over the opening credits sequence, as an image of a carved pumpkin is constructed on a computer screen.

The story, meanwhile, is more mature, revolving around adult characters and a vast conspiracy rather than teens and a killer with a butcher knife. The screenplay, also by Wallace (Nigel Kneale had an uncredited hand in its development), isn't always a beacon of airtight construction, however. A subplot connecting Cochran's scheme with a missing rock from Stonehenge is brought up and left dangling, while the film doesn't take into account the time zone differences that would put a snarl in his plan to simultaneously kill children from coast to coast. Discrepancies such as this are easily overlooked since, on the basis of its genre, the heightened emotions it works up, and the ambitions of its makers, the film is arguably the second-best in the *Halloween* series (following the Carpenter original). As protagonists Daniel and Ellie, Tom Atkins and the disarmingly voiced Stacey Nelkin are accessible and believable, the kind of people the viewer doesn't mind following for a couple hours. Though their relationship is hastily set up—they hop into the sack awful quickly once reaching Santa Mira—it comes to mean something by the end when one of them is taken away from the other, never to return. Garn Stephens also makes an impression as the personable, ill-fated Marge Guttman, who has come to town to pick up an order of masks, and Nancy Kyes (formerly Loomis) shows up as Daniel's ex-wife, Linda. It's interesting to consider that Kyes' character of Annie Brackett was killed in the first *Halloween*, and yet the actress still managed to appear in the next two sequels.

In a bleak but appreciable turn from the norm, *Halloween III: Season of the Witch* concludes with the suggestion that Daniel's adversity against Cochran and the Silver Shamrock brand is too much for a single person to stop. The final scene, open-ended but obvious what is to happen next, is a disturbing denouement worthy of the *Halloween* moniker. It is high time for viewers with a hang-up to reevaluate the pleasures that *Halloween III: Season of the Witch* has to offer. Michael Myers may only have a cameo—the first *Halloween* is seen advertising on a television—but he is replaced with an invigorating new narrative just as intriguing. Had the film been successful (and it deserved to be), Michael Myers wouldn't have been driven into the ground in lesser sequels and the anthology version of the series might still be going strong. If only.

Hatchet

2007 - Directed by Adam Green

A nearly two-year film festival favorite that finally received a nationwide 2007 theatrical release—and was subsequently followed by two sequels, to date—*Hatchet* is a zinger of a throwback to the days of barebones but purely fun 1980s slasher flicks. All of the hallmarks of such are on display: a group of diverse and frequently nubile characters, an isolated and threatening setting, ample nudity, socko death scenes, gore galore, a legend that the story is based upon, and a villain who, for the very first time in its decade, had what it takes to stand head and shoulders next to the likes of Michael Myers, Jason Voorhees and Leatherface. While many of the lesser and more derivative pictures of its ilk ultimately wallowed in poor production values, worse acting, and a so-bad-it's-good appeal, *Hatchet* has a leg up by being professionally made (on a modest $1-million budget) and knowledgeable about how to actually scare an audience. It's also not without some very funny moments that thankfully do not intrude on the seriousness of its thrills.

The film has a classic setup. Would-be Mardi Gras reveler Ben (Joel David Moore) is bummed out by being recently dumped by his girlfriend. Desiring to get away from it all, Ben, along with resentful but faithful best friend Marcus (Deon Richmond), pass up the New Orleans festivities in lieu of buying tickets to a haunted nighttime boat tour of the Louisiana bayou. Also onboard is inept tour guide Shawn (Parry Shen), touristy husband and wife Mr. Permatteo (Richard Riehle) and Mrs. Permatteo (Patrika Darbo), sleazy director Shapiro (Joel Murray), aspiring actresses Misty (Mercedes McNab) and Jenna (Joleigh Fioreavanti), and all-business loner Marybeth (Tamara Feldman). When the boat carrying them hits a rock and sinks, stranding them in the middle of the swamps, they come face to face with the murderous local legend that is Victor Crowley (Kane Hodder). Long thought to be dead, this half-deformed/half-disfigured psycho roams the bayous, murdering anyone who trespasses on his land.

Hatchet is the impressive directorial debut of Adam Green, a filmmaker with the talent to go far. His first film is a loving, rough-and-wild tribute to the kind of genre pics that saturated the marketplace as a result of the success of

1978's *Halloween*. Instead of spoofing the older movies, as in 2007's *Behind the Mask: The Rise of Leslie Vernon*, *Hatchet* mostly plays things straight even as Green delights in tweaking conventions and writing characters who are naturally humorous and all the more likable because of it. Unlike in Rob Zombie's 2007 reimagining of *Halloween*, where the viewer was at a loss when it came to caring about any of the obnoxious twits in front of the camera, the mincemeat fodder here are infinitely more appealing. When any of them meet a horrible end, one is sorry to see them go because of the valuable and easy dynamic they have created within the fast-dwindling ensemble.

Praise Adam Green's screenplay, too, for finally seeing fit to write a black character in a horror film who isn't a blatant racial stereotype, an excuse for cheesy one-liners, or the first person to die. As played by Deon Richmond, Marcus' sense of humor is amusing, but in a way that blends in with the other characters rather than calls attention to itself. Some of the other actors are also better than the '80s decade normally allowed. Of them, Joel David Moore is a curious choice for the lead role of Ben because he doesn't fit the typical mold—in short, he's long, lanky and a little nebbish—but that is part of why he's easy to relate to. Tamara Feldman, as Marybeth, is more along the line of what to expect from the female lead, but she shows fright and strength equally well and sells the role (modern "Scream Queen" Danielle Harris would later take over the part in the sequels). Mercedes McNab is a hoot as the airheaded Misty, who earnestly believes cops and police are two separate things when she tries to dial 9-1-1 on her cell phone. Parry Shen is an entertaining standout as the novice tour guide in way over his head. And Tony Todd, in a memorable cameo that would be expanded upon in 2010's *Hatchet II*, has a grand time hamming it up as Reverend Zombie, the runner of a voodoo shop who recommends the boat tour to Ben and Marcus.

As for Kane Hodder, he creates a new and genuinely unsettling slasher in the form of the monstrous Victor Crowley, as well as essays the melancholy part of Victor's father in a choice flashback sequence that depicts the Halloween holiday with more flair and atmosphere than the *Halloween* remake does. Huge in stature, vastly imposing, appropriately ghoulish and apt to spring up on his victims when they (and the viewer) least expects him to, Victor Crowley is a merciless psycho of the highest order. He's everything a villain in this breed of film should be, and used just sporadically enough that he retains his threat every time he shows up.

Moodily photographed by Will Barratt and with a music score by Andy Garfield that alternates between tense, creepy cues and a few upbeat, whimsical ones that are at wonderfully perverse odds with the mayhem about to occur—keep your ears open during the scene when the scare bus takes off for the tour—*Hatchet* is an affectionate ode to a time of simpler '80s-splatter diversions. Green makes no pretenses for what he has set out to make and, save for a few scenes where the on-and-off bickering between characters goes on too long, the pacing never flags. Certain moments toy with the audience in very effective ways, such as one lingering shot involving sounds coming from a bush, and there are at least four or five genuine jolts scattered throughout to keep the viewer on edge. Meanwhile, an easy setup for a sequel is, for once, welcome; Victor Crowley is too good not to get his own franchise, and it's no wonder he did. Whether seen as a stand-alone film or the beginning of a series, however, it makes no difference. For any self-respecting horror fan, *Hatchet* is an amusing, spooky, visceral, smartly crafted breath of fresh air.

Hellbent

2005 - Directed by Paul Etheredge-Ouzts

Hellbent follows the tried-and-true rules of any old body-count movie, but is groundbreaking all the same because its slew of heroes and victims are all gay males. It is a novel twist to the formula, to be sure, but the success of the film comes from the newfound layers and thematic undercurrents that resonate from this fact. Coming to terms with one's sexuality, the modern-day threats of HIV/AIDS, the common fear of being "out" in the workplace, the thin line between a harmless sexual encounter and outright death—it is all here, captured boldly by promising first-time filmmaker Paul Etheredge-Ouzts.

A playful tryst between two guys in a parked car leads to murder on the eve of Halloween, both of them gruesomely beheaded. As news of the crime spreads between a group of twenty-something friends, and even after believing they may have come into contact with the killer—a shirtless, musclebound phantom in a devil costume—they press on to the West Hollywood Halloween carnival. It is there, as the techno music swells, go-go boys dance around them, and the four of them flirt with crushes and possible hookups, that the killer lurks in the shadows, preparing for his next victims.

Hellbent is a competently made, atmospherically potent slasher flick that makes up for much of its lack of originality (outside of the gay angle, that is) with a style and know-how of generating good jump scares and a solid amount of tension. Although the very low budget is usually apparent, Etheredge-Ouzts works hard to give the project high production values, especially in having most of the action take place during West Hollywood's real-life annual Halloween carnival. This added authenticity, mixed with above-average performances from all the leads, lends the film an amount of foreboding and dread that it otherwise wouldn't have had.

When the central killings begin around the thirty-minute mark, the surprise comes not in the deaths themselves, but in the sadness that permeates from the loss of the characters, who are developed just enough to mean more to the viewer than most slasher movie victims. Joey (Hank Harris), for example, a comparative newbie to the gay scene who is kept a watchful eye on by his buddies, has a hopeful moment of connection with a nice, handsome guy at the party, his joy in getting his number silenced moments after by the devil's scythe. Another scene, in which cross-dressing Tobey (Matt Phillips) unfortunately decides to bare his soul to the killer (he doesn't know his identity at the time), is haunting precisely because Tobey's goodhearted intentions lead him to his awful fate.

As for lead Eddie (Dylan Fergus), whose hopes of a career in law enforcement ended when he lost one of his eyes in an accident, his burgeoning romance with a dark, brooding motorcyclist, Jake (Bryan Kirkwood), is treated seriously and with a sort of sweetness. That these two have just so happened to find their way into the middle of a violent and bloody horror picture is a case of bad luck. One of the most unsettling images Etheredge-Ouzts concocts is when the blade of the killer's weapon just barely scrapes against Eddie's glass eye—it's wickedly clever, perverse, and more disturbing than the bevy of decapitations on view.

As a novice indie effort, *Hellbent* tends to be a little rough around the edges—the pacing, while fast enough, flows unevenly from scene to scene, and the climax disappointingly lurches toward predictability and a last-second setup for a sequel—but remains an earnest, well-crafted throwback to the days of the '80s slasher craze. The moody camerawork especially deserves notice, undoubtedly influenced by John Carpenter's *Halloween* in the way lighting, shot compositions, and subtle background details keep the viewer off-balance and always with more to take in than originally meets the eye. Meanwhile, the villain's identity is wisely never revealed, leaving him an enigma all the more frightening because of the mystery surrounding him. *Hellbent* doesn't exactly reinvent the wheel with its narrative, but for horror fans (and that includes the heterosexual populace), it is smarter than the norm and delivers a crafty little twist to the conventions of the genre.

High Tension

2003 - Directed by Alexandre Aja

In a time when the motion picture industry skews marketing at any means necessary in order to attract a specific target audience, here comes a film whose very title is the ultimate truth in advertising. *High Tension* (or *Haute Tension*, as it was called in its native France when it was released in 2003) is exactly as its title proclaims, a near-breathless, nonstop study in unquenchable terror that knows just what the horror genre is all about, and puts those elements to use in a masterful cavalcade of suspense and dread. At the time of its U.S. opening in 2005, it may have been the most frightening, unshakable feature film since 1999's *The Blair Witch Project*.

Partially dubbed and very minimally pared down from an NC-17 to an R rating for the original North American theatrical release—thankfully, both the subtitling and the uncut version have been restored for home video—*High Tension* nevertheless lost none of its raw impact in translation. The dubbing was almost laughably unnecessary, anyway, as dialogue (in a taut screenplay by Alexandre Aja and Grégory Levasseur) takes a backseat to a non-verbal game of stalking and preying; even if this choice by American distributor Lionsgate Films doesn't get in the way, one must wonder just what their reasoning was behind the dubbing. No matter. At the time, the studio saw fit to present this down-and-dirty foreign masterpiece to as wide an audience as possible, and more power to them for that. *High Tension* deserves all of the attention and accolades it can possibly get, and probably more than it ultimately received.

Externally, the premise is simple and straightforward. College-aged best friends Marie (Cécile De France) and Alex (Maïwenn) travel to the French countryside to visit Alex's parents and little brother for the weekend. On the first night there, Marie narrowly escapes the wrath of a psychotic killer (Philippe Nahon) who breaks into the house and murders the family. In a brave attempt to save Alex, who has been taken hostage, Marie stows away in the killer's truck. Before the hellish night is over, the tables will be turned once more, with Marie becoming the hunted.

Stunningly directed by Alexandre Aja, the sheer brilliance of *High Tension* is how well it works on two completely different levels. Stripped of one or the other, it would still be a splendid example of how to make a horror film right, but, together, the two complement and strengthen each other, turning an exercise in scares into something deeper and more thought-provoking.

The first and more basic level is as a slasher picture, stripped to its purest and most unnerving core. An 85-minute cat-and-mouse chase between one of the most savagely disturbing villains in memory and a strong-willed, likable heroine whose plight is as gripping as they come, Aja spits on Hollywood's reliance on MTV-style cutting in favor of effectively long, lingering shots and a pace that simultaneously manages to be meditative and never let up. By choosing this route, and never relieving the audience's apprehension with humor, tongue-in-cheek or otherwise, the film cooks up a classical tone and look reminiscent of great horror movies of decades' past. It also gives viewers the appropriate time to allow their minds to work, anticipating one thing to happen in any given scene and then almost continually having their expectations be gloriously wrong.

Finally, Aja delights in not shrinking away from viscera; *High Tension* is violent and bloody, and graphically so, but not exploitative. What he has done is portrayed in as detailed a form as possible what it might be like—emotionally, physically, psychologically, and otherwise—if a person found him or herself horrifyingly faced with the sort of unspeakable circumstances Marie is. From the initial witnessing of the family's slaying, to her valiant, if failed, attempts to save her and Alex's lives, to her decision to ultimately take matters into her own hands, to her realization that she may be no match for her evil pursuer, the audience follows Marie every step of the way and is almost made to experience exactly what she is going through. As Marie, Cécile De France is a stunner, going through a range of both delicate and extreme emotions and physical demands with the ability of a master thespian. In addition, with all of the needless, awful violence in the world (it seems like every other day is met with a headline of kidnapping murders and whole families being killed at the hands of a fellow relative), the plot that *High Tension* recounts is sadly possible and, one assumes, authentic.

The second level that *High Tension* unveils itself to contain arrives in the final minutes, turning all that has come before on its head, and, likewise, making the preceding eighty minutes all the more eloquently profound. It needs to be said that the climactic revelation, which should not be given away, comes not as a cheap gimmick, as many like-minded American pictures have, nor does it fall into the trap of holding its viewers in contempt. When it comes, it makes perfect sense, and while one could pick out what might be considered plot holes, the content in question is so abstract, burrowing deeply into the darkest recesses of the mind and the grimmest corners of human relationships, that even the said holes begin to explain themselves away the more one thinks about them.

High Tension is a sinister, pitch-black masterpiece, as thematically deep and suggestively powerful as it is unforgettably scary. Those without strong stomachs and a small threshold for the most extreme of human behavior and capabilities will, no doubt, be turned off within the first fifteen minutes. For everyone else, this is a remarkably cathartic experience, a motion picture thick in mood and rich in actual ideas. Who could have guessed that a so-called slasher movie could be as psychologically haunting as this one manages to be? Alongside 2008's *Martyrs*, this is modern horror at its most primal.

Hitchcock

2012 - Directed by Sacha Gervasi

It has been extensively studied, pored over, written about and revered for over fifty years, but how many people know the genesis of slasher prototype *Psycho* and the story behind its creation? Adapted by John McLaughlin from Stephen Rebello's non-fiction book, *Alfred Hitchcock and the Making of Psycho*, *Hitchcock* is a motion picture for anyone who loves movies, revels in the art of filmmaking, and appreciates the special, one-of-a-kind, cathartic power of great horror cinema. Director Sacha Gervasi has made a film that not only beautifully peers into the behind-the-scenes creation of a future masterpiece, but also into the little-discussed lifelong romance between the so-called "Master of Suspense" and his dutiful muse of a wife, a woman who creatively consulted on all his projects but never received her rightful credit or accolades. It's endlessly entertaining, sweeping by in an effortless 98-minute gush, and also unexpectedly moving.

When *North by Northwest* is released in 1959 to rapturous reviews and robust box-office returns, the studios are suddenly clamoring for Alfred Hitchcock (Anthony Hopkins) to repeat the success with a similar follow-up effort. Fearful that he is becoming stuck in his ways and out of touch with the public consciousness at the ripe age of sixty, Hitch turns his attention away from spy and espionage thrillers and toward a different genre: horror. Sure, most are just considered low-rent B-movies, but what if a true craftsman behind the camera were to take the reins and treat such a project as more than just an exploitation piece? Inspired by Robert Bloch's novel, *Psycho*, itself loosely based on the crimes of notorious Wisconsin killer and cannibal Ed Gein, who kept the corpse of his overbearing mother in his house long after her death, Hitchcock proposes his new picture to Paramount, who balk at the subject matter and understandably are fearful of the censors. At first, his beloved wife (and frequent script supervisor) Alma Reville (Helen Mirren) is skeptical, too, but when she sees just how important it is to her husband, who yearns to reclaim the excitement of his earlier days as a director, she has no choice but to go along with him when he makes the decision to finance the $800,000 budget himself. If the gamble works, they'll be all the more on top. If it fails, it could be a real stab to their livelihood and Hitch's reputation.

A "born-to-play" type of part that rivals his Oscar-winning turn as Hannibal Lecter in 1991's *The Silence of the Lambs*, Anthony Hopkins wholly immerses himself into the daunting role of Alfred Hitchcock. Yes, the make-up that physically transforms him into the icon helps, but it is all Hopkins who sheds the things that make him so recognizable and seemingly embodies the very soul of Hitchcock in all his intensity, self-doubt, ambition and acidic humor. Helen Mirren matches her co-star step by step as wife Alma, bringing her out of the shadows she seems to stand in publicly, supporting Alfred while yearning to have her own creative pursuits. Their relationship, close and kindred but filled with passionate sparring, is poignantly depicted, Hitch's suspicions and paranoia about Alma when she begins collaborating on a script with writer Whitfield Cook (Danny Huston) like something out of one of his movies; he discovers she's been spending time at the beach by collecting the grains of sand on their bathroom floor. Neither Hopkins nor Mirren ever fall into the trap of actors obviously acting, but transcend impersonation to find the real people behind the personas.

If it is a treat to get an intimate glimpse into Alfred's and Alma's private lives, the insider's look at the preparation, shooting and post-production of *Psycho* runs enticingly parallel to the one-on-one scenes between these two. From Hitch's fights with the censors—elements seen as innocuous today were taboo in 1960, from the sight of two characters laying on a bed in their undergarments to the very sight of a toilet on screen—to his methods in provoking authentic responses from star Janet Leigh (Scarlett Johansson), to his breakthrough discovery of how Bernard Herrmann's chilling orchestral score could be the key to saving his picture altogether, viewers will no doubt learn a great deal they never knew about the production of *Psycho*. Meanwhile, in an example of crafty storytelling ingenuity, Hitchcock has occasional dreamlike conversations with Ed Gein (Michael Wincott) as the killer lurks around his farmhouse of horror, frightened of being found out—a literalized symbol of the filmmaker's own trepidations at being labeled a behind-the-times fraud and relic.

It is said that Hitchcock was instantly won over by Hollywood star Janet Leigh for the pivotal role of Marion Crane—a heroine who, in a twist of expectations, is killed off forty-five minutes in, at the end of the first act—when he discovered she had created an entire background and history for her character in preparation for meeting him. Scarlett Johansson is exceptional as Leigh, looking every bit the part while capturing the actress' kind and delicate essence. The filmmaker's working relationship with Vera Miles (Jessica Biel) was decidedly chillier, Hitch intentionally casting her in the relatively thankless part of Marion's sister, Lila, passive-aggressively burying her in bland, homely costumes as unspoken punishment for the actress dropping out of the role that went to Kim Novak in 1958's *Vertigo* due to her pregnancy. He never completely forgave her—Hitchcock's ego was easily ruffled, to say the least—a fact not exactly lost upon Vera. Jessica Biel is terrific as Miles, making the most of her screen time as she touchingly portrays a young woman disillusioned with her profession and hoping she may soon be able to escape it to concentrate on motherhood. Also in the universally well-played ensemble: Toni Collette, a vision of quiet, if somewhat harried, dedication as assistant Peggy Robertson, and James D'Arcy, perfectly cast as Anthony Perkins, who has no way of knowing just how unforgettable his transgressive character of Norman Bates is about to become.

"Thank God we have *Cinderfella* for the holidays!" Paramount reasons when prospects for *Psycho* turn bleak, a wickedly sly commentary on the Hollywood studio system and the unpredictability that comes with guessing which movies are going to click with audiences and which ones aren't. Fortunately, *Psycho* did click, despite there being no premiere and the theater count beginning at just two. With Alfred insisting that no one be allowed in the auditorium once the picture has started, a furor quickly builds. For film buffs (and particularly ones with a soft spot for horror), there will likely be few more purely joyous moments in recent cinema than the sight of Hitchcock anxiously waiting outside of one theater showing *Psycho*, his nervousness turning to giddy, childlike elation when the screams of the audience during the now-infamous shower scene carry into the lobby. Headlined by Anthony Hopkins and Helen Mirren in top form and draped in lush period tech details—lovely costumes, sleek art direction and production design (notice all of the bird imagery, a sly suggestion of what is to come for the director a few years later), and a fitting score from Danny Elfman—*Hitchcock* is a centralized biopic that brings newfound insight to an artist, his artistic wife, and the enduring legacy they left behind. The only disappointment is that it couldn't be twice as long.

Hocus Pocus

1993 - Directed by Kenny Ortega

Back in the 1980s, Walt Disney Pictures was responsible for some of the scarier horror movies—and they were marketed at kids. 1983's *Something Wicked This Way Comes* and 1985's *Return to Oz* are two that come to mind. One cannot imagine the Mouse House producing these films today. They were dark, frightening, perverse, and somehow rated PG. Still, watch *Return to Oz* today and try to imagine how little tykes in the audience must have reacted back in the day to the Wheelers (nasty punks who roll around on wheels in the place of hands and feet), to two young girls being chased through a foreboding mental hospital as lightning crashes outside, or to the scene where a room filled with spare heads in glass display cabinets are simultaneously awoken and scream for the disembodied witch Princess Mombi to catch Dorothy. *The Wizard of Oz* may have had the Wicked Witch of the West, but she was small potatoes in comparison to the nightmarish landscape that *Return to Oz* depicted. As family films have become increasingly watered-down and patronizing in the last ten years or more, they have lost their convictions out of fear of offending overly protective soccer moms.

Hocus Pocus isn't all that horrifying in the conventional sense—its tone is generally lighter and more humorous than the bleak, carnival-set *Something Wicked This Way Comes*, for example—but any movie that can involve witches, child murder and zombies and still be supported by Disney safely falls into that realm of family-targeted horror. Released in 1993 and, as far as can be remembered, attracting little to no controversy, the film somehow sneaked through the system without anyone paying much attention. Perhaps the type of parents who would potentially complain about *Hocus Pocus* were instead paying more attention to Bette Midler's 1,000-watt charisma and token brassiness. Whatever the case, for an 11-year-old boy already in love with horror movies, Halloween and Thora Birch, *Hocus Pocus* was my dream movie sprung to life. Memories of first seeing it back in the summer of 1993 are still firmly etched into my consciousness. It is hard to believe multiple decades have gone by since then, but not such a surprise to note that the film in question has built a big cult following (it's shown on television every October) and become a Halloween staple for many.

Bette Midler is in top form here in one of her most entertaining roles, playing well off comic foils Sarah Jessica Parker and Kathy Najimy. The three of them are the Sanderson sisters—leader Winifred, flighty Sarah and daffy people-pleaser Mary—witches in Salem, Massachusetts, 1693, who are hung for the killings of numerous children in the community. Before they die, they vow to return to life one day, conjured up the next time a virgin lights the magical black flame candle. Three hundred years later, 15-year-old Max (Omri Katz) is still brooding over his family's recent move from Los Angeles to New England, but has a crush on beautiful classmate Allison (Vinessa Shaw) to temporarily take his mind off things. While escorting precocious 8-year-old sister Dani (Thora Birch) around trick-or-treating, Max runs into Allison by chance and the three of them decide to pay a festive visit to the old Sanderson home. Upon Allison's telling of the black flame candle legend, Max makes the unwise decision to light it. The next thing they know, they are snatching the witches' spell book and going on the run as a newly revived Winnie, Sarah and Mary set out after them, determined to cast a bit of sorcery before dawn that will claim the lives of the children of Salem in exchange for giving them immortality.

Resourcefully directed by Kenny Ortega (who would later helm the popular *High School Musical* series), *Hocus Pocus* is almost three movies in one, and they're all a smash. The first is a thrilling, sometimes chilling Halloween story, wherein the Sanderson witches seek to lure children to their cottage so that they can suck the lives out of them as a means of living forever. Taken by itself, this doesn't particularly sound like fare for children, but they will eat it up. The film skirts the line between PG and PG-13, and, truth be told, the MPAA must have been asleep when they gave it the lighter rating. In addition to the (non-graphic) deaths of children and adults shown, there is a character named Billy Butcherson (Doug Jones), an ex-boyfriend of Winifred's whom she raises from the grave to do her bidding. Since Billy is tired of Winnie always telling him what to do, he eventually befriends Max, Dani and Allison. Still, it's a rotting corpse, and he loses his head on several occasions. Additionally, there is a heaping of peril and an intense sequence where Winifred, flying on her broomstick, attacks the three protagonists as Max drives down the road.

As Winifred, Sarah and Mary head out into a modern world far different than the one they knew in the seventeenth century, the picture becomes a spiked, clever fish-out-of-water comedy that imagines in inventive ways what it might actually be like for three old-time witches to suddenly find themselves in a vastly different era. Ortega and screenwriters Mick Garris and Neil Cuthbert give the villains naive personalities and an endearing love/hate sibling relationship that nearly make them lovable despite being so evil. Comedy is bright and frequent in these interludes, with the witches completely confused as to why people are wearing costumes around them (it takes them a while to even figure out they *are* costumes), mistaking a paved road for a black pond, and mortified when a little girl dressed as an angel curtsies to them and says, "Bless you." When a man dressed as Satan invites them into his home, they assume he's the real one, and even more convinced when they get into the kitchen, see the cooking utensils around them, and assume it's his torture chamber. That "Satan" and his monotone-voiced wife ("He has a little woman," Winifred observes) are played by real-life brother and sister Garry and Penny Marshall is either ingenious stunt casting or really, really sick.

Finally, when concentrating on Max, Dani and Allison, *Hocus Pocus* becomes a more typical live-action Disney feature. There's a nice bond that grows between Max and little sis Dani, with him realizing how much she means to him. The romance between Max and Allison is sweet and inoffensive. There's a talking cat, Binx (voiced by Jason Marsden)—really a teenage boy from three hundred years earlier who was turned into an undying feline by Winifred—that Dani adopts during their eventful evening. When Thackery Binx, once more in human form, reunites with his sister (a long-ago victim of the Sandersons), it is a bittersweet moment that touches upon the hopes we all have that we may one day get to see our loved ones who have passed on.

Bette Midler chews the scenery as the buck-toothed, lisping Winifred Sanderson, and she has a ball doing it. Midler is very funny, but also threatening when the script calls for it. She also performs a rollicking rendition of "I Put a Spell on You" as she, well, puts a spell on the guests at a costume party. As Sarah, Sarah Jessica Parker embraces her comic skills to play the prettiest, most boy-crazy, and arguably dimmest sister, and Kathy Najimy portrays Mary as a woman who would be completely affable and sweet if she weren't swayed to the dark side by Winnie. Omri Katz, a popular teen actor in the early '90s who disappeared from the acting world soon after, is the sympathetic hero of the piece. His Max is just the right mixture of rebellious, mopey and good. By the end, he has grown as a person, and as a brother. Thora Birch, child actress extraordinaire of the time period, is nothing short of a delight as Dani. Birch was to the '90s what Dakota Fanning was to the '00s. Finally, as Allison, Vinessa Shaw is personable, cute and down-to-earth.

Filmed on location as well as on Hollywood soundstages, *Hocus Pocus* is a visually tantalizing, nicely autumnal part-real/part-fantasy representation of Salem, Massachusetts. The film has probably helped to increase tourism to the area, though my personal experience in visiting Salem was that the movie version of the town is more peaceful and attractive than the actual place (at least during October's in-season). The whimsical music score by John Debney aids to the cause with rousingly memorable orchestrations, particularly of note during the opening credits where a flying witch's shadow can be seen on the water as the camera moves above the river. Ideal for Halloween and beyond—kids and adults alike should be taken by its sharp humor and intermittent scares—*Hocus Pocus* is the kind of entertainment that one can watch over and over and not tire of it in the least. Not many movies can make that claim, but this one does.

Hostel

2006 - Directed by Eli Roth

Seeing *Hostel* for the first time less than twenty-four hours after *BloodRayne* really put things in perspective. *BloodRayne* director Uwe Boll is a talentless hack, one whose passion for the art form is left null and void once he is put in front of a camera. Boll has no sense of timing, of how to handle actors, or of how to create the barest emotion within the viewer, and the other crew members he chooses to surround himself with are of the same level of ineptitude. In comparison, *Hostel* director Eli Roth is a true filmmaker in every sense; unlike Boll, he has a razor-sharp eye for texture, detail and character, not to mention how each scene should be carried out to reach its maximum possible effect. Roth, a die-hard horror fan since childhood, doesn't steal from better artists like Boll does, but uses his keen knowledge of the genre in exciting and original ways that pay respect to films and directors of the past—including Takashi Miike (2001's *Audition*) and Nicolas Roeg (1973's *Don't Look Now*)—without trying to mimic them.

With *Hostel*, a masterfully orchestrated, horrifically plausible terror show that ranks among the best of the *Grand Guignol* style, Eli Roth has only improved as a cinematic artist since his debut effort, 2003's flawed but auspicious *Cabin Fever*. Now comfortable enough to lay down his very own style and free of any remaining signs that he is still a novice at his craft, Roth details a novel premise based on a foreign organization he once read about on the Internet that may or may not have been a sham. In using this dirty business as the central conceit—a Slovakian mafia whom everyday citizens pay thousands of dollars to in order to know what it feels like to murder someone—it really makes no difference if it ever truly existed or not. The fact of the matter is that it very well could, its grim reality and underlying themes concerning severed foreign relations and the fear of the unknown making an unshakably haunting imprint.

The opening thirty-five minutes are sumptuously deceptive. Just-out-of-college American tourists Paxton (Jay Hernandez) and Josh (Derek Richardson), along with Icelandic drifter Oli (Eythor Gudjonsson), are feverishly backpacking across the seedier, wilder side of Europe. On a mission to have as much fun—

and as much sex—as possible, they move from nightclub to brothel to hostel and back again, surrounded by the most beautiful women they've ever seen. It is this hedonistic search for carnal pleasure that leads them to the Slovakian city of Bratislava, where the girls are promised to be as gorgeous and easy as they come. So far, the picture is in the vein of a crudely funny frat-boy comedy one step away from being the sequel to 2004's *Eurotrip*. If Paxton and Oli are chauvinistic in their conversations and actions, they are lewd in a lovable sort of way that suggests they just want to have a great time. As for Josh, he is the so-called "responsible" one of the group, a sensitive nice guy not as skilled with women as his pals and possibly even grappling with his own sexuality.

Upon reaching the Slovakian hostel, they end up sharing a room with Natalya (Barbara Nedeljakova) and Svetlana (Jana Kaderabkova), knock-out gals who instantly take a liking to Paxton and Josh. A damper is put on their trip, until now free of worries, when Oli suddenly disappears. The clerk at the front desk claims he already checked out, and Paxton receives a photo message on his cell phone telling him that he left for home, but something doesn't sit right about the situation. What is really going on—something that Paxton and Josh are soon involuntarily embroiled in—zooms safely past the average person's worst nightmares and onto a plane all their own.

Hostel is a disturbing, uncompromising descent into the blackest corners of human nature, where people are capable of shutting down their consciences in the face of strangers—strangers from other countries, no less—who they see solely as subjects to torture, slaughter and dissect. It's a horrifying notion, indeed, and one with some thought-provoking sociological elements that deepen its purpose beyond being a cheap thrill out to shock and nauseate viewers. *Hostel* is violent, gruesome and graphic, testing the limits of its R rating (beware scenes involving Achilles heels and vivisected eyeballs), but there isn't a moment that goes too far or feels exploitative. In the midst of its mounting tension is a truthful statement about how some people—not all, or even the majority, but some—classify foreigners as being almost of a different breed of human, or inferior to themselves. This xenophobia—the fear or contempt of that which is foreign—goes both ways, stemming from a sense of the unfamiliar. So, while Paxton, Josh and Oli parade around in surroundings different from what they know, merrily unaware that one wrong move could leave them hopelessly lost or in danger, the involved citizens in this Eastern European town take advantage of their Ugly Americanism—in Oli's case, Ugly Icelandicism—using them and their vulnerability for financial gain, culminating in extreme acts of brutality. Think of it as a gorier *Dogville* replacing race with nationality.

Writer-director Eli Roth treats each scene like a symphony, conducting it such a way that shows just enough of what needs to be shown and leaves the imagination to wander about the rest. The further toward the end Roth gets, the more he lies bare, courageous in overstepping questionable taste in favor of how things might really play out and how people would really react if put in the same unthinkable situation as Paxton, Josh and Oli. For the first time in memory, these movie characters, being faced with an infinite fear they have never known, their torture drawn out as death hangs over their heads, don't just cry and scream in reaction—they also puke all over themselves and no doubt shit their pants.

Jay Hernandez, without a role worthy of his capabilities since his breakthrough in 2001's *crazy/beautiful*, and Derek Richardson are credible best friends and strongly charismatic presences as Paxton and Josh, their unrelenting path toward make-or-break, life-or-death fates absolutely riveting because of their likability. That they feel like normal guys in their early twenties, on the verge of jobs and dreams and a whole future open wide to them, is crucial in following them as real people instead of scripted creations, and allows for a more powerful emotional impact. Hernandez is superb throughout, but especially good in a scene where he tells the traumatic childhood story of witnessing a helpless little girl's drowning—a creepy, savvy subtext that is counterbalance to Paxton's own helplessness in later scenes.

There will be audiences who will be offended by *Hostel*, both in content and context, and those who will be sickened by its explicit nature. They are the same people who will have preconceived judgments from the start and have no business seeing it in the first place. For everyone else (weak stomachs need not apply), *Hostel* is an extraordinary low-budget triumph that adeptly studies the threshold of one's own fear and endurance, and the fine line that makes up the boundaries between right and wrong, acquaintance and stranger. Additionally intriguing is the early picturesque cinematography by Milan Chadima, painting the European countryside in an exquisite, idealized light that gets turned on its head midway through when the settings and camera's stock become more grainy and threatening.

Hostel is an unapologetic, taut, brave thriller that puts the horror back in horror film, while simultaneously digging beneath the surface and into even grimmer areas of the human condition. If the ending seems a little too easy, it's only because what has come before has been so hard and despairing; the climactic moments are devilishly clever and logical in their inference. Finally, in Eli Roth is a stirring talent with the natural, invigorating filmmaking ability to become one of the horror genre's most reliable masters—a bloodier Alfred Hitchcock or a more radical version of old-school John Carpenter if you will. The equally smart and hair-raising *Hostel*, even more so than *Cabin Fever*, is our first unadulterated proof of this.

Hostel: Part II

2007 - Directed by Eli Roth

Hostel was the smartest, deepest and most effective horror film of 2006, an uncompromisingly merciless thriller with an unthinkable premise—an organization in Eastern Europe that traps out-of-towners and serves them up to customers who have paid money for the experience of killing someone—made all the more frightening because it was actually plausible. Besides that, the movie provocatively touched upon any number of thought-provoking themes and notions—Ugly Americanism, xenophobia, topographic dislocation, the mirroring of one's exploitative desire for sexual gratification with that of another's murderous impulses—that raised it above the level of just a typical, violent genre pic. At the consummate helm was writer-director Eli Roth, who cemented with only his second big-screen effort that he was one of the most knowledgeable and skilled filmmakers working in the horror arena.

With *Hostel: Part II*, conceived as the second and final entry in the series (a third, for what it's worth, was released direct-to-video in 2011 without Roth's participation), the director may not have detectably grown as an auteur, but he certainly has defied expectations. At first glance, the film looks as if it will be a retread of the original, with the only difference being the change in sex from male to female for the three central protagonists. Roth flirts with this presumed assumption of his audience, but gradually he turns the formula on its head. In superficial ways, yes, *Hostel: Part II* resembles *Hostel*. Tonally, however, the difference between them is incalculably vast. Whereas the first film began as a college kid's wet dream and ended as a nightmare, *Hostel: Part II* is cloaked in a blanket of dread and darkness from frame one. Even the lighter moments in the first act seem like taunting harbingers of doom.

Beth (Lauren German) and Whitney (Bijou Phillips) are American art students studying abroad in Rome who hop a train to Prague for a getaway weekend of partying and frivolity. Tagging along with them is classmate Lorna (Heather Matarazzo), a somewhat geeky outsider missing her home in Baltimore and hoping to fit in. After befriending local art model Axelle (Vera Jordanova) on the train, they alter their vacation destination with the exotic promise that Slovakia's natural hot springs are unlike anything they have seen before. Anyone who knows anything about the plot of the predecessor—or at least takes heed of the opening scenes involving the first movie's survivor Paxton (Jay Hernandez)—will have a pretty good idea what's coming. Sure enough, Beth, Whitney and Lorna check into the same infamous hostel and are lured to a nearby masquerade harvest festival. Several men show a liking to the trio of gals, and only Beth is cautious enough to realize the dangers of being left alone in a foreign country.

As these girls' story plays out in ways that range from predictable to clever to shocking, *Hostel: Part II* takes a step behind the curtains of the operation. Simultaneously detailing the reality-based ins and outs of the deadly business and the trek two new American clients, Todd (Richard Burgi) and Stuart (Roger Bart), go on when they receive the highest bids for Beth and Whitney, the film fills in all of the gaps and questions left by the original and partially tells the story from the bad guys' points of view. This brave plot decision on Roth's part initially appears to be risky, since the unknown is often scarier than having things spelled out. With just the right touch, though, Roth is able to build upon and enrich the ideas he introduced in *Hostel*.

The "Elite Hunting" corporation, their security noticeably beefed up since last seen, is portrayed in an eerily logical fashion that dodges the far-fetched. So, too, does the events involving Todd and Stuart, rich suburban family men bored by their safe-and-narrow existences and hoping that the act of homicidal slaughter will give them the thrill missing from their lives. That these two fellows are so different—Todd's anticipation is akin to a 5-year-old's on Christmas Eve, while Stuart is more hesitant and unsure of himself—leaves one actively curious about how things are going to play out when they come face to face with both their victims and the sheer enormity of what they have signed on the dotted line to do.

Hostel: Part II is equally as ambitious as *Hostel*, and frequently outdoes it in terms of the stark terror it ratchets. Still, it's a more flawed motion picture. Emotionally, the movie is colder and more unforgiving. This is fine in pulling a visceral response from viewers, but the end result is one of downbeat admiration rather than adrenaline-fueled excitement. Once the carnage has subsided and the end credits are rolling, it is easier to say that the film was extremely well-made than to admit you "liked" it. Additionally, the tone is more gravely serious, free of the frat-boy hijinks of the precursor's opening thirty-five minutes. The problem is that it was in that time frame that the viewer got to really know, relate to and care about the three guys. Here, lead actresses Lauren German, Heather Matarazzo and Bijou Phillips have less-rounded and complicated characters to work with, their roles barely rising above two-dimensional types. The strong established bond between the young men in *Hostel* was a key component in making them authentic human beings. By comparison, the friendships between these three girls is more sketchy and less palpable; they seem more like acquaintances than buddies.

With that said, it is far more difficult to witness a female meeting a nasty end on screen than it is a male, and this is where *Hostel: Part II* redeems itself for the less inspired writing of the characters. German, Phillips and Matarazzo are naturally charismatic and identifiable actresses; in other words, they have that crucial likability factor. In the setpieces where they are placed in harm's way, the film becomes uncomfortable in the extreme. This is no more in evidence than in a sequence of uncommon potency involving Lorna, played to the hilt by Heather Matarazzo. This scene is so cruel, so gruesome, so bloody, so sick, so twisted, so unfair and so heartbreaking that it may leave even the strong of stomach recoiling in physical fear and sickness. Eli Roth's unflinching work in this five-minute segment is either that of a genius or that of someone who, undeniable talent aside, crosses a line rarely before crossed in an R-rated film. In regards to the vulnerable and quirkily lovable Matarazzo, her naked, soul-baring performance is as courageous as any in memory given by a legitimate, mainstream actor. Lofty claims, indeed, but also warranted.

The MPAA must have fallen asleep when they screened *Hostel: Part II*, which is twice as violent and gory as the already-extreme *Hostel*, and more power to them. However Eli Roth got away with some of this material—for those familiar with 1978's hard-core *I Spit on Your Grave*, pick out what is widely regarded as the most memorable moment of the climax and imagine it even more explicit—he should be applauded for making the film he set out to make and not holding back from the bad taste that such a storyline honestly consists of. Sitting through it might cause a viewer to feel icky, but at least the movie delivers what he or she has paid to see. The bonus, then, is that a veritable craftsman like Roth is behind the camera; he doesn't make exploitation movies for exploitation's sake, but is an intelligent artist who brings a great deal of sociological layers to his projects.

Hostel: Part II has a dreamlike, operatic quality to its look and feel that is nothing like the half-vibrant/half-ashen landscapes of *Hostel*. Aided by Milan Chadima's brilliantly sumptuous, almost surreal photography, Roth has made a Grimms' fairy tale for a modern adult audience, and there is no doubt that this was precisely his intention. From the fantastical costumes at the harvest festival, to the stately mansion where the "wolf" takes the prey to pretty her up and give her a false sense of hope before she's "eaten," to the chilling, off-kilter production design of the torture chambers, to the image of a secret room lined with meticulously mounted severed heads, to the scenes at the hot springs that are as foreboding as they are beautiful, the correlation is unmistakable.

A quick bid for cash without an inkling of thought put into the story *Hostel: Part II* is not, and the imagination Eli Roth exhibits in lieu of merely repeating himself is a treat. Particularly intriguing this time is its fresh spin on the fight-or-flight method and the compelling comments Roth makes about gender relations—contrast the actions of the boys in the original, both before and after their capture, with the girls in this one—and the dangerously inestimable nature of a person's mental stability, seen most prevalently in the characters of Todd, Stuart and Beth. When all is said and done, *Hostel: Part II* is a very good film, relentless and difficult to shake. While it might have been one of the best horror efforts of 2007, it is also thoroughly unpleasant and will be borderline-inaccessible for all but serious genre buffs. You know who you are, and fortunately I am one of them.

House of 1000 Corpses

2003 - Directed by Rob Zombie

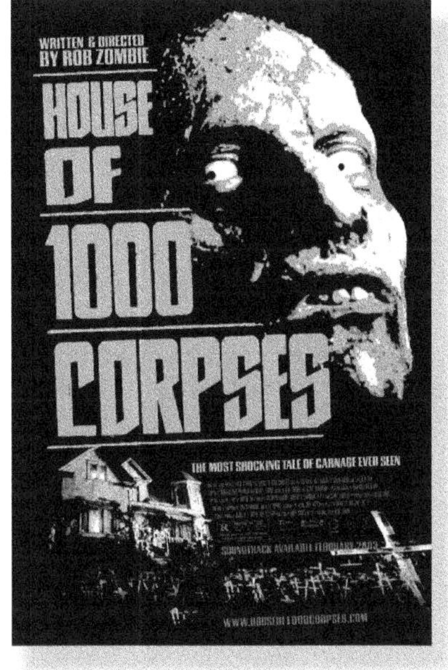

Three years and three film studios after it was originally supposed to be released in the fall of 2000, Rob Zombie's infamous-before-release *House of 1000 Corpses* was finally saved by Lionsgate Films. However, as is typically the case with filmic controversy, when the subject in question is eventually seen, one wonders what all of the uproar was about. Despite little in the way of actual gore, *House of 1000 Corpses* is unrelentingly violent and disturbing. Controversy or not, this loving, down-and-dirty throwback to the 1970s *Texas Chain Saw Massacre*-style horror flicks creeps under one's skin and stays there for its full 88 minutes.

Four twenty-something friends—Denise (Erin Daniels), Mary (Jennifer Jostyn), Jerry (Chris Hardwick) and Bill (Rainn Wilson)—traveling cross-country as they research weird roadside attractions stop for gas at "Captain Spaulding's Museum of Monsters and Madmen." The owner of the place, the clown-painted Captain Spaulding (Sid Haig), is only so happy to take them on a sort of carnival ride tour through the history of serial killers. Further up the road, they make the mistake of picking up a beautiful hitchhiker named Baby (Sheri Moon Zombie). When they run into car trouble, Baby suggests they come back to her family's house until their car is fixed by her mechanic brother, Rufus Jr. (Robert Mukes). Once inside and having also met matriarch Mother Firefly (Karen Black), the friends discover too late that the family welcoming them into their home are depraved serial killers, having trapped and slaughtered at least a thousand victims over the years.

Rob Zombie's ballsy, freakishly stylish, highly auspicious writing-directing debut, *House of 1000 Corpses* was a gratifying respite to what horror movies had become in the late-'90s/early-'00s—that of the sleek, overly self-referential era of *Scream*-inspired slasher films. Because Zombie is a die-hard fan of the genre, he knows exactly what he is doing, setting up his cast of unwitting victims and twistedly entertaining villains, and letting them run loose in his gruesome funhouse of carnage. The result is gritty, grimy, thoroughly unpredictable, and always unnerving. *House of 1000 Corpses* is a dream come true for those who have heard of and read *Fangoria*; if you don't even know what *Fangoria* is, then it's a safe bet you should stay far away.

In realizing his vision, Zombie has worked closely with production designer Gregg Gibbs to create a dazzling, spooky visual masterpiece. Set on Halloween, the movie does a better job of personifying the holiday than even Zombie's own 2007 *Halloween* reboot. Pumpkins, scarecrows, seasonal decorations and even trick-or-treaters fill each frame, deeply eliciting a certain time and mood. Editor Robert K. Lambert also does indelible wonders with flash-cuts, slow-motion, split-screens and the chilling use of film negatives. Mix all of this with a disturbing, candy-colored ride-cum-tour of serial killers, psychopaths in masks, severed doll heads, chickens in cages, clowns, operating tables, an arsenal of weapons, dead bodies, skeletons, bunny costumes and a deformed mutant, and what has been created knocks the socks off of every horror movie in this vein that had been made in the previous ten years.

The cast is not brilliant, but the over-the-top performances are, indeed, perfect. As the ominous Captain Spaulding, Sid Haig lords over the proceedings with overwhelming presence even when he isn't onscreen. Sheri Moon Zombie proved to be far more than Rob's significant other in this showy screen debut as the sexy, demented, childlike Baby, while Karen Black vamps it up as Mother Firefly. The quartet of normal protagonists, including Erin Daniels and a then-unknown Rainn Wilson, cannot compete with their flashier adversaries, and so do not stand out quite as much, but they do their jobs effectively.

At a time when former distributors Universal and MGM shied away from what was, in essence, exactly what a horror film should be, Lionsgate should be commended for having the courage to give *House of 1000 Corpses* the shot it deserved. That Rob Zombie was able to achieve this with such maniacal relish is, perhaps, what scared most studios off. It is rare in today's prim, proper, politically correct times to find a motion picture with the sort of pure visceral impact as *House of 1000 Corpses* has.

The House of the Devil

2009 - Directed by Ti West

The most criminally unsung genre moviemaker working today, writer-director Ti West got his start as a filmmaker with three great—not good, *great*—motion pictures over the course of just five years. All independently financed, all original ideas, and all acclaimed by the few who had been fortunate to see them, the films should have gotten West noticed by Hollywood, but, up to this point in 2009, his only foray into the studio system had been *Cabin Fever 2*, allegedly a horrible experience that distributor Lionsgate stole from him in the editing room. West may have lost control over that unnecessary Eli Roth-free sequel, but his masterly fingerprints are unmistakable throughout the rest of his résumé, from 2005's spine-tingling *The Roost* to 2007's chilling minimalist sucker-punch *Trigger Man*. His next impressive effort was no slouch, either. Far from some dumb spoof of the era, the potently ominous 1980s-set *The House of the Devil* actually looks and feels like a classic of that decade that has just now been discovered. Lively and frightful, deliciously slow-burning and yet all the more rattlingly effective because of its deliberateness, the picture continues Ti West's understanding love of building mood and a shiver-inducing sense of dread over cheap thrills. If ever the director orchestrates a jump scare—and he does, albeit sparingly—you better believe he earns every single one of them.

College student Samantha Hughes (Jocelin Donahue) is excited at the prospect of moving out of the dorms and into her very own first apartment, but she still needs three hundred dollars in order to pay the first month's rent. Answering a "Babysitter Needed" flyer that she spots on the campus bulletin board, Samantha finds herself that very night at the secluded Victorian mansion of Mr. and Mrs. Ulman (Tom Noonan and Mary Woronov). Once there, she discovers that they do not have any children at all, instead wanting her to be there in case an emergency pops up with Mrs. Ulman's elderly mother upstairs. Samantha senses something isn't quite right with this couple, but she also isn't about to turn down four hundred dollars for just a few hours' work.

The House of the Devil entrancingly builds in foreboding, slowly but surely, throughout its 95-minute running time. It is a joy to see films that trust the intelligence and patience of their audience, as West does, and even more pleasurable that genuine care has been brought to the multiple narrative and stylistic layers set up. As Samantha explores the house, watches television, orders pizza, tries to study, listens to music on her Walkman, and altogether attempts to keep busy lest a case of the heebie-jeebies get the best of her, the viewer knows the other shoe is bound to eventually drop. The not knowing of when, and how, is part of the fun and suspense. While a beginning screen of text hints at what is to come by mentioning the 1980s hysteria that occurred over the threat of satanic cults, it otherwise is left wide open as to where Samantha's overnight journey will lead her. Meanwhile, radio stations and news programs prattle on about the rare full lunar eclipse set to occur around midnight, adding further atmospheric texture to the proceedings.

If Ti West ever lulls his audience into feelings of the safe and mundane, it is but another tricky weapon in his arsenal. The insular worlds he creates for his characters are recognizable and authentic, but depicted or portrayed in a faintly askew fashion that suggests danger could be afoot around any corner. Certainly, his aesthetics add to one's edginess, normalcy colliding with the gothic. The opening credits dazzle with the nostalgia they elicit, freeze-frames, camera zooms and the introduction of a gnarly synthesizer score by Jeff Grace almost as inspired as John Carpenter's in 1980's *The Fog* all put to striking use. The cinematography by Eliot Rockett, making good with the wintry on-location shooting in Connecticut, is never less than sophisticated, evocative shots of barren tree branches casting shadows and unknown fingers opening a creaking attic door standing out amidst plentiful inspiration. Also complementing the story's specific time and place are period-appropriate but not overblown production and costume designs and a terrific, well-used handful of '80s songs (The Fixx's "One Thing Leads to Another," The Greg Kihn Band's "The Breakup Song (They Don't Write 'Em)," and Thomas Dolby's "One of Our Submarines").

Jocelin Donahue carries the movie—she's in every scene but one—and, for someone who had been better known for modeling than acting up to this point, she is faultless. Donahue's Samantha is identifiable and sincere, a likable protagonist whose one weak moment of greed—she demands four hundred dollars from the deceptive Mr. Ulman after he comes clean and offers her three—spells her potential doom. As the Ulmans, Tom Noonan and Mary Woronov play a middle-aged couple who might just be quirky, or might be seriously unhinged. By playing things close to the vest, Noonan and Woronov embody the nagging possibility of malicious intent—far scarier than if they were to be overtly playing whack-jobs. Making a splash just as she did in 2008's *Baghead* and every film since, Greta Gerwig gives her supporting part of Samantha's concerned friend, Megan, a depth of personality ranging from vivacious to fiercely loyal.

Ultimately, viewers are awarded for their efforts and attention spans with a blood- and violence-strewn climax that goes for the throat in more ways than one. It poses as a catharsis, to be sure, but where it ends up may be the least assured element, if only because Ti West never quite seems comfortable with his concluding moments. By then, however, the magic of a major talent undeterred by a limited budget and able to put to shame most major studio horror releases has already been spun. Classy even while getting down and dirty, unusually savvy about the importance of tension and character nuance over viscera and a soulless body count, *The House of the Devil* cogently suggests the sinister underbelly lurking in a world where complacency is just a temporary stop on the road to misfortune. And to think all Samantha wanted was an apartment and a little freedom.

House of Wax

2005 - Directed by Jaume Collet-Serra

House of Wax, a reinvisioning of the 1953 Vincent Price B-movie, borrows the general idea behind that film—a madman who turns his victims into wax figures for his ghastly museum—to concoct an affectionate throwback to the slasher genre of the '80s and '90s, albeit one eerier, smarter and more stylish than most. Indeed, former music video and commercial director Jaume Collet-Serra, making his splashy inaugural feature, brought to vividly ingenious life a premise that, in lesser hands, could have just been a schlocky waste of everyone's time. He makes expert and chilling use out of his macabre wax surroundings to bless the breathlessly taut proceedings with added layers of atmosphere and foreboding that horror aficionados should go wild over.

A group of college friends headed for a university football game are forced to take a detour off the beaten path and camp out for the night. The next morning, following a run-in with a mysterious trucker, easygoing Wade (Jared Padalecki) finds his car's fan belt ripped out. While Wade and his city-bound girlfriend, Carly (Elisha Cuthbert), set out for the nearest town to get a new car part, the rest of the friends—sexy Paige (Paris Hilton), her boyfriend, Blake (Robert Ri'chard), camera-wielding Dalton (Jon Abrahams), and Carly's troubled twin brother, Nick (Chad Michael Murray)—press on for the game. When Wade and Carly finally make it to the virtual ghost town of Ambrose, they are at first intrigued by the detailed wax house until they discover that it—and the town's inhabitants—are made up almost entirely of wax themselves. The exceptions are brothers Bo and Vincent (Brian Van Holt in a dual role), murderous psychopaths with designs to turn these two lovebirds, and later the rest of their unsuspecting buddies, into the town's latest deadly wax creations.

House of Wax is a gritty, bloody, violent, R-rated (thank you very much) return to what the genre is all about, at the time of its 2005 release possibly the most giddily inspired slasher pic since Rob Zombie's 2003 kaleidoscope of the macabre, *House of 1000 Corpses*. There are no ghosts in sight and, tellingly, the sight of practically hundreds of wax figures—really corpses engulfed in wax—populating a desolate, dusty town run by a pair of serial killers is far more disturbing than any old CGI-aided apparition.

House of Wax stands as an example of how an astounding production design, by Graham 'Grace' Walker, and sumptuous art direction, by Nicholas McCallum, can strengthen and even transcend what could have easily just been a hackneyed body-count movie. The entire fictional town of Ambrose was built from the ground up with such fervent attention to exacting detail that it becomes one of the lead characters of the film, and Collet-Serra uses his every set to its fullest potential. From the museum itself, constructed fully out of wax, to the body-strewn underground chamber, to the church, to the gas station, to, in one of the most unsettling and original sequences, the movie theater—where wax figures sit and watch 1962's *What Ever Happened to Baby Jane?* on a continuous loop—no expense has been spared in bringing to creepy life the sort of place that seemingly would only reside in the viewer's nightmares.

Whereas most slasher films fall apart when dealing with their characters and bringing their stories to a conclusion, *House of Wax* features people who may just turn out to be victims, but seem genuine as a group of college-aged friends who are unaware of the danger lurking right under their noses. Screenwriters Chad Hayes and Carey W. Hayes intelligently build this said danger slowly and methodically, drawing the viewer into the precarious circumstances faced by the characters before wholeheartedly unleashing the horror element. By doing this, the story gains a certain level of cinematic plausibility and becomes unpredictable in just when the stalking and killing will start. Once it does, the film never lets up, becoming a consummate, increasingly sinister ride offering up infinitely more thrills and good-time frights than most efforts of its ilk.

Also appreciative is the screenplay's wise decision to not overindulge the plot and killers' motives—a downfall of many like-minded features—giving the watcher just enough information so that the blanks can be filled in while always feeling like he or she is being treated by the filmmakers with respect. Refreshingly, there is no clichéd moment during the climax where the villains describe their devious plan to the final survivors. In this film, as it would more likely be if it were real, the maniacal wax sculptors have no interest in explaining themselves; their purpose is to kill the intruders, plain and simple. Thus, the grand-scale, ambitious finale is just as effective and go-for-broke as the preceding 100 minutes, pitting the final two protagonists against the murderers as the on-fire house of wax they are trapped in literally melts and disintegrates around them.

The performances are always professional and understated in their believable cogency, particularly Elisha Cuthbert, a talented, multilayered actress who, by this time, had proven on TV's *24* and 2004's *The Girl Next Door* that beauty and intelligence could very much go hand in hand. Cuthbert digs into the role of Carly with strength, determination and horrified realism; you believe as you watch her that she is going through these things and forget all about the actor playing the part, which is the biggest compliment of all. As brother Nick, Chad Michael Murray pushed away from the kid-friendly roles of his past (e.g., 2003's *Freaky Friday* and 2004's *A Cinderella Story*) and seemed to relish the opportunity.

Today, *House of Wax* may be best known for the major acting debut of Paris Hilton and, more specifically, her much-publicized death scene. Solely because of her appearance, some viewers hastily and unfairly wrote off the film altogether. What these same Paris haters may be disappointed to find, however, is a performance that isn't bad at all. Hilton meshes well with her castmates without drawing much attention to herself, and naturalistically plays a character that rarely even seems like her glitzy real-life persona. She's fun to watch onscreen, and is a good sport at slyly poking fun at herself, as in a moment involving a pile of cell phones that don't work.

One of the more satisfying releases from Robert Zemeckis' Dark Castle horror label, *House of Wax* is scary, scream- and squirm-inducing, and legitimately suspenseful, continuing proof that trends may come and go, but the slasher movie—a genre that has never gotten the respect it deserves—is alive and well. Taking its cue from 1996's *Scream*, it simply takes a masterful one to show how it can be done right. Stuffy, narrow-minded critics be damned, *House of Wax* is not only well-made and stylistically accomplished, but also unwilling to simply coast on name recognition alone. This is a very different film than the Vincent Price starrer, and in many ways more adept at taking advantage of its crafty central conceit.

The Human Centipede (First Sequence)

2010 - Directed by Tom Six

Xenophobic themes are nothing new in the horror genre, with countless cautionary fright tales telling of unsuspecting travelers abroad who don't return to their homeland in one piece—if at all. Indeed, there exists a fear in many, if even subconscious, of the foreign or unknown, and filmmakers of the macabre know exactly how to exploit this notion in their favor. Dutch writer-director Tom Six milks it to the hilt with *The Human Centipede (First Sequence)*, and then goes a step further into the sort of unimaginably bleak, despairing territory that actually makes the thought of death by hacksaw or harpoon sound desirable in comparison. At the forefront—when he's not hauntingly lingering motionless in the background, that is—is a villain so unforgettably chilling and believably maniacal that he alone does enough to smooth out the film's rougher edges and plaguing unanswered questions.

Young, nattering American friends Lindsay (Ashley C. Williams) and Jenny (Ashlynn Yennie) are traveling across Europe when, en route to a nightclub, their rental car gets a flat tire. Stranded on the back roads of Germany, they finally come upon a house in the clearing and seek the help of its owner, retired surgeon Dr. Heiter (Dieter Laser). They want him to call a tow truck, but he has other plans in mind. Coming to after being drugged, Lindsay and Jenny find themselves strapped to hospital beds, they and Asian kidnap victim Katsuro (Akihiro Kitamura) the three test subjects in Dr. Heiter's fiendish plan to construct a human centipede. Connected by their gastric systems and sewn ass to mouth, they now have two choices: submissively become the doctor's plaything, or rustle up all the willpower they've got to somehow escape their hellish ordeal.

If that synopsis sounds simply repulsive, causing your imagination to wander to the most nauseating of images, it should be said that *The Human Centipede (First Sequence)* does show a certain amount of restraint without ever going soft. Hence, Dr. Heiter explains the horrific procedure and consequences to his subjects beforehand (complete with projected illustrations) so that one is spared some—the operative word being *some*—of the graphic details when he puts his plan into action. Tom Six doesn't quite cover all the logistical queries audiences may have, such as the body's need for water to survive (a shot of Dr. Heiter intravenously giving it to middle and back sections Lindsay and Jenny could have quickly cleared this up) and the lack of necessary nutrients found in fecal matter, but he explores enough of them to be able to buy into it in cinema terms without things becoming patently ridiculous.

That the picture comes with a "100% medically accurate" stamp is probably stretching the truth a bit, but no matter. The film achieves exactly what it sets out to do—shock, disturb, disconcert, and force the viewer to ask what he or she would do in such a situation—and then grows to be a little more than just an exercise in revilement. Lindsay and Jenny are portrayed at the start as irritating and ill-equipped to be on their own in the real world, let alone in a place completely alien to them. Trapped along the road when their tire goes kaput, they are accosted by a fellow driver—a local, no doubt, speaking a language they do not understand—who pulls up and sexually harasses them. Thinking the worst is behind them after the perv speeds off, the two gals abandon their lone security—the confines of their car—and wander into a far greater danger than either can imagine. Their whiny personalities—or is it the performances of newcomers Ashley C. Williams and Ashlynn Yennie, far better when their mouths are sewn up and they must act with little more than their eyes, that are annoying?—do not exactly make them very sympathetic at the onset, but Six's achievement is in devising a destiny for them so awful in every way one wouldn't wish it upon their worst enemy. Thus, by the half-hour mark, the viewer is actively on Lindsay and Jenny's side, even when the former makes a numbskull decision in the midst of an attempted escape that will cause a few smacks to the forehead.

While it is sheer coincidence that the girls cross paths with the psychotic Dr. Heiter—the self-proclaimed "leading surgeon in separating Siamese twins," he has chosen in his retirement to test out the direct opposite, conjoining first Rottweilers and now humans—their Ugly Americanism seals the deal on their fates. Heiter's other victims, whom he actively hunts and shoots with debilitating darts in order to bring them back to his lair—e.g., a truck driver, then what appears to be a young Asian businessman—are interestingly also foreigners to the country, easier to make disappear without too many people asking questions. Bringing things full circle, Katsuro calls Dr. Heiter a Nazi at one point, stereotyping his nationality while at the same time figuratively equating him with a monster. He isn't far off in that particular judgment.

The Human Centipede (First Sequence) follows classic narrative conventions while putting a spin on genre expectations. Dr. Heiter isn't above killing if he has to, but that isn't his motive. No, what he purposes to do with his victims is far worse than any run-of-the-mill psycho with a knife. Jump scares, too, are mostly left out of the proceedings, not coming when they are most expected as a means of building up one's thick apprehension. It's fun to be on edge, expecting things that don't happen and vice versa. Adding to the picture's dread-drenched nature is a top-notch production design—the house chosen for

Dr. Heiter is, at once, a beacon of deceptively peaceful normalcy and a sterile, well-kept, off-center museum of white walls, large windows, abstract art, long hallways, rooms of the unknown, and a secret in the basement—and a close to brilliant performance from Dieter Laser. Laser's slim, tall frame, pale skin, and speckless white doctor's coat are imperative to his character, a lonely, deranged man whose past profession has given him a dangerous case of narcissism—in one scene, he gets lost in a hand mirror and kisses himself—and an outright God Complex.

Following the intentionally and impeccably conceived dismay and abhorrence of the first seventy-five minutes, what could one possibly be expecting for an ending? The finale of *The Human Centipede (First Sequence)* will not be given away, but it adds freshness to the usual climactic chase scene by leveling the score and forcing both parties to do something other than run, then leads toward a final scene far more psychologically terrifying, staggeringly tragic and plainly twisted than just about anything the horror arena has ever cooked up. *The Human Centipede (First Sequence)* is an inconsistent motion picture, stronger in certain areas than in others, but when it works, it works like a charm for the strong of stomach. The film burrows past one's defenses like a fungus and takes root in the mind, where one can scarcely believe what he or she is watching, yet can't help but be impressed by the audacity of it all.

I Am Legend

2007 - Directed by Francis Lawrence

In New York City, circa 2009, a cure for cancer was found that put the disease into turnaround for any patient that received the treatment. With this landmark discovery, however, came a catastrophic price, unleashing a physical and airborne virus that turned the infected into vampiric creatures of the night. Three years later, Manhattan is a deserted wasteland with one immune survivor, scientist Robert Neville (Will Smith). As far as he knows, he is the last man left on Earth, roaming around the city during the day with dog Sam and holing up in his home after dark, when the infected come out to prey. Haunted by his final tragic memories of wife Zoe (Salli Richardson) and daughter Marley (Willow Smith), Robert has thus far been unsuccessful in his attempts to find an antibody for the virus in his basement laboratory. There may not even be one.

Loosely based on the classic novel by Richard Matheson and the previous 1971 adaptation, *The Omega Man*, *I Am Legend* is a frightening film. What gets under one's skin, though, has nothing to do with the conventional horror elements involving, for lack of a better word, the vampires, who have been brought to life not terribly convincingly through CG effects. Indeed, the movie might have been better off excising these bad guys altogether and concentrating on Robert's eerily plausible plight in the face of mankind's extermination. That, above all else, is where *I Am Legend* excels, and it is the solitary day-to-day moments and rituals in the devastated lives of Robert and his trusty canine companion that are most unnervingly effective and dramatically potent.

To be sure, director Francis Lawrence and screenwriters Mark Protosevich and Akiva Goldsman have devised a number of more predictably tense and horror-centric scenes throughout. One setpiece, in which Sam chases a deer into the creatures' darkened lair and Robert must go in to find her, is genuinely nail-biting, as is another sequence where an injured Robert must crawl back to the safety of his truck before the sun goes down and the pack of infected dogs are set free. Still, these villains are too obviously the work of visual effects artists, and could have been improved upon by either using live-action actors or altering their design to make them look less like people and more like the savage, conscience-free monsters they have become. As is, they do not quite appear real or seamless enough in their surroundings to pose the level of threat intended.

Nevertheless, it is the quieter, subtler moments and details that the viewer's mind will likely keep returning to once the film is over. The way, for example, that Robert watches a recording of an old episode of the *Today* show each morning and night, clinging desperately to a connection with civilization that no longer exists. Or the way he devotedly listens to his Bob Marley album, serving to remind him of the hope that may still be in the world and as a dedication to his daughter, whom he named after the musician. Or his excursions to the video store, renting out DVDs from the mannequin he has set up at the cash register. Or his jaunts out to hunt for spare deer near Times Square, only, on one occasion, to come into contact with a family of lions who claim the game as their own. There is also an utterly heartbreaking scene between Robert and Sam, their last together, that will tear up all but the most stoic of audience members. In ruminative segments such as these, *I Am Legend* is note-perfect.

As the lone man of New York City, a scientist who holds himself responsible for the outbreak and who knows that he is the planet's final potential savior, Will Smith is extraordinary. The Smith of the twenty-first century bears little resemblance to the wisecracking performer from his days on sitcom *The Fresh Prince of Bel Air* or in decades-old blockbusters like *Independence Day* and *Men in Black*, and the steps he has taken to branch out as a multilayered performer while still making commercial projects is greatly admirable. There isn't a sign of mugging in Smith's deeply touching, often silent performance as Robert, and, left to act mostly with himself *à la* Tom Hanks in 2000's *Cast Away*, he is riveting to watch.

I Am Legend loses its way a little in the third act as a series of serendipitous, increasingly convenient plot developments take place. Though director Lawrence has trouble organizing a naturalistic conclusion, he should be commended for all of the things he gets absolutely right. The depiction of a desolate, post-apocalyptic New York City landscape is thoroughly ominous and believably rendered, while Robert's inner conflict as he scrambles to deal with what has happened and come to terms with where his own life has led him remains a truthful constant. *I Am Legend* is not without some stumbling blocks, but it also stands as a worthy achievement—an engrossing thinking-person's science-fiction tale with a mind and a heart.

Identity

2003 - Directed by James Mangold

It doesn't happen often, but once or twice every decade a motion picture comes along that redefines its genre—or, at least, deserves to. Complexly written by Michael Cooney and stunningly crafted by director James Mangold, *Identity* may not have lived up to the blockbuster success of 1999's *The Sixth Sense*, but, in certain ways, it did reinvigorate slasher movies the same way that picture jump-started supernatural thrillers. Similarities between M. Night Shyamalan's monster hit and this film are superficial, at best, but they do share a willingness to offer up something startlingly fresh, thoroughly unpredictable, genuinely creepy, and unshakably thought-provoking. By the time *Identity* reaches its heart-stopping final twist of a scene (never mind the corkscrew zinger that comes fifteen minutes earlier), it is safe to say not a single audience member will be able to pinpoint another film quite like the one he or she has just encountered.

Taking a page from Agatha Christie's classic *Ten Little Indians*, *Identity* places ten strangers within a secluded and ominous setting, and then proceeds to methodically bump them off at the hands of a mystery killer. It's a dark and stormy night in the Nevada desert. With the roads flooded, seemingly unrelated travelers are forced to check in at an out-of-the-way motel. The victims/suspects include a limousine driver (John Cusack) chauffeuring has-been television actress Caroline Suzanne (Rebecca De Mornay); a down-on-their-luck family consisting of a sincere stepfather (John C. McGinley), a critically injured mother (Leila Kenzle), and a mute son (Bret Loehr); an argumentative newlywed couple (Clea DuVall, William Lee Scott); a just-retired prostitute (Amanda Peet) headed for her Florida hometown to start over, and a police officer (Ray Liotta) transferring a convict (Jake Busey) across the state. As these people start getting killed off in what increasingly seems like a systematic fashion, they discover that they are all somehow linked. But who is the cold-blooded murderer? And what is their motive?

Reading the premise, you may think you've got it all figured out, or sigh with the feeling that you have seen a tried-and-true formula such as this played out countless times before. Think again. *Identity* may be a horror movie with a body count for its first hour, albeit a particularly chilling and faultlessly orchestrated one, but then it blindsides with the sort of plot revelations that turn everything that has come before and everything that follows on its head. It is utterly incalculable, even as you may scold yourself for not picking up on all the carefully placed clues along the way. More importantly, though, this novel twist does not pop up for the sole reason of fooling the viewer, but has a real purpose for being. It metamorphosizes *Identity* from what could have been just a high-gloss, unusually well-cast slasher item into something markedly deeper, substantially richer, and far more existential in nature. To say any more about the climactic truths uncovered would be blasphemy for those who have not had the pleasure of experiencing this compact, 90-minute gem.

In the first two acts, Mangold delights in toying with the typical body-count conventions, all the while cooking up something far closer in atmosphere and style to Alfred Hitchcock than, say, *Friday the 13th*. The killings, although occasionally bloody, appear more often after the fact than during the act, but it is in his classic-style setups that Mangold really comes into his own. He is aided by the sumptuously moody and detailed cinematography by Phedon Papamichael, superbly putting shadows and pouring rain to expert use, and the tight, meticulously woven editing by David Brenner. At around the 65-minute mark, Mangold suddenly pulls the genre safety net out from under the viewers, but in a good way. Yes, it forces one to look at everything differently, but it also strengthens rather than cheapens what has already come. And, best of all, it adds levels of poignancy and depth to the story, just as the second twist in the final minutes returns the movie with a bang to its veritably scary and disturbing lineage.

The cast, filled from all sides by real talent, fit right in. John Cusack is perfect in his laid-back, everyman kind of roles, and his Ed makes for an enthralling protagonist. As former prostitute Paris, who just wants to get to Florida and start an orchard, Amanda Peet matches Cusack scene for scene, developing her role far more than what is expected of a female heroine, usually on hand to just run and scream (although she does these quite well, too). As the questionably on-the-level motel clerk, John Hawkes brings an unforced, distinguishable energy to his scenes. Everyone else, especially the wonderful Clea DuVall, the always interesting Ray Liotta, and bright young newcomer Bret Loehr, are standouts in purposefully archetypal roles.

The third act of *Identity* does not offer simple answers, nor does it always follow through with what is expected of a spooky whodunit. For those who aren't paying close attention, the film's intricate pleasures will be rendered useless. For anyone tired of the "same old thing," however, *Identity* makes for a surprisingly challenging and rewarding motion picture experience, as contemplative and difficult to forget as it is thrillingly wicked and suspenseful. Move over, *Psycho* and *Rosemary's Baby*—*Identity* has every last thing it takes to join the ranks of these classic horror watermarks.

Idle Hands

1999 - Directed by Rodman Flender

A late-'90s horror-comedy directed with devilish glee by Rodman Flender, *Idle Hands* came and went in theaters, proving too quirky for immediate mainstream success. A potentially nostalgic experience for children of the VHS era, the film proved a fun and twisted throwback to the goofy slasher flicks of old while also knowing exactly how to have a good time, political correctness be damned.

The picture gets off to a fabulous start, as a kooky middle-aged married couple (Fred Willard and Connie Ray) has just settled down in their beds for the night. Seeing the words, "I'm under the bed," sprawled on the ceiling, they immediately hear a noise downstairs. The husband goes to investigate and never returns. Then she goes down to see where he is. Anyone familiar with the staples of horror are intimately familiar with this procedure, but, instead of feeling clichéd, the scene is both genuinely intense and hugely funny as the first wave of sick, over-the-top humor is unleashed.

The next morning, we meet slacker Anton Tobias (Devon Sawa), a clueless teenager who spends his days loafing on the couch watching television and smoking pot. After noticing that he hasn't seen his parents for a couple days, he tells his friends, Mick (Seth Green) and Pnub (Elden Henson), but doesn't really think anything of it. The discovery of their bodies (whose location in the house will remain unsaid so the surprise will be kept) coincides with Anton's discovery that his right hand is possessed by Satan and is starting to control him. Killing anybody in its path, including Mick and Pnub, a harried Anton confronts his dark, brooding neighbor, Randy (Jack Noseworthy), about the unfortunate situation. "Idle hands are the devil's playground," Randy responds. "Just keep them busy." Ultimately, the ensuing murderous rampage of Anton's appendage collides with the high school's elaborate Halloween dance.

Idle Hands is a delirious, no-holds-barred attempt at creating a slasher movie with lots of campy and outrageous humor. While some of it fails (including the whole subplot dealing with Mick and Pnub, who return from the grave), much of it really is funny and difficult to not be reminded of the so-bad-they're-great '80s horror flicks that this film obviously gets its inspiration from. Back in those days, there were very few redeeming qualities, just gory killing after gory killing, intermingled with a helpful dosage of gratuitous nudity. In the '90s, however, things began to mature a bit, there was usually a mystery aspect to who the killer was, and T&A was rare. With *Idle Hands*, Flender went back to basics, albeit with his tongue firmly in cheek.

For one thing, the film does a terrific job of portraying the All Hallows' Eve holiday, the very first shot in the film an instant bravura moment as the camera starts on a brightly lit pumpkin, travels through a heavily Halloween-decorated front yard, and finally rises into an upstairs window. Due to this example and several other impressively shot scenes, the cinematography is distinctive and well-done. Also memorable: composer Graeme Revell's cool, edgy music score.

Once Anton's hand is taken over by Beelzebub, *Idle Hands* unfortunately begins to meander with an overemphasis on slapstick. After his hand is cut off and sets out for the dance, though, the film returns to its high-energy mode and is a treat thereafter. The rock band Offspring makes an appropriate cameo at the dance as they sing the Ramones song, "I Wanna Be Sedated," while nubile teens are dispatched in gruesome ways. In one great scene, two girls being pursued—one whom happens to be Anton's new girlfriend, Molly (Jessica Alba)—must escape through the ventilation system and crawl through a sharp, spinning fan that has been halted (but for how long?) by a shoe wedged in its blades.

Devon Sawa is an adequate protagonist as Anton, given plenty of opportunities to show off his talent for physical comedy. Seth Green and Elden Henson have some fun with their respective roles, especially after they have been killed (with Mick having a beer bottle lodged in his forehead, and Pnub actually carrying around his severed head). In one of her earlier screen appearances, Jessica Alba is nice eye candy—in a ditsy sort of way—while fulfilling her duties as a damsel in distress. Finally, Vivica A. Fox is hysterical in the smallish role of Deb, a spicy druid priestess who sets out to find the possessed hand.

Idle Hands is bloody, violent, and smart in its dumbness, boasting a round of clever ideas amidst the rising death toll. It may not be a great movie, but it is one of the most amusing and happily different byproducts that came out of the post-*Scream* horror panorama.

I Know Who Killed Me

2007 - Directed by Chris Sivertson

Say what you will about Lindsay Lohan's erratic and admittedly sad troubles with the law, but her mature, poignant performance in *I Know Who Killed Me* was unfortunately overshadowed when the film's release coincided with the start of her real-life personal struggles. Regardless, the girl has talent. A true testament to her abilities is that, save for a few unavoidable life-imitating-art reminders, Lohan so effortlessly slides into her multiple characters that the viewer forgets all about the baggage being carried behind her.

As for the film itself, it's not that *I Know Who Killed Me* is a great work of art. It isn't, and the more one thinks about it after the fact, the more the seams start to show. Even so, director Chris Sivertson and screenwriter Jeff Hammond deserve credit for tackling such an edgy, uncompromising project. Defiantly turning their backs on all things cookie-cutter, Sivertson and Hammond have crafted a lurid erotic thriller, a dark and violent horror-mystery, and a spookily whimsical fairy tale all in one.

Community college student Aubrey Fleming (Lindsay Lohan) is a serious-minded aspiring writer who disappears without a trace, leaving the quiet suburban town of New Salem in fear that she is the latest victim of an on-the-loose killer. A few weeks later, she is miraculously discovered alive alongside a road, one of her forearms and one of her legs so badly mutilated that they require amputation. As the police detectives attempt to unravel the crime and profile the culprit, they face an additional obstacle in the young woman's insistence that she isn't Aubrey at all, but Dakota Moss, a parentless exotic stripper straight from the school of hard knocks. Aubrey's concerned parents, Susan (Julia Ormond) and Daniel (Neal McDonough), believe their daughter is suffering from a form of amnesia, but Dakota refuses to accept that the very different life she has led is simply a figment of her imagination.

I Know Who Killed Me plays with common expectations—a jump scare here, a red herring there—but is also unorthodox, and the highlight of the entire enterprise is the seductive and haunting visual scheme. The images, flooded in deep blues and reds, are vibrant and just plain gorgeous, turning even empty moments into chances to aesthetically wow the viewer. Production designer

Jerry Fleming has outdone himself, giving the sets a real yet quirkily off-center moodiness. The cinematography by John R. Leonetti is just as eloquent, the fluidity, assuredness and imagination of the camera movements favorably bringing to mind old-school Brian De Palma and John Carpenter. Another standout scene in which the camera follows the floating petals of a flower into a bedroom mirror, past an owl, and down to a tranquil wooded stream is (1) singularly beautiful and (2) like something out of 1986's *Labyrinth* or 1984's *The Company of Wolves*. Meanwhile, the stormy music score by Joel McNeely pulsates with the incessant tone and energy of Hitchcock-era Bernard Herrmann.

The dialogue and plotting are unfortunately not at equal footing with the movie's style. The story's developments, though unpredictable and certainly intriguing, are preposterous even by the standards of the thriller genre. The climax, as exciting as it does get, is overly convenient. Conversational exchanges between characters occasionally feel forced, which may be the reason for the stilted acting from the normally reliable Julia Ormond and Neal McDonough. Ormond and McDonough lack chemistry both as a couple and as the parents of Aubrey; the emotional distance might be intentional since they are dealing with someone whom they are not even positive is really their daughter, but there's something still off about what they do with the roles.

By comparison, Lindsay Lohan commands the screen as the more reserved Aubrey and shows off her range in the culminating scenes as the damaged, sexually uninhibited Dakota. For what it's worth, Lohan's stripteases and pole-swinging theatrics at the gentleman's club are notable for being genuinely steamy, sleekly shot and choreographed, and suggestive in their surroundings of the seediness and underlying perils that go along with such a job.

I Know Who Killed Me will likely go down in history as the stripper movie released the same week that Lindsay Lohan was charged with her second DUI in six weeks. Distributor TriStar Pictures must have thought just as much, releasing it without advance screenings for critics or much notable fanfare, but the film does not deserve such dubious distinctions. Blemished though it is and prone to a handful of leaps in logic, the enthralling, elegantly mounted *I Know Who Killed Me* should instead be thought of as the film that reiterates what many know to be true: for all her real-life foibles, Lohan is a chameleonic young actress with a rare depth and intuition to equal her captivating screen presence.

In Dreams

1999 - Directed by Neil Jordan

Every great once in a while, a mainstream, big-budget studio picture will come along and miraculously restore one's faith in Hollywood, its ingeniously fresh ideas and the courage to not stick with the practicalities of any certain genre attributes worth celebrating. One of the most consistently disturbing, surprising, visually beautiful motion pictures of the 1990s, Neil Jordan's *In Dreams* came and went in theaters in January of 1999, earning less than $12-million domestically. Even at this writing nearly fifteen years later, it is a criminally overlooked film, begging for a rebirth.

In the eerily gorgeous opening sequence, it is learned that the town of Northfield was completely flooded in the 1960s to make way for a reservoir, the 30-year-old ghost town now but an underwater graveyard that a group of forensic investigators are exploring. Soon afterward, it is disclosed that they are searching for a little girl who was recently abducted by a serial killer. We then meet Claire Cooper (Annette Bening), a generally satisfied woman living in New England with her pilot husband, Paul (Aidan Quinn), and young daughter, Rebecca (Katie Sagona), the child anxiously preparing for her school play of *Snow White and the Seven Dwarfs*. For a long time, Claire has been having a recurring dream about the missing girl, whom she sees in an apple orchard being led away by a person with red hair. She has reason to believe that she may, actually, hold the key to the child's disappearance until the murdered body of the girl is found nowhere near an apple orchard.

Since *In Dreams* is so completely unpredictable and pleasing from beginning to end, it is important to tread carefully concerning what happens next. When a tragedy occurs in Claire's life, she gradually becomes more and more haunted by the killer. Though the people around her, including psychiatrist Dr. Silverman (Stephen Rea), believe she is going out of her mind, Claire is convinced the psychopath has found a way into her brain, her very dreams holding the crucial answers to what will happen in the future.

After 1991's *The Silence of the Lambs* took audiences by storm and won five Academy Awards in the process, a blitz of serial killer thrillers became the latest trend. Most, like 1997's *Kiss the Girls* and 1999's *The Bone Collector*, were inferior, flimsily disguised knockoffs. A rare few, however, such as 1995's *Se7en* and the marvelous *In Dreams*, served to wondrously rejuvenate the well-worn subgenre when it needed it most. So entirely imaginative and original is *In Dreams* that it is almost difficult to know how to react while watching it. For anyone who sees a lot of movies of every type, it is easy for one's senses to wilt with all of the recycled junk that Hollywood puts out. *In Dreams* is the complete polar opposite, filled with enough savvy and inventiveness for five movies. Not only that, it is authentically frightening.

The cast in *In Dreams* is uniformly great, particularly Annette Bening, able to gain our outright sympathy despite her inevitable demise into madness. Bening has sparkled before and since, but this remains one of her most challenging and emotionally demanding roles, to date. Before he became Tony Stark/Iron Man and rose to the A-list, Robert Downey Jr. was a hard-working character actor who didn't allow his personal struggles with drugs get in the way of his onscreen performances. When he finally shows up late in the picture, he comes off as one of the most believably menacing villains in memory.

Additionally of note, the cinematography is close to unsurpassed. Seldom before has a director of photography captured such unforgettable and devastatingly ominous images as Darius Khondji does in this film. Every single shot is brought to glorious light, with sequences set in the apple orchard, the underwater town, at the outdoor school play on the edge of the woods, and around the Carlton Hotel especially vivid in their realization. For the whole 100-minute running time of *In Dreams*, the film places the viewer in a state of awe and rapture, slyly subverting any and all predictions one might have for where the narrative is leading. One particularly brilliant and intricately constructed sequence involves the same thing occurring to two different people in two different time periods, the stories seamlessly intercut while paralleling each other.

It is not too often a picture is released that actually has so many wonderful ideas, and it is an even more precious occurrence that these ideas are actually carried through all the way to the end. Too many chefs in the proverbial kitchen can screw up any feature film, but *In Dreams* miraculously escapes such a wrath, only getting better as it moves toward its unsettling climax. For once, here is a film that does not condescend to its audience in any way, nor does it try to sugarcoat dark themes touching upon fate and destiny, cognizance and mental illness. As far as director Neil Jordan goes, this nightmare-laden, extraordinarily harrowing thriller remains one of his most accomplished pieces of work, right up there next to 1992's *The Crying Game* and 1994's *Interview with the Vampire*. It is certainly his most underrated.

Inland Empire

2006 - Directed by David Lynch

Whatever David Lynch has been smoking, let us all respectively pray that he never goes to rehab. If ever there was a director who represented the desire as a filmmaker to be independent-minded and visionary in all of his projects, sticking to his guns and never streamlining his ideas to accommodate mainstream audiences and make a few extra bucks, it is him. In all that Lynch does, he works without compromise—he self-distributed *Inland Empire* in lieu of selling it to a major studio. Besides being a great maker of movies, it is this adamant claim he has made for true individuality that is most admirable. Sure, Lynch has been getting more out-there the older he has gotten and is an understandably acquired taste, but not even those viewers who dislike his stuff can deny that there is talent behind his creative madness.

One would almost have to assume *Inland Empire* is Lynch's final step toward reaching a plane of cinematic existence never before captured in a theatrical release. The film, at once seeming to have been created on the spot and meticulously designed, is a phantasmagoric embodiment of one's nightmares. It defies description, burrowing to corners of the human psyche so dark and unsparing that many people (read: Lynch's non-supporters) won't want to go there. For the rest of us, it is a masterpiece of narrative layers, hidden meanings and semiotics so heady, imaginative, frightening, freakish, devastating and brain-twisting that it makes the viewer want to start from the beginning and rewatch it the second its three-hour mind trip is initially over.

Serving as a complementary piece to 2001's equally stunning *Mulholland Drive* that touches on many of the same thematic elements—the Hollywood milieu of struggling actresses and power-hungry movers and shakers; the breaking-apart of a person's mental state; identity crises—*Inland Empire* nonetheless carves out a place for itself in the Lynchian fold that is staunchly and uninhibitedly one of a kind. Viewers who like easy answers and a concrete A-to-B-to-C plot might as well look elsewhere, as even the partially inscrutable *Mulholland Drive* is as straightforward as *Notting Hill* in comparison. *Inland Empire* looks and feels like an actual dream that somehow was shot with cameras, the memory of it vivid in parts and fuzzy in others. Frustrated or not, adventurous filmgoers may just end up talking about it for hours after seeing it. I, for one, would take such an experience any day over a generic hack job that leaves the viewer with nothing to discuss afterwards.

In a too-rare leading role, Laura Dern dominates the screen in a hugely demanding performance of blinding beauty and wrenching heartbreak. At the start, she is Nikki Grace, a fading actress who gets a chance to revitalize her career when she wins the main role in a Southern gothic melodrama titled *On High in Blue Tomorrows*. She and her co-star, Hollywood hunk Devon Berk (Justin Theroux), are ominously told by director Kingsley Stewart (Jeremy Irons) prior to shooting that the movie, its story based on a piece of Polish folklore, is actually a remake to a picture never finished when the original actors were murdered.

Against their good judgment—Nikki is mentioned to have a jealous husband (Peter J. Lucas)—she and Devon sleep together. It is at this point that Nikki's identity is stripped from her. Suddenly she is Susan, an emotionally broken and physically abused woman who may or may not be the character Nikki is portraying. She may be a prostitute in Poland, or might not. She is interrogated by the police about a murder, and could very well be the culprit, brought on by the tragic loss of a son and an oafish husband who didn't understand her. As Susan's sense of self fractures into pieces, she makes her way around a labyrinth of rooms, each doorway leading to horrifying revelations about a life that stopped being her own long ago.

Shot with an economy-grade video camera, *Inland Empire* is gritty, quixotic and intoxicatingly ominous. Although lacking in the clarity that good old film provides, this turn toward low-end digital imaging is the only way this story could be told while still retaining the grim mysteries hiding within the darkness of every corner Nikki/Susan turns. Made over a period of three years—Lynch is said to have written scenes and had the actors perform them without indicating what would be coming before and after—the movie indelibly burrows in like a tick and stays there long after the end credits have rolled.

Understanding the picture as a whole isn't anywhere near the top of David Lynch's list of priorities—in fact, it probably doesn't exist on such a list—and that is as it should be in this instance. The cinematic world is filled with so many cookie-cutter affairs that it is a welcome respite to be presented with something that plays like a puzzle box not meant to be solved. And yet, profundity does emerge amidst its impenetrable nature. In one respect, *Inland Empire* is about the Hollywood world in general and the need to be accepted within it, where aging or unpopular actresses can be spit out just as fast as their souls are eaten up by the allure of fame. Nikki yearns for the glory she once had—she lives in a stately, gated Los Angeles mansion whose deceased past owners haunt the property—but, along the path to reclaiming it, she deteriorates into a shell of a woman who has no idea who she is and who she once was.

Cynical but truthful, the film is also about the robotic reprogramming of society, where consumers are trained like animals to swallow whatever is placed in front of them. This is no more evident than in the eerie sequences of a three-person family of people in rabbit costumes, their inane, disconnected and unfunny dialogue answered by the stale sounds of a canned laugh track. In another scene, a mortally wounded woman lays dying on the street as strangers waiting for the bus carry on a conversation between her, their beings so desensitized that they hardly have time to acknowledge the life being lost under their noses. And then there's the Lost Girl (Karolina Gruszka), who sits in front of a TV in a darkened room, acting as spectator over what is transpiring in the film and weeping forlornly. There are various reasons for her crying, gradually unveiled as her past indiscretions come to light, but she could just as well be weeping for the state of uninspired, mass-produced entertainment in today's society.

Inland Empire is unlike anything else one is likely to have seen—to be sure, this includes the sight of disaffected Polish hookers doing a zombified dance to the sounds of Little Eva's "The Locomotion"—and is additionally body-flinchingly scary in a way that the creator of *Blue Velvet, Lost Highway*, *Mulholland Drive* and TV's *Twin Peaks* only knows how. When a strange visitor (Grace Zabriskie) shows up at Nikki's door in the first act and gives her a portentous prophecy, Nikki shudders alongside the viewer, unknowing of the nightmare in store for her. It is this critical scene and another, in which Devon tries to track down a possibly evil presence lurking on the soundstage where he is rehearsing, that sets up the shiver-inducing, endlessly fascinating tone of the rest of the film. In the marvelous, internally naked Laura Dern is the Alice of the picture, tumbling down the rabbit hole, bypassing Wonderland altogether, and finding herself through the looking glass of a world she scarcely recognizes. *Inland Empire* isn't just a brilliant motion picture; it's a work of staggering art.

The Innkeepers

2011 - Directed by Ti West

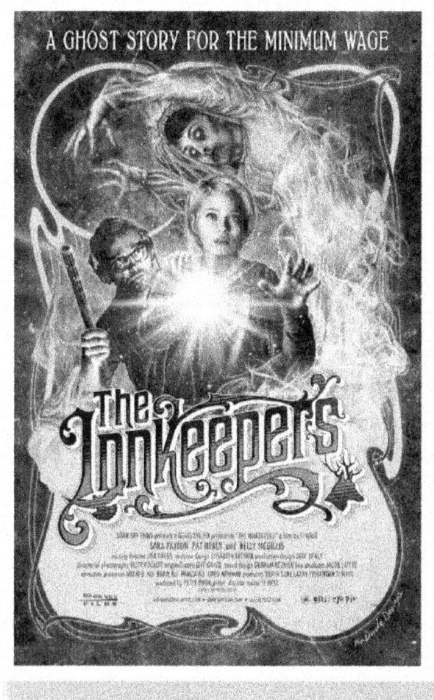

Ti West is the best-kept secret of modern day's horror landscape, a filmmaker of both unbridled passion and meticulous skill with not a single less-than-impressive motion picture on his filmography (well, okay, there was *Cabin Fever 2*, but he was so displeased with the studio-mandated final cut that he unsuccessfully attempted to have his name taken off of it). Working with minimalist budgets, he is able to create sucker-punches of breathless mood and tension that put to shame the vast majority of genre efforts released within the major studio system each year. His debut feature, 2005's *The Roost*, featured vampiric bats and a lonesome rural barn with the power to send chills down a person's spine. 2007's *Trigger Man* auspiciously, chillingly and methodically turned an innocent daytime hunting trip into a nightmare of all-too-real terror. And 2009's *The House of the Devil* paid loving, gripping, frightening homage to the "babysitter-in-peril" and "satanic panic" subgenres of the 1970s and early '80s with nary a wink in sight. West knows how to conceive terrific ideas, for sure—and he still has yet to come close to repeating himself—but where he really earns points is in his simple, detailed, airtight delivery of sumptuous atmosphere and suffocating suspense within the deceptively mundane. It's about time more than a handful of devoted fans discovered Ti West's breadth of talent; he's every bit the genuine article as John Carpenter, Wes Craven and Sam Raimi were thirty or more years ago.

With *The Innkeepers*, West dips his feet into supernatural waters while, again, remaining in the wheelhouse of what can be believed without too much strain. The limited characters, as real as can be, are not living in a fantastical world, but in our own, grappling with the same questions and internal conflicts as we all sometimes face. For Claire (Sara Paxton) and Luke (Pat Healy), the last remaining workers left as Connecticut's 100-plus-year-old Yankee Pedlar Inn prepares to close its doors for good, they have no idea what to do next. Juggling twelve-hour shifts while choosing to stay in rooms on the property, Claire and Luke will be newly unemployed once the weekend is over. For now, however, they occupy their time trying to find hard evidence that the hotel is haunted.

Legend has it that Madeline O'Malley, a jilted bride who hung herself there many decades before, still lurks about, but is it true? One thing is for sure: a fresh EVP recording would be great for Luke's website about the ghostly goings-on at the Yankee Pedlar.

Shot on location at New England's non-fictional Yankee Pedlar Inn, *The Innkeepers* features an invaluably authentic setting and an equally distinctive triple threat (writer-director-editor) at the helm. If the film does not quite match West's best of the best, this has more to do with the somewhat restricted expansiveness he can bring to said otherworldly material without allowing it to become far-fetched or too silly. There's restraint in what West does, but also an understanding of how to fulfill audience expectations so that his films cannot be accused of being cheats. In the middle of it all are ordinary protagonists whose lives and personalities are filled in through their interactions, conversations and observations. By taking the time to care about Claire and Luke, the viewer is able to more fully invest in the story and what happens to them. It also makes the scares all the sweeter, the threat of horrific possibilities (like one scene involving an opened cellar door) often more nerve-jangling than the more overt physical payoffs.

Sara Paxton is appealingly quirky as the curious Claire, in the midst of doubting her decision to drop out of college and not really needing to hear the snide judgments of Leanne Rease-Jones (Kelly McGillis), an aging actress-turned-mystic staying at the inn while attending a nearby convention. Claire is a fan of Leanne's, which only makes it worse when she snips back at her rather than kindly taking a compliment. For her part, Leanne recognizes her prickly side and attempts, in her own way, to eventually make amends. A discussion the two of them share about life, death, states of being and the vastness of the universe is altogether more comforting than anything in Terrence Malick's 2011 study in existentialism, *The Tree of Life*. Kelly McGillis, once an ingénue back in her *Top Gun* days, has developed into a far more interesting character actress as she has grown older, lending wisdom, texture and emotional truth to supporting parts. Such is the case with her take on Leanne. As Luke, Pat Healy warmly essays the kind of guy who talks himself up more than actually takes action; he and Paxton's Claire share a comfortable short-hand with one another that clicks. There is little doubt that he has a crush on his co-worker, but also the sad-but-honest suspicion that they would never be friends were it not for working together.

The Innkeepers is never slow because it's never boring, but Ti West does enjoy extending the quiet spaces in between the horror for maximum effectiveness. It is a style that works exquisitely for an auteur with his expertise. That his films are independently produced, giving him full control over all aspects of the screenplays and their production, is not to be taken for granted, nor are his trusted collaborators, from cinematographer Eliot Rockett's elegant lensing to composer Jeff Grace's richly foreboding music score to Graham Reznick's complex sound design. The third act of *The Innkeepers* assuredly raises the stakes a notch—the scenes with an elderly man (George Riddle) coming to stay in the room where he once shared his honeymoon with his late wife are pitch-perfectly elusive and poignant—and then goes full-tilt, destined to send everyone with a pulse jumping up and recoiling in apprehension. Do the last few beats live up to all that has come before? Not quite, no, but it's the getting-there that's worth sitting up and taking notice. *The Innkeepers* is a beguiling entertainment as it deals out its grab-bag of soul-searching, good-willed humor and particularly serious gasps.

Insidious

2011 - Directed by James Wan

The first shot of *Insidious* displays the screen-spanning opening credit, "A James Wan Film," in large, bold letters the viewer can't miss. At the end of those same titles, "Directed by James Wan" lingers for several beats longer than the norm. Prominently advertising himself with the sort of event-like fervor that would make even M. Night Shyamalan get red in the face, Wan had a hit-and-miss track record with his films leading up to *Insidious* (2004's *Saw*, 2007's *Dead Silence*, and 2007's *Death Sentence*) and hadn't yet proven what the credits slyly suggested: that a master filmmaker of noted importance was in charge. Roughly 100 minutes later, Wan had, indeed, moved closer to displaying just how astute he can be at working his audience to a fever pitch. As uneven as *Insidious* sometimes is, it can also be dread-inducingly, cling-to-your-armrest scary. As a vessel that mischievously provides some seriously petrifying images and roughly five huge jump scares spread throughout, Wan and screenwriter-actor Leigh Whannell do their most important job—to set audiences on edge—admirably.

Aspiring musician Renai (Rose Byrne) and school teacher Josh (Patrick Wilson) have just moved with their three kids to a spacious, attractive, somewhat creaky new house. It should be a fresh start for all of them, but then their intuitive eldest son, 8-year-old Dalton (Ty Simpkins), falls into a sudden coma that leaves the doctors baffled by its cause. This would be a stressful, upsetting time for any parent in the same situation, but it's made all the worse when Renai is soon overwhelmed with unexplainable occurrences and terrifying visions of people lurking with her in the house. Non-believer Josh reacts by withdrawing into his work until Renai puts her foot down and insists they leave. Mistakenly believing their problems are finally behind them, the couple soon discover, with the help of medium Elise Rainier (the underrated Lin Shaye), it isn't their house that is haunted, but their son.

A ghost story with a setup that matches scene for scene the apparent blueprint of the genre, *Insidious* tries to fool the viewer into thinking that the characters and the lives they lead—Renai's music-writing and piano-practicing, for example—are more important than they really are. The pacing is slow and measured at first, biding its time until it's ready to pounce. When it finally does, it startles with its sheer abruptness and force and hauntingly simple *mise-en-scène*. Suddenly transformed into what it genuinely is, the film stops paying much interest to the people and becomes all about the scares. Because they usually work like gangbusters and aren't just unimaginative throwaways, that's not necessarily a criticism. A large portion of the picture, especially in its superior first half, repeats the formula of a character—usually Renai—walking down hallways and peeking in rooms. Most of the time there is nothing there. When there is, it is so effective it is sure to elicit jumps, if not screams, in the nervous audience. Were that not enough, Wan unforgettably incorporates Tiny Tim's "Tip Toe Through the Tulips" into the proceedings in a way that is goosebump-forming and possibly genius. Tiny Tim's legacy might not have been to petrify the living hell out of people, but that is what it will be once this movie gets done with him.

Lest it be assumed that the picture will continue following a predictable plot, Wan and Whannell do, to their credit, concoct story motives and a third act that diverge from typical haunted house movies. Astral projection, demons and a dark realm called "The Further" all figure into the mix, but so do two ghostbusters (Angus Sampson, Leigh Whannell) who ought to have been excised. The fantasy-laden dip into the subconscious near the end is more ambitious than wholly successful, but remains visually interesting and at least different. For a film that partially works so well because of its use of practical effects, make-up and costumes over a reliance on CGI, one shot involving a creature climbing sideways on a wall instantly dissipates the intensity and takes the viewer out of the situation. Without giving things away, a last-scene twist is also misguided in its identity reveal of a certain character.

Insidious is akin to a particularly macabre funhouse ride, the viewer (in the place of the passenger) taken on a tour where the threat of spooky things popping out at any second doesn't alleviate until it's over. The achievement in boasting a high scare quotient evens out the movie's numerous trouble spots. Patrick Wilson is trifled by murky motivations as Josh, a skeptic even when it's blatantly obvious something supernatural is going on. He is outshone by Rose Byrne, committed and believably frantic as her Renai starts seeing things she can't believe, yet can't deny. While son Dalton plays an important role in the goings-on, their other two kids all but disappear by the second half, leading one to wonder why they were put in the screenplay at all. Barbara Hershey, too, is wasted as Josh's worried mother, who has had her own recent experience with a specter in her dreams. When *Insidious* is just concentrating on empty spaces and the propensity for something nightmarish to be lurking about, the film is exceptionally good. When Wan tries to open up the scope, introduce more characters, and expand the mythology, its focus tends to get lost now and again. The real story is and should be the one about the average family whose lives are threatened and psyches left unbalanced by forces greater than they can imagine. It is this little corner of the unknown where actual fear and dread reside, and Wan knows that all too well.

In the Cut

2003 - Directed by Jane Campion

Based on the novel by Susanna Moore, *In the Cut* is a fascinating psychological character study wrapped in a murder mystery where the identity of the villain hardly seems to be the point. Although it will likely displease and bewilder filmgoers used to the more conventional side of cinematic thrillers, it holds so much depth, so much innovation, and such a crystal-clear vision of what its intentions are, that more learned film buffs are in for a treat. And, as written and directed by Jane Campion, *In the Cut* is pitch-black in its tone and admirably unsparing in its character portrayals and narrative details. It was easily one of the most haunting motion pictures of 2003.

In a startling change from her usual frothy romantic comedies, Meg Ryan delivers the kind of powerful, courageous, multidimensional performance that expands and strengthens careers (think Nicole Kidman, who produces here). That the film originally did not receive the attention it warranted is a shame. Ryan received much publicity for baring it all, and that she does, but what is so very astonishing and risqué about her Oscar-worthy turn has nothing to do with nudity.

In her portrayal of English professor Frannie Thorstin, Meg Ryan sheds her blonde hair and perky demeanor for a faded brown mop and an imploding personality whose stark realism cuts right to the bone. Frannie, an intelligent lover of words, discovers at the most seemingly inopportune time in her life that she has a sexual hunger that has gone unsatisfied for too long. After witnessing a man in shadow receiving oral gratification in the basement of a New York City bar, her pent-up sex drive gets a sudden fetishistic jump-start of its own. Unfortunately, her attraction toward Detective Giovanni Malloy (Mark Ruffalo) surfaces just as his investigation into a local serial killer—parts of whose latest victim were found in Frannie's garden—leads him to her. As the killer threatens to strike again, Frannie embarks on an exceedingly dangerous carnal relationship with Malloy, despite her better judgment and the rising suspicion that the psychopath in question may very well be him.

What Meg Ryan has done with her complex, demanding role is not some cheap ploy to be taken seriously as an actress, but an example of a performer expanding her reach and testing herself. In Frannie, she creates a true-to-life, flawed human figure, and has done it flawlessly. Her character is not naive; she recognizes that her sexual dealings are unhealthy and her relationship with Malloy is inappropriate, but she gains a sort of corporeal satisfaction and internal strength from her own discovered masochism that is difficult for her to give up. In what looks to have been emotionally draining, Ryan gives a brilliantly fascinating performance, one that was robbed of Oscar recognition.

Campion has crafted a formidable piece of work that falls somewhere between art and entertainment, while garnering the right to be both. Along with top-notch cinematographer Dion Beebe, Campion evokes a dreamlike quality as Frannie delves into matters she is inexperienced in and unsure about, but that may have serious, life-changing repercussions. The camerawork, intentionally jittery and seemingly at a constant struggle to capture focus, effectively foreshadows Frannie's personal journey, aiding in the uncomfortable atmosphere. Moments of symbolism, including a recurring running bystander on the street, a bride with a cast on her arm, and wordless black-and-white flashbacks to Frannie's parents ice-skating on the day they got engaged, avoid pretentiousness and rely on the power and subtlety of their indelible images to get their existential purposes across.

The meticulously chosen music also plays a major role in the film, opening with a wistful version of "Que Sera, Sera (Whatever Will Be, Will Be)" that acts as a cogent contrast for what is to follow. A beautifully written and acted sequence between Frannie and close half-sister Pauline (Jennifer Jason Leigh) garners even more humanistic weight with the use of Annie Lennox's "Waiting in Vain." And the way in which The Partridge Family's "I Think I Love You" plays a disturbing role in a despairing scene near the end is downright ingenious.

Enriching Meg Ryan's startling work even more is the support she gets from two other superb performances by Mark Ruffalo and Jennifer Jason Leigh. As Detective Malloy, Ruffalo hits every note perfectly in creating the right balance between suave, seductive coolness and a more threatening underlying side. Leigh brings sympathy and a quiet mournfulness to Pauline, whose desperate attempts to find her one true love have led to her getting stalking charges put on her.

Although the identity of the killer is unveiled at the climax of *In the Cut*, it arrives as a sidebar to the real conflict facing Frannie, whose life has spiraled out of control as a result of her quest for sexual fulfillment and a need for personal purpose in her everyday life. Throughout the film, Frannie gains further satisfaction by reading the poetry postings on the walls of the subway car. What starts as a hobby, however, gradually turns into a statement as the lines become intermingled with what is occurring in her own life. It is just another lovely little detail in a motion picture rich with ideas, exact characterizations and visual artistry. *In the Cut* is a major cinematic achievement—simultaneously scary, heartbreaking, unpredictable, sexy, grim, provocative and eerily plausible.

In Their Skin

2012 - Directed by Jeremy Power Regimbal

The home-invasion horror-thriller subgenre is very nearly as rampant as the current found-footage fad, but, as with any kind of movie, the secret to success is in the level of skill and intelligence with which it is done. Taking this into account, *In Their Skin* ranks up there with 2008's *The Strangers* and 2007's *Funny Games* in terms of its jittery, supremely uncomfortable potency. It helps that the onscreen family, already in crisis long before sociopaths enter their lives, are so credibly empathetic, their dynamic and the way they initially react to off-kilter outsiders intruding upon their turf instantly identifiable. First-time director Jeremy Power Regimbal and screenwriter Josh Close generally stick to formula, but change the details enough for its familiarity to not overwhelm the hair-raising journeys of its characters. That the film ultimately reveals itself to be about redemption and the process of healing over hopelessly succumbing to evil also gives the story an added layer of worth and freshness.

Still grappling with the recent death of their young daughter, Mary (Selma Blair) and Mark (Josh Close) travel to their family's country home with 8-year-old son Brendon (Quinn Lord) in the hopes of spending some much-needed private time together. The morning after a strange encounter with a truck that pulls up to their property's gate before driving off, they are woken by neighbors Bob (James D'Arcy) and Jane (Rachel Miner) and their 9-year-old son, Jared (Alex Ferris), who have brought over firewood as a kindly gesture. Something is a little off about them, but they seem harmless enough that Mark doesn't think much of it when they more or less invite themselves over for dinner. From there, Bob and Jane make no bones about butting into Mark's and Mary's business. They appear to be the ideal family, and it isn't long before these intruders have decided they want to become them. Literally.

In Their Skin is nothing if not exceedingly skillful in placing an uneasy cloak over the viewer just as it descends on Mary, Mark and Brendon. From the opening scenes, the stark cinematography by Norm Li paints a desolate, claustrophobic picture of their surroundings, where no one could hear them for miles around if they were to need immediate help. When Bob, Jane and

Jared come over for dinner, the prying questions that are asked of the hosts are intimate and invasive long before more sinister intentions are revealed. When the other shoe does drop—and, yes, the family dog is naturally the first one to go—the tone only grows more chilly and unsparing. Through this life-or-death tribulation, however, is the very real sense that Mary, Mark and Brendon realize what it is they stand to lose if they don't find a way to fight for their survival.

In Their Skin is frightening, but also, in its own way, inspiring. Performances are top-notch throughout—in her career, the underrated Selma Blair has rarely been asked to delve into such raw emotions, while Rachel Miner is exceptional as the meekest of the unhinged interlopers, a woman who incessantly apologizes while fearfully going along with all that her lunatic "husband" does—and everything comes to a boil in time for a finale that surprisingly shifts from the conclusive norm of these kinds of films. *In Their Skin* isn't reinventing the language of cinema or anything of that sort, but it is very good all the same at putting its audience in the place of a family whose identities, as well as lives, are at stake. There is a reason they must never give up, and it is this newfound drive that ends up being their emotional savior.

I Saw the Devil

2010 - Directed by Kim Ji-woon

Revenge tales are tricky to pull off and even more difficult to lift above formula. By and large, they all follow the same basic blueprint, end up in the same place, and usually misjudge or overlook the story's moral implications. Director Kim Ji-woon, responsible for 2004's skin-crawling supernatural mystery *A Tale of Two Sisters* (remade for the U.S. in 2009 as *The Uninvited*), is aggressive and resourceful enough to play with expectations. *I Saw the Devil* is ceaseless in its goals to devastate, infuriate, nauseate and finally challenge (in roughly that order) audiences used to more pandering, watered-down treatments of tragedy and vengeance.

The careful attention to detail is apparent from the startling prologue. Stranded alongside the road with tire trouble, the lovely Joo-yeon (Oh San-ha) is approached by Kyung-chul (Choi Min-sik), who at first looks like he wants to help. As Joo-yeon sits in her automobile, her fluffy, white steering wheel cover, mirroring the blanket of snow outside, proves a subliminal sign of her false security. She might as well not even be sitting behind a pane of glass. Before she knows it, Joo-yeon has been bashed over the head with a hammer and is faintly coming to in a grimy warehouse. She pleads for her life and the life of her unborn child, but it's no use reasoning with a deranged psychopath. The next time she is glimpsed, she is but a pile of dismembered body parts. Suddenly, before any proper plot has been introduced, the viewer is already ruminating on a deeper level than the norm about how precious and profound life is and how quickly and easily it can be snuffed out.

When an ear is found in a field beside an overpass, it is only a matter of time before Joo-yeon's decapitated head is recovered from a nearby riverbed. Her detective father, Squad Chief Jang (Jeon Gook-hwan), is devastated, remarking to her grief-stricken fiance, Soo-hyeon (Lee Byung-hun), how he has been professionally solving crimes for thirty years, but couldn't even save his own daughter. Using the skills he's picked up working as a special agent, Soo-hyeon embarks on a cat-and-mouse game with Kyung-chul that traverses much more than just the final goal of killing him. No, before he does that, he wants to destroy every facet of his life and give him a glimpse at the well-deserved hell he has brought upon himself.

After Soo-hyeon asks for a two-week leave of absence and sets out on his blazing path of insatiable payback, *I Saw the Devil* carries on for two more hours of unwavering brutality that rarely abates. They first come face to face while Kyung-chul is about to rape and murder his next victim, a school girl he has kidnapped from the after-school bus he drives and taken to a desolate nursery. Soo-hyeon beats him to a pulp, breaks his wrist, and has him unknowingly swallow a small GPS device before letting him go. When he pulls himself out of unconsciousness, Kyung-chul can't believe he's survived and foolishly believes he's escaped. Not so fast. Soo-hyeon returns again just as the killer is about to attack a nurse, this time focusing his wrath on his Achilles tendon. These two encounters are only the beginning of what becomes a hunting game for Soo-hyeon. Once Kyung-chul has figured out his pattern, the stakes raise again. He's more than willing to play along with his pursuer.

Written by Park Hoon-jung and directed with twisted glee by Kim Ji-woon, *I Saw the Devil* flirts with exploitation, but never crosses the line (it crosses it plenty of other ways, though). Not simply a film that gets its kicks from the depravity it portrays, Ji-woon instead uses violence and the increasingly out-of-control actions of Soo-hyeon to comment on how easy it is for the line between good and evil, justice and criminality to become blurred. Yes, Kyung-chul deserves what is coming to him, but at what point will Soo-hyeon completely lose sight of the reason he wants to destroy this man little by little? Who else might he have to sacrifice to fulfill his blood mission? Is he in perilous danger of becoming no better than the killer he hunts? By the end, the innocent, ill-fated Joo-yeon is a distant memory—an epiphany that rushes over Soo-hyeon in a sudden, despairing burst. It is in that moment that he realizes he not only lost his future wife, but himself, as well.

I Saw the Devil is a crackerjack thriller, present and in-the-moment with a fair share of surprises up its sleeve. It is also not without its contrivances. Soo-hyeon's finding of Joo-yeon's ring in a drain within Kyung-chul's lair is far-fetched and patly handled, a furthering of the narrative at the expense of plausibility. Additionally perplexing is the distressing snapshot of Korea as a place filled with murderers and deviants, extending beyond Kyung-chul to also include a serial killer friend of his, a woman whose own rape gradually turns her on, and two deadly thieves he coincidentally hitches a ride with at one point. These trouble areas aside, the picture is supremely well-made and in Lee Byung-hun, as Soo-hyeon, and the chilling Choi Min-sik, as Kyung-chul, are two performances of stunning commitment and effectiveness. *I Saw the Devil* is a title that refers not to a literal figure of malevolence, but to the dark nature in each of us. Soo-hyeon ultimately recognizes this in his own doing. He knows he must finish what he started, but isn't so sure who he'll be once he's reached the other side.

I Spit on Your Grave

1978 - Directed by Meir Zarchi

Meir Zarchi's infamous *I Spit on Your Grave* is inarguably one of the most controversial films ever made. At the time of its release, the film was critically lambasted, audiences were largely outraged, and it was banned entirely from the UK and Germany. What mostly got under people's skin about the picture was its extremely graphic and brutal depiction of rape, and the violent consequences that follow. Although watching this movie in a theater with others would be understandably uncomfortable, that is simply human nature. What occurs here is very difficult to watch regardless, and Zarchi doesn't so much as flinch in his harrowing depiction.

Sure, *I Spit on Your Grave* is not for everybody and certainly deserved its original X rating. It's neither a "fun" nor "entertaining" film, nor should it be, its examination of cruelty and violence both during and after the fact fairly thoughtful and realistic. To single one certain critic out, the late Roger Ebert rated the film zero stars at the time of its release, and, like everyone, was in a frenzy over what takes place during the 100-minute running time. With such passionate feelings, however, it made little sense that just a few years earlier he had raved about 1972's *The Last House on the Left*, which has more or less the same plot and a wildly inappropriate, up-tempo banjo-laden soundtrack to accompany it. What *The Last House on the Left* strangely makes light of is precisely what *I Spit on Your Grave* treats with the seriousness it deserves. Aside from being loosely based on Ingmar Bergman's *The Virgin Spring*, the earlier Wes Craven film is far more exploitative and includes a fairly ridiculous plot gimmick: that the rape offenders unknowingly spend the night at the victim's parents' house. How one could love the more cheap and manipulative picture, and then turn around and criticize this one boggles the mind.

I Spit on Your Grave has a fairly straightforward story. A young, attractive writer named Jennifer Hills (Camille Keaton) leaves her home in Manhattan and travels upstate to stay in the country at an idyllic, remote cabin she has rented for the summer. Her goal is to write her first novel, but everything changes when she is accosted by four men while boating on the lake, forced into the woods, and raped repeatedly. Left for dead in her cabin, Jennifer instead miraculously survives and slowly begins to recuperate from the ordeal. She certainly doesn't want the men to get away with what they did, and finally decides to take matters into her own hands.

I Spit on Your Grave could have easily fallen into the manipulation of *The Last House on the Left*, but is more somber in its treatment. The main female character is an intelligent woman who could easily go to the police about what happened, but what good would that do? The reasoning she comes up with is that even if they went to prison, they would eventually be released, free to do such a thing again to someone else. One of the major misconceptions that many people have about *I Spit on Your Grave* is that it is a horror film, but it isn't—at least, not in the typical sense. Instead, it is a horror story about the human condition, and how far some people can actually go if they do not have any respect for other human life. There are no murders in the film, either, until the climax, but those aren't carried out in the same way that, say, Michael Myers' or Freddy Krueger's death toll might. On the contrary, the killer in *I Spit on Your Grave* ultimately turns out to also be the heroine, and she has a real reason for doing what she does. In a particularly affecting sequence right before she goes through with her revenge, she pays a visit to the local church where she prays for forgiveness of what she is about to do. Now when exactly was the last time you saw that in a so-called low-rent, irresponsible film of this nature? Zarchi, like Jennifer, understands the gravity of the situation and the moralistic line about to be crossed.

An early independent film bordering on the artsy, *I Spit on Your Grave* is meticulously shot by cinematographer Yuri Haviv. One scene, for example, lasting a couple minutes, is filmed entirely in a long shot as the camera tries to distance itself from the hurtful things happening on the screen. Another smart move on Zarchi's part is that he does not paint the four men as outright monsters and spends a lot of time with them. One of them, the mentally challenged Matthew (Richard Pace), is actually touching in the way that he is pulled into participating in a crime he does not fully understand and, through a chain of events, becomes the outcast of the group. It also comes as an unexpected twist to find out later on that the leader of the clan, Johnny (Eron Tabor), is married and has two children, whom he loves. What these men do is vile, cruel and unforgivable, but, thanks to the director, they are not in any way treated in two dimensions.

I Spit on Your Grave is a striking and courageous motion picture, gravely misunderstood, but it does have a few noticeable problems. For one, we do not really get to know the female protagonist very much. After being raped and bruised and cut up, she gets well very fast—too fast, perhaps—and although she murders the men for vengeance, she never quite is able to fully emulate the breadth of emotion that might come with such a personal plight. Maybe what Zarchi was attempting to do by choosing to go this route in the finale was to show that she had become numb inside from what had happened to her. Indeed, it is not out of the realm of possibility that she very well could be on the edge of a nervous breakdown. Another problem finds Johnny making some very stupid decisions as Jennifer lures him toward his just desserts, though it wouldn't be the first time he acts with a certain body part other than his brain. This scene, exceptionally gory and to never be forgotten, is the most suspenseful of the film. As *I Spit on Your Grave* draws to its rapt conclusion, there is no false hope provided for Jennifer. She may have lived through a nightmare and, from her point of view, made right a terrible wrong, but there is no pretending that she will now be okay. The road ahead of her is forever changed and her former assumptions about safety and security have been shattered beyond repair.

Jeepers Creepers

2001 - Directed by Victor Salva

A nasty, crafty little item that forgoes the glossy style of today's slasher movies for genuine scares and almost nonstop suspense, *Jeepers Creepers* stood, at the time of its release in September 2001, as the best thing to happen to the horror genre since 1999's groundbreaking *The Blair Witch Project*. A welcome, gritty throwback to the era of grindhouse-style horror classics like *The Texas Chain Saw Massacre*, the film offers up a generous helping of edgy gore and violence to tell the story of two normal, everyday college kids who find themselves inexplicably being stalked by the most vicious, unrelenting psychopath this side of Leatherface.

It's spring break, and siblings Trish (Gina Philips) and Darry (Justin Long) have bypassed the boring freeway to travel home on the back roads of rural America. Following a nasty run-in with a trucker with serious road rage issues, Trish and Darry spot a dark figure getting out of the very same automobile (license plate reading "BEATNGU") a few mile down the road, as it dumps two bloodied, life-sized objects wrapped in sheets down a drain pipe. Making the serious mistake of going back to investigate, Trish and Darry are hurled further and further into a whirlwind of terror as they try, and fail, to escape the cleaver-wielding, trench-coat-wearing, possibly inhuman maniac.

Borrowing its title from the classic 1930s Louis Armstrong song (*"Jeepers Creepers/Where'd you get those peepers?/Jeepers Creepers/Where'd you get those eyes?"*)—a running theme throughout—*Jeepers Creepers* couldn't have come at a more opportune time. A gratifying return to the days when horror movies weren't about selling pop/rock soundtracks and starring the latest television starlets, the picture is unapologetic in its singular goal to scare audiences out of their wits.

Wasting no time in setting up the premise, savvy writer-director Victor Salva quickly hurls our two realistic protagonists, and subsequently the viewer, into a freakish phantasm that cannot be snapped out of. At a fast, highly appropriate ninety minutes, *Jeepers Creepers* runs at a clip pace that makes each scene all the more ineradicably absorbing and tense. The tight, expert editing by Ed Marx helps to make the goings-on all the more nail-biting.

Virtually a two-character show, Justin Long and Gina Philips make for a believable, charismatic brother-and-sister pair. Credit Salva for choosing to make his leads related; it makes the situations they get in all the more real, and does away with the inevitable romantic subplot that usually hinders films of this type. Their love-hate relationship is set up with many delightful nuances in the early scenes as they hold conversations and bicker childishly while driving in the car. Even when arguing, however, it's obvious they love each other as siblings only can. In small roles, Patricia Belcher is a standout, not to mention subtly funny, as a local psychic who has visions of what is in store for Trish and Darry, while Eileen Brennan memorably plays an ill-fated backwoods local they seek help from. As she describes, she's got "more than a couple" cats.

With atmospheric cinematography by Don E. FauntLeRoy that paints the back country roads as a location one would never want to get stuck on alone, *Jeepers Creepers* cleverly taps into the deep-seated fears everyone has about feeling helpless in the eyes of great danger. And like the excellent dessert that comes after a fine main course, the film saves its most unforgettable image for last—a horrifyingly disturbing, surprisingly touching final shot that courageously proves, once and for all, good does not always prevail in the face of pure evil.

Joshua

2007 - Directed by George Ratliff

An old-school thriller in the style of 1968's *Rosemary's Baby* and 1973's *Don't Look Now*, the sublimely unnerving *Joshua* embraces the simple power of suggestion over cheap jump scares and an overabundance of gore. In their observant and tragic portrait of an upper-class family in a state of collapse, writer-director George Ratliff (2002's excellent documentary *Hell House*) and first-time co-writer David Gilbert manage to shake and alarm without so much as one scene of violence. The creep-factor is all in the details—the mood, the character depth, the multilayered story complexity and appropriate lack of easy answers. Indeed, the abysmal 2006 remake of *The Omen* could have learned a thing or two from what *Joshua* serves up.

9-year-old Joshua Cairn (Jacob Kogan) is a little different than most of the other boys his age. A piano prodigy more interested in reading books and learning about Egyptian history than playing sports and rough-housing around, his insulated Manhattan lifestyle with loving parents Brad (Sam Rockwell) and Abby (Vera Farmiga) is dramatically altered when a newborn baby sister is added to the equation. No longer the center of attention, Joshua is suddenly faced with doubts about whether his mom and dad love him and how he fits within the family dynamic. As his behavior becomes stranger, Abby's mental state deteriorates under the pressures of caring for a restless, crying infant during all hours of the day and night. Brad, often busy at work, isn't too concerned until it becomes readily apparent that young Joshua may be capable of far darker acts than he could ever imagine.

Joshua is a masterful study in subtlety that proves horror films don't necessarily require gouged eyes and decapitations to earn their place in the higher echelons of the genre. Take the now-largely-forgotten Elisha Cuthbert-starring *Captivity*, for example, which was seen by myself less than an hour before my initial viewing of *Joshua* back in 2007. The former spared no expense on the red stuff, but that apparently didn't leave enough money for acquiring a good script. The end result was a movie that was unscary and dramatically cold. By comparison, this modern-day "bad seed" tale expertly weaves a spell of genuine frights and jittery tension even in the most innocuous of scenes.

As a character, Joshua is neither demonized nor two-dimensionalized; he isn't a descendant of the devil like Damien in *The Omen*, but a human child who is psychologically disturbed and, to make matters worse, feeling neglected at the same time that he is exposed to a number of damaging revelations that force him to reevaluate the way he sees his parents and the world at large. Joshua unveils himself, little by little, to be devious and calculating, but even these turns are ominously plausible. He's an alternately horrifying and devastatingly tragic title figure, dangerous and in need of help, and Jacob Kogan, in his film debut, is perfectly cast in the role. Kogan has the talent and lack of affectations that he can be unsettling without trying too hard and then turn around and break your heart. It's a stunning debut turn for someone so young.

Joshua is the main attraction, but it is his parents whose eyes we as the audience see through. Vera Farmiga is an emotional wreck for the bulk of the running time as mother Abby. It initially seems as if she is the crazy one in the family, prone to unpleasant mood swings and at her wit's end over dealing with her fussy new daughter. As she fights to keep it together for the love of her son, the question becomes: is Abby losing her mind, or is it all being meticulously orchestrated by Joshua? The answer is left somewhat ambiguous—my inclination is that her problems stem from both—and that is as it should be. A scene in which Abby and Joshua play hide-and-seek is dripping with the kind of suspense rarely seen and captured, and it's a testament to director George Ratliff that he achieves this despite little in the way of action occurring.

As father Brad, Sam Rockwell is an unsung dramatic actor who finds the truth in each moment and holds on it. The way in which his character transforms is disconcerting and yet absolutely electrifying, going from a happy-go-lucky dad with undying love for Joshua to a beaten-down soul on the verge of losing everything and questioning who his son really is. In a nicely nuanced and understated supporting turn, Dallas Roberts deserves notice as Abby's brother, Ned. That Ned is pretty obviously gay but it is sparsely brought up and never made issue of is a pleasing sidenote to the strength of the material.

Intelligent and realistic about its subject matter, the running themes, including sibling jealousy, familial dissidence, and parent-child relations, consistently hit a relevant note. Ultimately, it is the knowledge of all the horrific possibilities for what could happen rather than the foresight of what does happen where the film ratchets up and then maintains its entrancing levels of fear and dread. Sleekly photographed by Benoit Debie and brilliantly scored by Nico Muhly—the use of the off-key piano chords are an invaluable atmospheric addition—*Joshua* is a haunting and evocative motion picture that stays with the viewer.

Joy Ride

2001 - Directed by John Dahl

In the early 1990s, my dad had a CB radio in his truck that I would often turn on, attempting to make contact with the truck drivers nearby, or just to eavesdrop on their sometimes oddball conversations with one another. I never got myself into trouble with the CB, but the reality is that it could realistically be turned into a tool, much like the Internet, used to terrorize people. That possibility of danger, intermixed with the idea of being left helpless on a long, lonesome, flat stretch of highway, is fearfully and expertly tapped into in *Joy Ride*, a seemingly conventional horror movie that surprises and creates palpably felt scares by not always playing by the rules.

Having just completed his freshman year away at college, Lewis Thomas (Paul Walker) has made a deal with longtime best friend Venna (Leelee Sobieski) to pick her up in Colorado so that they can spend some time together while traveling cross-country to their home back east. Buying a used car on a spur-of-the-moment impulse, Lewis stops along the way to bail his troubled older brother, Fuller (Steve Zahn), out of jail in Salt Lake City. Reunited for the first time in five years, Lewis and Fuller make the mistake of buying a CB radio at a truck stop for their trip. Impersonating a woman they label "Candy Cane," they pass the time flirting with a lonely, gravelly-voiced trucker named "Rusty Nail" before inviting him for a late-night motel rendezvous. Lewis and Fuller, staying one door over from where "Candy Cane" is supposed to be, witness the shadowy figure make his way to the room, followed by the sounds of a muffled struggle. They are alarmed to find out the next morning by the police that the man staying next door to them was found in a coma with his jaw completely ripped off. It seems "Rusty Nail" is a lonely phantom of the back roads who has just snapped, out to prove to the two brothers, and later Venna, just how deadly playing games can be.

Edited with the strength and tautness of a vise grip, *Joy Ride* is an impeccably visceral cinematic experience that never, or rarely, stops long enough to allow the viewer to take a much-needed breath. A sort of take-off on Steven Spielberg's nerve-jangling 1971 film, *Duel*, in which a man is terrorized by a severely unhinged trucker, *Joy Ride* might accurately be described as an extension on the opening twenty minutes of *Jeepers Creepers* to feature-length standards (do note that it is not, however, a copycat, their theatrical releases coming only a few weeks apart in 2001).

Directed by the meticulous John Dahl, who excels at telling noirish stories of murder and mayhem, *Joy Ride* is an absolutely merciless thriller—exciting, marvelously crafted, strongly acted, and with more than a few moments destined to increase one's heartbeat. Taking a short premise that could be described as "three victims menaced by a giant truck," Dahl and screenwriters Clay Tarver and J.J. Abrams thankfully do not clutter the ingenious storyline with lots of subplots, nor do they feel it necessary to ever visually unveil the psychopath behind the big rig. Not knowing exactly what Lewis, Fuller and Venna are up against makes for an even more unshakably eerie experience.

Paul Walker and Steve Zahn make for a winning, believable combination as siblings Lewis and Fuller, who haven't seen each other in a while, but remain close-knit. They are likable and attractive protagonists, with Walker (who has never been better than he was here) playing someone a bit less outgoing than he is usually accustomed to, and Zahn managing to steal scenes with his barbed dialogue exchanges. Rounding out the trio, Leelee Sobieski adds welcome femme support to counterbalance the boys, and, as always, delivers an on-target, convincing performance in a role that refuses to appear underwritten (even if it is on the written page).

Director Dahl, complemented by a stirring music score by Marco Beltrami, successfully ups the ante with so much genuine tension that it occasionally becomes almost unbearable. An extended action sequence in which the three are tracked down in a cornfield by the truck, and the nerve-racking climax set at a rural, roadside motel, are especially impressive. With unsettling cinematography by Jeff Jur that casts the characters and their dire surroundings with shadows and brightly colored neon lights, *Joy Ride* is a marvelously executed fright film that offers up more effectively horrific moments than the genre usually provides.

Let Me In

2010 - Directed by Matt Reeves

In 2008, critics and audiences—you know, those not turned off by subtitles—went gaga over Tomas Alfredson's lyrical coming-of-age vampire movie, *Let the Right One In*. It's a well-made, even affecting, film, but one that was a little overrated. Besides not being particularly scary—it was billed as a horror picture, after all—there was an underlying chilliness to it that had nothing to do with its wintry, snow-drenched setting. Even as the love story between the two 12-year-old leads—one of them who had been twelve for a long time—was about as unexpectedly gentle and honest as a relationship could be that involved serial killing and bloodsucking, they stood at an emotional distance from the viewer. This is not the case with the resolute—and dare it be said, superior—American remake, *Let Me In*, which burrows deeper into the characters' points of view to find the achingly true pangs that come with both growing up and having no choice but to remain the same. Whereas the previous version was sweet in its own way, this one is, at once, genuinely touching, tragic and chilling.

In the small town of Los Alamos, New Mexico, circa 1983, an Amish schoolboy has been found brutally murdered. As Ronald Reagan talks on the television about evil existing in the world and the notorious "satanic panic" craze heats up, a local policeman (Elias Koteas) takes heed of both and suspects a cult might be involved. For 12-year-old Owen (Kodi Smit-McPhee), he has his own problems to deal with. Incessantly bullied at school by Kenny (Dylan Minnette) and his two sidekicks and dealing with the ramifications of parents who are in the midst of divorcing, Owen daydreams of committing violence against his antagonizers while quietly yearning for a friend. He gets his wish when Abby (Chloë Grace Moretz) moves with her father (Richard Jenkins) into the apartment next to his. They first meet on the snow-covered playground outside the building—when Owen asks Abby if she's cold when he notices her not wearing shoes, she responds, "I don't really get cold"—and, despite Abby's initial protests about getting close, are soon something akin to best friends. As Los Alamos is shaken by more mysterious deaths and Owen gains the courage to finally stand up to Kenny's taunts, he begins to suspect—and for good reason—that Abby is no ordinary 12-year-old girl. She may not be a girl, or really twelve, at all.

Based on the novel by John Ajvide Lindqvist and adapted by both the author himself and writer-director Matt Reeves, *Let Me In* is a gripping tale that owes just as much of its inspiration from the original film, *Let the Right One In*, as it does from its literary source material. Reeves faithfully borrows certain key shots from the earlier picture—this is no coincidence—and his version follows the same basic plot trajectory. Where the filmmaker excels is in his economical, intelligent tweaks of the narrative—his placement of the story within a specific historical context; his streamlining of unnecessary characters and subplots that would have taken the viewer away from the complicated, sympathetic psyches of Owen and Abby, and his impeccable choices in period details and music complement the setting. A rule should be made that "The Breakup Song (They Don't Write 'Em)" by The Greg Kihn Band be in every movie, whether it's set in the 1980s or not. Furthermore, the Now and Later candy jingle, an "It's 10:00, do you know where your children are?" public service television ad, and David Bowie's "Let's Dance" all play sly roles in the proceedings.

The hiring of Greig Fraser was also an ace move, the cinematographer gorgeously lensing a winter wonderland turned fatally upside down. Fraser additionally manages the expert feat of shooting his two pre-teen subjects with such a compassionate intimacy that he threatens to pierce their very hearts whilst all the while transforming his camera into an unseen onlooker spying upon their lives. At once tender-hearted and threatening, Reeves' film is a satisfying balancing act between a *Romeo & Juliet*-style love story (Owen reads the Shakespeare play on the bus even as he is about to go through a similar experience) and a ghastly horror tale that draws a fine, sometimes indistinguishable line between light and dark, goodness and malevolence. With Abby needing blood to survive, her father figure disappears into the night, a black trash bag with beady eye holes pulled creepily over his head, in search of fresh victims. A queasily brilliant setpiece in which he attacks a teenage boy in a car outside a convenience store and, in trying to get away, gets into a nasty accident, is showstoppingly elevated through the use of Blue Öyster Cult's "Burnin' for You" and the decision to film the entire crash from inside the automobile.

The casting of young actors to fill the emotionally demanding roles of Owen and Abby must have been a daunting proposition, but Reeves has struck gold with Kodi Smit-McPhee and Chloë Grace Moretz. Both are astounding, delivering performances so untarnished and true they remind of no one less than Jean-Pierre Leaud in Francois Truffaut's 1959 coming-of-age landmark, *The 400 Blows*. Smit-McPhee devastates as a meek young boy who gets lost spying on the lives of the other residents of his apartment complex to escape from his own. A scene where he calls up his dad on the phone and struggles to find a solace he is no longer getting from either of his parents is remarkably moving. So, too, is the shot of happiness he finally finds in his relationship with Abby. When he asks her to go steady and she agrees, the look on his face says it all.

As Abby, Moretz has an even tougher assignment. Wise beyond her years, vulnerable, seemingly innocent yet capable of ruthless murder, Abby is full of contradictions. She loves Owen, but is she also using him the way she has used her "father" for the last fifty years? Indeed, she is destined to remain a child for the rest of eternity while Owen ages into adulthood. This knowledge brings a mournful undercurrent to the bond they share, and Moretz and Smit-McPhee seem to fully understand the complexity within their parts. Supporting turns from Richard Jenkins, sad as Abby's "father;" Elias Koteas, in the newly invented role of a policeman sniffing too close to a truth that could seal his fate, and Dylan Minnette, menacingly charismatic as bully Kenny, spouting off the same taunts and put-downs that he receives from his cruel older brother, all impress without stealing the rightful spotlight from Smit-McPhee and Moretz.

With his dad never more than a voice on a phone and his distraught mother (Cara Buono) never clearly captured in full on camera—her face is always either blurred, turned away, or just out of frame—Owen's isolation and disconnect to the grown-ups around him is indelibly felt. He finds the companion he needs in Abby, but it is one that comes with a price he may ultimately live to regret once he gets older and recognizes the cost of the decisions he's made. Until then, the two of them are soul mates. Free of compromise if not consistently of its own individuality—director Matt Reeves owes a lot to *Let the Right One In*, particularly a climactic swimming pool scene that is almost shot-for-shot identical—*Let Me In* will have fans of the original questioning this one's purpose until they see it and realize alterations have been made for the better. Altogether more confident and dramatically sound, this is the rare remake that makes a convincing case for existing by exceeding expectations in nearly every way.

Let the Right One In

2008 - Directed by Tomas Alfredson

A unique revisionist take on the classic vampire tale, *Let the Right One In* received heapings of accolades when it opened theatrically in the U.S. and its native Sweden in 2008. A love story between two lonely 12-year-olds, one of them a vampire, is certainly different, not only because of their pre-teen age, but because the film treats the dark plot with a maturity and uncompromising forthrightness that makes it very much within an R-rated realm. That the backdrop is the frozen, snow-covered setting of Stockholm, 1982, lends the picture an otherworldly, fable-like quality. All of this is deserving of praise, even as the experience as a whole doesn't quite come together in the way its biggest supporters have suggested.

Like a pint-sized, decidedly cuter relative of Nosferatu, Eli (Lina Leandersson) arrives in the middle of the night to the wintry Swedish suburb of Blackeberg, moving into an apartment complex with an older man, Håkan (Per Ragnar), in tow. The bullied, sad-eyed Oskar (Kåre Hedebrant) watches their arrival from his bedroom window, and meets Eli proper a night or two later out in the courtyard. Oskar's offering of a Rubik's cube for her to play with touches Eli, and she in turn instructs him to start standing up for himself against abusive classmate Conny (Patrik Rydmark). As their relationship closens and they start to "go steady," Oskar begins to suspect what the viewer already knows: Eli is a bloodsucking vampire, herself and Håkan responsible for a series of murders rocking the community. When he presses her on her age, she replies, "I'm twelve, but I've been twelve for a long time."

Elegantly directed by Tomas Alfredson and written by John Ajvide Lindqvist (based on his own novel), *Let the Right One In* is most affecting when the focus is solely on Oskar and Eli. Although they are technically ages apart, the vampiric Eli is forever trapped in the outer shell of a child, and her bonding with Oskar is gentle and touching in the way first love often is. Their relationship is not about sex—they are, after all, only twelve—but about much-needed companionship in a world that is cold without having anything to do with the frosty temperature outside. Oskar's reaction to learning what Eli truly is is one of initial caution, and quick acceptance; for him, it does not make a difference, and is certainly preferential to a father who comes in and out of his life and to a mother who has no idea how to connect with him.

Where *Let the Right One In* is on wobblier ground is in the rest of the narrative. There is a spooky segment involving a confused woman, Ginia (Ika Nord), who is saved from an attack only to start turning into a vampire herself, but otherwise the film isn't scary in a conventional horror sense. The townspeople, despite being well aware of the brutal murders happening around them, are almost nonchalant about the occurrences. Håkan's identity is never divulged—is he a father figure to Eli, or being controlled by her?—and Oskar does not ever press Eli about her past and where she comes from. Oskar's home life is underdeveloped; he appears to be a latchkey kid, but his mom is home much of the time and their uneven relationship is in need of some fleshing out. As for the ending, it is lyrical and satisfying in its simplicity, but does not bother to question what will happen when Oskar grows up and Eli remains in her prepubescent form.

Kåre Hedebrant and Lina Leandersson equip themselves admirably as Oskar and Eli. They are both striking in their looks—Hedebrant is blond and fair-skinned, Leandersson brunette and with the astonishing ability to appear as a kid and an old soul simultaneously—and their untrained performances (this is the first time either one acted) lend an aching honesty to the roles. It is because of the naturalism and chemistry of Hedebrant and Leandersson, and also because of the striking imagery courtesy of cinematographer Hoyte Van Hoytema—his predominant use of white and red is eye-popping, as is a climactic scene set in a swimming pool—that one can overlook the seemingly missing pieces of the film's storytelling. *Let the Right One In* is not the be-all-end-all groundbreaker some are labeling it as, but it does put a new, sweet spin on a subgenre long in need of some freshening up.

Lisa and the Devil

1974 - Directed by Mario Bava

First, a disclaimer. When Mario Bava's lush, cerebral *Lisa and the Devil* premiered at the Cannes Film Festival in 1973 and released internationally in '74, it was a financial failure (the U.S. did not even distribute it). In the hopes of making a return on their investment, the producers hired director Alfredo Leone and set out to shoot additional footage in 1975, tacking on a satanic possession plotline that copied off of William Friedkin's *The Exorcist* and retitling the film *House of Exorcism*. This new and completely different cut didn't do much better at the box office and served to almost erase the existence of *Lisa and the Devil* until the original version was put out on video in the 1990s and Blu-ray in 2012. *House of Exorcism* is trashy and exploitative, and should be avoided by all except those who wish to compare how a true artist's vision can be resculpted and downright desecrated by money-hungry, quality-deficient studio executives.

Equal parts resplendent and haunting in its dreamlike logic, *Lisa and the Devil* is an unheralded gem, a motion picture of breathtaking beauty that casts an intoxicating spell over viewers who delight in being treated as equals rather than as imbeciles who demand everything be spelled out for them. Nothing, really, is spelled out in *Lisa and the Devil*—the narrative is open to interpretation in the same way a painting or a photograph might—and that is part of its savory, unforgettable charm. For Italian filmmaker Mario Bava, 1971's *Twitch of the Death Nerve* (a.k.a. *Bay of Blood*) may be his most famous effort, paving the early way for the '80s slasher bonanza and notoriously helping to inspire several death sequences in the early *Friday the 13th* movies. It is the lesser-known *Lisa and the Devil*, however, that is his paramount achievement. Not only did Bava finally receive full control over the script and production, but it is said to have been the project he always wanted to make. Judging from the rule-breakingly imaginative, creepingly seductive final product, it's easy to see why.

Vacationing in the ancient Spanish city of Toledo, Lisa Reiner (Elke Sommer) wanders away from her tour group and stumbles into a shop where she meets Leandro (Telly Savalas), a maker of lifelike dummies who strongly resembles the portrait of the Devil she has just seen on a nearby fresco. Upon exiting the store, Lisa is unable to find her tour group as she immerses herself all the more into the cobblestone labyrinth of streets, alleyways and looming old buildings surrounding her. She finally comes upon a car and is able to flag the riders down—wealthy married couple Sophia (Sylva Koscina) and Francis Lehar (Eduardo Fajardo) and their chauffeur, George (Gabriele Tinti)—but automobile trouble leaves them stranded. The lot of them are invited to stay the night at a mansion owned by the blind Countess (Alida Valli). It is here that Lisa's nightmarish ordeal only deepens. As the guests begin dropping like flies, the Countess' son, Max (Alessio Orano), is taken by Lisa's uncanny resemblance to his former deceased lover, Elena. If that weren't enough, it is revealed that Leandro is working as the butler, his handmade puppets of deceased people morbidly tied to the funeral parlor he is running on the property's grounds.

Lisa and the Devil is a mesmerizing, singularly one-of-a-kind experience. The story, driven by an artistic eye for stunning imagery and quixotic cinematography by Cecilio Paniagua, is spellbinding to watch unfold. Deliberate pacing is mixed with striking *mise-en-scène* compositions and floating camerawork that also incorporates low angles, representing Lisa's foreign landscape crushing down upon her, and a number of startlingly effective zoom-ins—a calling-card of Mario Bava's work. Symbolism is quite prevalent—note the heavy use of clocks, many of them broken, as well as the use of reflections within a lake and spilled red wine on the floor—adding texture to the film that only increases with each viewing. Surrealistic touches permeate each scene, too, and keep a close eye on the way Leandro's dummies are intermittently and scarily replaced with human actors, foretelling of the characters' threatened mortality.

As Lisa's night proceeds, the film methodically breaks ties with reality altogether, the complexities within each of the characters' pasts and current motivations not immediately explaining themselves. Blunt and brutal murder setpieces are orchestrated—in one scene, bright-red blood nearly covers the lens—in between Lisa's horrifying voyage throughout the buildings and property. When she comes upon an ornate room populated by the lovingly displayed heads of the dummies, it calls to mind 1985's *Return to Oz*, which must have used this picture as inspiration. The sheer unorthodox otherworldliness of the piece additionally cements the influence Mario Bava has on David Lynch's modern work (e.g., 2001's *Mulholland Drive* and 2006's *Inland Empire*).

The highly photogenic Elke Sommer is a well-cast heroine as Lisa Reiner. Not a whole lot is asked of Sommer outside of reacting to an unthinkable plot happening to her, but she holds the camera's attention and manages to build her character through charisma and actions rather than concrete details about her life. The standout of the cast is Telly Savalas (most known from his 1973-1978 television drama *Kojak*), who, as Leandro, depicts one of the most sinister, skin-crawlingly shady villains in memory. In every look, glance, dialogue exchange and lollipop lick, Savalas is deeply frightening as only the Devil himself could be. The rest of the actors commit to their roles and fill them nicely, but this is Sommer's and Savalas' show all the way.

An indelible horror film of a remarkably original nature, *Lisa and the Devil* is overflowing in atmosphere and suggestion. The ending will not be given away, but I would be remiss not to mention a finale set on Lisa's airplane trip back home that is unshakably eerie and thoroughly ingenious, bringing the tale to a close that keeps with the off-kilter rationale of the rest of the picture. The culminating image before the end credits is unforgettable. *Lisa and the Devil* is over forty years old, but just as contemporary and relevant today. That it has been overshadowed by the junky *House of Exorcism* is sinful. *Lisa and the Devil* is the real deal, a masterfully poetic journey into darkness and dislocation that is long overdue in finding the audience it so desperately deserves.

Mama

2013 - Directed by Andy Muschietti

It is exceedingly appropriate that *Mama* begins with the age-old story opener, "Once upon a time...," for the film wastes not a moment taking on the appearance and feel of a beautifully macabre fairy tale. Set in the real world yet fraught with foreboding whimsy, it's a supernatural thriller in the classic vein, relying on crafty suspense and an eloquently unfolding plot that aims to disconcert and frighten, then unexpectedly touch, the viewer. Executive produced by Guillermo Del Toro—his stamp of approval is always reassuring—this curious tale of a specter's dangerous motherly love has been directed and co-written by Andy Muschietti, clearly taking great responsibility in expanding his much-acclaimed 2008 short to feature length. That he has a healthy budget, a top-notch technical crew, and the Oscar-nominated Jessica Chastain in the lead role only help his cause. *Mama* is a scream, and deliciously so.

For five years, struggling artist Lucas (Nikolaj Coster-Waldau) has searched for his two young nieces, spirited away by his unhinged brother following the murders of two business associates and his estranged wife. Though hope of finding them alive has dwindled, he gets the surprise of a lifetime when 8-year-old Victoria (Megan Charpentier) and 6-year-old Lilly (Isabelle Nélisse) are found alone in a wooded cabin, malnourished and emotionally stunted, but nevertheless alive. Working with child psychologist Dr. Dreyfuss (Daniel Kash), the girls gradually improve their communicative and verbal skills until the day when the courts allow Lucas and girlfriend Annabel (Jessica Chastain) to take them home. With the opportunity to move out of a cramped apartment and set up in a suburban two-story under the condition they retain a certain anonymity, Lucas is gung-ho about taking care of Victoria and Lilly, while Annabel, a member of a rock band going nowhere, is more reluctant to take on the role of a parent. When Lucas is hospitalized after a bad fall down the stairs, Annabel is suddenly thrust into the position of the girls' temporary sole caretaker. The responsibility is far more than she bargained for, but one she is willing to fight for when the mysterious presence Victoria and Lily call "Mama" turns out not to be imaginary after all.

Intentionally or not, *Mama* takes worthwhile inspiration from 2002's *The Ring*, 2003's *Darkness Falls*, and 2011's *Don't Be Afraid of the Dark* while cooking up its own gothic standalone fable. The screenplay, credited to Andy Muschietti, Barbara Muschietti and Neil Cross, doesn't play coy when it comes to Mama's existence; she is established as very much real and something of a supernatural entity before the opening credits. Instead, the question becomes who, exactly, Mama is, where she came from, and why she wants Victoria and Lilly as her own. Annabel would be the first person to admit she's not maternal—in her first scene, she very nearly jumps for joy when her pregnancy test comes back negative—but as she spends more time with Lucas' nieces and sees how troubled and vulnerable they are, her natural protective instincts begin to come out. Getting close to the girls, though, could also spell doom. "She'll get jealous," Victoria warns Annabel, and at the time Annabel only asks enough questions to know she'd better take a step back. When so many films of this kind demand their characters remain disbelieving cynics even as danger corners them from all directions, Annabel—and, for that matter, a sleuthing Dr. Dreyfuss—are quick to trust the girls and open their minds to the possibility that an otherworldly force is at work.

Jessica Chastain refuses to play weak characters or those that are informed by the men in their life, and so it goes with Annabel. Sure, she's the "girlfriend" of Lucas, but she's also very much her own person with her own ideas and feelings. With Lucas laid up in the hospital for the better part of the picture—arguably he's in there too long, one of the movie's more obvious plot devices—it is Annabel who is left presumably alone with two children to take care of. Director Andy Muschietti, accompanied by Antonia Riestra's arresting cinematography and Anastasia Masaro's brooding production design, knows how to fill a screen with suggestive threats and thematically loaded imagery so that even an exterior establishing shot of an otherwise standard house is somehow transformed into a place few people would want to ever step foot in. At times, there are one too many setups ending in a jolt or pop-up scare, but these more predictable moments are offset by the control of Muschietti's clear genre know-how and the restraint of a filmmaker who doesn't dare reveal all the cards he's playing with at once. Consequently, the anticipation of what's to come is one of its most effective assets, the sordid story of Mama and the crazed figure she came to be leading toward a third act that combines a rustic, cliffside *mise-en-scène* so imaginative and hair-raising it could make Tim Burton jealous with a sympathetic side that finds the tragic humanity within a monster.

Audiences who flock to see *Mama* will think they know where things are headed. On the way to this destination, there are obligatory scenes of characters slowly walking down darkened hallways, reaching to open doors they shouldn't, and sticking their noses in situations that could get them killed. What goes in between these conventions is where the film quakes, rattles and provokes, spacing out Mama's gasp-inducing reveals while slowing down to weave a layered narrative where one mother's mental instability and another's trepidations and inexperience ultimately lead them to a single common bond: their love of a child. Jessica Chastain is fantastic as Annabel, her hair shaggy and dark, her persona totally unlike any other character she's played, while Megan Charpentier and newcomer Isabelle Nélisse are equally transformative as children torn between domestication and the feral natures they've grown used to. And then there's the lady of the title, played to the same chilling hilt that spindly male actor Javier Botet put to unforgettable use as Nina Medeiros in 2007's *[REC]* and 2010's *[REC]²*. That Mama is a live-action creation, with CGI used only to complement in subtle, unobtrusive ways, makes her all the more perilously plausible. She's the stuff of nightmares, and what fairy tale worth its salt doesn't inspire a few bad dreams to go along with the hope of a happily ever after?

Martyrs

2008 - Directed by Pascal Laugier

Director Pascal Laugier has gone on record apologizing for *Martyrs*, and he was only partially joking. This is not to suggest that he thinks he has made a bad film, but one that works all too effectively, daring to go to places so despairing and bleak that few prospective viewers will be able to aptly prepare themselves. Indeed, one cannot passively watch *Martyrs*; it is too strong, too bold, and too thematically loaded for apathy. For those who would prefer a cinematic walk through the proverbial park, look elsewhere. All others willing to go on an experience that transcends the unthinkable, gird your loins.

When Lucie (Mylène Jampanoï) was a child, she was abducted and held captive for a year, facing daily physical abuse before narrowly escaping with her life. The people responsible were never apprehended. Sent to live at a youth home during her recovery, she is befriended by the compassionate Anna (Morjana Alaoui). Although Lucie is safe, she is unable to escape from her terrifying traumatic memories caused by the experience. Fifteen years later, a seemingly normal family—a mother (Patricia Tulasne), father (Robert Toupin), son (Xavier Dolan) and daughter (Juliette Gosselin, heartbreaking)—sitting down to breakfast are interrupted by the doorbell. Standing outside is Lucie, looking to make all four members pay with their lives for the parents' sins. She is convinced they are her kidnappers from the past, but has not fully thought out her plan. When Anna arrives, she tries to take control of the situation and clean up the mess, but her attempts to help her best friend are lost on a mentally tortured young woman who will never be able to escape her past and the incontrovertible damage already done to her.

What has been described so far takes up, maybe, the opening thirty minutes of a part-ghastly, part-meditative barrier-breaker that defies easy categorization and lets no one involved off the hook. Powerfully blunt violence begets rapid-fire intensity begets a transformative second half delving into nothing less than the literal search for God. Tough to take but imminently rewarding, *Martyrs* is one of those films that is impossible to guess where it is going. Grabbing viewers, and grabbing them hard, the early moments where a family sees their loved ones and their own life systematically wiped out in a flash is petrifyingly authentic. The more one learns about them, though, the more it becomes apparent that looks are most definitely deceiving. From there, Laugier plows forward, his sympathetic if uncompromising handling of the characters making the horror elements all the more impactful. He knows exactly where he is headed, and he doesn't dare disclose it until it's happening on the screen.

For much of the film, Morjana Alaoui and Mylène Jampanoï are front and center, carrying the twisty narrative to places forbidding and austere. These are demanding roles in all conceivable senses of the term, and the bravery with which the actors approach the harsh realities of their protagonists' circumstances is not to be marginalized. As Lucie, Jampanoï heads up the first act, the flurry of emotions she goes through—grief, shame, rage, terror—tipped over by haunting hallucinatory visions of the malnourished, mutilated fellow victim she left behind all those years ago. Alaoui, as Anna, is given an even more demanding task, baring her soul as nakedly as she does her body. In a key supporting turn that fiercely haunts the picture's closing moments, Catherine Bègin portrays Mademoiselle, an aging woman willing to go to extremes to find out whether or not there is something beyond the physical plane of life.

Harrowing and unforgettably ambiguous in its final stretch, the French-Canadian *Martyrs* (it was filmed in Québec) yanks the viewer into a world both unthinkably vicious and unfair, but also transcendent. If evil exists, so, too, does humanity's fear of the universe's natural process. Some people may turn toward faith as a means of coping with what they do not finitely know, while others concentrate on science. The film imagines a third group, bred out of desperation, who will do whatever it takes to know what awaits them on the other side of their last breath. Do they get their answer? The screenplay's last words, "Keep doubting," linger tenebrously in the air even after the credits have rolled. *Martyrs* is one of the loftiest achievements the horror genre has seen in the twenty-first century.

May

2003 - Directed by Lucky McKee

The astonishing debut of writer-director Lucky McKee, *May* was a critical hit when it premiered at the 2002 Sundance Film Festival and continued its acclaim via other fests and Internet word-of-mouth, but distributor Lionsgate Films treated it like an ugly stepchild and gave it zero support. Why is it that studios so often sit on gems such as this—or, to give more examples, the also much-delayed *The Cabin in the Woods*, *All the Boys Love Mandy Lane* and *Trick 'r Treat*—while wasting no time in tossing to the masses any old disposable, derivative piece of mediocrity? *May* was one of the most auspicious and original independent features of the twenty-first century's inaugural decade—particularly for a first-time filmmaker—and continues to build over time as a classic in training.

First and foremost, the film is an incisive and touching character study about a young woman (Angela Bettis) whose childhood insecurities have carried over into adulthood. It is an often enormously funny comedy, in which the humor stems from both natural and offbeat human behavior and emotions. And then, finally, it takes a turn toward the grimmest recesses of the mind in the third act, when May's best friend—a sacred, eternally encased porcelain doll—is accidentally broken, and psychotic tendencies eventually alienate her from her only two living friends, the darkly sexy Adam (Jeremy Sisto) and wildly sensual co-worker Polly (Anna Faris). In a desperate attempt to rekindle the relationship she shared with her doll, May sets out to steal her favorite body parts from acquaintances and assemble a new life-size companion.

May is a horror film, and it is one both inventive and genuinely disturbing, but it offers up another characteristic more rare for the genre. Through Lucky McKee's impassioned direction and alternately delicate and merciless writing, he gets the viewer to put a rooting interest into the story and characters, and then gets them to care. It is safe to say that May eventually careens over the deep end into madness, but through the careful setup of her character, one understands why she does what she does in the third act, even if one cannot necessarily relate to it. In May's eyes, the murder of imperfect human beings is only a means in which to make a perfect doll out of each person's best physical features. May is a sick individual, but she is almost as much a victim as she is the villain. The viewer fears what she may do next, even as he or she empathizes with her lonely plight.

Perhaps what McKee achieves most beautifully is his three-dimensional presentation of May within a film that offers almost no horror scenes in the first hour, yet still has the viewer recoiling in apprehension at every encounter she has with someone, simply out of fear of what she may be capable of doing. At one point, May goes to work with a group of blind children at a daycare center, but it remains unclear if she has offered her services as a way of doing genuine good, or for more devious reasons. She is also deeply attracted to Adam, especially his hands, and she carries around a pack of cigarettes he once gave her as some sort of treasured entity. "Do you think I'm weird?" May asks Adam. "I like weird," horror movie buff Adam responds, but he follows that up later with, "not that weird," when she tries to reenact a scene from his latest student film, about cannibalism. Likewise, Polly is a free-spirited lesbian who shows a definite romantic interest in May, but unintentionally hurts her feelings when she later makes it clear that she doesn't practice monogamy. May is constantly searching for acceptance in any way she can get it, only to be let down time and again by the people around her.

In a talent-defining role that reminds a bit of what 1976's *Carrie* did for Sissy Spacey (is it any wonder she followed this role up with that Stephen King adaptation's television remake?), Angela Bettis is note-perfect as the mousy and dangerous May. Bettis has made the wise decision to play up May's crumbling self-esteem and yearnings to fit in rather than her villainy, which causes the story's development to be all the more heartbreaking when she is driven mad. Meanwhile, May's doll, which she confides in and thinks of as a miniature version of herself, looms over the scenes even when it isn't present, the cracking of the glass it is encased in a chilling symbol of May's own fracturing sanity. In key supporting roles, Jeremy Sisto effectively chooses to play Adam with an attractive swagger he doesn't recognize and a relatively normal personality that spars with May's more adventurous and pushy side, while Anna Faris is a delight as the almost-as-offbeat Polly who, nonetheless, refuses to be faithful to May. Faris plays her last scene, especially, with a frightening vulnerability, its cumulative effect proving unshakable.

The climax of *May* is nearly unbearable in its assured intensity and unforgettable in its unblinking views of psychological sickness, ruthless serial murder, and even darker possible areas of the human condition. The first full hour of exposition and setup brilliantly paves the way for what finally occurs, even if one cannot quite believe McKee's bravely grim and poignant intentions. The final image *May* cooks up is its most courageous. In the wrong hands, or in a more exploitative movie that had not allowed its audience to care about the main character, the shot may have inspired bad laughs. It does not, however, and McKee earns its subtle implications. Simply put, it was the most bone-chilling sequence seen in 2003, more disturbing than anything in *House of 1000 Corpses*,

Wrong Turn, *Identity* or *28 Days Later*. Lionsgate may have ruined its chances of gaining a large following through theatrical bookings, but *May* has become a cult favorite in certain circles, much like 2001's initially overlooked but finally found *Donnie Darko*. As a stirring drama, a marvelously developed character piece, a sly black comedy, a taut psychological thriller, and a gory, scary, unflinching horror film, *May* is a cinematic masterwork, a film with the ability to do all five things at once, or apart, with pitch-perfect grace.

Monster

2003 - Directed by Patty Jenkins

In today's world, right is right, wrong is wrong, and someone who kills another person in cold blood is instantly viewed as an evil, irredeemable entity. It's really as simple as that, and there is little gray area when it comes to this popular census. Based on the true story of Aileen Wuornos, labeled "the first female serial killer" after murdering six johns in the 1980s, *Monster* does not try to compensate Aileen's heinous actions, nor does it ask that she even be sympathetic. Instead, in her bold directing debut, Patty Jenkins' goal is for the viewer to simply understand how someone like Aileen might be pushed to commit such crimes, especially when the entire world around her becomes a consistent disappointment with few other options. The film's ultimate emotional effect is something of a passionate, unflinching *tour de force*.

A highway prostitute in Daytona Beach, Florida, since her early teens, thirty-something Aileen Wuornos (Charlize Theron) is an eternal lost soul about to end her own life when fate intervenes at a lowly gay bar in the form of 18-year-old Selby Wall (Christina Ricci). Selby is something of a lost soul herself, a lesbian still discovering her sexuality who has been kicked out by her dad for coming out of the closet. Aileen defensively denies being gay when Selby approaches her, but, after a few rounds of drinks, they have made a connection that quickly turns to genuine love. Aileen has never had another person care about her in the way that Selby does, and she clings to it, using her new relationship as a sign to go straight in her life and do away with hooking. Unfortunately, a legitimate job is not as easy to come by as Aileen expects, particularly with a police record attached to her name. When one of her liaisons goes bad and Aileen is assaulted and raped, she manages to kill her attacker in self-defense. Miserable in her dead-end profession and frustrated with men, Aileen's dark unconscious is suddenly unleashed from this fatalistic incident. In its wake, Aileen gradually creates a bloodbath across Central Florida that has no way of ending but badly.

Monster is not a serial killer movie in the sensational sense of the term, but one that feels all too real, and was. In her powerful, multifaceted portrait of Aileen Wuornos, Jenkins does not absolve Aileen of her crimes, but does make a convincing argument that her actions were at least partially the result of a life that was basically one bum deal after the next. By the time Aileen grows aspirations to do more with her life, her past actions have already sealed the deal on her grim fate from which there is no escape. In one painfully frank moment, Aileen goes to an employment agency and is told point-blank that with her police record the best she could ever possibly hope for is a minimum-wage factory job. After she gets away with her self-defense murder (the newspapers state that there are no leads), Aileen comes to the conclusion that she doesn't need to demean herself in order to get paid; in her mind, it is easier and more convenient to simply dispose of her oily clients in exchange for their car and all of their money. In turning to killing, however, Aileen gets in way over her head, eventually leading to the death of a well-meaning, would-be savior (Scott Wilson) who only wanted to help her out.

There are no deserved words to describe the performance of Charlize Theron, one of the most gorgeous actresses in Hollywood, who has gone through a physical transformation like few others. Outside of her weight gain and the flawless make-up effects by Toni G, Theron's work is a fearless powerhouse. She does not simply mimic her real-life counterpart, but somehow has cosmically burrowed herself into Wuornos' own skin, becoming her. Theron had been very good in the past, but never given a role that allowed her to unveil how much acting talent and range she really had. This part, for which she won an Academy Award, was the turning point in her career. From her body language, alternately self-imploding and filled with an underlying rage able to pop at any time, to her speech, to even the way she handles and smokes her cigarettes as if they are a utensil for showing off, Theron embodies from the inside out someone other than herself, and uncompromisingly does it with the depth, the foresight and the humanity that can only be said of the best-ever performances in the history of cinema. Like Hilary Swank's in 1999's *Boys Don't Cry*, an equally brilliant and tonally similar drama, Charlize Theron's turn as Aileen Wuornos is one for the record books.

In the less showy but critical part of Selby Wall, Christina Ricci's performance is a revelation that may be overlooked in favor of Theron's, but shouldn't be. In some ways, Ricci has the trickiest role. Selby is a quirky, somewhat gullible young woman still trying to find her place in the world, but she is not stupid, and suspects what Aileen has been doing long before she openly acknowledges it. How else to describe the constant change in car and the sudden increase in cash flow? Selby desperately loves Aileen, but as the stakes are raised she becomes frightened for the both of them, and realizes how in over her head she is. Like Theron, Ricci's every action, every piece of body language, and every line of dialogue paints a distinct, fleshed-out, richly drawn true original of a character. She is phenomenal.

Monster, which gets its name from a giant carnival ferris wheel Aileen was scared to get on as a child, has to be one of the most humanistic portrayal of a serial killer in the annals of fictional cinema, filled with raw power and unsuspecting beauty. The production design by Edward T. McAvoy, costumes by

Rhona Meyers, cinematography by Steven Bernstein and precise music choices create such an unmistakable time and place that they effortlessly refuse to call attention to themselves. And the vital use of "Don't Stop Believin'," by Journey, is poignant and magical bordering on downright brilliant. Executed by lethal injection in 2002, there is no doubt Aileen Wuornos was guilty of the crimes for which she was committed, but *Monster* heartbreakingly yearns for all of us to consider the circumstances that led to her downfall. We do not have to like Aileen Wuornos, director Jenkins seems to be saying, but we should at least consider her life's path as a tragedy in and of itself in a world that refused to give her a break. *Monster* is a fair, thought-provoking, unwavering masterpiece.

Monsters

2010 - Directed by Gareth Edwards

Monsters is one of the top cinematic achievements so far this century. That is not to say it is necessarily a great film, only that, for what was achieved on a reported budget of less than $100,000, it is very nearly mind-blowing. The canny writing-directing debut of Gareth Edwards (who also pulls off cinematography and visual effects duty), *Monsters* was made with a crew of two behind-the-scenes people, two actors, and a lot of glorified extras. Its stunning production values and almost seamless computer-generated effects work make it look as if its budget were seven hundred times as large, putting to shame plenty of big studio films that cost $100-million-plus.

A cross between 2004's *The Motorcycle Diaries*, 2005's *The War of the Worlds*, and 2009's *District 9* with plenty of 1934's *It Happened One Night* thrown in, *Monsters* is, collectively, like no other feature film in memory. Set in a world where a space probe in search of alien life crashed upon re-entry over Central America, infecting a portion of Mexico with giant roaming creatures, Andrew Kaulder (Scoot McNairy) is a professional photographer in search of that one outstanding shot that will win him a magazine cover. Roped into escorting his boss' grown daughter, Samantha Wynden (Whitney Able), from Costa Rica to transportation that will send her safely to the U.S., Andrew quickly discovers this trip is going to be tougher than expected. When their train announces it is turning back, Andrew and Samantha hop out and make their way to a ferry station. Tickets are $5,000 apiece—money they barely have—and the only other option is to take their chances traveling across the "Infected Area" toward the American border. As the two of them bond over a tough situation and develop feelings for each other, they inch ever closer to an unavoidable revelation and fate.

From the outside—and based on its marketing campaign—*Monsters* looks to be a sci-fi/horror effort about two people being stalked by alien invaders across an apocalyptic landscape. Instead, it's a road movie and a love story that just so happen to take place amidst a horrific backdrop. The invasion occurred six years ago and, for the residents of Mexico, life has almost gone back to normal (save for the occasional destruction of a building or two). Most of the creatures are confined within the "Infected Area" bordering North America and are only glimpsed a few times throughout. Because they are so sparsely used yet constantly looming ominously over the story, when they make their appearances it's so jolting and realistic that the impact is truly disconcerting. The conceptual design of the creatures and the visual effects used to bring them to startling life are close to photorealistic, made even more impressive because they were rendered on Edwards' own computers for next to no money. If ever there was proof that movies no longer require enormous budgets in order to have an enormous scope, this is it.

Andrew and Samantha start off as strangers with only one connection—her father and his boss—but, as opposed to not getting along at first, they hit it off fairly well. Samantha is engaged to be married, but that doesn't stop her from feeling jealousy (that she none too convincingly hides) when she discovers Andrew has had a one-night stand the evening before she is to set sail through the hot zone. As they are isolated further and must rely solely on each other to make it to the border, the film increases in quiet intimacy to the point where one begins to question the very title of the movie. The sights and sounds Andrew and Samantha are faced with are filmed with a lonesome poeticism, but that doesn't always take away the fact that this is a deliberately paced movie requiring patience and trust that Edwards knows where he's going. He does.

Scoot McNairy and Whitney Able are the sole human attractions in a cast otherwise made up of walk-ons and a lot of open land. They are well-equipped in their roles, natural and never showy. Their romantic chemistry is admittedly about room temperature, but they do come off as opposites who unexpectedly connect on a deeper level under strenuous circumstances. In an amusingly accurate exchange, Samantha asks photographer Andrew how he feels about relying on bad things happening in order to profit from them, to which Andrew replies, "You mean like doctors?" Later, when they come within sight of the man-made structure separating Central America from Texas, they comment how different it is to look at America from the outside. It's a little on the nose, but a testament to who they are and how good they never realized they had it.

Simmering with tension the closer Andrew and Samantha move toward their destination, *Monsters* culminates in the sort of confrontation between man and alien that audiences will have been waiting for all along. Not one to go down an oft-traveled road, Edwards upholds his end of the bargain by veritably spooking the viewer—a shot in which one of the creatures looms over a nighttime gas station, lit only by lightning flashes, is astoundingly nightmarish, reminding of something out of H.P. Lovecraft—but then jerks in a different last-minute direction that finds a compassionate commonality between man and beast. Not feeling the need to answer every question posed, *Monsters* is, at once, rousingly independent and technically very much a part of the mainstream. What it isn't is conventional, the final image all the more tragic if one has paid close attention to the picture's prologue. Suddenly, all that has come before is put into perspective. *Monsters* is adamantly uncompromising—a certain attentive commitment is demanded of the viewer—but what is destined to be its biggest claim to notoriety is how much money it makes $15,000 seem like. All of Hollywood ought to be green with envy.

Mother's Day

1980 - Directed by Charles Kaufman

If *Mother's Day* isn't the most adept and accomplished motion picture ever released by Lloyd Kaufman's exploitative Troma Entertainment, then this writer hasn't seen the one that's better. Its low-budget may shine through now and again—in one scene, a speckled-with-blood character reacts and screams at a beheading that is still seconds away from taking place—but these little production flaws only serve to add a bit of charm to the anything-goes, guerilla-style filmmaking process. So much more than a common slasher film from the early '80s, *Mother's Day* blends unthinkably nasty horror elements with perverse comedy, intimate drama, and outrageously on-target satire without missing a beat.

In the ten years since graduating from Wolfbreath College, best friends Abbey (Nancy Hendrickson), Jackie (Deborah Luce) and Trina (Tiana Pierce) have gone their separate ways but vowed to meet for an annual surprise getaway vacation. With Abbey tending to her overbearing mother, Jackie constantly used by a coke-sniffing boyfriend who doesn't appreciate her, and Trina off in Hollywood meshing with the rich and famous, the trio are happy to get away from it all for a week of relaxation and catching up. This year, Jackie's choice in location—New Jersey's isolated Deep Barons—turns out to be their undoing. Attacked and kidnapped in the middle of the night, Abbey, Jackie and Trina find themselves at the mercy of Mother (Beatrice Pons) and her beloved grown sons Ike (Frederick Coffin) and Addley (Michael McCleery), backwoods yokels who delight in systematic torture and killing.

Frequently mean-spirited but with alternately comical and earnest slants, *Mother's Day* works on multiple levels. As a satirical comment on gross consumerism, domesticity and the unintended effects of self-help groups, the film is overflowing with underlying thematic intent. Opening at a motivational seminar called E.G.O. ("Ernie's Growth Opportunity") that Mother attends in Manhattan, the picture then segues to her giving a lift to two other group members about to meet their maker. "You live really far out," one of them comments. Mother's response: "I take what's good from the city, and the rest you can keep." The intentional ludicrousness of this statement is wickedly funny, for the "good" that Mother has apparently taken from the city is the ability to rape, kidnap and murder innocent people. Meanwhile, she lives in a house where the walls are spray-painted with sexual references, televisions are turned on 24/7, name-brand junk foods are consumed as if they were vegetables—"Eat your cheese spread, Ike, it's good for the liver," Mother says at one point—and a *Sesame Street* Big Bird alarm clock sits inches away from a rotting corpse hanging in the closet. Suffice it to say, *Mother's Day* is full of the kind of winking bite either lost upon most of today's cinema, or not pulled off nearly as well.

On another level—as a deviously violent and unsparing horror effort—the film is morose and poignant, detailing a threesome of old friends whose happy-go-lucky vacation leads to one of them dead and the other two fighting back for vengeance and survival. Surprisingly feminist in nature, director Charles Kaufman sets up protagonists who are no shrinking violets. Forced into a valid transformation from whimpering victims to no-holds-barred fighters, they signify the model of a modern woman who can take care of herself and doesn't need to just be eye candy or a trophy wife. Before this can occur, however, the movie must get through its most uncomfortable segment: the brutal raping and physical abuse of one of the gals. That this goes down within a role-playing sex game that Mother affectionately labels "the Shirley Temple," the victim forced into the part of a schoolbooks-carrying little girl accosted by a stranger hiding behind a park bench set up in their yard, signals that Kaufman's tongue is at least planted firmly in cheek.

When the film wants to get down and dirty, it knows how. Violence and bloodshed are plentiful; when a rope Abbey is pulling cuts deeply into the palm of her hand, the viewer feels it. Special effects used to pull off the innumerable bodily injuries inflicted are mostly professional if occasionally coarse. And the climax, in which three well-deserved comeuppances take precedence, is involving and appropriately ruthless in its savagery. The sight of Mother being suffocated by plastic blow-up breasts speaks loud and clear of the sadism she has chosen to surround herself with.

Speaking of Mother, Beatrice Pons (a veteran actress of television and the stage who chose to be credited under the alias "Rose Ross") is unforgettable in a one-of-a-kind performance that is sick, funny and touching all at once. Her love for her sons and the normalcy-cum-squalor that she has raised them in actually gives her a flawed human touch. She's a monster, for sure, but she still cares for her family. As heroines Abbey, Jackie and Trina, Nancy Hendrickson, Deborah Luce and Tiana Pierce are uniformly strong. None of them went on to big acting careers, and that's unfortunate; the relationship between the three of them is endearingly developed—there's even a sweet flashback to their college days scored to Tommy James and the Shondells' "I Think We're Alone Now"—and each one slides into a character specifically individual from the other two.

Mother's Day is gritty and grimy—a bath may be in order after watching it—but it is not without merit. Whether viewed as a stark horror pic, a wildly offbeat comedy, a female-empowerment saga, or a cutting depiction of consumerist society gone woefully wrong, the film has something to offer all but those with weak stomachs. The socko surprise ending—let's just say it involves Mother's deranged, forest-prowling sister, Queenie—is the perfect capper on a relic of the 1980s slasher craze that still, oddly enough, feels awfully relevant.

The Mothman Prophecies

2002 - Directed by Mark Pellington

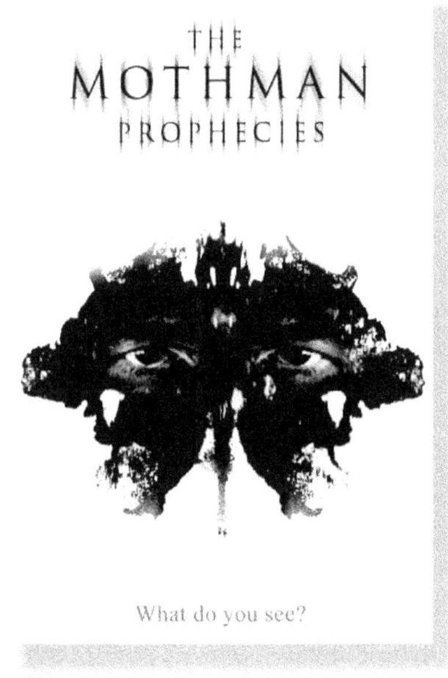

An ominously puzzling mystery, *The Mothman Prophecies* gains much of its visceral power not from onscreen violence and bloodshed (there is very little of both), but from the fact that it is based on a stunning true story that occurred in Point Pleasant, West Virginia, in 1966-67. Director Mark Pellington wisely recognizes that not all scary movies require an ax-wielding maniac chopping people's heads off; instead, he uses a thick undercurrent of atmospheric dread and truly creepy sound effects to keep the tension high.

Based on the supernatural non-fiction book by John A. Keel, the story has been updated to the present day but has kept most of its plot points intact. *Washington Post* journalist John Klein (Richard Gere) and his wife, Mary (Debra Messing), are a couple very much in love and looking for a bigger place to move into. On their way home one night, Mary sees something that horrifies her so much she crashes their car and is seriously injured. While in the hospital, it is discovered that she also has an irreversible brain tumor.

Switch to two years later, John still hasn't fully recovered from the loss of his wife. While traveling to Richmond, Virginia, to interview a politician, his car breaks down. After seeking help from a nearby house, the inhabitants, Gordon (Will Patton) and Denise (Lucinda Jenney), call the police on him, claiming that he has knocked on their door at 2:30 a.m. for three nights in a row. More mindboggling is John's realization that he is in the sleepy town of Point Pleasant, located 400 miles in the opposite direction from his target destination in Richmond. With the help of local police officer Sgt. Connie Parker (Laura Linney), John is drawn into an investigation concerning the residents' recent claims of seeing bright lights in the sky, receiving spectral phone calls, and glimpsing an eight-foot-tall moth-like creature—the same one the now-deceased Mary claimed she saw the night of their car wreck. Are these otherworldly sightings dangerous phenomena or merely warning signals to impending disaster?

Because the real-life sightings were never solved in the 1960s, culminating in the fatal collapse of Point Pleasant's Silver Bridge, *The Mothman Prophecies* poses a great deal of questions and very few answers. This is how it should be. Credit Pellington and screenwriter Richard Hatem for not crafting a bogus conclusion that neatly ties all of the plot points together, but allows them to remain true accounts of the still-unknown. The key to the film's ultimate effectiveness is in its methodic pacing, drawing the viewer into the perplexing circumstances surrounding the characters. Save for a stunningly orchestrated finale set on the town's bridge, there is little action to be found. Pellington has smartly chosen to tell this particular tale by way of a static-laden, frightening use of sound; blustery cinematography by Fred Murphy that takes full advantage of its blue hues, and an escalatingly dire set of horrific developments that are rarely seen, but often heard.

Underscoring the central premise is the sensitive story of a man learning to come to grips with the loss of a loved one. Richard Gere is an underrated actor who brings a sensitive, heartfelt aura to the mourning John, and Debra Messing makes a haunting impression as the ill-fated Mary. Messing has limited screen time, but her character hangs over the film like a ghostly apparition that won't go away. Joining Gere and Messing are Laura Linney, as Connie, the woman who halfheartedly joins John on his crusade to find out the truth. She does the most with a modestly underwritten role. And, as Gordon, Will Patton does exemplary supporting work.

If there is a disappointment with the final product of *The Mothman Prophecies*, it is that the film might have been even more frightening were we to have gotten at least a glimpse of the title phantom that the townspeople claim to keep being visited by. Except for a one-second flash of it in the first act, it is never visually seen again, only depicted through a set of drawings. This filmmaking decision is not necessarily the wrong one by any stretch of the imagination, but it deserves being suggested that it might have made for a more satisfying denouement since so much of the picture is left dangling in the air at the end. As with 1999's excellent study in paranoia, *Arlington Road*, director Mark Pellington once again has made a thriller that goes against the conventions of the genre, yet loses none of its overall power in the process. Sure to give almost anyone a hefty case of the willies, *The Mothman Prophecies* is not only very scary when it wants to be, but also a movie with far loftier, thought-provoking themes than the premise might suggest at first glance.

Mulholland Drive

2001 - Directed by David Lynch

A heartbreaking tale of the dark side of Hollywood and the way life doesn't always turn out as expected, *Mulholland Drive* is just about as perplexing and foreboding a motion picture as one is likely to see. Innovatively written and directed by David Lynch, the film is an even more baffling cinematic experience than 1997's *Lost Highway*, but is also more ambitious and complex. Filmed in a nonlinear fashion that sets everything up as a pleasant dream that quickly turns into a hellish nightmare, *Mulholland Drive* leaves the viewer with more questions than answers, but also a whole lot to discuss, investigate and debate long after its unforgettable journey reaches an end.

The narrative begins with an attempted murder during a pitch-black night on Los Angeles' Mulholland Drive that turns fatal when a carload of partying teenagers hit their limo. The targeted victim, a luscious brunette beauty (Laura Elena Harring), is the sole survivor. Stumbling away from the wreckage, she seeks shelter in a gorgeous nearby apartment that has been left vacant by a vacationing actress. The following morning while taking a shower, she is discovered by the chipper Betty Elms (Naomi Watts), an Ontario native who has come to stay at her aunt's place in Hollywood as she attempts to start an acting career. The woman, who has no memory, tells Betty that her name is Rita after seeing a poster for *Gilda*, starring Rita Hayworth. Betty and Rita become self-appointed detectives, deciding to find out who Rita is and what happened on Mulholland Drive. In an interweaving storyline, a young hotshot director named Adam Kesher (Justin Theroux) is preparing to cast his latest picture. Although several big-name actresses are knocking on his door for the part, mysterious forces begin inundating pressure on him to cast a new ingenue named Camille, or pay the possibly deadly consequences.

This is the basic setup of *Mulholland Drive*, although to give anything else away is to, conflictingly, steal the pleasures of discovering the film as it plays out, and to not give much away at all. Suffice it to say, roughly 105 minutes into the movie, something both shocking and bewildering occurs that turns everything that has come before on its head. Characters suddenly take the identities and personalities of other characters, scene after scene abruptly cuts off before it conventionally concludes, and the whole world becomes an alternate reality where one is left unsure if any of the movie has been real, or just a frightening, disorienting dream.

Mulholland Drive has been highly publicized to have originally started off as a television pilot that was rejected by the network. Foreign financier Studio Canal offered Lynch $7-million to reshoot and further develop the story into a complete feature film. Doing such a thing could have proved horribly uneven, but the halves blend so seamlessly into a whole that one would never be able to guess the history of the project without already hearing about it. An almost epic-sized picture with a huge cast of lead characters, supporting ones, and memorable cameos, the movie offers scenes in the first half that seem potentially unnecessary, as if Lynch has decided to just shoot material that is freakily "out-there," but everything masterfully and satisfyingly reemerges in the later sections, leaving the viewer giddy to see what the master filmmaker has up his sleeve next. One such sequence, in which a nervous man tells his friend about a horrifying nightmare he had the night before about the diner they're eating in, only to minutes later see his fears come true in reality, leads later on to a small, eerie blue box that is found by Betty and Rita. What powers the blue box holds is best left undisclosed, but it paves the way for the disturbing final forty minutes.

As protagonists Betty and Rita, Naomi Watts and Laura Elena Harring are brilliant, giving multilayered turns that complement the off-kilter, intricate plot. Watts is, at once, innocent and bright-eyed, but has an obscure, sexual side that is discovered as the film progresses and her intentions change. Harring is just as boldly good, making Rita into a person both scared out of her wits and curious of her forgotten, concussion-induced past. Justin Theroux is appropriately high-strung and self-absorbed as rising filmmaker Adam Kesher, who suspects his life may hang in the balance based on who he decides to cast in his new movie after a mystifying meeting he has with a stranger named The Cowboy (Monty Montgomery).

James Karen, as a studio casting director; Lori Heuring, as Adam's cheating wife; country music singer Billy Ray Cyrus, as the man she is having an affair with; Monty Montgomery, as The Cowboy; Robert Forster, as Det. Harry McKnight; Dan Hedaya, as a peculiar studio exec; Missy Crider, as a waitress whose name inexplicably changes from Diane to Betty—a mirror image of what also happens to Watts' character—and Melissa George, as debut actress Camille Rhodes, round out the fine supporting cast. Finally, Rebekah Del Rio performs Ray Orbison's "Cryin'" in a nightclub completely in Spanish, the performance so overwhelmingly powerful that she leaves onlookers Betty and Rita in tears.

Mix in an elderly couple who have demented smiles plastered on their faces at all times; a rotting corpse in a motel room whose identity isn't fully discovered until the end; a wheelchair-bound dwarf (Michael J. Anderson) in a glass room who listens in on the conversations of movie studio bosses, and a psychic who comes to Betty's door speaking of horrible things she senses are coming to either her or Rita, and the surface has still only barely been scratched within the alternately inventive, confusing, thought-provoking world that David Lynch has created here. With a superb, offbeat music score by Lynch regular Angelo Badalamenti, *Mulholland Drive* is a masterpiece that leads Betty and Rita down a path that leaves neither of them sure who they are anymore. What it all means is up to the audience to decide. For the adventurous sort who can handle an uncompromisingly direct assault on their senses and mind, an absolutely great time is nearly guaranteed to be had trying to piece everything together. *Mulholland Drive* is tough to forget, and why would a person want to?

A Nightmare on Elm Street

1984 - Directed by Wes Craven

Before he got his own syndicated television anthology in 1988 and before he turned into a virtual stand-up comedian in later installments, Freddy Krueger was a truly unnerving screen villain. This is no more true than in the motion picture that started it all, 1984's classic *A Nightmare on Elm Street.* Of the "Big Three" slasher series'—*Halloween, Friday the 13th* and this one—the very premise of *A Nightmare on Elm Street*, in which a child molester and murderer's spirit lurks within the dreams of the teenage offspring whose parents burned and killed him in vengeance twenty years earlier, warrants a greater artistic license. Part-fantasy, part-horror, the films are free to move beyond the plane of conscious reality, partially taking place in surrealistic dream worlds where anything is possible and the chance for escape is slim. Sleeping, after all, is a necessary part of one's life, and it's only a matter of time before we all must succumb to it.

Getting a studio to agree to finance writer-director Wes Craven's dream project was no small feat. In an era when the horror genre widely consisted of flesh-and-blood psychopaths picking off kids in everyday surroundings, *A Nightmare on Elm Street* proposed to take this convention to a fresh, imaginative level, introducing a supernatural killer who was only able to claim his victims after the lights were out and their eyes were closed. Enter New Line Cinema, an upstart company that had nothing to lose and everything to gain by taking a gamble on Craven's idea. A surprise financial success, the original film not only began a lucrative franchise for the studio, but it more or less established their presence among the Paramounts and Universals of Hollywood.

Even taking into account Freddy Krueger's increased wisecracking ways as the 1980s pressed on, *A Nightmare on Elm Street* has not lost any of its unquenchable power and ingenuity in the intervening years. Dark and forbidding, chilling and refreshingly non-jokey, the picture takes seriously its fantastical plot and treats its characters, particularly resourceful lead heroine Nancy Thompson (Heather Langenkamp), with an empathy and fairness that was often missing from teen movies of that time period. His scarred face hidden mostly in shadows, his red-and-green sweater and the screeching of his handmade fingerknives along metal taking visual and aural prominence, Freddy Krueger remains a ghastly spectral figure throughout. He is, indeed, precisely what nightmares are made of.

15-year-old Tina Gray (Amanda Wyss) has begun having vivid, restless dreams of a mysterious man stalking her. Afraid to be alone when her single mother heads out of town with her newest schlub of a boyfriend, she invites best friend Nancy and Nancy's nice-guy boyfriend, Glen (Johnny Depp), to spend the night with her. When Tina's own leather-clad boyfriend, Rod (Jsu Garcia), shows up, they retire to the bedroom. Before the night is over, Freddy will come to Tina's sleep once more, this time brutally clawing her to death. Rod is arrested for the crime, but Nancy is sure that he didn't do it. She, too, has been having bad dreams of the same man Tina described, and is adamant about getting to the bottom of who he is and how to stop him before she and the rest of her friends wind up dead.

A Nightmare on Elm Street masterfully blends authentic teen life and experiences—relationships with the opposite sex, the demands of school, and, for Nancy, dealing with a mother (Ronee Blakley) who is slipping deeper and deeper into alcoholism—with intermittent flights of horrifying fancy. The dream sequences, which require memorable but not overpunishing special effects, are the horror centerpieces. Tina's final sleep, where she is called out of her house and into the dank alleyways by a long-armed, finger-slicing Krueger, is freakishly riveting, as is another scene where Nancy dozes off in her English class and follows a body-bagged Tina into the school's basement boiler room.

One of the scariest moments is also one of its subtlest; when Nancy bumps into a scowling female classmate with a nosebleed (really Krueger in disguise), she receives a mischievous warning. "Hey, Nancy," the girl says in Freddy's deep-throated voice, her fingerknives scraping together, "no running in the hallways." Other details, as when Nancy runs up her stairs and her feet sink into holes of sticky white goo, or when she falls asleep in the bathtub and is yanked under the water by Freddy's hand, display a creativity and truth about the randomness that we all tend to dream about.

The climactic one-on-one battle between Nancy and Freddy—having set up boobytraps all over her house, she plans to grab hold and pull him out of her dream—strains a bit of credibility with its coincidences and flawed timeframe. The ending is also left open to interpretation and is a little confusing—was it all just a dream, and if not, then why are characters who have died suddenly alive again?—but this is a minor quibble to a film that takes chances and creates an appropriately thick veil of anxiety. The cinematography by Jacques Haitkin (who would work with Wes Craven again in 1989's *Shocker*) is innovative and atmospheric, and the superb music score by Charles Bernstein (also responsible for 1986's *April Fool's Day*) uses synthesizers and creepy sound effects to nerve-jangling effect.

Heather Langenkamp makes Nancy her own. A cute girl-next-door type—in one of the few unintentionally funny lines of dialogue, she gazes at herself in the mirror and remarks that she looks (gasp!) twenty years old—Nancy sticks to her values, isn't afraid to stand up for herself, and becomes exceedingly inventive in her path to stopping the monster haunting her dreams. As Nancy's worried, not-all-together mother, Marge, Ronee Blakley does a fine job essaying a boozy woman paying the price years later for the violent murder she had a hand in committing. John Saxon has less to do as Nancy's sheriff father, Lt. Thompson, but has several good moments with his daughter that help to build their fractured relationship (he has moved out of the house). And, in a film debut that would lead to one of the most coveted careers in Hollywood, Johnny Depp is characteristically charismatic as Nancy's boyfriend, Glen. His demise, involving a bed and a river of blood being catapulted to the ceiling, is still one of the most unforgettable screen deaths in cinema history.

As often occurs in low-budget features, some of the acting around the fringes is slightly amateurish, and the ending suggests post-production tinkering, but *A Nightmare on Elm Street* works gangbusters in all the ways it really counts. Terrifically spooky and original—at the point in which the movie was made, there had never been anything like it—the film continues to feel completely modern despite being well over a quarter-century old (for this reason, the weak 2009 remake was unnecessary in the extreme). In veteran actor Robert Englund, whose name would become synonymous with his character, he would be responsible for bringing to life a horror villain as iconic to the 1980s zeitgeist as any other in memory. Freddy Krueger was never more palpably sinister than in the first (and best) *A Nightmare on Elm Street*.

A Nightmare on Elm Street Part 2: Freddy's Revenge

1985 - Directed by Jack Sholder

As is the prevalent case with most sequels, *A Nightmare on Elm Street Part 2: Freddy's Revenge* is inferior to its predecessor. It is still very, very good, however, more so than most viewers give it credit for. And, in its own way, it is just as groundbreaking, as wealthy in substance and downright courageous as any horror film released in the mid-'80s. Taking over for Wes Craven, director Jack Sholder and screenwriter David Chaskin opted to not repeat the formula of *A Nightmare on Elm Street*, but take it in a notably different direction. It still has Freddy Krueger as its central opposing figure, but otherwise is the *Halloween III: Season of the Witch*-style black sheep of the series. Its moment in the spotlight is long overdue.

Set five years after the events of the first film, 16-year-old Jesse Walsh (Mark Patton) has moved with his family—iron-fisted father Ken (Clu Gulager), doting mother Cheryl (Hope Lange), and precocious little sis Angela (Christie Clark)—into the residence on Elm Street formerly lived in by Nancy and Marge Thompson. The infamous legend of Freddy Krueger would seem to have faded completely if not for one hitch: tossing and turning in an overheated sleep state brought about by the house's faltering air-conditioning system, Jesse has begun to dream about him. Itching to break free into the real world, Freddy wants to take over Jesse's body and have him do his murderous bidding. Without a detectable way of stopping him, suddenly no one in Jesse's life—among them, friends Lisa (Kim Myers) and Grady (Robert Russler), and hardass gym teacher Coach Schneider (Marshall Bell)—is safe from Freddy's wrath.

A Nightmare on Elm Street Part 2: Freddy's Revenge opens with a stunner of a prologue, as Jesse and two catty teenage girls are terrorized on a runaway school bus with no way of escape after the ground falls out from beneath the vehicle. This is all just a dream, of course, but the first to signal to Jesse that something strange is afoot. As his nightmares intensify and the mystery surrounding Freddy's identity and past are clarified through a diary written by Nancy that Lisa finds in his bedroom closet, Jesse is faced with the frightening realization that he may no longer be in control of his body.

It is at this point that the film itself goes down a path far removed from simple, cookie-cutter horror fare. Jesse's friendship with Lisa—"he's just my ride to school," Lisa defensively says when pal Kerry (Sydney Walsh) presses her on their relationship—appears to be building toward a romance, but it is one that Jesse doesn't seem all that interested in. He is more in his skin when hanging out with hunky male classmate Grady, whom he semi-regularly shares afterschool detention with on the sports field, lorded over by the skeevy Coach Schneider. Plagued with bouts of sleepwalking, a partially clothed Jesse leaves his house in the pouring rain and ends up having a drink at the local gay bar. It is here that he runs into leathered S&M enthusiast Coach Schneider, who bizarrely takes him back to the high school to run laps. In the locker room showers afterwards, Freddy enters Jesse and serves up a setpiece that is unmistakable in its homoerotically charged inferences. Seeking safety from all forms of balls telepathically flying his way, Schneider runs into the locker room, where he is stripped down, tied up with jump ropes, and bloodily whipped on the bare backside by towels.

Keeping in mind all the evidence in between and what has come shortly before this curious sequence—Jesse dances in his bedroom to "Touch Me (All Night Long") by Wish (feat. Fonda Rae), the sign on his door reading, "No Out-of-Town Chicks"—and it becomes obvious that the film isn't really about Freddy Krueger at all, but about a confused teenage boy unsuccessfully trying to come to terms with his sexuality. At the pool party Lisa throws in the third act, Jesse feels out of place and seeks refuge in the cabana. Lisa comes in to comfort him, and they have an awkward sexual encounter that abruptly ends when he runs out on her and heads to Grady's house. Here, Jesse pleads for Grady's help—"something is trying to get inside of me!"—his friend more than a little confused why Jesse has abandoned Lisa and shown up to spend the night in his bedroom.

The picture eventually returns to its horror roots, with Jesse (in the form of Freddy) attacking Lisa at her home before crashing the party out back—in a portentous segment, Freddy raises his arms before a crowd of scared teens and says, "You are all my children now." The climax culminates at the creaky abandoned factory Freddy used to work at before his death, with Lisa following Jesse there and adamantly telling him that he has to fight to stop the urges inside him. In the end, a surprising shock that harkens back to the school bus opening confirms that Jesse's fight with Freddy (symbolic of his homosexual urges that are a part of him, and that he cannot run away from) is far from over.

Viewed strictly on the surface, *A Nightmare on Elm Street Part 2: Freddy's Revenge* is a well-made and suspenseful possession-laden thriller that drops some of the rules distinguished by the first *A Nightmare on Elm Street* in order to avoid being a mere lazy redux. Performances from Mark Patton, strongly cast as protagonist Jesse, and Kim Myers, emanating sweetness and light as Lisa, help to make accessible the story's leaps in logic. For all of this, the movie is more than admirable. For its underlying message about sexual oppression in a cynical world, though, the film endeavors to go one step deeper. Psychology majors could have a field day with *A Nightmare on Elm Street Part 2: Freddy's Revenge*. So much is left to open-ended interpretation that it couldn't have possibly been by accident that the picture plays not only as slasher fantasy, but as poignantly felt coming-of-age story in which the hero's complicated struggles to find himself and be accepted by others aren't so easily wrapped up with a tidy ribbon.

Night of the Demons

1988 - Directed by Kevin S. Tenney

Dexterous, savvy and in some ways ahead of its time (the '80s hairstyles and fashions are not two of those ways), *Night of the Demons* is a teenage possession flick that also works as stylish slasher fodder and as a guide to Halloween myths and traditions. Director Kevin S. Tenney displays impressive ambition in creating a definite mood and identity to the piece, starting with a lovingly rendered animated opening credits sequence—practically unheard of in the annals of low-budget horror releases—scored to the memorable, propulsive synthesizer chords of Dennis Michael Tenney's music score. What his few unpolished actors occasionally lack in thespian prowess, Tenney and screenwriter Joe Augustyn make up for with a barrage of imaginative ideas and tight pacing that lift the film well above the norm.

As the live-action movie proper begins, the viewer is inundated with the calling cards of the holiday, from pumpkins, to costumes, to prankish scares, to candy and seasonal appetizers, to television specials (1936's vintage cartoon short, *The Cobweb Hotel,* makes an appearance), to parties, and so on. Speaking of parties, Angela (Amelia Kinkade) is hosting one at Hull House, a spooky abandoned funeral parlor at the edge of town. In attendance are demure, sweet-natured Judy (Cathy Podewell) and her date, player Jay (Lance Fenton); Judy's ex-boyfriend, Sal (Billy Gallo); Judy's fun-loving friend, Frannie (Jill Terashita) and her boyfriend, Max (Philip Tanzini); Angela's guy-crazy best friend, Suzanne (Linnea Quigley), and the odd trio of loud-mouthed, piggish Stooge (Hal Havins) and superstitious Helen (Allison Barron) and Rodger (Alvin Alexis). Dancing and good times at the cobwebbed mansion lead to a séance where, lo and behold, they manage to stir up the demonic forces living on the property. As the characters scatter around the house, they one by one fall victim to Angela, possessed by the spirits and set on transforming the rest of them into minions of Hell, too.

Night of the Demons is funny in an anything-goes way, but also rather exciting when the action sets in and Judy and Rodger are chased through the dark hallways of the house by a fast-multiplying population of demons. That one of the heroes of the piece is black, well-educated and not treated as a victim or comic relief is pretty groundbreaking—and admirable—for its time. As sensitively played by Alvin Alexis, the pirate-costumed Rodger is one of the most positive portrayals of an African-American in a horror movie in memory. As Judy, dressed as the title character from *Alice in Wonderland*, Cathy Podewell (who would go on to play Cally Ewing on TV's *Dallas*) is attractive, dignified (she stands up for herself when Jay pressures sex on her), and sweet as apple pie. These two, bonding as would-be victims might if being hunted by demons, are protagonists worth rooting for.

As Suzanne, '80s-horror staple Linnea Quigley embraces her eye-candy status and character's flaky persona while also, in the picture's most infamous scene, disrobing on cue and turning titillation into terror when she does something unthinkable with a tube of lipstick. Quigley has never been the best of actresses, but she has used her assets to the benefit of an enduring B-movie career. And, as head villain Angela, Amelia Kinkade (who would reprise the character in the hugely inferior 1994 and 1997 sequels) is creepy as a possessed Goth chick who performs a strobe-lit dance to Bauhaus' "Stigmata Martyr" and really means it when she toasts her hands by the fire. The make-up effects by longtime ace designer Steve Johnson greatly contribute to the atmosphere, bringing to rotting, malevolent life the demons of the title.

The tattered, haunted-house production design by Ken Aichele never really looks like anything but sets on a studio lot, but it is a detailed feast to gaze upon all the same. Cinematography by David Lewis is top-notch, making indelible use of shadows, intricately set-up reflections in broken glass, and a superior tracking shot that barrels through the interior of the funeral parlor. Special effects are generally chintzy, but that's to be expected for the decade in which it was made. *Night of the Demons* doesn't have anything of importance to say and offers no deep messages. Instead, it's got violence, sex, nudity and a good-humored script. There are all different types of genre films, and this one was purely made to entertain. Its technical and creative savvy is but a plus on the scorecard, and its wraparound sequence, involving a grouchy old man who has the tables turned on him when he slips razorblades in the trick-or-treaters' apples, is a bewitchingly grim capper. *Night of the Demons* isn't free of flaws, but it is practically dripping with the blood, sweat and tears of those who set out to make a genuinely good party movie, and they did exactly that.

Nosferatu

1922 - Directed by F.W. Murnau

Vampires are as large a part of the horror—and, sadly, teen romance—landscape as any other form of cinematic villain. Long since gone mainstream and enduring over the decades, fanged bloodsuckers have been further popularized through modern fiction writing by Anne Rice (e.g., *Interview with the Vampire, Queen of the Damned, The Vampire Lestat*), Stephen King (e.g., *Salem's Lot,* short stories *The Night Flier* and *Popsy*) and Stephenie Meyer (The *Twilight* series), as well as on television (Alan Ball's HBO series, *True Blood,* and "The V Word" episode of Showtime's anthology series, *Masters of Horror*). Before them all was Bram Stoker's classic 1897 novel, *Dracula*, loosely based on the real-life case of Vlad the Impaler, and the first film out of the gate to be (unofficially) adapted from that work was 1922's *Nosferatu*.

A landmark motion picture—in addition to being one of the first horror movies to delve into the mythology of vampirism, it's one of the first horror movies, period—*Nosferatu* still holds up surprisingly well. Taking into account that it is of the silent era, and that subsequent horror films were able to learn from this one and mold more effective ways of frightening an audience through the evolving conventions of the genre, *Nosferatu* is not so much scary anymore as it is a valuable milestone in the history of cinema. It is additionally a fascinating study of mood and carefully constructed *mise-en-scène*, using chiaroscuric shadows, mirrors and a gloom-induced set design to weave a weighty sense of impending doom.

Hutter (Gustav von Wangenheim) is a bright-minded realtor living in the peaceful town of Wisborg, Germany. When his shady boss, Knock (Alexander Granach), tells him that Count Orlok (Max Schreck) is interested in buying property in their cozy community, Hutter packs his bags, leaves worried wife Ellen (Greta Schröder) with friends, and sets off for Transylvania. Once welcomed into Orlok's castle, buried deep within the Carpathian Mountains, Hutter senses that something isn't quite right with his host. When he accidentally cuts his finger at dinner, Orlok grabs his hand and sucks the blood away. Sleeping all day and awake at all hours of the night, the Count eventually signs the necessary papers and sets out for his new home in Wisborg. Stowing away on a ship with his coffin and claiming the lives of the captain and his crew, Orlok finally arrives in town—an event that few seem to notice as fear of an invading plague sweeps over the village. Ellen, however, whose feverish sleep has led to sleepwalking and psychic visions, has stumbled upon her husband's book about vampires, and knows that the only way to stop the evil is for a woman to willingly sacrifice herself.

Nosferatu is a film that almost wasn't. When German expressionist director F.W. Murnau chose to adapt *Dracula* without permission, changing the characters' names but otherwise unmistakably following the narrative of Bram Stoker's tale, Stoker's widow was none too pleased when she found out. She consequently sued Murnau and demanded that all copies of the picture be destroyed—an order that obviously was not carried through. The film fortunately survived, becoming a vital bridge between cinema's heyday and the horror genre that would follow.

By present-day standards, *Nosferatu* is tame. Violence is largely inferred rather than shown, and the only blood glimpsed is on Hutter's finger when he slices it with a knife. Acting, as was customary in silent films, is animated, boasting exaggerated emotions as a means of making up for words that cannot be audibly spoken. Dialogue, of course, is relegated to intertitles. There is a poeticism and innocence to this antiquated format, though, one that sadly has been all but forgotten (or never learned at all) by modern generations.

Watching *Nosferatu* in the twenty-first century, what stands out is Murnau's keen filmmaking sense. Special effects to represent the sun rising, or doors opening by themselves, are simplistic but savvy, and his back-and-forth cutting between places and characters far apart from each other within the same scene is ahead of its time. Murnau also intriguingly suggests how paranoia can overtake a population of people—the residents of Wisborg mistake a plague for Orlok's murderous vampiric power over them—and further clearly articulates the fight between the pure and tainted halves of one's human nature. His stark yet inevitable climax, wherein Count Orlok's hunched body and long, twig-like fingers are personified by the shadows of him walking up a staircase and reaching for a doorknob to claim his latest victim, remains indelible and disquieting.

Mentioning Max Schreck's unforgettable portrayal of Count Orlok serves as a fitting final word on *Nosferatu*. Whereas vampires usually are viewed as seductive, dangerous creatures whose sexuality goes hand in hand with their need for blood, Orlok is just as grotesque on the outside as he is on the inside. That his insatiable hunger prevails despite his off-putting demeanor lends the film an added macabre touch missing from future vampire stories. Schreck doesn't so much play the character as he seemingly becomes him. It is because of him, above all else, that ensures *Nosferatu* will live on in the annals of horror's history forever.

November

2005 - Directed by Greg Harrison

An official 2004 selection at the Sundance Film Festival (where it deservedly won the Best Cinematography award), *November* is a compact 73-minute masterpiece. An awesomely constructed puzzle of a movie that, when finished interlocking all of its carefully woven pieces, creates a deeper and more three-dimensionally substantive whole than originally expected, director Greg Harrison has made a dream picture for both psych majors and anyone with a taste for more offbeat, narratively complex fare reminiscent of David Lynch's abstract storytelling.

November will not be easily digestible for mainstream audiences who require things spelled out for them, but step back and run through the scenes and details in your mind once it's over and the film begins to make perfect sense. Because of that valuable element of unknowing that Harrison relies so heavily on to garner intrigue for the duration of the running time, it is difficult to discuss what is real, what is symbolic, what is imagined, and what is dreamed—if, in fact, anything is. What can be said is that screenwriter Benjamin Brand has developed a beautifully intricate maze of scenes, all faultlessly conceived and placed, never cheating his audience or getting too showy and cute. Each moment has a distinct purpose, and they collectively paint a heartrending portrait of the difficult grieving process and the unpredictable frailty of each singular life.

In a significant departure from the lighter work she usually receives, Courteney Cox is mesmerizing in an understandably low-key way as Sophie Jacobs, a somewhat mousy photographer and college professor having a difficult time coming to terms with the untimely murder of her boyfriend, Hugh (James LeGros), during a convenience store robbery. The therapist Sophie has just begun seeing, Dr. Fayn (Nora Dunn), believes her recent headaches might be due to the guilt she feels for secretly cheating on Hugh in the month preceding the tragic incident. Her mother, Carol (Anne Archer), advises that she make a fresh start beginning with a new haircut when all Sophie wants to do is find Hugh's killer. And, during a slide presentation given by one of her students, she is horrified to discover a stray picture in the machine taken outside the convenience store on the night of the murders, complete with Sophie's car parked in the foreground and a figure inside the window that might be Hugh. Who took the picture? Is someone stalking her, or just trying to drive her crazy? As the circumstances grow ever more surreal, the film backs up twice more, portraying the robbery and its aftermath in very different ways as Sophie herself moves closer to the truth.

Separated into three sections, each with its own title card—"Denial," "Despair" and "Acceptance"—that clarify themselves by the devastating final sequence, *November* begins for the first forty minutes or so as a classic mind-bender of a psychological thriller that is creepier and more harrowing than anything found in most straight horror movies. There is an unshakable feeling of voyeurism in what Harrison fills his scenes with, making such potentially banal settings as a classroom, a restaurant and an average-looking apartment ominous beacons of threat. Paying close attention to every frame can only work in the viewer's favor, as the first hour or so is overflowing with details and happenings big and small that eventually reveal an ingenious master plan.

As Sophie, Courteney Cox is outstanding in a difficult performance of quietly simmering guilt, fear and regret that is ready to explode at any time. She is onscreen from the first scene onward, and carries it off by creating a very real, distinguishable character that will instantly make one forget she was ever Monica Geller on TV's *Friends*. This is what stretching as an actress and working because of passion is all about, and it has paid off handsomely for an actress smartly looking to move in different creative directions (the film's entire production budget was a measly $150,000, or roughly one-sixth of what used to be Cox's one-episode salary on *Friends*). As Sophie's devoted boyfriend Hugh, the invaluable James LeGros is so charismatic opposite Cox that the two of them fulfill exactly what was intended—a cerebral, dread-filled tale that is also a lyrical and tragic love story, their relationship, for various reasons left to be discovered, cut dramatically short. Other supporting cast members are strong in small roles, with Nora Dunn, as Sophie's concerned therapist; Anne Archer, as Sophie's mother, and Nick Offerman, as Officer Roberts, whom Sophie confides in about the robbery-murder investigation.

Masterful digital photography by Nancy Schreiber, the deep blues, blacks and reds popping off the screen to suffocate Sophie's imploding surroundings (each section has its own color scheme), and a grimly memorable music score by Lew Baldwin that is perfectly mixed with the movie's tricky juggling of sound and silence, are the final chess pieces in a one-part disturbingly abstruse, one-part emotionally sublime motion picture of stunning eloquence and wisdom. Director Greg Harrison knows and captures the feeling of loss and the sense of something being taken away in startlingly understated and honest ways that make his movie more than just a study in style. *November* is a film reaffirming that ideas and creativity more often than not are found in the smaller releases that, for one reason or another, big studios have passed on in favor of the umpteenth television-to-feature remake and pointless sequel. It is the real deal, subtle and alarming and touching and profound and unforgettable all at once, its enigmatic aspects scrupulously chipping away at the viewer's consciousness via airtight filmmaking and pure force of will. The entire experience is something of a revelation.

Orphan

2009 - Directed by Jaume Collet-Serra

Prospective viewers who believe they have seen enough scary movies about evil children to last a lifetime will be forced to eat their words after watching *Orphan*, a deliciously macabre humdinger of a horror film that puts a skin-crawlingly ingenious spin on what may seem at first sight like hackneyed material. As the idiom goes, the devil's in the details, and director Jaume Collet-Serra (2005's underrated *House of Wax*), along with astute first-time screenwriter David Leslie Johnson, are certainly up to the challenge in twisting expectations while building upon critical elements, like character development, a palpable foreboding, and provocative subtexts, often missing from modern mainstream genre fare. Once all the mysteries are sorted out and revealed, it is safe to say no one will be able to claim they have seen this picture's devious bag of tricks before.

Kate Coleman (Vera Farmiga) has been having nightmares of the stillborn birth of her daughter, masked doctors and proudly videotaping husband John (Peter Sarsgaard) cheerfully going about the delivery as if it were normal to present a mother with the shriveled, blood-drenched corpse of her new baby. During her wakeful hours, Kate's life isn't quite so traumatic. A dedicated mother to son Daniel (Jimmy Bennett) and mostly deaf daughter Max (Aryana Engineer), Kate is a recovering alcoholic one year sober, visiting a therapist (Margo Martindale) every week and attempting as best she can to make amends for her mistakes and move on with her life. Still, Kate senses that there is a missing hole still waiting to be filled, and her and John's decision to adopt sounds like a good way to do that.

Upon visiting the St. Mariana Home for Girls, Kate and John are drawn to Russian-born 9-year-old Esther (Isabelle Fuhrman), keeping to herself as she practices her painting skills in an otherwise empty upstairs classroom. Three weeks later, Kate and John are welcoming home the newest addition to their family. Extremely well-mannered and insisting upon wearing dressy clothes and ribbons in her hair and around her neck at all times, Esther is a little quirky, but that is to be expected for a child who has had such a tough go of things. The more time Kate spends with Esther, however, the more she begins to question how little they actually know about her and her past.

An unnerving psychological thriller with the atmospheric elegance of classics like 1968's *Rosemary's Baby*, 1973's *Don't Look Now*, and 1980's *Dressed to Kill*, *Orphan* is meticulous in its blends of style and substance, violence and mayhem. With the exception of one or two predictable jump scares, director Jaume Collet-Serra bypasses the negative trends and clichés that tarnish most studio-produced horror filmmaking and instead concentrates on the very real struggles, both internal and external, of its characters as they are faced with a terrifying mounting situation. Because Collet-Serra spends time with the Coleman family and all the different relationships within it—there is a beautiful bedtime scene, so gentle and poignant, where Kate reads a children's book to Max that explains what happened to her deceased younger sister—the viewer feels genuinely invested in them by the time Esther enters the equation.

For a while, Esther is utterly charming, a dream come true who is well-behaved, wise beyond her years, and delights in singing "The Glory of Love." When she pushes bratty, mean-spirited classmate Brenda (Jamie Young) off the playground equipment, the viewer stays on her side; Brenda, we believe, had it coming to her, what with her snot-nosed remarks about Esther's wardrobe and her cruel destruction of her Bible. With the torn-up shreds of the religious tome, a grave miscommunication between right and wrong is unleashed, if not literally than certainly between the lines and in the face of a spiritual teacher who ultimately become the first murder victim. This, it would appear, is not merely coincidence on Collet-Serra's part. As Esther plays mind games with Kate, Max and Daniel, in their own private ways being seriously threatened and blackmailed with their lives, she moves all the closer to John, who doubts the severity of his adopted daughter's troubles and starts questioning his wife's own mental health.

From 1956's *The Bad Seed*, to 1976's *The Omen* (skip the terrible 2006 remake), to 1992's *Mikey*, to 1993's *The Good Son*, to 2007's *Joshua*, to the terrific 2009 British chiller, *The Children*, there has been no lack in motion pictures serving to turn the angelic innocence of childhood into examples of demonic manifestations and old-fashioned antisocial behavior. Superficially, *Orphan* does not break fresh ground except for in the graphic viciousness with which Esther is capable. The trajectory of the plot goes about as expected up to a certain point, then reveals added layers heretofore gone unseen. Esther's surgical intelligence, from a scene where her sisterly bond with the hearing-impaired Max is revealed for the ruse it is to another scene where pre-teen Daniel is intimidated in ways unimagined, are destined to shock the viewer as much as they send a shiver down his or her spine. The cruelest actions, however, are saved for Kate, with Esther toying with her where she knows it will sting, pulling flowers in the family's greenhouse that signify the spirit of their late daughter and calling attention to the fact that her other children do not—and, in Max's case, cannot—share her love of music. The disappointments and regrets that go along with being a parent and raising children who aren't quite the fantasy picture of who he or she had in mind are faced with an unblinking straightforwardness. So, too, is the prolonged aftermath of something as disturbing as losing a child during birth, and Kate's subsequent battle throughout between the love for her family and her own personal demons.

The performances are as impressive as the bold, sleek cinematography by Jeff Cutter and frosty, snowswept Ontario surroundings (standing in for New England). Vera Farmiga brings both a ferocious desperation and heartbreaking fragility to Kate, a mother and wife whose protectiveness of her family is at odds with John's growing mistrust in her. As John, Peter Sarsgaard gives depth to a comparatively underwritten part that requires he doubt Kate's warnings about Esther. John's beliefs, while frustrating for the viewer, are also plausible; we must remember that, from his point of view, Esther has done nothing wrong and given off no signs to him that she is troubled. As the initially jealous, soon imperiled Daniel, Jimmy Bennett racks up another professional turn from an already impressive résumé, and newcomer Aryana Engineer genuinely impresses as Max. Engineer, hearing-impaired in real life as well as in the picture, is a total natural without an ounce of kid-actor unctuousness.

The star attraction of *Orphan* also happens to deliver one of the most momentous examples of acting from a child performer in years. From her freckled, perfectly coiffed brunette appearance, to her flawless Eastern European accent, to her ability to switch from sympathetic to ice-cold to veritably creepy in the same breath, Isabelle Fuhrman is astonishing as Esther. Not merely a one-note villain, Esther is a complex creation whose motives are subject to interpretation and whose secrets, when discovered, do nothing if not haunt the viewer's conscience. Fuhrman understands the part through and through—all the more amazing for a 12-year-old—and presents a fascinating case study for a probably incurable diseased mind. If Linda Blair and Jodie Foster warranted Oscar nominations for 1973's *The Exorcist* and 1976's *Taxi Driver*, respectively, then it is quite the shame that Isabelle Fuhrman did not receive the same recognition.

With Esther's artistic aspirations and preternatural sexual blossoming additionally paying off in disturbing ways by the end, the questions of who this girl is and where she comes from loom over the proceedings. The answers will dare not be revealed—the central revelation is as inventive and unpredictable as it is truly horrifying, reminding one of the effectiveness of seeing 1999's *The Sixth Sense* for the first time—but they shine a newfound light on all that has come before, demanding a second viewing in the process. Brave in the places it goes and more than commendable in its refusal to shy away from difficult, controversial subject matter, *Orphan* is hard to shake and impossible to deny its effectiveness. An original thought in Hollywood is rare in a world of borrowed ideas and remakes galore, but story creator Alex Mace, writer David Leslie Johnson and director Jaume Collet-Serra have achieved just that. It's worth celebrating.

The Orphanage

2007 - Directed by Juan Antonio Bayona

In 2009, *The Orphanage* (released as *El Orfanato* in its native Spain) comfortably joined the ranks of 2001's *The Others* and 2005's *Dark Water* as one of the superior cinematic ghost stories of its decade. Going above and beyond the empty-headed, boo-laden trappings that plague many films within the genre, *The Orphanage* is first and foremost a weighty, at times agonizing, existential study of the delicacy of life, the mystification of death, and the knowledge of one's own mortality. It is also very, very scary—boy, is it scary—but the frights go much deeper than the things-that-go-bump-in-the-night variety, and actually are there to service the story rather than the other way around.

Laura (Belén Rueda) and husband Carlos (Fernando Cayo) have just moved with 7-year-old adopted son Simón (Roger Príncep) to the long-abandoned seaside orphanage that she stayed at as a child. Their goal is to offer a spacious and loving home for special needs children, something near and dear to their heart as they struggle to come to terms with Simón's illness (he is HIV-positive). As Laura and Carlos grapple with telling him about his condition, Simón learns the truth through a new group of imaginary friends he meets in a nearby cove. When he suddenly goes missing without a trace and Laura, distraught over the disappearance, starts hearing eerie sounds within the house, she begins to consider the possibility that Simón's friends weren't a figment of his imagination after all.

Upon release, *The Orphanage* was touted as the new film from director Guillermo Del Toro, a sneaky marketing ploy to reel in the same audience won over by his own 2006 hit, *Pan's Labyrinth*. While fans of that adult fantasy will surely appreciate what *The Orphanage* has to offer, in actuality Del Toro merely produces while fresh new filmmaker Juan Antonio Bayona takes the helm. What Bayona has crafted is nothing short of entrancing, a rapturously gripping and superbly taut horror film that garners a lot of its lingering impact through its story of a desperate woman who refuses to accept the loss of a child while doing everything in her power to locate his whereabouts. In doing so, she gradually is forced into considering the limitless possibilities of life (a different realm of life, but still a life) proceeding death. Further thought-provoking themes emerge, too, including the not always ideal actions people sometimes take toward others and the regret and guilt that go along with not being afforded the chance to do things differently.

Bayona keeps a tight-fisted grip on the revelatory, multilayered narrative, in full control over the emotions he elicits at any given moment. Drenched in threatening moodiness and an unshakable sense of impending despair, the picture's human element nonetheless is not overpowered by these things. Still, one cannot deny how chilling the production is. By retaining a subtle tone up until the slightly too-on-the-nose final minute or two, comparatively innocuous moments, such as the loose flapping of a shed door, a masquerade party, and the image of a small figure standing before an enveloping cave in the distance, take on an off-balance and jittery life of their own. More obvious attempts at shocks, such as the grisly aftermath of an auto accident or the slamming of a closet door by a possibly spectral force, are additionally so expertly achieved that they feel new again.

In virtually every scene, Belén Rueda is mesmerizing as Laura, never playing the emotions too broadly while rawly emanating from every look given and piece of dialogue spoken the sheer tragedy befalling a woman who sees the life she has built for herself crumbling down around her. As young Simón, Roger Príncep is a fine child actor, natural and touching in his relationship with mother Laura; when he exits before the midway point, the viewer feels his loss and, along with Laura, actively yearns to uncover what has happened to him. Also memorable is Geraldine Chaplin, who steals her screen time in the colorful supporting role of a medium called upon to investigate the supernatural presence Laura insists is in their home.

Hauntingly shot by Óscar Faura, every frame composed with the precision of a photograph, *The Orphanage* is a distinctly affecting psychological drama that also works splendidly as a shiver-inducing horror tale. The oceanside setting (complete with rocky cliffs, sandy beaches and a lighthouse) and the desolate title location are characters unto themselves, drawing the strong-willed but fallible Laura into an ever-terrifying web that may provide her with answers she is not prepared to learn. Movies such as *The Orphanage* do not frequently come around, and they should be applauded for what they achieve. One minute the viewer may be shrinking down in his or her seat or startled with a jump, and the next he or she might be fighting off the urge to shed a tear. It's fun to be scared, especially when a film has the mind and intelligence to back it up.

The Others

2001 - Directed by Alejandro Amenábar

The Others, directed by Alejandro Amenábar, is a gorgeously woven motion picture that manages to be as emotionally rewarding as it is genuinely spine-chilling. An eloquent and deeply affecting ghost story, the film bears a superficial resemblance to 1999's *The Sixth Sense*, yet distances itself from that equally fine movie by imposing upon the viewer its own personal layers of shivering atmosphere and signs of approaching dread that could only be classified as its own.

Set almost entirely within a mansion on Britain's Channel Islands, circa 1945, Grace (Nicole Kidman) is a stringently religious woman living with her two precocious children, Anne (Alakina Mann) and Nicholas (James Bentley). With a husband (Christopher Eccleston) presumably lost amidst the horrors of World War II, she is greeted one day at the door by three people who have come to act as her servants—kindly, no-nonsense Mrs. Mills (Fionnula Flanagan); reserved Mr. Tuttle (Eric Sykes), and young, mute Lydia (Elaine Cassidy). Grace promptly explains to them that Anne and Nicholas have a rare photosensitive disorder that bars them from ever being exposed to sunlight, and so whenever they enter a room, the curtains must be closed on all the windows and each door must be locked before opening another. As they begin to settle down into a pattern of normalcy, Anne refuses to keep quiet about her sightings of others hiding in the house, which she labels "intruders." A devout Catholic, Grace refuses to believe her daughter's seemingly made-up stories until she, too, starts having frightening experiences that gradually lead her to believe in the existence of otherworldly entities.

The remarkably fascinating achievements permeating throughout *The Others* are due solely to Alejandro Amenábar, who not only has directed the film—his first English-language feature—but also written the multidimensional screenplay and composed the subtly chilling music score. As a classic horror picture, *The Others* is the best kind, weaving its spell in a deliberately slow fashion that penetratingly involves the audience in its central characters and their unfortunate plight. The film is without overt violence or bloodshed, but one-ups these elements by creating a masterful ambiance of both mood and unshakable trepidation that is far more haunting than the sight of a masked killer hacking away at a pretty teenaged cast.

If *The Others* is an example of sheer cathartic artistry, then it excels even more as it maturely grapples with themes of faith and religion. Most intriguing of all is the beliefs which Grace possesses—beliefs that she starts to question as the circumstances within her home grow progressively more dire. Teaching her children about the Bible, Grace assuredly discusses its topics with the directness of a person who is positive what she believes is true. Grace is very serious about her Catholicism, so, when things begin occurring that contradict everything she has ever learned and studied, it is all the more distressing. Serious faith-based issues are rarely tackled head-on in the horror genre, and the fact that this one does only allows for a more wholly satisfying experience. The movie is scary fun, to be sure, but also offers up various stimulating evocations that raise it up a few notches further.

For Nicole Kidman, 2001 was a banner year for the actress, who starred in a pair of very different critically lauded and financially successful films that also, incidentally, marked two of her career-best performances. In *Moulin Rouge*, she played her part—that of a high-spirited, dreamy courtesan unknowingly dying of tuberculosis—to perfection while revealing a glorious singing voice. With *The Others*, Kidman is more emotionally unhinged, more serious, more insecure about the entire world around her. Easily the star attraction as she inhabits almost every scene, Kidman rises to the challenge, passionately portraying Grace as a woman who is as internally weak as she is externally strong. As Grace's children, Anne and Nicholas, newcomers Alakina Mann and James Bentley are extraordinary. It is rare to get so much unblinking reality and nuances out of child performers, especially those making their acting debuts, but Bentley and, especially, Mann are the real deal. Their roles are not easy, either, with Mann wisely projecting a childlike playfulness with an air of stern maturity beyond her years.

With lush cinematography from Javier Aguirresarobe, who excels in giving the surroundings a dank, eerie feel that perfectly complements the desolate, fog-enshrouded outdoors, *The Others* is a marvelous entertainment with a depth that gives viewers a little something extra to chew on long after the end credits have rolled. While one of the climactic twists isn't terribly surprising, the final corkscrew in the plot is nearly impossible to predict, and also ingenious. Kudos must go out to Amenábar, whose expertise and intelligence help to make *The Others* more than "just another supernatural thriller." It is a disquieting, classy, superbly realized horror tale that should not, and will not, be forgotten.

Paranormal Activity

2009 - Directed by Oren Peli

Originally shot for a shoestring $15,000, *Paranormal Activity* premiered at the Screamfest Film Festival in 2007 and was picked up by Paramount and Dreamworks with the original intention of remaking it on a bigger budget. When test screenings led to rapturous talk and acclaim and a bigwig by the name of Steven Spielberg watched it and allegedly became freaked out afterwards, the distributors wisely tossed out those plans and agreed that they already had something potentially special on their hands. Their release plan was unorthodox—releasing the film in ten random college towns for midnight screenings only, and then widening it to other cities based on a "Demand It!" website voting system—but positive buzz and word of mouth turned it into a similar lightning-in-a-bottle success story as its forefather and most obvious inspiration, 1999's *The Blair Witch Project*.

Paranormal Activity is no *The Blair Witch Project*, still one of the most frightening first-time viewing experiences of my life, and it is difficult to imagine that this new film would have been made without the existence of the other one. One is set in a house, the other in the woods, but their narrative progression is nearly identical, as are the terrorized characters' deteriorating mental states as they face an unimaginable situation they have no idea how to get out of. Additionally, both movies are told through the lens of a household video camera, purportedly edited from found footage, and share a number of similar shot compositions. Whereas *The Blair Witch Project* was a tad bit more gritty and raw, ratcheting up an uneasy blanket of dread that became almost suffocating by its final ten minutes, *Paranormal Activity* does not have quite the same steady momentum. Its grab-bag of frights are of a spottier, start-and-stop variety, but when they are pulled off, they work like magic.

Young San Diego couple Katie (Katie Featherston) and Micah (Micah Sloat) sense a supernatural presence in their home and have decided to start shooting surveillance in their bedroom overnight in the hopes of maybe picking something up. For Katie, she has been haunted off and on since the age of eight, where she lives making no difference. A psychic (Mark Fredrichs) agrees to try and bring insight to their problem, and quickly lets them know that he not only senses negative energy in the house, but that the haunting is of demonic forces rather than ghostly ones. Unable to escape the horrors happening around them, Katie and Micah's relationship is put to the test as Micah insists on continuing to film and the preternatural encounters become more frequent and violent.

Paranormal Activity might have been slightly overhyped when it was released, but that comes with the territory. Clearly, everyone involved did something right since it made $107-million at the domestic box office. Seen for what it is—a movie made in a week's time for a budget of next to nothing—the film is close to phenomenal. First-time feature actors Katie Featherston and Micah Sloat sell their onscreen reality by not seeming to act at all, becoming their characters without any traces of artifice. Their relationship, intensifying and becoming rockier as the stakes are raised and desperation takes over, is uncommonly truthful, the sympathetic foundation for which to pile on the spookiness. Debuting filmmaker Oren Peli knows what it takes to scare the viewer, and achieves this feat over and over with the subtlest of tactics, from a door moving by itself to the sound of stomping edging closer. The threats grow ballsier and more extreme, to be sure, and all the while it is the lingering fear of what might come next that leaves the most chilling of impressions. A scene where Katie and Micah wake up to find inhuman footprints in the baby powder they have methodically placed across the hardwood floor is creepy, but it is what follows—a discovery that the attic hatch is askew and Micah's investigation of what may or may not be hiding up there—that really makes one's skin crawl.

Millions of dollars and countless seat-jumping scare tactics mean nothing if there aren't characters worth caring about and a story that understands the value of using restraint to build genuine tension. Peli achieves all of these things with far fewer resources, and he is all the better for his minimalist touch. When the mere opening of a curtain or entrance into a room can cause audience gasps and recoiling, it is clear said film is in reliable hands. Only in the aforementioned derivative recalls to *The Blair Witch Project* and in an ending that startles, but happens too quickly to be anything other than anticlimactic, does the spell falter. The viewer walks out of *Paranormal Activity* wishing there was more to it (nothing in it compares to the nightmare-personified last minutes of 2007's *[REC]*), while acknowledging all the same that the picture's cumulative impact is formidable, lingering long after the lights have come up.

Paranormal Activity 2

2010 - Directed by Tod Williams

When *The Blair Witch Project* was released theatrically in 1999, it became a breakout phenomenon, earning $140-million against an estimated budget of $60,000. Ten years later, *Paranormal Activity* repeated the same sort of success based on its Internet promotion and a grassroots campaign urging moviegoers to "Demand It!" in their nearby theater. Made for the nothing price of $15,000 over a week's time, the film went on to rustle up over $100-million, thoroughly outshining *Saw VI* at the box office and leading the folks of that long-running franchise to seriously question if there was any juice left in the series. Favoring subtlety and imagination over blatant violence and special effects, *Paranormal Activity*, like *The Blair Witch Project* before it, proved how much scarier and effective the simple power of suggestion can be.

Also like that lost-in-the-woods nerve-jangler, a sequel has been rushed into production and is arriving in theaters just one year later. While 2000's *Book of Shadows: Blair Witch 2* was admirable in its bold decision not to repeat the first picture's faux-documentary, POV-shot style, it also turned off most fans of the original and promptly did a financial belly-flop. By comparison, *Paranormal Activity 2* wisely stays faithful to its predecessor's format, albeit with a few minor tweaks and some ramped-up frights. Yes, this is the rare continuation—more a prequel than a sequel, actually—that wholly lives up to what came before.

Several months after bringing home newborn baby Hunter, the Rey family—father Daniel (Brian Boland), mother Kristi (Sprague Grayden), and her teenage stepdaughter, Ali (Molly Ephraim)—are alarmed when they come home to a ransacked house. Naturally assuming it was a break-in despite only a necklace given to Kristi from big sister Katie (Katie Featherston) missing, they install six surveillance cameras around the inside and outside of their suburban Carlsbad abode. Over the next three weeks, they will discover that the culprit is actually living inside the house, and very likely isn't human.

Directed by Tod Williams with an emphatic grasp of how to expertly build quietly simmering suspense toward a collection of jump-out-of-your-seat payoffs, *Paranormal Activity 2* is a rousing success, at least as good as its forefather. Increasingly imperiled couple Katie and Micah (Micah Sloat), both of them making return appearances, were stronger, more indelible characters than this one's leads, but this only minimally lesser element is evened out by an increase in spooky tension that brutally goes for the throat while staying blood-free. Time and again, major studio horror flicks fail with their overblown seat-jumping tactics and thunderous, annoyingly obvious music cues, spelling out how the viewer should feel. Efforts like *Paranormal Activity 2*, however, understand far better that silence, simple sound effects and the anticipation that something bad is about to happen are usually far more affecting. A falling pan, a toy truck moving on its own, blowing curtains, slamming doors and the mere sight of the grainy nighttime surveillance footage is enough to put one on edge or leave him or her outright screaming, whichever the case may be.

Told through the lens of a home camcorder and the fixed security cameras, *Paranormal Activity 2* takes on the eerie sensation that the characters are being constantly watched. Acted with almost constant naturalism as the film's oppressive dread escalates—Molly Ephraim is especially arresting as the understandably alarmed Ali, who takes to recording the goings-on and investigating the possible cause of the haunting—the picture moves ever closer toward revelations that conjoin the story with that of the original film. Notwithstanding a clunkily placed piece of information that shows up as unnecessary text exposition in the middle of one scene (did director Williams really need to spell this out for audiences?), *Paranormal Activity 2* is designed with unexpected cleverness and a mind toward strengthening the new franchise's mythology. It serves up both exactly what one expects and then leads a step further by going places one cannot anticipate. What's certain is this: if you were taken by the first film, it's pretty much a done deal that you'll leave the second on an even greater jittery high.

Paranormal Activity 3

2011 - Directed by Henry Joost and Ariel Schulman

With Lionsgate's seven-part *Saw* series having worn out its welcome and wearied moviegoers, Paramount's *Paranormal Activity* films swept right in to replace it as Halloween's go-to horror franchise, a new entry appearing each successive October. Whereas the *Saw* movies were riddled in blood and guts and torturous acts of violence, *Paranormal Activity* relies on a more psychological creep factor, the power of drawn-out suspense and the sheer anticipation of something eventually popping into the frame enough to give anyone a stern case of the heebie-jeebies. Made for thousands rather than millions of dollars and relying on the power of social media sites and word of mouth to create buzz, 2009's supernatural found-footage chiller, *Paranormal Activity,* earned over $107-million in the U.S. alone. Hot on its heels (and arguably even more effective) was 2010's slyly set-up prequel, *Paranormal Activity 2,* making over $84-million at the box office. Another year later, directors Henry Joost and Ariel Schulman, they of 2010's *Catfish* fame, and returning screenwriter Christopher Landon spin further back into the past to depict how the demonic haunting of two doomed sisters began. Judged wholly on its own merits, *Paranormal Activity 3* one-ups both of the previous films in quality and quantity of its scares. Returning fans will get what they came for, and then some. As a connective piece of the puzzle, however, it doesn't begin to add up to what has been established, calling into question the memories—and even the authentic identities—of the grown-up Katie (Katie Featherston) and Kristi (Sprague Grayden).

The year is 1988, and 8-year-old Katie (Chloe Csengery) and 5-year-old Kristi (Jessica Brown) live with mother Julie (Lauren Bittner) and her wedding videographer boyfriend, Dennis (Chris Smith), in a spacious upper-middle-class home in Santa Rosa, CA. When an earthquake caught on camera reveals dust falling from the ceiling and settling on an invisible figure before dropping to the floor, Dennis is understandably perplexed and intrigued. Setting up two camcorders upstairs (one in each bedroom) and another one jerry-rigged to an oscillating fan downstairs, he begins to record the alarming goings-on as they rapidly escalate. Julie is skeptical, mostly because nothing overt has happened to her yet, but Kristi, who claims to have begun talking to an old man in the house named Toby, knows all too well that a supernatural presence is among them.

Stylistically, *Paranormal Activity 3* is more of the same, inventing a plausible explanation for why these characters' lives are once more being captured on tape. Within this framework, Joost and Schulman display a fantastically inspired sense of showmanship, building tension to a heightened, breathless level and coming up with a real humdinger of a new filmmaking scheme with the introduction of the fan-mounted camera. As it swivels ever so slowly back and forth, the audience shrinks in their seats, giddy yet anxious of what might be revealed in the living room and kitchen. There are at least three huge scares conceived from this expert gimmick, one involving a mysterious figure under a white sheet stalking babysitter Lisa (Johanna Braddy) that is nothing if not a loving homage to 1978's John Carpenter classic, *Halloween*. If you're going to borrow from other movies, you might as well borrow from the best. The use of a Teddy Ruxpin doll (a fixture of 1980s kids' toys), a storage area in the girls' bedroom, and a Bloody Mary game involving Katie and Dennis' assistant, Randy (Dustin Ingram), that goes malevolently awry all add to the mischievously nerve-rattling fun.

When things get too tense at home, the family members find themselves taking shelter at the cozy country cottage of Katie and Kristi's grandmother (Hallie Foote). They think they're safe, but what follows alerts them to the contrary. One particular extended climactic shot is an astounding, willies-inducing showstopper, with Dennis' search for the rest of the family through the darkened rooms of the house turned into a first-person nightmare of the shadowy unknown and things—not all of them otherworldly—that go bump during the witching hour. As satisfying as this finale is, it does open itself up for one legitimate problem: what occurs does not match up with what Katie and Kristi, as adults, have described of their childhoods in the first two movies. Where is the house fire, or the dark figure that supposedly always appeared at the foot of Katie's bed? Furthermore, watching the final theatrical trailer afterwards reveals that many of these story holes were filmed and just cut from the finished product. It's the one disappointment in an otherwise exceptionally well-made movie, the ending practically demanding that a fourth picture fill in these gaps and continue the sordid tale of these sisters in 1988 (indeed, *Paranormal Activity 4* came to fruition a year later, but disappointingly answered none of the questions this predecessor posed).

Faultlessly and naturalistically acted by its mostly unknown cast—Lauren Bittner is particularly good as mother Julie, kept out of the loop for too long about what is occurring around her—*Paranormal Activity 3* is a fitting continuation to a series that often raises the stakes without needing to resort to unnecessary gore and extreme violence to freak out the viewer. Beyond that, it adds to the lore of Katie's and Kristi's hauntings even when posing more questions than answers. The ambiguity is what adds to one's fear. As Samhain approaches, *Paranormal Activity 3* is an ideal choice for viewers yearning to get into the holiday spirit.

ParaNorman

2012 - Directed by Chris Butler and Sam Fell

For lovers of the dark, otherworldly and macabre, delighting through the 93-minute *ParaNorman* will be akin to attending a horror-themed amusement park, exploring a desolate and foreboding haunted house, and simultaneously watching 1985's *The Return of the Living Dead* and 1993's *Hocus Pocus* all rolled up into one. The writing-directing debut of Chris Butler with co-director Sam Fell, this project, produced by LAIKA (the same studio behind 2009's *Coraline*), is filled to bursting with a passion and love for the horror genre that assures the story and characters are taken very seriously, even when the tone or the seldom ingeniously acerbic dialogue and visual cues also give it a rich, potent brand of unkiddified humor. Spooky, charming and poignant besides—the movie fearlessly touches upon the subject of death in a way that does not pander to children, remaining mature yet accessible—*ParaNorman* arrives as every bit a one-of-a-kind creation. Simply put, it is no less than the most confident, fully realized, and just plain imaginative stop-motion animated feature since 1993's holiday classic, *The Nightmare Before Christmas*.

From the outside looking in, the sleepy New England burg of Blithe Hollow would appear to be just the right hometown for 11-year-old Norman Babcock (voiced by Kodi Smit-McPhee) to live in. He sees and talks to spirits everywhere he goes—dearly departed Grandma (Elaine Stritch) continues to knit away on the couch—but no one, not even parents Sandra (Leslie Mann) and Perry (Jeff Garlin) and snooty older sister Courtney (Anna Kendrick), believe him. The idea of being able to communicate with the afterlife doesn't sound like such a stretch for a community best known for the impending 300th anniversary of a witch's death, but so be it. Prepping for the school play (wherein Donovan's moody-cool "Season of the Witch" shall be sung) and dealing with bully Alvin (Christopher Mintz-Plasse) is what Norman currently fills his days with—that is, until he is visited by his hobo uncle, Mr. Penderghast (John Goodman), and warned that the witch's curse is about to be unleashed. Pretty soon, the zombified bodies of the founding fathers responsible for alleged witch Aggie's (Jodelle Ferland) death are sprouting from the graveyard and attacking the town. If Norman and new best friend Neil (Tucker Albrizzi) do not find a way to defeat them by sunset and put Aggie's angered ghost to rest, it could mean the end of Blithe Hollow as everyone knows it.

The art of stop-motion is the most painstaking of all animated mediums—if film moves at twenty-four frames per second, that means there are over 1,400 required setups per minute—so it is especially fulfilling to come upon a movie that lives up to the dedication with which it was mounted. Appropriately jerky like a Ray Harryhausen creation and sumptuously atmospheric with mysteries of the unknown going bump in the night, each character and landscape has a personality, each mold of the clay an irresistible homegrown quaintness belied only by its sheer technical wonderment and complexity. The town of Blithe Hollow is a triumph of art direction, inspired, no doubt, by Salem, Massachusetts, by way of a fictional hamlet where Halloween lasts pretty much 365 days per year. The town's "welcome" sign features a motto—"A nice place to hang!"—alongside an illustration of a pointy-hatted hag in a noose. All of the stores are appropriately themed. The town square features a statue of the infamous 300-year-old witch in question. And the specters whom Norman chats with, while unseen by others, sure are a lively bunch.

Film references range from fairly obvious to sly as can be, from the opening cheesy '80s horror movie that Norman watches on TV, the zombie's yelling out for "Brainnnnnns!" to the cell phone ringtone that plays John Carpenter's immortal *Halloween* theme (this latter detail is followed up by a *Friday the 13th* nod even whilst still aping a direct scene from Carpenter's 1978 slasher watermark). Every image of *ParaNorman*, in fact, is dripping with "blink-and-you'll-miss-them" flourishes and Easter eggs, and that extends past horror, too; the movie is also an affectionate ode to coming-of-age teen cinema of the John Hughes ilk, from Norman's daily grind at school to sister Courtney's instant gaga crush on Neil's buff, dumb-as-a-nail older brother Mitch (Casey Affleck). In Norman is a kid who just wants to fit in, along the way realizing that to be average, or "normal," is no way to live at all. At the start, his parents chalk up his claims of talking to spirits as that of a kid who just wants attention, who hasn't fully come to terms with his family member's death. "Your grandmother's in a better place," his mom tries to reassure him. "No, she's not," Norman replies. "She's in the living room."

If *ParaNorman* has a mischievous comedic side, it also has a surprising amount of heart. Norman's disbelieving parents come around, to be sure, and so does Courtney, a teenybopper nightmare who learns to value her family more than petty material objects. At the start, she sees Norman as a pest—not because he is one, but because it's the law of 16-year-old girls to be terminally annoyed by 11-year-olds. Funny, how a few lives in danger can turn around a person's outlook. Lo and behold, Courtney genuinely cares about Norman and is willing to fight for him. So, too, is friendly fellow outcast Neil, who has a container of spicy hummus at his disposal and isn't afraid to use it on creepy uncles or marauding reanimated corpses. The finale, busy but coherent, the chaos of a spirit-driven tornado refusing to get in the way of the story's deeper, relevant themes, is as winning as what has come before it, making a valuable point about the silliness and potential societal dangers of believing in superstitions. Bandwagons are a harmful thing to jump onto, and it was this very mistake all those centuries ago—just like it was during the Salem witch trials—that led to untold lives being destroyed and ruined.

A dream sprung from autumn personified, *ParaNorman* is vibrant even in its gloom, a ray of light at dawn bringing hope to a doom-laden evening none of the residents of Blithe Hollow will soon forget. For all of its thrills, its creeptastic imagery, its ominous sorcery and ancient curses, the film, in its purest form, boils down to the tender human story of a pre-teen boy searching for reason and acceptance in a world that doesn't have all the answers. Impressionable younger children will be scared out of their minds—directors Chris Butler and Sam Fell aren't shy about the gory details of life and death—but for everyone else, *ParaNorman* is one of the biggest animated treats—stop-motion or others—in years. For a picture focusing so heavily on the ghoulish underbelly of history and nature, its propensity for compassion and empathy is immensely unexpected, and comforting.

Passengers

2008 - Directed by Rodrigo Garcia

In October 2008, *Passengers* was quietly released without press screenings, without any advertising of note, on only 100 random multiplex screens across the country. What TriStar Pictures was hoping to accomplish by tossing away a film headlined by popular talents Anne Hathaway and Patrick Wilson is anyone's guess. At the time, Hathaway was coming off of consecutive box-office hits and simultaneously had *Rachel Getting Married* (for which she went on to receive an Oscar nomination) in theaters, while Wilson had also been rising to the A-list over the previous several years. It would be one thing if the finished product were a fiasco of some sort and the studio was cutting their losses by burying it, but it wasn't. At all. With the proper promotion and wider push, *Passengers* could have earned a tidy little profit.

First of all, it should be noted that the film is not very surprising from a storytelling perspective. An existential mystery-cum-romance, director Rodrigo Garcia and screenwriter Ronnie Christensen construct the plot in such a way that all the threads come together at the end for a revelation that resets its entire trajectory. The problem is that they are not very sneaky in doing this, and the audience is aware from the beginning that a big climactic twist is ultimately in the cards. For me, I was able to pretty much guess what was going on ten minutes into it. If the script were just a flimsy clothesline of deceptive turns with no substance, this might have spelled disaster. Fortunately, there is more—much more—to take away from one's viewing than just the last-act reveal.

When a plane crashes on a Vancouver beach and only nine passengers survive out of over a hundred, grief counselor Claire Summers (Anne Hathaway) is called in by her trusted mentor, Perry (Andre Braugher), to help work them through their trauma. As she sees the population of her group therapy sessions dwindle, the survivors seemingly vanishing, Claire suspects that there must be some kind of airline cover-up going on. After all, while investigators are blaming the crash on a maintenance problem, those that were onboard largely seem to recall a burst of light and an explosion before they hit the ground. One of Claire's patients, Eric (Patrick Wilson), is hesitant to speak about the event at all, his life rejuvenated as he believes he was miraculously given a second chance. The more time Claire spends privately with him, the more she begins to open up. There's a bond between them, but paranoia eventually takes over after a series of ominous occurrences start taking place.

It is difficult to discuss *Passengers* without giving key things away, but suffice it to say the film is a ruminative examination of coming to terms with things that cannot be changed and learning to value the human connections that satisfy and fulfill our lives. Through her relationships with Eric and a kind neighbor in her apartment building, Toni (Dianne Wiest), Claire comes to recognize that her troubled relationship with sister Emma (Stacy Grant) is one that she'd like to fix rather than see fall apart for good. She also cannot help but be drawn to Eric, who makes his intimate feelings clear to her. There is a gorgeously lit and performed scene between them where they take a dip in the chilly waters off of Vancouver, the city glowing in the distance behind them. A later love scene is tastefully composed and edited without falling into the choppy trap that most PG-13-rated movies do.

If *Passengers* is being billed as a supernatural thriller—the poster certainly suggests this—it really isn't. Garcia cleanly and proficiently tells his story without throwing in cheap jump scares or wavery apparitions. Instead, the director concentrates on making the film a character piece above all else, as well as a romantic drama set against a subtly eerie backdrop. The British Columbia locations, looking palpably cold and overcast, are sumptuously shot by cinematographer Igor Jadue-Lillo and also turn out to serve a bigger purpose. Thinking back on the settings of certain scenes, they initially feel a bit superfluous, only to take on greater meaning as the story's smaller secrets are discerned. The music score by Edward Shearmur is additionally simple and elegant, making an impact without going for thundering orchestrations.

Anne Hathaway's turn as therapist Claire Summers is not a disappointment. Always searching for logic and truth, Claire butts heads with airline pilot Arkin (David Morse) when she has reason to believe that what really happened to cause the plane to crash is something he's trying to hide. Hathaway essays the role with a pent-up vulnerability to befit a young woman not yet completely comfortable within the profession she has chosen and hesitant to take chances or get too close to anyone. Her chemistry with Patrick Wilson, an enduring presence himself as Eric, is low-key and soulful, growing to mean more than the viewer anticipates. Dianne Wiest, as the wise Toni; Clea DuVall, as crash survivor Shannon, and David Morse, as Arkin, also receive effective character arcs and commit to their parts with classy panache.

Passengers grabs one's attention even when the plot details feel familiar, and does a nice job of closing off all the possible loose ends. Despite already predicting what was to occur, the last fifteen minutes have the power to blindside with their resonant emotional power. It is not what happens, per se, but how it happens. Fighting back tears and being manipulated in a way that refreshingly didn't feel condescending was something that could never have been guessed in advance, and the final shots of a beautiful world in its natural flow strike a lingering chord. With a storytelling sensibility more common in foreign films than mainstream ones, *Passengers* is a compact, thought-provoking tale that challenges the viewer while shedding light on one's own life, and how he or she has chosen to lead it.

Perfect Sense

2012 - Directed by David Mackenzie

Smell. Taste. Hearing. Sight. Touch. For those of us with all of our senses intact, we tend to take for granted just how important they are, both collectively and apart, in our day-to-day experiences. Playing undeniable roles in our lives, all of them have the power to unlock memories and contribute pleasure and, occasionally, pain. People who suffer from a loss of any one perception have an automatic handicap, but can easily survive and press on to have a full life. The disappearance of most, or all, of them, however, would be catastrophic. Directed by David Mackenzie with a chilling, matter-of-fact candidness, *Perfect Sense* presents a horrific "what-if?" scenario and bravely allows it to run its natural course. A raw, character-centric hymn to the apocalypse, the film reminds of 1999's *Last Night*, 2006's *Children of Men*, 2011's *Contagion* and 2011's *Melancholia*, but brings its own angle and ideas to similar subject matter. The immense empathy Mackenzie and screenwriter Kim Fupz Aakeson afford their characters and the population of the planet as a whole ensures that their interest lies not in the world's destruction, but in the giant, messy beauty of love and existence, and what the human race has to lose if such an unthinkable pandemic were to pass.

Michael (Ewan McGregor) is a London-based chef with commitment issues who still beats himself up over a past relationship he knows he didn't handle well. Susan (Eva Green) lives in the flat across the street from the restaurant, an epidemiologist feeling restless and kind of sad in her currently lonely here-and-now. Upon the two of them meeting, there's a chemistry akin to the strike of a match. They get along amazingly well and seemingly understand each other even in shorthand. Alas, their tight bond is one with either perfect timing or the worst ever. A mysterious outbreak has suddenly begun to sweep the globe, intense feelings of grief paving the way for a person's complete loss of smell. Scientists are baffled over its cause—is it ecological? Biological? Religious? Supernatural?—but when the bulk of the world's sense of taste also vanishes overnight, it becomes clear that no one is safe from impending events that will soon, too, strip them of their optical and auditory functions. With nothing left but to feel, both physically and internally, might Michael and Susan still have a chance to be saved by each other?

Engrossing before packing a staggering emotional wallop as its full implications are revealed, *Perfect Sense* dabbles in the soft-spoken and radical, an intense spectrum that makes this very much a universal story rather than a centralized one. Michael and Susan are damaged thirty-somethings. They've made mistakes before and, if given the chance, would probably make new ones in the future. They're also innately good people, just trying to get by. Together, though, they are something more than that. It's an unexpected sensation that sneaks up on them, but how can one deny such a kindred connection? If their lives are about to be ripped apart and imminent death is the only option, at least they might have each other to hold onto until nothingness takes over. This, then, is both the savior and tragedy of the entire picture, the gradual realization that without senses and some kind of palpable reciprocated love, we do not really exist at all. Michael and Susan will, until they're no more. Dust in the wind.

The screenplay—and director Mackenzie's treatment of it—is much more than just a love story set against the backdrop of doom. If we were to begin systematically losing our senses, yet had to forge a path to keep going, this is how it would probably be. Visionary yet steadfastly logical, the story takes into account everything from the act of dining out when one's taste and smell are gone, to the common need to hear music once sound is no more (the answer to this latter question is miraculous in its unforced comment on the dynamism of human nature). Another scene, in which a food critic rates Michael's cuisine not by the most obvious traits—he can't—but by temperature, texture and presentation, is simple yet immensely clever. While some people rebel and loot, most keep going. To collapse and submit to the end is not a part of our fight-or-flight tendencies.

Ewan McGregor and Eva Green make for a fervent pair as Michael and Susan, living lives so closely to each other but only meeting recently by pure chance. Their time together, first as new friends getting to know one another and then as more, is not cause for instantaneous love, but more significant of the undeniable binds moving them closer. When they fall, it means something, and when they agree to tell each other a sort of secret that few people know, it is their comfort in being honest and bare that only proves how right they are as a couple. It is this knowledge that gives such sudden unforgettable urgency to the last scenes. What happens cannot be discussed, but the enormity of its suggestions hit the viewer like a truck, its concluding moments transformative and electrifying.

Perfect Sense is an expert study in paranoia, the fleetingness of one's past, and the memories that make us who we are. It all boils down to the connection between emotions and senses, and the fuse that could so easily short-circuit if one of them cut off. A smell of a room, the taste of lemon, or the aroma of a cold winter's day may snap a person back to a nostalgic vision of childhood or a family member no longer with him or her. A song can instantly remind of the time a person first heard it. To no longer be able to access these thoughts and senses is indescribably frightening, Michael's and Susan's fates coming down to the compassion and, yes, love they'll be able to hold onto for as long as breath escapes their mouths. *Perfect Sense* captures all of this with the tenderness of a star-crossed romance that ends with an embrace, and the bitterness of it being the last one either of them shall ever take.

Pet Sematary

1989 - Directed by Mary Lambert

A horror movie that has done its job correctly will set a person off-balance, leaving one either disturbed or fearful about what is about to come next. Most of the time, the scare factor lasts for the length of the running time and then goes away as the viewer finishes the film and moves on with his or her hectic real life. The imprint that *Pet Sematary* makes is more lasting. Director Mary Lambert and screenwriter Stephen King (adapting from his own novel) introduce an idyllic family at the onset who are identifiable, happy and likeable, and then proceed for the next 100 minutes to viciously rip their world apart. The audience, in turn, is left sucker-punched and devastated by the events that unfold, afraid to watch any longer the destruction of the characters, yet unwilling to turn away from the screen. Lambert and King sharply hook the viewer in their gaze, spinning the story in unfathomably horrific directions while never losing sight of their dramatic compass. Above all, *Pet Sematary* is a remarkably mature and thoughtful look at the mysterious nature of death and the complexity of the grieving process.

The Creeds arrive at their new home in Maine with the same sort of high hopes the Lutzes had when they first pulled up to their dream house in Amityville, New York. Louis, a doctor, has uprooted the family for work, and he and wife Rachel (Denise Crosby) cannot help but notice upon getting there that the road beside their property is a favorite for truckers. When young daughter Ellie (Blaze Berdahl) points out a path into the woods behind their house, kindly neighbor Jud Crandall (Fred Gwynne) offers to show them where it leads—back to the incorrectly spelled "Pet Sematary," where heartbroken children and families have buried their beloved animals over the years. Soon after, the Creeds' luck begins to sputter out. On his first day on the job, Louis is unable to save the life of Victor Pascow (Brad Greenquist), a university student wounded in a freak accident. Though deceased, Pascow shows up in what might be Louis' dream or something else, warning him of the Indian burial ground located beyond the pet cemetery. "The border wasn't meant to be crossed," Pascow tells him. "The land is sour." Louis doesn't yet know what he means.

When the family cat, Church, is hit and killed by a truck while the rest of Louis' family is visiting Rachel's parents for Thanksgiving, Jud suggests that Ellie isn't ready to lose her favorite pet. They travel together up to the Micmac burial ground and lay Church to rest there. Hours later, Church shows back up at the house, smellier and more irritable than usual, but undeniably the same feline. Death will proceed to find its way into the Creeds' lives again and again. When their housekeeper, Missy (Susan Blommaert), suffering from a long-standing illness, hangs herself in her basement, it kicks up old traumatic memories Rachel has had since childhood of the passing of her own sister, Zelda (Andrew Hubatsek). When tragedy eventually strikes closer to home and Louis and Rachel find themselves mourning their beautiful 2-year-old son, Gage (Miko Hughes), Louis is unable to stop thinking about what might happen if he buries his baby in the same dirt that brought Church back. "The soil of a man's heart is stonier," Jud portentously tell him at one point, "and what you own always comes back to ya'."

Disregarding 1986's disparate coming-of-age classic, *Stand by Me*, *Pet Sematary* quite possibly is the best film adaptation of Stephen King's work. 1980's *The Shining* comes close, but that iconic effort is infamous for the creative license Stanley Kubrick took in translating it to the screen. By comparison, King wrote the script for *Pet Sematary* himself, and, with only a few minor exceptions, has remained truthful to his source material. This is a horrifying movie, but not without flashes of humor. The picture is set in the real world, portrays a conceivably authentic familial unit, and is piercingly human in the often raw emotions it rattles up. The story takes the occasional flight of fancy, for sure, but Lambert reels in its over-the-top elements or approaches them from a skewed hellish point of view.

Before the more overt grisliness has begun, Lambert has treated the characters as those of a straightforward drama. Missy's unexpected suicide allows the Creeds to put their own lives into perspective and acknowledge the inevitability of death. Rachel knows all about losing someone close. When she was a little girl, her sister, Zelda, suffered from spinal meningitis. Kept away in the upstairs bedroom like a "dirty secret," Zelda's emaciated body grew distorted and her mental health turned to clinical insanity. Rachel, meanwhile, was left alone to care for her sister—a child herself who had begun to take the shape of a monster—and was the one who witnessed Zelda's ultimate death by choking. At the time, in the back of her mind, Rachel was glad. Zelda, depicted in flashback before popping up twice more as a spectral purveyor of danger, is the most unnerving film creation in memory, and that is not just merely some emptily grandiose statement, either. Brilliantly performed by Andrew Hubatsek (a male actor), Zelda's upsetting, tormented, skin-crawling presence weighs down on the proceedings like a hideous wraith, the very embodiment of every fear and hang-up a person can conceivably have in relation to guilt and death.

The untimely loss of toddler son Gage is ruinous to the Creed family. There is a chance for them to move on, but Louis' denial over what has happened and his knowledge of the burial grounds' power proves too tempting an equation.

Indeed, what returns is not his son, and it is Louis' fatal misjudgment in messing with the laws of nature that spells doom for him and almost everyone he has ever cared about. Filled with anguish, heartbreak, veritable frights and an escalating sense of approaching calamity, the third act of *Pet Sematary* works magnificently as both horror and tragedy, nearly Shakespearean in its bleak turn of events and avalanche of dramatic force. When Louis decides to go back to the burial ground with a third body, all along knowing what has happened before, it is logical for viewers to become skeptical of the character's intelligence. What they fail to realize is that Louis has already unwittingly committed such atrocities that he is at the point of no return. When he buries that third body, he is burying himself, and he knows it.

Dale Midkiff, a consistently working actor who has, for reasons unknown, never hit it big, is close to faultless as Louis Creed. The journey Midkiff takes in his character's shoes would be demanding for any actor, and he pulls off every emotion with a gritty honesty and vulnerability that few performers could have played so well. As wife Rachel, Denise Crosby does an equally fine job, displaying the love she has for the life she has built and the discomfort of a woman who has never been able to accept death or wrap her mind around it. Fred Gwynne is a standout as neighbor Jud Crandall, down-to-earth, wise and conversational in his reading of the sort of guy one would like to sit on the porch with and shoot the breeze. And, as kids Ellie and Gage, Blaze Berdahl (and twin sister Beau) threatens pushing too hard at times, but handles difficult scenes like a pro, and Miko Hughes, two years old at the time of filming, is downright amazing. Even if his performance is the product of an expert editor, this can still not discount Hughes' naturalism in front of the camera.

A motion picture of loss and regret, *Pet Sematary* imagines the worst in its view of the permanent disintegration of a family. Haunting, sorrowful and reverberatingly eerie, the film is also complemented by the punk-rock flair of The Ramones (who perform the title track over the end credits) and the thoroughly unsettling, gothically enhanced instrumental score by Elliot Goldenthal. That *Pet Sematary* is as creepy as it is without bogging down in genre trappings is a rare miracle in horror circles. Director Mary Lambert trusts in the universality of her characters, their tightly drawn relationships with each other, and the insurmountable conflicts they face to carry the story forward. It is these things that most resonate—these are what we relate to and can connect with, after all—and the reason why *Pet Sematary* has endured and not been forgotten in the decades since its release.

Poltergeist

1982 - Directed by Tobe Hooper

The archetypal American Dream—having a family, making a living, and becoming a homeowner—is perilously pulled out from under the Freelings in *Poltergeist*, one of the post-1970s watermarks of the supernatural horror subgenre. A reputable classic, more modern than one might suspect from a 1982 release, the film offers up the complete package: well-defined, down-to-earth characters; giant scares galore that prey on both grown-up and childhood fears; superb special effects that still hold up decades later, and an overhanging mystery that pulls the audience from one terrifically nail-biting situation to the next. Spawning two respectable but less well-received sequels—1986's *Poltergeist II* and 1988's *Poltergeist III*—the *Poltergeist* series has been the bearer of a number of myths and controversies over the years. Some people claim that co-writer and producer Steven Spielberg directed certain scenes rather than credited helmer Tobe Hooper, who, at the time, already had two solid genre efforts under his belt with 1974's *The Texas Chain Saw Massacre* and 1981's *The Funhouse*. There also has been a fair share of documentation about the series' alleged curse, what with real skeletons being used as props in certain scenes of the first and second pictures and six cast members dying in the half-dozen years between the making of the original film and the third. While this sort of conjecture might be fun to talk about, the dazzling skill that *Poltergeist* possesses deserves to not be overshadowed by Hollywood gossip. Its influence undeniably reverberates thirty-plus years later through virtually every haunted-house story that sees the light of day.

5-year-old Carol Anne Freeling (Heather O'Rourke) shuffles downstairs in her pajamas as the living room television concludes its daily broadcasting with the late-night playing of "The Star-Spangled Banner" before cutting to static. She is drawn to the screen, closer and closer, placing her little hands on the glass of the tube. She seems to be communicating with someone, or something, but who, or what? "They're here," she simply utters. Carol Anne has recently moved with her family—father Steven (Craig T. Nelson), mother Diane (JoBeth Williams), moody teenage sister Dana (Dominique Dunne), and over-imaginative 8-year-old brother Robbie (Oliver Robins)—to a brand-new tract housing development called Cuesta Verde. All appears to be relatively happy-go-lucky until Diane witnesses things in the kitchen moving around on their own. At first, she is more excited than scared, believing that there must be some sort of gravitational explanation for these strange occurrences. When she turns her back and sees that all of the chairs in the kitchen have stacked themselves on top of the table like a pyramid, however, it becomes fairly clear that their house is haunted. How could a construction that has just been built have ghosts? With the help of a group of parapsychologists led by Dr. Lesh (Beatrice Straight), Steven and Diane are drawn into investigating this very question when Carol Anne suddenly goes missing, trapped in another dimension as she communicates to her family the only way she can: through the television.

Written by Steven Spielberg, Michael Grais and Mark Victor, *Poltergeist* is a quintessential paranormal thriller pitting a normal, sympathetic middle-class family against extraordinary circumstances. When Carol Anne's tweety-bird dies and Diane helps her to bury it behind their house, the young mother has no way of guessing that she will soon be facing the potential loss of her daughter through means outside of her control. It is an unthinkable situation for any parent, to be sure, and the film approaches this subject with an uncompromising poignancy while bringing an intimidating reality to the more irrational fears that kids and adults often experience. As the Freelings are clued in on the cause of what haunts them—Cuesta Verde was built by money-hungry investors atop a cemetery, the headstones moved while leaving the corpses behind—Tobe Hooper works a consistently mounting level of giddy apprehension while hitting his imaginatively conceived scares out of the ballpark. A lifelike tree outside Robbie's window and a seriously daunting clown doll sitting in a chair across from his bed are milked for all the tension they're worth. Eating a leg of fried chicken immediately after the movie would be out of the question.

The cast is superlative all around, though there is a shade of melancholy with the knowledge that two of the three young actors playing the Freeling children met with untimely deaths. As eldest daughter Dana, a typical teenage girl whose relatively frivolous concerns come to an end when she witnesses her family battling powers beyond their comprehension, Dominique Dunne reveals a charismatic sparkle that would have served her well as her career flourished. Tragically, she was strangled to death by her real-life boyfriend mere months after the film's release. As little Carol Anne, Heather O'Rourke (who would go on to reprise her role in the two sequels before passing away from intestinal stenosis at the age of 12) is adorable. Heading up the ensemble are Craig T. Nelson and JoBeth Williams, bringing a pleasing warmth to their relationship. The viewer actively comes to care about them and want to see them through their ordeal. By being able to connect so intimately with the Freelings, it is easy to imagine if one's own family were in their shoes. In a standout supporting turn, Zelda Rubinstein is a delight as diminutive, fervently no-nonsense clairvoyant Tangina, called in to help the family get Carol Anne back.

Poltergeist climaxes in a morbidly fantastic rush of emotional catharses, its marriage of the entertaining and the horrific grandly paying off as the root of the manifestations come back for vengeance and all hell more or less literally breaks loose. An extended stormy setpiece of crowd-pleasing payoffs commence, a scene in which Diane is terrorized in the mud-drenched swimming pool by unearthed dead bodies especially hair-raising. A big summer movie of the sort that doesn't usually get made any more, the film never loses sight of its closely observed characters or the mainstream spectacle closing in on them. It's a spectacular ride, relying on exquisitely orchestrated suspense over violence and topped by composer Jerry Goldsmith's vivid musical accompaniment. As far as motion pictures about the spiritual unknown and things going bump in the night (and day) are concerned, *Poltergeist* is tough to beat.

Prince of Darkness

1987 - Directed by John Carpenter

If *Prince of Darkness* isn't writer-director John Carpenter's most personal cinematic work, it certainly feels that way while watching it. Idiosyncratic in the best, most thought-provoking and creepy-crawly senses, the film was made at a time (in 1987) when the horror genre's slasher fad—which, coincidentally, had rose to popularity with Carpenter's own 1978 masterpiece, *Halloween*—was fading fast. Audiences were showing with their dollars that they wanted something new, and, while there is a case to be made that *Prince of Darkness* found its most fervent following later on home video, the filmmaker gave them exactly that. Steeped in religious iconography while perceptibly revising and reimagining the history of Christianity, the picture covers many thematically loaded bases, and does it screamingly well. What if, Carpenter asks, the world had not been created by God, but by Satan, and what if there was an ancient otherworldly evil lying in wait for the chance to bring its granddaddy from down below back to Earth? These very notions are petrifying, and Carpenter is clever and wise enough to know just how to milk his intimidating subject matter.

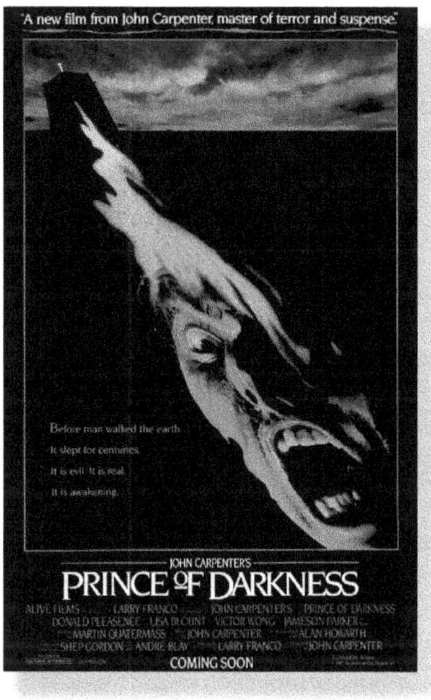

When an elderly priest passes away and leaves behind a diary and key, Father Loomis' (Donald Pleasence) investigation into the items leads him to an abandoned East L.A. church housing a mysterious canister of green liquid in the basement chapel. Seeking the help of physics professor Howard Birack (Victor Wong) and a team of graduate students, Loomis and his assistants convene on the church for a weekend of research. As their translation of ancient texts begins to terrifyingly contradict everything they've ever thought they knew about the creation of the universe, the seven-million-year-old substance—Satan's son in liquid form—is unleashed upon the group, one by one infecting and possessing them while preparations gear up to welcome the Devil himself back to the physical land of the living.

Coinciding with news of the explosion of a supernova, its anti-God particles dropping into the planet's atmosphere, *Prince of Darkness* is a heady, provocative study of faith, religious mysticism and revisionist history. The film's ideas, threaded throughout a collection of icky and horrific setpieces that pit the characters, including physics classmates and new lovers Brian (Jameson Parker) and Catherine (Lisa Blount), against nearly indomitable odds, appear to be a symbolic—if fictional—representation of Carpenter's own internal debate about religion. The villain of the piece, an all-encompassing power that finds a way to pass through human hosts, begins to seep into the consciousness of the movie's protagonists as they start to share the same dream of a cloaked figure in shadow edging ever closer from the corridor entrance of the church. Meanwhile, the homeless derelicts outside surround the building, insects crawling over them and the leader (musician Alice Cooper) not afraid to use a sharp bicycle spike on anyone who attempts to escape.

Back in his 1970s and '80s heyday, Carpenter's music scores were some of the top compositions around, his methodic, deceptively simple use of the piano and synthesizers serving to create iconic aural melodies that were every bit a character in his films as the actual actors. In *Prince of Darkness*, Carpenter and co-composer Alan Howarth rarely let up, their ominously propulsive orchestrations carrying the viewer from one scene to the next. Although some audience members claim the picture moves slowly, this criticism is difficult to understand since there is a constant rhythmic forward motion to the narrative, the indelible compilation of music and image and taut editing rivaling the cadence of a feature-length montage. All the same, there is an attention to detail, to the unraveling of the story's nifty developments, and to the interplay between different personalities that bless the proceedings with far more layers than the average horror film. It isn't surprising, then, to learn that the auteur made the movie independently, with full creative control (only after the fact did Universal Pictures buy the title and distribute it to theaters the week before Halloween).

When student Kelly (Susan Blanchard) bruises her arm in the company of the malevolent canister, she thinks nothing of it even as a bizarre symbol slowly appears in the black-and-blue mark. While lying down for a quick nap as the already-zombified Susan (Anne Marie Howard) and Lisa (Ann Yen) look on, Kelly's sleeping body absorbs the remainder of the green liquid, the fluid pouring into her facial orifices as an unspeakable transformation starts to take place. The last fifteen minutes of *Prince of Darkness* are akin to a runaway train with a faulty break line and a cliff up ahead, the clamorous circumstances raising to edge-of-your-seat degrees while not only threatening the lives of all involved, but also suggestive of a coming apocalypse—or, more specifically, Hell on Earth. With Walter (Dennis Dun) trapped in the closet of the room, the viewer is placed alongside him, given a first-person seat to Kelly's metamorphosis from bubbly young woman to the living embodiment of Satan's child. The climax, lifting off with the opening of her eyes as Walter cries for help—"I don't want to die!" he exclaims, looking unadulterated horror squarely in the face—is quite enough to leave one visibly aghast. Needing a portal to bring her "Father" through, the changed, demonic Kelly, her body a bubbling collection of slimy red lesions, turns to a full-body mirror when her make-up compact won't do. As Kelly grabs hold of Satan's hand in the blackness of the mirror, the brave, intelligent Catherine sees what is taking place and, in an instant, knows what she must do.

Prince of Darkness is a taut, deliciously grim jewel of the horror genre, not quite like any other film in memory. Violent but also restrained, the film proved further—as if it still needed to be proved at all by this point in his career—why John Carpenter attained the moniker of "Master of Suspense" alongside forefather Alfred Hitchcock. Delving into a plot with the greatest, and gravest, of all imaginable stakes, he was able to make an elegantly photographed, legitimately frightening tale that does not shirk away from its controversial concepts. Having watched the woman he had started to care about and perhaps love make the ultimate sacrifice, Brian is left alone with his thoughts, his belief system inexorably stricken and rearranged by the awful things he has witnessed. In a motion picture overflowing with iconic imagery, the last shot of Brian's finger reaching toward a mirror, the screen cutting to black before the glass has been touched, is a thrillingly enigmatic, devastatingly suggestive final comment on the mysteries of the world yet to be discovered and humankind's lifelong struggle over all of that which we do not know.

Psycho

1960 - Directed by Alfred Hitchcock

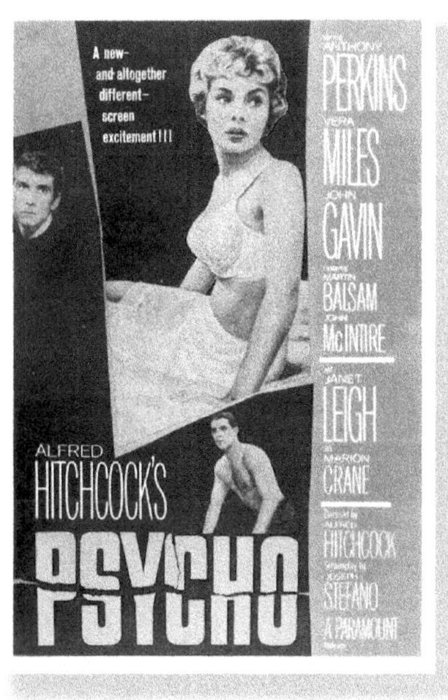

From the original "Master of Suspense," *Psycho* is Alfred Hitchcock's most widely known and talked-about film, a towering achievement for a relatively low-budget horror picture that, at the time it was made, cost only $800,000. Based on the novel by Robert Bloch and loosely inspired by cannibalistic Wisconsin serial killer Ed Gein, the movie came at a time when Hitchcock was tired of helming variations on the same old spy plots and longed to stir things up. Deferring his usual salary for a slice of the hoped-for earnings, he went out on a creative limb and, as a result, forever altered the future of an entire genre. *Psycho* terrified audiences in 1960 and, surprisingly, still holds up today. This is a scary and immersive motion picture, both entirely potent and enormously entertaining.

Tired of the life she's been living and wishing to be able to marry longtime boyfriend Sam Loomis (John Gavin), Marion Crane (Janet Leigh) makes a rash decision to steal $40,000 in cash from the Phoenix bank she works at. Filled with paranoia and a little guilt, Marion trades in her car and skips town. Having driven all day and into the wee hours, she makes the fateful choice to stop off for an overnight stay at the rustic Bates Motel. Before the evening is over, she will meet the end of a very sharp knife while taking a shower. When motel manager Norman Bates (Anthony Perkins) discovers the body, he believes it is the work of his invalid mother, her silhouette peering out from the upstairs window of the house overlooking the motel. Not knowing what else to do, Norman disposes of the body by putting her in the trunk of her car and driving it into a nearby swamp. When Marion never shows up, older sister Lila (Vera Miles) grows concerned and enlists the aid of both Sam and police detective Arbogast (Martin Balsam) to investigate her disappearance.

At the time of its release, *Psycho* was viewed in certain circles as a rule-breaking, wildly explicit film, dealing in brutal murder, risqué (for 1960) sexual situations, and themes involving Norman's Oedipal complex and transvestitism (never mind it was also the first time a flushing toilet was seen on film). Although these elements are not nearly as shocking in the twenty-first century, Hitchcock's *Psycho* remains a miraculous motion picture of bravery and innovation. It is no wonder it consistently ends up on any—and sometimes at the top—of the list of all-time horror greats.

The screenplay by Joseph Stefano is way ahead of its time in both its dialogue and construction. For those unfamiliar with the iconic shower scene (is anyone?), it would come as a huge surprise that the character of Marion, who has been established as the protagonist of the story, dies within the first hour. There are actually two murder setpieces in *Psycho*, and they are both dazzlingly executed. The sequence where Arbogast is attacked as he mounts the staircase in the Bates' home is exceptionally composed and cut together, powerful enough to still creep viewers out and cause them to jump in their seats.

The character of the occasionally charming, partly threatening Norman Bates will always be associated with the late, irreplaceable Anthony Perkins, who never had a role as memorable as this one. He is perfect as the tall but slight, somewhat shy Mama's boy who isn't yet aware of—or doesn't want to face up to—the bitter truth about himself and his mental state. As the film's anticlimactic heroine Marion, Janet Leigh was deservedly nominated for an Oscar for this monumental role. Her Marion is a tragic figure of poor decisions and circumstance; she is not a bad person—realizing that she has made a terrible decision, she plans to return the next morning to Phoenix and face the consequences moments before heading to shower—but one whose misguided actions have led her to a destination of doom. Long before the film's more macabre aspects kick into gear, Leigh manages to vibrantly come alive, her character faced with so many dreams for her future it has culminated in a crisis of conscience.

Transcendentally influential as a cinematic masterpiece and a piece of artwork in motion, *Psycho* continues over a half-century later to capture the attention, respect and adoration of new generations of moviegoers. Hitchcock weaves a spell of command and tension that begins in the first half—a scene where Marion stops at a car dealership and believes a policeman across the street is watching her is as nail-biting as any of the more perilous later moments—and doesn't stop until the final revelatory minutes. Additionally, John L. Russell's black-and-white lensing is superlative, bringing a great deal of atmosphere, foreboding and mystery that might not have had the same haunting effect in color. It almost goes without mentioning the flawless string-laden music score by Bernard Herrmann, ripped off many times since but never equaled. As in *Halloween* eighteen years later, it is impossible to imagine *Psycho* without that music, its striking orchestrations sending an unavoidable shiver up one's spine. As a groundbreaking horror film that paved the way for what was to follow, *Psycho* is a richly modulated study in the darkest regions of a person's psyche and a paragon of style, mood and undeniable terror.

Quarantine

2008 - Directed by John Erick Dowdle

When Hollywood studios acquire foreign properties and try to remake them, the results are famously hit-and-miss. It is for this reason that expectations were not very high for *Quarantine*, based on the smashing Spanish horror film, *[REC]*. Would an American crew dumb things down for audiences, going for cheap thrills and condescending storytelling over the original's more penetrating and cerebral aura of fright? The answer, it is heartening to declare, is no. Promising writer-director John Erick Dowdle and co-writer Drew Dowdle stay mostly faithful to *[REC]* while diverging just enough to make this new version their own. They have managed to improve upon certain aspects while not living up to other things that its predecessor did better. Measured out overall, they are close to equals.

Told exclusively from the point of view of a cameraman's lens, the film immediately introduces Angela Vidal (Jennifer Carpenter), host of a television show called *Night Shift*. She is at a fire company, all set to spend the overnight hours there as she reports on the profession of firefighters. After interviewing the employees and getting particularly chummy with one of them, Jake (Jay Hernandez), the alarm bell sounds. Angela and cameraman Scott (Steve Harris) excitedly ride along with them to answer the call of an apartment building where screams from an elderly neighbor have alarmed the other residents.

No sooner have they entered and gone up to Ms. Espinoza's (Jeannie Epper) apartment that the woman, foaming at the mouth and disoriented, suddenly attacks one of the rescuers. Escaping back down to the building's atrium, the group discover that police and government officials have surrounded the building, quarantining the inhabitants and refusing to let any of them leave with their lives. As sickness spreads among them—Lawrence (Greg Germann), a veterinarian, surmises from the symptoms that it's an extreme, highly contagious form of rabies—Angela, Jake and Scott desperately attempt to find a way out.

Quarantine follows the basic outline of *[REC]* while tweaking it here and there. At 89 minutes, the screenplay has been expanded, adding in a few more scare scenes, a few more clues as to what is going on amidst the chaos, and a few more character moments. This latter addition is certainly an improvement; whereas the characters in the earlier film mostly blended together, not really getting a chance to stand out from the crowd, the ensemble here are much more individualistic and their almost wholly dire fates more coherent and effective. Tiny inserted details, such as the pet that is seen running out of Ms. Espinoza's apartment, or the hostile rat that Scott stomps on with his shoe, are welcome, building upon the mysterious, bone-chilling mystique of the viral outbreak.

By and large, the creep factor is also increased, the suddenly villainous, no longer completely human antagonists more unsettlingly zombified in their features. With the camera swirling frantically and madness taking over the people's DNA, the film will take some viewers back to the same feeling they got as 7-year-olds attending a radio-sponsored Halloween attraction. Afraid to inch around corners but demanding rapidity as drooling lunatics pop out from every direction, the audience tightens their grip and edges to the end of their seats. Director Dowdle is terrific at building intensity levels to near-unbearable crescendos, and also throwing in subtle hints and background action that may not be caught the first time through.

Jennifer Carpenter, as Angela, deserves credit from venturing far and beyond the typical call of duty in a horror film. Not content to just scream and look frightened, Carpenter goes one step further by hyperventilating and falling into helpless bouts of pure hysteria. Some viewers may accuse her of overdoing it, but the actress embodies a despairing, authentic range of emotions that someone in her situation really would experience. With that said, Carpenter is not as personable or warm as first pic's lead actress Manuela Velasco, and her news reporting skills suggest that she's been on the job for less than a week. The rest of the cast is superb, making the most of their fleeting screen time as the camera roams this way and that to catch all the goings-on. Of them, Jay Hernandez makes the sharpest imprint as Jake, an upstanding professional at the end of his ropes.

The biggest flaw of *Quarantine* is the crucial climactic scene that was easily the highlight of *[REC]*. For a movie that thus far has done a better job of trying to explain what is happening, the brothers Dowdle go in the opposite direction with the ending and makes the unfortunate choice to cut out some of the crucial backstory of a key last-scene character. Because of this, the tension comes not from anticipating what is about to show itself to Angela and Scott, but from the unholy levels of mess-your-pants terror Jennifer Carpenter exhibits and spills out into the audience. This nightmarish figure that does ultimately appear, by the way, is nowhere near as horrifying as in *[REC]*, looking more like an unkempt man than the emaciated abomination that haunted the earlier movie. Of all that Dowdle gets right, he gets this unfortunately wrong.

Notwithstanding the most shameless example in memory of a theatrical trailer giving away a movie's very ending, *Quarantine* is unnerving, jolting entertainment that, lo and behold, mostly does *[REC]* proud. The film is completely unnecessary, to be honest, but if a remake must be made in lieu of original thoughts and ideas, one could do far, far worse. Putting to complete and utter shame a film that was released around the same time in the fall of 2008—George Romero's manipulative, badly acted, insultingly conceived POV zombie film, *Diary of the Dead*—*Quarantine* is the real deal, a primal, uncompromising vision of insanity run amok.

[REC]

2007 - Directed by Jaume Balagueró and Paco Plaza

When *Quarantine* came to theaters in October 2008, the film from which it was remade, the Spanish-language *[REC]*, had yet to be released in America. This is a shame for a great many reasons, but none more so than the fact that the majority of casual viewers going to see *Quarantine* were likely not aware that basically the same movie was made just a year earlier. Hollywood likes nothing more than to take original motion pictures from other countries, snatch up their ideas, and reap the financial benefits. Why expend energy in coming up with imaginative ideas of your own when you can just copy off of the strong genre work coming out of Spain, Japan and Taiwan? One supposes that's their skewed way of thinking, and it's close to despicable.

Indeed, *[REC]* eventually hit North America in 2009. As effective as *Quarantine* ultimately was, this earlier-made feature deserves accolades for coming first. *[REC]* is a well-made funhouse ride of pure terror and near-breathless dread, on the short side at only 75 minutes but making up for its brevity through directors Jaume Balagueró's and Paco Plaza's knowledge in how to go for the jugular and scare an audience. Inspiration for the picture's style, told completely from the POV of a character's camera, likely comes from 1999's *The Blair Witch Project*. Conceptually speaking, the films share a definite similarity, but the use of the aforementioned camera becomes more than just a gimmick as it is plausibly explained why the photographer continues to shoot even in the face of unthinkable horror.

The setup is ingeniously clever. Reporter Ángela (Manuela Velasco) is the sunny host of a late-night television program called *While You're Asleep*, in which she travels to different workplaces and uncovers the ins and outs of their daily overnight routines. On this fateful evening, she is visiting a local fire company. The expectation is that it's going to be a largely uneventful episode, but, when the fire alarm rings out, Ángela tags along with her cameraman in tow to an apartment building where a resident is disturbing the peace. No sooner have they gotten inside that the police arrive and quarantine the building, locking everyone inside with no route of escape. The suspect, an older woman, has seemingly gone crazy, and proceeds to mortally wound one of the policemen by biting off a chunk of his neck. Explanations are slim and the atmosphere among the inhabitants is understandably chaotic as they, one by one, are taken over by a contagious virus that transfers rage and delirium via each other's saliva.

[REC] is the sort of cinematic experience that breeds nightmares. The picture starts innocuously enough, with Ángela interviewing the employees, jokily trying on their heavy fire suit, and passing the time by joining in on a basketball game. When the call arrives and Ángela becomes entrapped in the apartment building, the film takes a startling turn. The viewer remains right there with the reporter at all times as confusion turns to frustration, and then outright fear. By the end, the apartment has descended into hell, monstrous beings lurking throughout the building as Ángela and her trusty cameraman plot an exit or safety (whichever comes first). Since the only footage captured is from the show's camera, much, but certainly not all, of the mayhem is left off-screen, the viewer attempting to piece together what is happening, what has already occurred, and the grim fates of the other snared souls, from an elderly couple, to an Asian family, to a mother and daughter.

Performances are naturalistic at all times, never tipping their hat to obvious acting or melodrama. There is no music score, as it should be. These are key elements crucial for bringing realism to the so-called "found-footage" subgenre. *[REC]* gets the formula right, and Manuela Velasco is exceptional as tour guide Ángela, effortless in her reporting skills early on and accurately embodying the sheer panic and dismay of a person stuck in a hopeless situation. Additionally, Velasco is instantly so personable and cheery that she is immensely likable. We, as spectators, care about what happens to her.

[REC] leads to a final fifteen minutes destined to produce goosebumps on the arms of the most jaded of viewers. Locking themselves in the penthouse apartment of a doctor who has abandoned the premises, Ángela and her cameraman stumble upon newspaper clippings and audio recordings that begin to piece together the truth behind the viral (or is it supernatural?) outbreak. When the light on the camera breaks, stranding them in complete darkness save for the lens' greenish night-vision, they are visited by a horror beyond anything they could have imagined. The story's path isn't groundbreaking, but in the unknown aspects of what Balagueró and Plaza have conceived is where it leaves one most excitingly ill at ease. Consequently, *[REC]* boasts an uncommonly cathartic power to shake the viewer to his or her very core.

[REC]²

2010 - Directed by Jaume Balagueró and Paco Plaza

This is how you make a sequel. Instead of just being a tacked-on continuation or brazen cash-grab, *[REC]²* builds upon the mythos set up in 2007's *[REC]*, then twists it in rousingly unanticipated ways as the characters—and viewers—learn more about what they are dealing with. Returning to the directors' chairs, Jaume Balagueró and Paco Plaza find logical ways to also retain the POV style of the original. This "you-are-there" feel, aided by superb actors who never seem as if they are acting, creates a strong sense of disquiet and foreboding. Anything could be lurking around the corner or at the edges of the frame, and half the fun is in the diverting of this anxious anticipation just as the real scares prepare to pounce when you least expect them to.

A city apartment building has been quarantined from the outside world, some kind of contagious virus having turned its inhabitants into raving, drooling madmen. Enter a SWAT team equipped with helmet cameras who, led by Dr. Owen (Jonathan Mellor), are tasked to make their way inside, search for survivors, and find a possible antidote hiding somewhere in the attic apartment—the root of the outbreak. Dr. Owen knows far more than he's letting on, however, and it doesn't take long for all hell to once again break loose. Meanwhile, three teens (Andrea Ros, Pau Poch, Àlex Batllori) wielding a camera find their way inside via the underground sewer system, not realizing just how fatal this decision is about to become.

A study in bad-dream realism, *[REC]²* comes off as a natural extension to its raw, startlingly creepy predecessor. Whereas *[REC]* and the American remake, 2008's *Quarantine*, took their time setting up the story and pulling the viewer in before their gradual ascension into pure terror and horror, *[REC]²* is faster and more unstoppable—an edgy, frightening thrill ride sometimes reminiscent of a (really good) first-person video game. By the start of the picture, the crap has already long since hit the fan, and now it is up to Owen, the SWAT team—and later, the three teenagers who have broken in—to survive the ordeal long enough to capture a blood sample from the virus' source, an emaciated, zombie-like girl named Niña Medeiros (Javier Botet) who is lurking about the property.

The scenes set in the penthouse apartment are, once again, thick with overwhelming tension, and a setpiece taking place in an air shaft is enough to suffocate the most strong-willed of audiences. It goes without saying that the inevitable appearance of Niña Medeiros—the physical embodiment of one's greatest fears—is just about as teeth-chatteringly scary as it was the first time around. Javier Botet, ultra-skinny and lanky and no doubt draped in top-notch make-up effects, is stunning in the most chilling of ways as Niña Medeiros. Also at the top of their games: newcomer Jonathan Mellor as the determined Dr. Owen; Andrea Ros as Mire, the most reluctant and vulnerable of the teens, and Manuela Velasco, welcomely returning as reporter Ángela Vidal, lead protagonist of the first *[REC]*, who has survived within an inch of her sanity.

There is very little that is thematically deep about either *[REC]* or *[REC]²*, but they both make up for it in their educated, tightly crafted know-how of the horror genre. Balagueró and Plaza are well aware of how to toy with their audience, tossing them through the veritable wringer. With *[REC]²*, they do not merely repeat themselves, but bring added insight to the plot, turning an unthinkable biological hazard into something that, as it turns out, is also hauntingly supernatural. With suspense raised to the rafters, the film concocts a number of climactic revelations that deliciously expand the scope and seemed to be paving the way for a third film in the series. Said follow-up, 2012's wedding-set *[REC]³: Génesis*, ultimately went in a different, blackly comedic direction that did not tonally work for this particular franchise. The first two, though, are apexes in modern Spanish-made horror.

Red State

2011 - Directed by Kevin Smith

If *Red State* isn't necessarily Kevin Smith's best picture (for this writer, 1997's *Chasing Amy* still holds that title), it most certainly is his best-directed, signaling a vast leap forward for the filmmaker. It couldn't have come at a better time, either; his previous movie (his first that he didn't script), the Bruce Willis-Tracy Morgan buddy comedy *Cop Out*, was an unthinkably lame, incompetent, entirely laughless waste of resources. Smith has a lot on his mind with *Red State*, so credit is due that he never spells out his messages or mixed moral implications, allowing each viewer to take from it what he or she will. Yes, he touches heavily upon the dangers of religious extremism, but he doesn't make a mockery of it so much as a pointed comment on hypocrisy, rotting fanaticism and the tragedy of psychological conditioning. Most of the would-be "good guys" are deeply flawed and unsavory in their own ways, too, leading to an underlying discussion about how skewed right and wrong can get when people's belief systems and self-interest get in the way of their humanity.

Travis (Michael Angarano), Jarod (Kyle Gallner) and Billy-Ray (Nicholas Braun) are three randy teenage boys living on the outskirts of Middle-American town Cooper's Dell who think they're setting out to hook up for sex with a 38-year-old woman they've met on the Internet. What they don't realize is that it's all a setup by the Coopers, a Phelps-like family of extreme fundamentalists who lure sinners to their compound and brutally do away with them. The madness is presided over by sermon-spouting patriarch Abin (Michael Parks), who welcomes death but isn't about to go quietly when ATF agents led by Joseph Keenan (John Goodman) show up on the edge of their premises and a standoff-turned-shootout begins.

Independently financed and wholly made outside of the studio system, the $4-million-budgeted *Red State* did not have to answer to any pre-set parameters during its creation, nor did writer-director Kevin Smith have to deal with any controlling producers' identity-snuffing whims. That's good, because the final product would probably look a lot different than it does now.

Taking inspiration from the works of Joel and Ethan Coen (hints of 2007's *No Country for Old Men* are unmistakable), Rob Zombie (the guns-blasting third-act skirmish resembles 2005's *The Devil's Rejects*) and Eli Roth (the very plot is but a religious-themed variation on 2006's *Hostel*), the film ultimately averts genre expectations, starting off as a raunchy teen comedy, moving into ghastly horror territory, detouring into a bullets-whizzing action pic, and concluding with a perfect satiric exclamation point. For a director whose visual sense wavers little beyond a bland point-and-shoot style, Smith's more ambitious vision for *Red State* is thrillingly accomplished, aided by cinematography from David Klein that is predominately handheld but controlled. Cohesively edited and affectingly stark, the camerawork lends an authentic immediacy to the narrative. Especially chilling is the way the camera sticks with Jarrod in an early scene, trapped in a covered cage as the haunting sounds of fevered hymns being sung from outside are heard.

The first half is its better portion. Had the narrative continued down this path, remaining intimately with the crazed Cooper family and the three teenage boys' heinous experiences within their clutches, it no doubt could have ratcheted apprehension to hyperventilatory levels. After the guys are drugged and captured, Abin's ensuing sermon to his brainwashed followers down in an underground church is as icky and unsettling as one would expect (and also a little too short; Smith should have probably rethought the edits he made following the Sundance Film Festival premiere). What happens next, beginning with the horrific, torturous murder of a gay man (Cooper Thornton) the Coopers have also ensnared, is harrowing stuff, Smith's one mistake being his decision to cut out of this sequence midway through and sever the rising tension. This aside, the picture pulls no punches and defies convention as no one—not even the protagonists—is safe, deaths occurring just as they so often are: sudden, messy and without glorification. Furthermore, people who deserve comeuppances don't receive them as expected, and the actions of certain characters force one to always be reassessing whether or not they're purely despicable or worth our sympathies. This unsure appraisal most definitely pertains to Cheyenne (Kerry Bishé), the grown granddaughter of Abin who decides she wants out of her current bleak situation even if that means turning her back on her elders.

The introduction of Joseph Keenan as the next honorary "hero" of the film is where things take a turn away from outright horror. With the ATF squad surrounding the building, a careless action on the part of philandering police chief dunce Wynan (Stephen Root) is the catalyst for an unnecessary casualty, a subsequent rashly immoral decision from those who should be in charge, and a shoot-to-kill standoff. With the Coopers no longer the only villains and the authority figures proving irresponsible and bloodthirsty in an entirely different way, only the kids—those who have grown up with their minds polluted, and those whose only downfall has been letting their sexual curiosity get the best of them—are anything approaching innocent. With so many warring viewpoints and diseased psyches, however, senseless violence is the only result. The second half of *Red State* is riveting, to be sure, but does start to grow repetitive as consecutive scenes threaten to turn into a whirr of bullets. Fortunately, there are detectable thoughts behind it and inferences to the characters' decisions that keep the viewer questioning in the best way Smith's intentions. It is easy at first to point the finger at how rotten and evil the fundamentalists are, but when the rest of the ensemble reveal less savory shades, too, there is no choice but to reevaluate what is being said underneath the surface, and why.

Michael Parks brings enough fire and brimstone to his juicy role of Abin Cooper that it's difficult to envision him as an actor. He sinks his teeth into the part, chilling throughout but with a truly disquieting entrance as he's first glimpsed standing motionless alongside his family, who are picketing a gay man's funeral. Travis spots him as he and his mother (Anna Gunn) drive by, and it's enough to give him—and us as the audience—the willies. John Goodman first appears halfway through the running time as Agent Keenan before taking over as the lead. One of Goodman's juiciest roles in years, he gives a world-weary charm to a man who sees first-hand what can happen when someone takes an elitist stand on religion without bothering to understand or respect other people's beliefs. Melissa Leo, at the time of release fresh off her Oscar win for 2010's *The Fighter*, is dryly funny as the trailer-park woman the boys travel to meet, then wickedly cutthroat when it's soon revealed that she is Abin's abiding daughter. Michael Angarano, Kyle Gallner and Nicholas Braun are dragged through some emotionally high places as the teens who get the story in motion, making a decision that will severely and grievously change the course of what's left of their lives. And, as the most morally unpeggable figure, Kerry Bishé indelibly plays Cheyenne, whose desperation leads to what could either be construed as deception or a wake-up call.

Red State is a brazenly liberated motion picture about psycho-ultraconservatism, the lingering effects of shame, and the contemptible ease of corruption in a free country that somehow lost its way during its journey to the present day. The film is not without problems, certainly. Kevin Smith's love for his own words shines through several times, edging toward pretentiousness when the dialogue gets a little too verbose (this happens twice during scenes when Agent Keenan is talking on the phone). There are also two parts in particular—one set in a classroom, the other during Abin's sermon—where information is unnaturally and rather clunkily stated for no purpose other than to provide exposition to the viewer. As mentioned, the momentum is also harmed when the film shies away from its more overt horror elements almost as quickly as they're introduced. With all that said, *Red State* is defiantly and admirably its own being, drawing from other directors and works in tone and style and archetypal plot elements, but daring to confront hot-button topics like religion and politics in a fresh, non-preachy way. It's a smart, mature film from a man who, at long last, had artistically come of age.

The Ring

2002 - Directed by Gore Verbinski

Every scene and every shot of *The Ring*, the smart American remake of the popular 1998 Japanese horror film, *Ringu* (itself based upon the novel by Kôji Suzuki), prompts a nearly asphyxiating aura of dread. It weighs down heavily on the characters' lives and viewers' heads, refusing to let up. Directed by Gore Verbinski with a sharp eye for visual detail and a keen sense of generating suspense, the film is a creepy and considerably unsettling experience that works its way deeply under one's skin.

The startling, deliberately paced prologue is a real attention-grabber. During a sleepover, two teenage girls, Katie (Amber Tamblyn) and Becca (Rachael Bella), discuss an urban legend wherein watchers of a cursed videotape immediately receive a telephone call informing them they have only seven days to live. After Katie confesses to Becca that she watched it exactly a week ago, things readily grow dire. Enter news reporter Rachel Keller (Naomi Watts), a single mother who is asked by her sister (Lindsay Frost) to investigate the circumstances surrounding daughter Katie's mysterious sudden death. Rachel's research ultimately leads her to the infamous tape in question. When she views it and, to her horror, receives the cryptic phone call, the countdown to her impending death begins. Unless Rachel can find out where the tape originated and put a stop to the curse, she faces the same fate as her unfortunate niece.

The Ring is a superbly crafted horror film that, rare to form, does not dumb down or lessen the impact of its foreign counterpart. Not overly violent and with almost no gore, the unshakable effectiveness it musters comes from what is hinted at, but not seen. This tactic works magnificently since the characters themselves are faced with something that they do not understand. The opening scene, for example, has a setup similar to 1996's *Scream*, but, instead of ending in an evisceration, opts for nothing more than a horrific sense of being nervously unsure of what to expect. Another sequence involving a crazed horse getting loose on a barge en route to Pacific Northwest's Moesko Island is spectacularly tense and imaginative.

Her first leading role in a prestigious studio-produced release following her breakthrough work in 2001's David Lynch-directed *Mulholland Drive*, Naomi Watts does not disappoint. As Rachel, whose situation grows even grimmer after her ex-boyfriend, Noah (Martin Henderson), and young son, Aidan (David Dorfman), watch the tape themselves, Watts' performance is fresh and likable, contemplative and typically layered. Great character actor Brian Cox is a welcome addition as a man with close ties to the tape, while Daveigh Chase is unnervingly good as a child somehow behind the videocassette's origin.

The Ring is a merciless thriller, threateningly beautiful to look at and eerie to behold. Verbinski and screenwriter Ehren Kruger refuse to let their possibly doomed protagonists—Rachel, Noah and Aidan—off the hook, cleverly setting up a falsely predictable ending bred in conventions before pressing on for another fifteen minutes as they totally bulldoze expectations. The picture's top-notch technical attributes are additional characters in and of themselves. Bojan Bazelli's atmospheric cinematography is marvelous, full of vivid fog-shrouded locations and rain-drenched landscapes, its color scheme with a moody penchant for indelible gray and blue hues. Likewise, Hans Zimmer's music score and Craig Wood's taut editing serve to keep the audience on edge. In his description of Alfred Hitchcock's work on 1960's *Psycho*, the late Roger Ebert once famously wrote that the director "plays his audience like a piano." The same could be said for Verbinski's laudatory work here. As with the "conundrum"-causing videotape at the center of the film, once *The Ring* has been seen, there is no unseeing it. The deliciously distressing spell has already been cast.

The Roost

2005 - Directed by Ti West

A pulpy, grainy, Super-16mm creature feature made on a budget that far belies its savvy ambition, *The Roost* marked the acclaimed but underseen film debut of über-talented writer-director Ti West. Though the auteur has grown in many different facets as an artist in the years since (with impressively diverse efforts as varied as 2007's hunting-gone-awry thriller *Trigger Man*, 2009's nostalgic, '80s-set throwback *The House of the Devil*, and 2011's ghost tale *The Innkeepers*), one only has to see the movie that started his career to witness what a true, unadulterated genre talent he already was. Soaked and dripping in atmosphere both intimidating and thrilling, *The Roost* tells its story simply and elegantly, drawing out one's apprehension with deliberate lingering beats before pouncing at bravura unexpected moments.

In an act of shrewd inspiration, *The Roost* is positioned as a classic horror picture of the B-movie variety, introduced by the ghoulish, pun-heavy host (Tom Noonan) of WDIE-TV Channel 13's *Saturday Frightmare Theater*. These bookends—with a brief interlude just prior to the third act—are an invaluable inclusion that only add to the schlocky yet scary-fun Halloween-heavy vibe. Set during the witching hours of October 31st, four friends are headed to a wedding when something suddenly flies into their windshield and causes them to run off the road. Unable to get their car out of the mud, they decide to get help at a secluded nearby farmhouse. When Brian (Sean Reid) wanders off and disappears into the barn, siblings Elliot (Wil Horneff) and Allison (Vanessa Horneff) and buddy Trevor (Karl Jacob) go to find him. What they discover aren't just a flock of standard-issue bats lurking in the darkness of the rustic building, but vampiric ones, their bite turning anyone they come across into the walking undead.

The occasionally stilted performances from the actors playing the four central protagonists in *The Roost* are a small price to pay for a film that tosses substance on the back burner and cranks the darkly sumptuous style up to 11. Every shot is carefully, lovingly composed by Ti West and cinematographer Eric Robbins, the palpable locations and detailed production design giving the rural setting a memorable personality that leers threateningly over the in-peril characters. With the exception of a cell phone in one scene, there is also a timeless feel to the proceedings, with the *Saturday Frightmare Theater* framework and the use of a Halloween-centric radio news report and storytelling program bringing invaluable flavor to the periphery. Little details, such as the friends' car passing by a roadside memorial with four crosses rising from the ground, offer up distinct but sly foreshadowing, confirming that multiple return viewings will be richly rewarded. At 81 minutes, there isn't a second of fat to trim from the editing; every shot is there for a reason, and West unhurriedly knows how long to hold in order to work up maximum unrest in his audience.

The classy score, filled with screeching strings and a *Psycho*-esque aura, complements the story's sure-footed rise in tension as the full extent of encroaching danger is revealed. For a movie made for very little money, the effects work is so seamlessly integrated that it puts to shame any number of studio pictures costing millions. Mixing the practical and a light touch of opticals, the swarm of bloodthirsty bats come convincingly alive. There is not a wire attached to their flapping wings in sight. How did West pull these off with such limited resources? It might be better to not know, lest the magic be spoiled. As if malevolent winged creatures weren't enough, the narrative introduces an additional threat in the second half that informs this root of evil, the reliance on what is happening in the background of shots often just as important as the foreground.

With *The Roost*, Ti West relies on solid, old-fashioned yarn-spinning while avoiding the temptation to blatantly explain or spell out what is happening. Indeed, the viewer only learns what the characters do, the spare parts coming satisfyingly together while still allowing for there to be a purveying enigmatic quality to the plot's developments. West's control of every aspect of his cinematic tableau is in full force, proving that the financial side of moviemaking has next to nothing to do with how well a film is made. Either the people behind the scenes have that special something, or they don't, and West and his crew most certainly do. Their passion bleeds over every frame of *The Roost*, leading to an experience as creatively and aesthetically inspiring as it is deliciously gasp-provoking.

Satan's Little Helper

2005 - Directed by Jeff Lieberman

Satan's Little Helper is an unsung gem, a film that premiered to positive notices at the 2004 Tribeca Film Festival, but bypassed theaters and was sent directly to DVD. This typically signals that a movie was deemed not to be theatrical material, but don't let that fool you this time. Smoothly marrying politically incorrect comedy with horror without losing an ounce of laughs or creepiness in the process, *Satan's Little Helper* deservedly should garner a wider audience and a high regard among Halloween-set thrillers.

9-year-old Douglas "Dougie" Whooly (Alexander Brickel) is obsessed with a violent video game he has recently received called *Satan's Little Helper*, so much so that he has dressed up as the title character—a pint-sized cohort of the Devil himself—for Halloween. When he and mom Merrill (Amanda Plummer) eagerly go to the ferry station of their small New England town of Bell Island to pick up his college-aged sister, Jenna (Katheryn Winnick), Dougie is angered to find that she has brought along new boyfriend Alex (Stephen Graham). Bummed about the turn of events, Dougie runs off. While walking through a nearby neighborhood, he watches as a figure dressed in a Satan costume drags a dead woman with a slit throat out of her house and props her up on the porch next to a scarecrow decoration. Satan then moves on to the next house, stabbing a man and laying him out in his front yard next to a mock burial plot. Of course, the passersby in the community don't even bat an eyelash, noting the October 31st date. Dougie, however, is enamored by what he sees. Thinking that this is the Dark Lord from his video game, he approaches the killer and asks to be his helper. Satan Man silently obliges.

Satan's Little Helper was written and directed by Jeff Lieberman, a talented cult director who once helmed 1976's *Squirm*, 1978's *Blue Sunshine* and 1981's *Just Before Dawn*. His sense of humor is blackened to a crisp, and his intuition at filming setpieces that throw the viewer off-balance while building tension is on the money. This is an applause-worthy example of originality and delicious morbidity that follows the viewpoint of a child not yet able to decipher fiction from real violence that is being committed before him. When Dougie suggests that Satan kill Alex so that he can once again have his sister to himself, he makes the potentially grievous decision of guiding him to his home and allowing him to hide out in the basement. After Satan does away with Alex while he and Dougie are out hunting for a costume, he returns home with the child. Jenna and Merrill naturally think the person in front of them is simply Alex in the guise of his Halloween get-up, unaware of the imminent danger before them.

Dougie is twisted in many ways, but he isn't without his naive innocence. He thinks it is all just a game, for example, when Satan pushes him in a shopping cart, running over a pregnant lady, a baby carriage and a blind man in the parking lot of a grocery store. As Dougie cheers at the carnage laid before them, the natural comedy of the situation is so wrong and yet undeniably funny. Satan, smartly never revealed as either a homicidal maniac in a costume or the genuine article, isn't absent of a playful, mischievous side. When he rings the doorbell of an elderly lady with a walker, he motions with his hands that he is asleep and then checks his watch after it takes her too long to reach the door. He subsequently wastes no time in hanging her with a rope off the side of her home as trick-or-treaters pass by in the night.

Alexander Brickel is adorable as young Dougie, likable even when he is portrayed as overly gullible, and later touchingly truthful when he realizes the murders are no joke and his family members are next on Satan's target list. As sister Jenna, Katheryn Winnick is a winning presence who has trouble convincing her mother it's not just a prank when she tells her Alex isn't behind the Satan garb. The always-quirky Amanda Plummer essays one of her more down-to-earth roles as mother Merrill, but still plays the part with an endearing dippiness. Finally, Joshua Annex is unnerving as Satan Man, downright brilliant in his body language without once taking off his mask or uttering a syllable. He does change his costume, however, and when he shows up at the door dressed as Jesus Christ immediately after Dougie has prayed to God for help, the results are beyond chilling.

The low budget of *Satan's Little Helper* is apparent in spots, and it's a shame that the ingenious idea Jeff Lieberman had for the final scene, wherein Dougie and his family are killed and set out on their porch like decorations, was never shot. Still, with a solid cast lined up and a strong script, the film exhibits how much can be achieved with limited resources. The autumnal atmosphere of Halloween in New England is effectively established, especially considering that the movie was shot in the summer, and the tone never oversteps its boundaries between what is meant to get laughs and what is meant to disturb the viewer. *Satan's Little Helper* is an uncompromisingly wicked, subjectively brave chiller practically crying out to be discovered.

Scream

1996 - Directed by Wes Craven

Scream opened on December 20, 1996, and raked in a paltry $6.3-million over its first three-day weekend, opening well behind fellow new release *Beavis and Butthead Do America*. Being a genre enthusiast, I remember excitedly going to see the film on opening night. The theater was empty, but the film was groundbreakingly original, as good as the then-dying horror landscape had been in years. I went back and saw the film a week later, and there was scarcely an empty seat to be found. I went back a third and final time the following weekend, and the theater was so packed that people were sitting in the aisles. Cultural cinematic phenomena are often like that, taking consumers by surprise and building quickly upon rabid word-of-mouth.

Written by Kevin Williamson and directed by Wes Craven, who went on to also helm the series' subsequent installments, *Scream* arrived at the perfect moment. Many people, most notably studio execs, had long begun writing horror movies off as a form that was no longer commercially viable. Creativity was at an all-time low, and box-office receipts were no better. *Scream* changed all that, taking audiences (and Hollywood) by surprise in a way that only happens a few times every decade. The film, at once a pointedly knowledgeable, frequently funny satire on slasher conventions and a terrifically scary, joyously suspenseful horror picture itself, treated viewers with a rare intelligence not often seen. By outwardly making note of the rampant clichés found in the genre even as it sometimes intentionally mimicked the very things it was deriding, the movie was not quite like anything that had come before it (coincidentally, 1994's *Wes Craven's New Nightmare*, seamlessly melding fiction with reality, is probably its closest cousin).

The opening ten minutes of *Scream* are masterfully conceived and horrifyingly pulled off, likely as well-known as the shower scene in 1960's *Psycho* or the shark attack that started 1975's *Jaws*. Although the prologue has been spoofed numerous times since, most notably in 2000's *Scary Movie*, it has not lost its unblinkingly terse power. Casey Becker (Drew Barrymore) is home alone, making popcorn and readying herself for a night of watching horror flicks, when the telephone rings. She at first flirts with the unknown caller as they chat about their favorite scary movies, but becomes increasingly nervous when she senses the person on the other end of the line might be closer than she thought. Terrorized by a horror-trivia game the culprit has concocted, Casey answers the question incorrectly ("Name the killer in *Friday the 13th*...") and finds herself running for her life.

By the next morning, the media has descended upon the sleepy campus of Woodsboro High School as buzz about Casey's brutal murder spreads. Virginal teen Sidney Prescott (Neve Campbell), who cannot help but be reminded of her own mother's slaying a year earlier, tries to go on as usual, but cutthroat journalist Gale Weathers (Courteney Cox), sensing a connection, won't let her forget the past. As Sidney's pals—boyfriend Billy Loomis (Skeet Ulrich), cinephile Randy Meeks (Jamie Kennedy), over-caffeinated Stu Macher (Matthew Lillard) and sympathetic best friend Tatum Riley (Rose McGowan)—hypothesize about who the killer might be, Sidney almost becomes the next victim when she is attacked in her home and narrowly escapes. Wearing a flowing black robe and Ghostface mask, the psychopath next sets his or her sights on a party at a secluded farmhouse where all the principle characters, including Gale and Tatum's smitten police officer brother, Deputy Dewey (David Arquette), have converged.

The plot may sound like more of the same, but it is in its conception and delivery that *Scream* becomes something special. Instead of populating the film with big-breasted bimbos and brainless jocks, Williamson and Craven have imagined a world in which horror movies exist and the characters are all too aware that their lives are becoming one. Sharp references to pop culture and all things scary movie-related naturally litter the dialogue, with Randy particularly adamant that the authorities would be able to solve the crime if they paid attention to the slasher films filling the shelves at the video store he works at. Timeworn traditions—sex equaling death; the notion that saying, "I'll be right back," is a death sentence; victims running up the stairs when they should be fleeing out the front door—are all lovingly mocked here, and then turned on their heads. Snappy and always smart, the writing allows the characters to be identifiable, existing as human beings rather than just chopping blocks. Despite knowing what they know, they do not always make the best decisions when placed in harm's way, and that's part of the fun (and the point).

If *Scream* were but a winking nod to horror's past, it would only be half the film that it is. The key to its exceptional success is the effortless blending of humor with genuine terror. The story is taken seriously, and so are the characters' fates. Tension is high throughout—the costumed killer lurks in the background of the proceedings, waiting to strike—and the violence, some of it quite graphic, is sobering and dark. When Randy watches *Halloween* and pleas for Jamie Lee Curtis to turn around at the moment where Michael Myers is right behind her, the Ghostface maniac perilously looms behind Randy. It's an ingenious moment, perfectly commenting on how knowing the rules of horror movies will not always save a person when faced with the real thing. The finale, wherein the identity of the killer(s) are revealed, is unexpected, though a little too talky and explanatory. Fortunately, the film returns to its glory in time for the shrewd closing moments.

The ensemble cast is speckless. As heroine Sidney Prescott, Neve Campbell (at the time riding high from TV's *Party of Five*) is strong-willed and vulnerable—two characteristics necessary in essaying an endangered protagonist whose mortality is at stake, but who also has what it takes to overcome the evil headed her way. That Sidney is still in the midst of trying to move on after the death of her mother adds a rich texture to the character, and Campbell hits all the right notes. Courteney Cox (who shot this when TV's *Friends* was still in its infancy) is superb as tabloid reporter Gale Weathers, willing to do almost anything for a story but with occasional signs underneath that she still has a beating heart. Cox's sizzling chemistry with David Arquette, then a virtual unknown who would later marry his onscreen love interest, gets a lot of mileage from their scenes together.

Memorable supporting performances from Rose McGowan, as Sidney's closest friend, Tatum; Skeet Ulrich, as Sidney's suspicious boyfriend, Billy; Matthew Lillard, as Tatum's boyfriend, Stu, and Jamie Kennedy, as the acerbic Randy, gave most of these actors the careers they have today in film and television. As for Drew Barrymore, the biggest star of the cast, she uninhibitedly throws herself into the brief but emotionally demanding role of ill-fated Casey Becker, getting the film off to a rousing, unforgettable start. Barrymore's scene alone still has the effectiveness to send chills down one's spine.

Technical credits are the icing on the cake. The cinematography by Mark Irwin is tight, slick and still gritty, taking suburban and rural settings and making their idyllic innocuousness seem threatening. The editing by Patrick Lussier doesn't waste a second of film, keeping the pace moving and knowing when to slow down to orchestrate taut suspense. The music score by Marco Beltrami is additionally top-tier, with alternately mournful and eerie cues complementing the silences. The soundtrack, too, is just right, with Gus' cover of "Don't Fear the Reaper," Nick Cave and the Bad Seeds' "Red Right Hand," and SoHo's "Whisper to a Scream" (the latter over the end credits) ideally chosen and placed.

Scream was so enormously successful, not only personally but financially, that it single-handedly jump-started a whole new slasher era the likes of which hadn't been seen since the late-'70s/early-'80s. 1997's *I Know What You Did Last Summer* (and its sequel), 1998's *Urban Legend* (and its sequel), 1998's *Disturbing Behavior*, 1998's *Halloween: H20*, 2000's *Cherry Falls* and 2001's *Valentine* were just a handful of the efforts that were clearly inspired by and modeled after "Scream" before the tides once again turned and supernatural thrillers and remakes became all the rage. The horror genre is like that, reinventing itself every few years, but never going away. Audiences like to be scared—fear is perhaps the most cathartic emotion that cinema offers—and *Scream* was one of those lightning-in-a-bottle miracles that proved why horror will continue to endure as long as movies are made.

Scream 2

1997 - Directed by Wes Craven

Rushed into production after *Scream* hit blockbuster status at the box office, *Scream 2* is a better follow-up than it has any right to be, especially considering that Kevin Williamson's script wasn't even finished when filming got underway. Arriving in theaters one week shy of a full year after its predecessor—a word-of-mouth sensation that resurrected the slasher genre from a long-dormant slumber—this sharp-tongued sequel has a lot of ground to cover as it catches up with the surviving characters, introduces a new roster of supporting players, and must devise a plot that stays true to the first while building upon the increasingly elaborate chain-events mythos sparking from the affair and subsequent murder of Sidney Prescott's (Neve Campbell) mother. While the picture sometimes lacks the sense of freshness that the original displayed, it more than makes up for it with director Wes Craven's undaunted weaving of suspense and terror with innately human moments.

Two years after the events of *Scream*, survivors Sidney Prescott and Randy Meeks (Jamie Kennedy) are now students at Windsor College, happy to have the tragedies from their pasts behind them. When two classmates, Maureen (Jada Pinkett Smith) and Phil (Omar Epps), are murdered at an advance screening of *Stab*, based on Gale Weathers' best-selling book, *The Woodsboro Murders*, Deputy Dewey Riley (David Arquette) wastes no time in coming to check on Sidney's safety. Detecting a good news story when she sees it, Gale also promptly arrives on campus to report on what she suspects may be a copycat slayer. What none of them yet realize is that a whole new killing spree is about to begin, with Sidney once again the prime target.

Scream 2 is wit-filled and a whole lot of fun, building panicky apprehension more so than leave-the-light-on-at-night scares. It's also sometimes breathlessly intense, as when Sidney and friend Hallie (Elise Neal) must climb over the knocked-out Ghostface psychopath in order to escape from the back of a crashed police car, or a slam-bang setpiece where Gale is stalked through the maze-like corridors of the university's visual arts building. One thing the *Scream* series has always done expertly is the juggling of self-aware satire and knowledge of cinema tropes while treating the central protagonists with the sympathetic respect they deserve. Jokes are made in the spry interactions between diverse personalities (and it was a stroke of genius to cast Tori Spelling as Sidney in film-within-a-film *Stab*, the very actor she jokingly said would play her in the first *Scream*). However, when lives are in danger, it is tackled with the *gravitas* that would come from these events occurring in the real world.

The cast is punchy and look to be having a ball. By the nature of what she is going through, Neve Campbell's Sidney doesn't have as much time to be light and cheery. At the start, she has moved on and has even managed to have a sense of humor about her lot in life—when she receives a prank call from the supposed killer, she wastes no time in checking her Caller ID and responding with the guy's full name and number. Campbell plays the part with all the qualities someone would want in their horror heroine, and her new pals, from roommate Hallie to supportive boyfriend Derek (Jerry O'Connell), are colorful but grounded. Laurie Metcalf deliciously goes against-type as awkward news reporter Debbie Salt, unable to live up to what Gale's vision of an intrepid journalist should be, while Courteney Cox is at her facetious best playing a cutthroat career woman who has simultaneously gotten an even bigger head even as she cannot stop herself from caring about the people she has shared a previous life-or-death experience with. Also making an impression, Liev Schreiber goes from cameo to one of the leads as Cotton Weary, falsely convicted murderer of Sidney's mom who has been released from prison and is looking to take advantage of his part in the sensationalistic media hype; Timothy Olyphant, as film major Mickey, a camera always in his hand before YouTube and the concept of reality shows had even been born yet, and Sarah Michelle Gellar, whose sorority sister Cici is menaced as a parallel scene from F.W. Murnau's *Nosferatu* plays on the television screen.

Scream 2's high body count threatens to leave one a bit jaded by the end, but then comes a showdown where the culprit(s) are revealed and Sidney, trapped on the school's auditorium stage, must live out the role she has been preparing to portray, as Cassandra in *Agamemnon*. It is a savvy, unmistakable detail that the college production is a Greek tragedy. If not tragedy, what kind of life has Sidney's become? *Scream 2* is the weakest entry in the franchise, running a little long and ungainly, but it is still smarter than the majority of studio horrors that get released each year. For a film where death runs rampant, its creative and financial success proved that there were plenty of avenues yet to explore with these now well-loved characters and their fight to make it in a world where anyone, at any time, can be the unwelcome recipient of a very sharp knife.

Scream 3

2000 - Directed by Wes Craven

In 1996, screenwriter Kevin Williamson and director Wes Craven created *Scream*, a low-budget slasher satire that revitalized the horror genre due to its innovative approach of having the characters be "in-the-know" about the conventions of movies concerning killers hacking away at nubile victims. Thus, when a psycho really does begin to dispatch of the teenage residents in the town, they know how they should handle it. Even more than that, though, *Scream* was the very first horror movie in a long time that was actually smart, scary and genuinely suspenseful, a twist on the "stalk-and-slash" films from the late-'70s/early-'80s. The $14-million picture ultimately went on to gross $103-million in the U.S., a whopping number that is virtually unheard of for this type of movie.

But lightning struck twice, as *Scream 2*, with most of the same cast and crew, was released exactly one year later and set new box-office records on opening weekend. The $25-million sequel ended its cume at $101-million. Although it made virtually the same amount as its predecessor, the film left audiences divided, with some saying it was actually superior and others claiming they were a little disappointed. My opinion fits somewhere in the middle. While *Scream 2* didn't even come close to the level of craftiness that the first one had, looking as if it had hurriedly been thrown together (with less than twelve months separating their releases, *it was*), it still had enough of its token wit and intensity to be a satisfying venture.

At the time intended as the final piece in the financially and creatively successful series, *Scream 3* arrived a little over two years later. To say it was well worth the wait would be an understatement. Despite the disappearance of Williamson as screenwriter (Ehren Kruger was handed script duties), Craven remained faithful as the top-notch filmmaker of the series, as did ongoing stars Neve Campbell, Courteney Cox, David Arquette and Liev Schreiber. In its own way, *Scream 3* is a groundbreaking motion picture itself—a second sequel that has somehow accomplished the daunting task of being almost as fresh and thoroughly gratifying as the now-classic film that started it all. The hanging story threads from the previous ones are brought to the forefront, as the natural evolution of the characters, as well as the series itself, skillfully come around full circle.

It has been several years since the bloodbath that occurred at Windsor College, and Sidney Prescott (Neve Campbell) now lives in a secluded rural Californian home, working from her house as a crisis hotline counselor under a false name. Unable to lead a regular life anymore and plagued with nightmares of her deceased mother, Maureen, Sidney is distraught to find that one of the people from her past has been murdered (seen in the token opening death scene) in Hollywood, where *Stab 3: Return to Woodsboro* is well underway in its production on a studio backlot. Determined cutthroat news reporter Gale Weathers, now hosting a television show called *Total Entertainment* after her brief gig on *60 Minutes II* fell through, is contacted by Detective Kincaid (Patrick Dempsey) to join him in his investigation of the multiple murders. Illegally getting onto the set of the film, Gale has a surprise run-in with Dewey Riley (David Arquette), recently retired from the police force due to his handicap and currently an advisor for the movie. Although they briefly had a relationship with each other after the goings-on in the second pic, their varied personalities have since broken them up. It is obvious the spark between them is still very much alive.

One of the elements that is so inventive in *Scream 3* is its movie-within-a-movie approach (there is a stunning, show-stopping sequence in which Sidney finds her way to the sets from the production, all of them spitting images of real places in her hometown of Woodsboro), and in the way the mystery killer—once again dressed in that spooky Ghostface costume—kills off the characters in the order in which they are whacked in *Stab 3*. Adding confusion to the mix, (1) three different versions of the screenplay were created in order to throw off fans on the Internet, but it is unclear which one the killer has gotten hold of, and (2) with the real Gale, Sidney and Dewey in Hollywood alongside their three actor counterparts, will the killer want to get rid of the real people, the performers portraying them, or both?

Whereas any old second sequel to a slasher franchise would be more than showing its age by now, *Scream 3* is that rare case in which it is not merely here to cash in on the big bucks, but was all along planned as a three-parter. One could possibly question if this is actually true, or just an excuse by the filmmakers once the original struck pay-dirt, but *Scream 3* does a fabulous job of wrapping things up and filling in the missing pieces, all the while delivering what fans have grown accustomed to: scares, snappy dialogue, believable characters, and some sort of unique spin on the otherwise clichéd formula. While *Scream 2* was the most straightforward of the series in terms of its violence and occasionally messy plot developments, *Scream 3*, like its 1996 precursor, is a multilayered funhouse of chills that does a more than sufficient job of keeping the surprising twists coming. The final unveiling of the killer is not only unanticipated, but the details for his/her motive come off as more plausible than they have any right to be.

Aside from the aforementioned scene where Sidney stumbles upon the soundstage and, subsequently, is chased by the killer as she relives her past, there is a clearly innovative and exciting sequence coming every ten to fifteen minutes. The 40-minute climax, set in an eerie mansion complete with secret passageways and dark corridors, is literally nonstop in its intensity—and in the perverse delight Craven, Kruger and the gang are obviously having toying with expectations. Moreover, the in-jokes about moviemaking and Hollywood are occasionally satirical and often biting, with a few people turning up in enjoyable cameos.

Neve Campbell, fresh-faced and well-cast in *Scream*, had continued to develop into an even more talented actress with clear star qualities within the three-and-a-half years since she was chosen for the role. Wisely choosing to downplay the sullen Sidney from the middle chapter, her character is now a young woman stuck in a rut in her life, filled with understandable paranoia that she can never be safe until she has completely disappeared from the rest of the world. The progression Sidney goes through is both touching and truthful, and Campbell is able to surpass her performances in both of the other pictures. Courteney Cox and David Arquette, married to each other at the time of filming, are both up to par with their consistently entertaining turns as Gale and Dewey. Of the three central characters in the series, it is Gale who has gone through the most changes. Starting off as a fairly heartless wench in *Scream* and still very much ruthless in *Scream 2*, Gale's sweet relationship with Dewey has humanized her into a slightly warmer individual. In the latest addition, Gale has finally learned there is more to life than just getting a juicy story, helping out the police in the investigation of the increasing death toll and rekindling her romance with Dewey—now the two things most important to her.

A wide array of new faces are introduced, as usual, and the actors all have great fun. The highlight is easily Parker Posey, as Jennifer Jolie, a vapid, relatively ditzy actress who has been cast in the Gale Weathers role, taking pride in portraying the character even better than Gale herself. Posey is a comic delight, stealing almost all of the scenes she is in. Relatedly, there is a very funny rapport that develops between Jennifer and Gale, who are stuck together like glue through the second half. When it is Gale who is to die next in the script, Jennifer figures that if they are always side by side, the killer will just attack Gale and leave her alone. Also in a memorable appearance is Jenny McCarthy, as Sarah Darling, an aging 35-year-old starlet tired of always being cast as teenagers and especially angered that her character in *Stab 3* only appears in two scenes and then is killed off (guess which real actress appears in only two scenes in *Scream 3* and is killed off?). Rounding out the cast is Patrick Dempsey, before TV's *Grey's Anatomy* helped to recharge his career, as Detective Kincaid; Scott Foley, big-headed and appropriately pretentious as *Stab 3* director Roman Bridger; Emily Mortimer, as Angelina Tyler (Sidney in *Stab 3*); the always-beguiling Matt Keeslar, as Tom Prinze (Dewey in *Stab 3*), and Lance Henriksen, as Sunrise Studios producer John Milton (who may or may not have known Maureen Prescott years before). Also showing up is Liev Schreiber, the fourth returnee from the other *Scream* movies, as Cotton Weary.

In the director's chair, Wes Craven has somehow been able to keep the energy level as high as possible in *Scream 3*, as if it was the first movie he has directed in the series. This being his third go-round, in retrospect, may actually be nothing but a positive thing, as Craven has treaded similar horror territory so many times in the past that he could do it in his sleep. What cannot be denied is that Craven is a master at setting up absorbing horror setpieces and adding a stylish flare to the proceedings. With the wholeheartedly satisfying conclusion of *Scream 3*, one of the most widely popular horror movie series of all time had seemed to come to a purported close. The way each of the surviving characters' lives receive closure is an excellent touch, and the final few shots are filled with subtle, yet remarkable, power. Who would have guessed that the ending of a film called *Scream 3* could be so poignant? Certainly not I, but it is. Now how's that for an unexpected twist?

Scream 4

2011 - Directed by Wes Craven

In 1996, director Wes Craven and screenwriter Kevin Williamson broke barriers and resuscitated a dying genre with *Scream*, a post-modern, part-satirical, part-scream-worthy comment on characters well-versed in pop culture and the so-called rules of horror movies who find themselves at the center of their very own slasher film. Mixing in a clever whodunit aspect to the carnage, the picture bred so many imitators that it is easy to forget just how groundbreaking *Scream* truly was when it initially came out. It racked up over $100-million at the box office and was followed by two solid sequels, 1997's *Scream 2* and 2000's *Scream 3*. With the end of *Scream 3* was a sense that the story—for all intents and purposes, a trilogy—had come to its natural, fitting conclusion, the very last shot of an open door not suggesting that there were more follow-ups to come, but symbolic of surviving protagonist Sidney Prescott's (Neve Campbell) newfound safety and empowerment.

Eleven years later, the official announcement that there would not only be a *Scream 4*, but that all of the main players—in addition to Craven and Williamson, also steadfast leads Neve Campbell, Courteney Cox and David Arquette—would be returning was met with unavoidable excitement, but also a fair amount of trepidation. The previous film had finished out on a high note, and a lesser fourth chapter might very well feel like a betrayal of the now-loved characters' earned defeat against evil. After all, what could another slasher flick in the series possibly do that hadn't been done before? Would the whole thing come off as tired and desperate, a last-ditch clinging to a formula long past its sell-by date? As it turns out, there was absolutely nothing to worry about. Equipped with an uncanny, innovatory, at times brilliant screenplay by Kevin Williamson, *Scream 4* is in many ways just as much a wholehearted revitalization of the again worn-out slasher genre as *Scream* was a decade and a half before. Because horror movies go through fads with audiences and technology has grown and developed so much in the interim, *Scream 4* not only has a brand new arsenal of material to speak about, but also works as an astute, thought-provoking commentary on the world we now live in. It's whip-smart, it's auspiciously savvy, it's full of escalating tension, and it knows just how to juggle humor with frights without either tone lessening or overshadowing the other.

The complex opening setpiece is a bravura expression of imagination and showmanship that approaches meta levels of self-referential ambition. No more details can be given, because part of the fun comes in the discovery of what its filmmakers have up their sleeves. As the plot proper gets underway, Sidney has returned to her hometown of Woodsboro on the fifteenth anniversary of the original massacre to promote her best-selling memoir, *Out of Darkness*. Her joyous reunion with Sheriff Dewey Riley (David Arquette) and retired news journalist Gale Weathers (Courteney Cox), now married, is promptly cut short when two teenagers are found brutally slain. Forced to stay in town during the investigation after a bloody scene is found in the trunk of her rental car, Sidney is welcomed into the home of her late mother's sister, Aunt Kate (Mary McDonnell), and semi-estranged teenage cousin, Jill Roberts (Emma Roberts). Sidney cannot help but see herself in Jill, her circle of close peers—best friend and closet film aficionado Kirby Reed (Hayden Panettiere), next-door neighbor Olivia Morris (Marielle Jaffe), ex-boyfriend Trevor Sheldon (Nico Tortorella), know-it-all cinema club president Robbie Mercer (Erik Knudsen), and Robbie's softer-spoken sidekick Charlie Walker (Rory Culkin)—reminding her of her own ill-fated high school pals. When it becomes increasingly clear that a new psychopath behind the Ghostface mask has begun a fresh killing spree, Sidney and Jill are put in immediate danger while Gale, lured by the memories of her old cutthroat profession, decides to one-up Dewey's police force and start up her own investigation.

If *Scream* tore through slasher clichés with self-aware mischievousness, *Scream 4* just as shrewdly sends up the never-ending stream of remakes, torture porn and high-numbered franchises the film industry had been inundating audiences with over the previous decade. All the while—and most innovative of all—it intentionally poses as its own loose remake of *Scream* while delightfully subverting expectations at every turn. To see how this expertly constructed house of cards plays out was one of the most significant cinematic pleasures of 2011. The ideas and subtextual depth lurking just beneath the surface never seems to end, its look at the wolf-pack nature of current press and media colliding with a perceptive and all-too-valid observation of how the gravity of calamitous events, and what they mean, fades over time. Indeed, Woodsboro was once a small town with a stain in its history, and now the residents go out of their way to celebrate the anniversary as if it were some sort of local holiday. When Dewey quite eloquently states, "One generation's tragedy is the next one's joke," it rings resoundingly true. One might look at the original *Scream* the same way; for those young enough to not remember its theatrical release and the imprint it made, there is no way for them to understand just what kind of sensation it was, a cultural zeitgeist for people who had never seen anything like it before.

It might sound corny, but enough years have gone by that dropping back into the same characters' lives—namely, that of Sidney, Dewey and Gale—is like revisiting long-lost, well-liked acquaintances. There is no awkwardness to their interactions, either, the old chemistry they shared still very much in abundance. With over ten years' worth of perspective behind her, Sidney has come into her own as a fully grown woman who has now gotten her feelings out and expunged her deepest emotional scars. With the knowledge that it's all happening again and her life once more in danger, she is afraid, but no longer shaken, by what she knows she must face. For Dewey and Gale, their relationship endures despite the rough patches they've braved. Gale, who is trying her hand at being a novelist with thus far little success, has begun to grow a little stir-crazy. She isn't happy by the new murders, but also hasn't rid herself of her opportunistic side; she knows a sign when she sees one, and if that means defying Dewey's official investigation and "going rogue," as she amusingly calls it, so be it.

Craven handles the narrative with an artful skill he hadn't shown in a while, proving he still had what it takes, at the age of 71, to still grab and thrill viewers. False-alarm jump scares are his one lingering unnecessary vice, though the handful that there are work if one sees them as cognizant of another enduring horror convention. Sensitive character moments smoothly blend with self-deprecating humor and suspense-laden mad-stalker scenes, the latter not extraneous but always used as a means of motivation and moving the plot forward. The aforementioned prologue is right on target, handily establishing how vastly things have changed since the mid-1990s. A parking garage chase and assault involving Sidney's cheerily callous personal assistant Rebecca Walters (Alison Brie) is classily orchestrated. Visually potent flourishes, like a shadow Sidney sees reflected in a window and a cute bit with wind chimes, help to build the threat and atmosphere. Gale's pursuance of a story that leads her to a secluded barn where the third annual Stabathon—a marathon screening of all seven *Stab* movies—is being held ratchets up tension while simultaneously calling to mind the rural house-party climax of *Scream* and the opening scene from *Scream 2*. From this point forward, the movie is menacingly nonstop as it sneakily averts from and pays loving homage to high-throttle third-act norms and the typically tacked-on nature of alternate endings and rejiggered finales.

With a collection of new faces surrounding the central trio, Neve Campbell, Courteney Cox and David Arquette don't miss a step sinking back into their closely defined roles of Sidney, Gale and Dewey. Oftentimes it is difficult relocating the soul of a past character and the results feel superficial, but that's not the case here. Freshman standouts abound, each of them distinctive enough to make their own respective mark. Hayden Panettiere is having a ball playing the infinitely cool Kirby, whose love for classics like *Suspiria* and *Don't Look Now* reveal a learned cinephile. Erik Knudsen and Rory Culkin adroitly portray two sides of the same movie-geek coin, with Knudsen's Robbie wafting through his days with a snarky attitude, a camera pinned to his head, and a truth about himself he hasn't yet admitted, and Culkin pining away for longtime crush Kirby. Bringing a surprising dose of comedic verve to the proceedings are Marley Shelton, embracing her offbeat side and an unspoken longing for acceptance as Deputy Judy Hicks, Dewey's partner and old classmate of Sidney's, and Alison

Brie, stealing her scenes as Sidney's inconsiderate assistant, Rebecca. Finally, Emma Roberts, as Jill, stands as both forerunner and effective counterpoint to the Sidney from the first *Scream*. Even while getting to play a nice girl, there is an edge to Jill that intrigues and stands out. For someone who used to be best-known for kid-friendly family pics and a Nickelodeon sitcom, Roberts relishes the chance to go against the grain with this finitely R-rated change of pace. She's better than a lot of people will probably be expecting.

Where *Scream 4* goes cannot be divulged, but let it be known that the film entertains hugely for the duration, reinventing itself with each new reel in ways that are excitingly unanticipated. The final twenty minutes go down some grisly paths, even for this series, and what is so fascinating is how disturbing it becomes not from the blood and violence, but from its harrowing, thematically stacked inferences. The film's sturdy technical specs are guided by returning cinematographer Peter Deming's in-tune lensing and composer Marco Beltrami's appropriately diverse music score, incorporating several of the most memorable themes heard in previous installments. And standing in for Northern California's vision of fictional burg Woodsboro, the use of Michigan locations are seamless most of, if not all, the time. A particularly pronounced middle finger at the tendency to remake every horror movie with the vaguest name value—a scene where Kirby lists as many remakes as she can think of in quick succession is downright staggering in what it says about the dirge of creative inspiration in present-day Hollywood—the picture defies all rules by being a post-trilogy sequel as vividly original and resourceful as any horror film released in years. At a point when most series have gone stale, run out of ideas, and worn out their welcome, the bold, exhilarating *Scream 4* replenishes itself anew.

Session 9

2001 - Directed by Brad Anderson

By and large, every horror subgenre relies heavily on setting and mood, so finding a great location is half the battle. Writer-director Brad Anderson outdid himself in this department with *Session 9*, a methodically paced psychological chiller that starts slowly and ends with the viewer's heart racing. The film shakes and stirs in a way that few films do, exploring the most fragile and potentially bleak corners of the human mind. That Anderson manages such a feat not with violence, but through suggestion, editing and the invaluable use of crackly voice-over recordings permeating over images both benign and threatening, shows what a firm grip he has on filmmaking. This is, to date, his most resounding cinematic achievement.

Hoping to receive a tidy bonus for their efforts, an asbestos cleaning crew headed by overworked new father Gordon (Peter Mullan) and right-hand man Phil (David Caruso) give their word that they'll be able to finish their three-week job at Massachusetts' abandoned Danvers State Hospital in only five days. It's a daunting proposition—the mental institution, erected in the 1870s, has been closed for fifteen years and is in crumbling, dilapidated shape—but one that Gordon is confident they will be able to pull off. As the hours and days tick by in a place where untold amounts of tragedies and atrocities have occurred, the men's relationships and psyches gradually begin to crumble. For Gordon, he is faced with troubles at home and a rising mistrust in his co-workers after weasily hotshot Hank (Josh Lucas) doesn't show up for work on Wednesday and allegedly has skipped town. Meanwhile, Gordon's wet-behind-the-ears nephew, Jeff (Brendan Sexton III), tries not to let his uncle down, and Mike (Stephen Gevedon) becomes enraptured with listening to the case studies of now-deceased multiple personality sufferer Mary Hobbes after stumbling upon the doctor's recordings.

Shot on location at the sprawling real-life Danvers State Hospital—a building that infuriatingly was demolished in 2007 to make way for an apartment complex—*Session 9* is a sometimes brilliant study in restraint. Writer-director Brad Anderson and co-writer Stephen Geveden (who also essays the role of

Mike) aim to scare their audience, but they do this by turning their backs on modern-day horror trappings and allowing their characters and story the room to breathe and develop in a natural fashion. Is the asylum haunted? Perhaps not in the conventional sense, but the pasts of the mentally insane patients who resided and often died there live on within the walls of the imposing structure. They also survive through the existing audio reels that Mike finds and listens to, the horrific tale of Mary Hobbes playing out over nine sessions that culminate in a revelation as truly unnerving as the one that occurs between the five men presently working there.

The ins and outs of the relationships of working crews is captured with a keen and provocative eye, offset by the sinking suspicion that something isn't quite right between them. With Gordon unable to hide how overextended he is with a new child and a rocky marriage, Phil grows worried about his abilities on the job. Gordon, in effect, questions Phil's ulterior motives, particularly after spotting him talking to two unknown men on the hospital's property and later finding him with a valuable coin that may or may not have come from a stash located in the walls of the underground tunneling system. When Jeff discovers the thought-to-be-gone Hank lurking incoherently in the stairwell, he is wise enough to know something far more ominous is going on.

The unique setting is the fifth and just as important character in *Session 9*, Anderson and cinematographer Uta Briesewitz taking full advantage of their almost unearthly surroundings. From the patients' rooms, littered with old pictures stuck to the walls from decades' past, to the dank surgical areas, where lobotomies were performed, to the complex maze of tunnels underneath the building, the film's portentous atmosphere is thick enough to strangle. All of these places and several others play a part in a third act as thought-provoking as it is veritably frightening. With the camera gliding along hallways, amidst the outside property and from the sky, the picture's aesthetic style reminds favorably of Stanley Kubrick's 1980 classic, *The Shining*. Additionally, the music score by Climax Golden Twins is rich with the sorts of unidentifiable sounds and instruments that only add to the shiver-inducing tone.

The top-tier cast is as good as expected. Peter Mullan runs off with the most glory—his character of Gordon is for all intents and purposes the lead, and also the most intricately layered—and he is exceptional as a man who either could be coming unhinged or just having a bad week. As Phil, David Caruso does nicely low-key work without all of the histrionics and silly voice inflections he used on TV's *CSI: Miami*. And Brendan Sexton III leaves an impression as Jeff, a normal kid having to work with people who look down on him because he's young and hasn't yet learned all the ropes.

Audiences expecting a more-of-the-same type of horror story may not latch onto or have the patience for the quietly rattling pleasures of *Session 9*. Playing to a classier tune, the film is one that is immersive even in its understatedness, weaving a tale that is all the more effective because of how believable it is. Everything that happens could happen in the world we live in—some of them even did in Danvers State Hospital—and that's the scariest thought of all.

The Shining

1980 - Directed by Stanley Kubrick

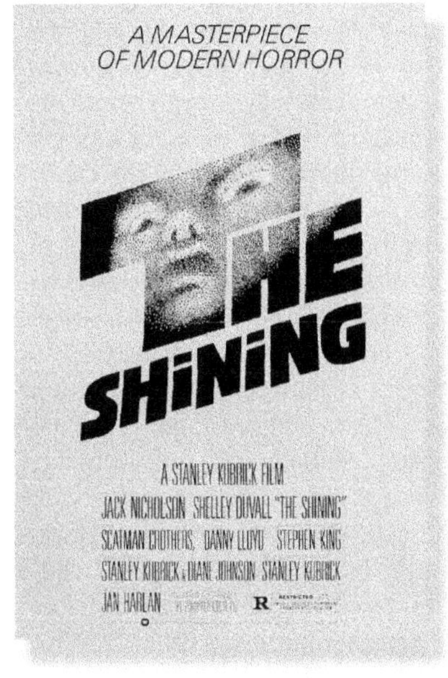

When *The Shining* was released in the summer of 1980 to box-office acclaim but split critical reaction, Stephen King spoke out against the creative liberties writer-director Stanley Kubrick and co-scribe Diane Johnson had taken in adapting his work. Claiming that the soul of the story had been lost, King also wasn't thrilled with the casting of Jack Nicholson, whom he said seemed crazy from the beginning rather than an everyman who gradually goes off the deep end. As with many great motion pictures, *The Shining* took some time to receive the praise and respect it deserves, its place in the annals of horror cinema steadfast and undeniable. So what if Kubrick didn't follow King's 1977 novel to the letter? The author wrote his own film version, a 1997 network miniseries starring Steven Weber, and it was a clunky, oft-tacky mess. Any writer should be so lucky as to have a master filmmaker of Kubrick's caliber tackle their work. His obsessively meticulous vision for *The Shining* is what has made the movie what it is today: a terrifically frightening, supernaturally tinged deconstruction of a family in imminent jeopardy.

With the off-season approaching, Jack Torrance (Jack Nicholson) has been hired as the winter caretaker of Colorado's secluded Overlook Hotel. He, wife Wendy (Shelley Duvall) and five-year-old son Danny (Danny Lloyd) are looking forward to some quality time together in between the planned writing of Jack's novel. Having free roam of a cavernous hotel in the mountains as snow forever falls outside sounds like a one-of-a-kind adventure. As the days and weeks pass by, however, the solitude slowly starts to eat away at Jack's mind. As Danny rides his little three-wheeler around the maze of hallways throughout the building, his special precognitive abilities open him up to ghostly visions hiding just around the corner. The Torrance family isn't truly alone at the Overlook, and it's only a matter of time before Jack, like a former caretaker who went crazy and slaughtered his family there, snaps.

The opening titles of *The Shining* are heavy with portent, a seamlessly intoxicating precursor to what is to follow. As director of photography John Alcott's camera glides across the water and swoops above the rocky terrain, a car driving on a winding mountain road comes into focus. Underscored by composer Wendy Carlos and Rachel Elkind's unearthly music, enough to put a chill down anyone's spine, Kubrick's ready vision has already created a uniquely off-kilter tone and a treacherously picturesque sense of location. The pacing is deliberate, to be sure, but under full control as the Torrances arrive at the Overlook and are given a tour of the property as the last of the guests check out and the staff prepares to close down. Once alone, the family's day-to-day routine begins peacefully enough before the snow sets in and Jack grows frustrated over a nasty bout of writer's block. When Wendy finds bruises on Danny, it strikes her as the ultimate betrayal; she cannot believe her husband would hit their little boy, but all signs point to the affirmative. And, when it is revealed what Jack has been spending his days pounding away at the typewriter, the frailest of threads holding these people together breaks. Jack is no longer himself; he is the living embodiment of an extraordinarily sick hotel that has claimed its latest victim.

For all of its methodical build-up, *The Shining* delivers again and again as it enters its third act. If Jack's decision to see what lurks in the off-limits room 237 is a wince-inducing appetizer to the potential carnage to follow, the point of no return, perhaps, is his entry into the Gold Ballroom, where he takes his first drink since going sober. In the restroom, he has a conversation with Delbert Grady (Philip Stone), the ill-fated caretaker from the past who talks in forward, chilling words about "correcting" his wife and daughters. With Wendy and Danny in mortal danger while trapped on the premises with Jack, the malevolent chanting on the soundtrack rises as the Overlook unveils its true macabre nature. The lobby transfers into a cobwebbed catacomb full of skeletons. Jack chops his way through a door as Wendy, knife in hand, screams bloody murder. The rushing elevator of blood that Danny has already imagined comes to fruition. And who, pray tell, are the old man and the figure dressed in the furry dog costume that Wendy spots through an opened doorway?

Does Jack Nicholson play his early scenes as a man who is already simmering with psychopathic tendencies, or does it just come off that way? No matter, there is a weirdly unsettling undercurrent to his Jack Torrance from the start. As his mental state deteriorates, Nicholson pulls off a performance as committed and frantic as it is believably deranged. For all of Stephen King's misgivings over his casting, this is quite possibly the actor's most iconic role. There is a reason for that. As Wendy, Shelley Duvall brings a quirky affableness and vulnerability to her part, facing a calamity she is not at all prepared for as she struggles to protect her son. In his only feature film, a mop-topped Danny Lloyd is just right as Danny Torrance, still too young to quite grasp what his special ability signifies and how he can control it. Finally, Scatman Crothers emanates wisdom and kindness as Overlook chef Dick Hallorann, who notices right away that Danny shares his gift of "shining."

The Shining has earned a feverish following over the years, the kind that has elicited so many theories and personal readings into Stanley Kubrick's underlying themes and subliminal messaging that it has spawned its own movie, a boundlessly fascinating 2012 documentary from director Rodney Ascher called

Room 237. From the semi-convincing notion that the story is an allegory about the genocide of Native Americans, to the belief that the auteur is copping to the rumor that he was responsible for faking the moon landing, to the discovery that the serpentine floor plan of the hotel (which was shot on a soundstage) doesn't make any conceivable sense, *The Shining* eerily consumes the viewer as its multilayered narrative plays out. Proving even more captivating to discuss and debate after the fact, the film is clearly in the hands of a master at every turn. Kubrick may have tried to drive his actors and crew crazy as he demanded upwards of one hundred takes of certain shots, but his perfectionism paid off. Nothing in front of the camera happens by chance, and it is this painstaking attention to detail that keeps drawing audiences back into its labyrinth of familial crisis and paranormal madness.

Signs

2002 - Directed by M. Night Shyamalan

In his note-perfect artistic vision, M. Night Shyamalan was once superficially compared to Steven Spielberg and Alfred Hitchcock. While it is true he evokes those directors in his stunning ability to enrapture audiences with finely modulated, excitingly original stories and deeply humanistic characters, Shyamalan ably stands as an individualistic, first-rate filmmaker in his own right. 1999's *The Sixth Sense* captured much-deserved acclaim for its assured storytelling and expertly woven twists, and 2000's *Unbreakable* put a fresh spin on the usual superhero mythology that remains more or less unrivaled in terms of its innovation. There was once a time when going to see "An M. Night Shyamalan Film" meant something special, a virtual guarantee to audiences that what they were about to experience would pack just as much of an emotional wallop as a visceral one. A victim of his own notoriety, Shyamalan has fallen on hard times in more recent years, in miscalculated duds such as 2010's *The Last Airbender* and 2013's *After Earth* unable to come close to matching the sort of acclaimed work he was once known for.

Before this unfortunate creative descent, *Signs* marked what was arguably Shyamalan's most accomplished work, to date. Under the helm of a Roland Emmerich or a Michael Bay, the film would offer nothing more than a cast of stereotypes and clichés doing battle with a cut-and-paste enemy. Shyamalan, time and time again, has extraordinarily more up his sleeve. In *Signs*, he takes the very frightening possibility that we are not alone in the world as a mere jumping-off point to tell a more highly personal story about characters harshly struggling with their faith and beliefs. In doing so, he has constructed a bone-chilling horror film in the classic sense, where the old adage that less is more most satisfyingly applies, and a devastating drama about a family that has quickly begun to deteriorate after having met with tragedy.

Set in the farming community of Bucks County, Pennsylvania (45 miles outside of Philadelphia), former pastor Graham Hess (Mel Gibson) awakens one morning to the disturbing sight of crop circles in his cornfield. Although police officer Caroline Paski (Cherry Jones) assures Graham, younger brother Merrill

(Joaquin Phoenix), and children Morgan (Rory Culkin) and Bo (Abigail Breslin) that these intricate designs are a hoax, they have reason to believe otherwise when crop circles suddenly start appearing at a rapid-fire rate across the globe. Almost immediately, the family hears running on their roof and rustling within the corn, their dogs start acting strangely, and they pick up what sounds like another language on an old baby monitor they have. For Graham, a man who has lost all faith in God and religion after the horrible death of his wife six months earlier, he expects nothing but the worst to come to them.

Signs is as skillfully made as genre films come. It's also about as genuinely scary. Shyamalan meticulously has planned out and crafted his motion picture so that nary a single shot seems extraneous or wasted. As Steven Spielberg did with 1975's *Jaws*, Shyamalan teases the audience throughout with the physical appearance of the aliens, choosing to show a single claw or a darkened silhouette over a full-on glimpse of the intruders. In doing this for the majority of the running time, he cunningly builds a feeling of incomprehensible dread so thick that it occasionally becomes almost unbearable in the most thrilling of ways.

When Merrill witnesses on the news the first footage recorded of one of the aliens (taken at a child's birthday party in Brazil), his gasping response of horror carries over into the viewer. After that unshakably disturbing moment, it is understandable to suspect that Shyamalan has hit his ultimate crescendo, but one would be terribly mistaken. Credit Industrial Light and Magic for their impeccably realistic and subtle visual effects work in bringing these creatures to life.

Where the majority of Hollywood films in this sci-fi/horror vein would be happy to leave it at that—no more than a brilliantly executed scare picture—Shyamalan has grander sights in view. Indeed, when it comes to frightening an audience one minute and making them cry the next, there are few better auteurs. The stark poignancy of these characters and their situation is not melodramatic, nor does it violently plug at one's heartstrings in an obvious manner. As he did with the fragile relationship between son (Haley Joel Osment) and mother (Toni Collette) in *The Sixth Sense*, Shyamalan has made another keenly observant and touching portrait of a dysfunctional family that feels authentic and unscripted. Tellingly, a highly charged dinner scene that comes just before the film's climax is so raw it becomes difficult to take.

Mel Gibson is at the top of his game as the grievously conflicted Graham Hess. Nuanced and understated, Gibson turns in Oscar-caliber work as a man slowly imploding from the inside out. He carries on an easy, believable rapport with Joaquin Phoenix, who equally impresses. Unlike so many movie siblings, Gibson and Phoenix emulate the feeling of being actual brothers rather than actors who happen to be playing close relatives. Carrying out his tradition of winningly directing child actors, Shyamalan coaxes exquisitely fine performances from a then-12-year-old Rory Culkin and 5-year-old Abigail Breslin (in her big-screen debut).

While there is a revelation at the end of *Signs*, it is not the kind of obvious twist that made *The Sixth Sense* and *Unbreakable* so noteworthy. Nonetheless, it brings together many of the earlier plot points (Bo's belief that all their water is contaminated; Merrill's failed minor league baseball career; Morgan's asthma) in an ingenious way that strengthens the characters' plights and the story's whole reason for being. A cracklingly intense music score by James Newton Howard and shadowy, threatening cinematography by Tak Fujimoto only add to the looming atmosphere. *Signs* is a masterpiece of human emotions and seemingly unrelenting terror. Coincidentally, the trauma that the Hesses must go through turns out to also be their savior.

Silent House

2012 - Directed by Chris Kentis and Laura Lau

A much-improved U.S. remake of the far-fetched 2011 Uruguayan suspenser, *The Silent House (La casa muda)*, directed by Gustavo Hernández, *Silent House* embraces the elements that worked the first time while shaking up or deleting altogether the things that did not. What was originally little more than a flimsy, exceedingly ludicrous plot wrapped in a stylistic gimmick—it was purportedly filmed in a single unbroken shot—has been transformed here into a psychologically loaded, altogether more coherent example of crafty low-budget filmmaking. It's still not entirely airtight for every second, but, considering the lackluster feature they had to adapt, writer-directors Chris Kentis and Laura Lau have excelled beyond all conceivable expectations.

College-aged Sarah (Elizabeth Olsen) has returned to the old country house she and her father, John (Adam Trese), used to stay at when she was a child. Their goal is to fix the place up enough to put it on the market. With the power turned off and the windows boarded up to keep out squatters, the building has become an ominous maze of darkness and decrepitude, lit only by the lanterns they carry with them. When Sarah senses someone else is in the house with them, her suspicions turn to outright fear after John turns up badly wounded. With the place securely locked and the keys missing, Sarah will have to find a way to escape while evading the intruders if she hopes to make it out alive.

Hopes were not high walking into *Silent House*. The original film, released by IFC Films, was a major disappointment, so numb-skulled that the idiotic characters and their nonsensical actions kept getting in the way of the film's technical skill and ability to create tension. It is a happy surprise, then, that Kentis and Lau have bettered their source material in every way. Gone is the contrivance of having Sarah and John arrive at the house just in time to prepare for sleep while it's still daylight outside; in this telling, they have been there for days and are still in the midst of packing and throwing things out. Here, there is always a logical reason for why the characters are in the house, even when they have the chance to get out. Upon finding an exit the first time, Sarah is nearly run over by the truck driven by her Uncle Peter (Eric Sheffer Stevens). She's relieved to have reached safety, but then cannot believe it when Peter insists they go back to the house to rescue her injured dad. "You've gotta be fucking kidding me!" Sarah says in disbelief. It's the perfect reaction for a person who knows better.

Contributing enormously to the overall looming, nightmarish effect is a fleshed-out narrative with far more going on underneath the surface than meets the eye, traumas from Sarah's younger days resurfacing and reaching a head in the final twenty minutes as ghastly sexual and violent imagery collide with the mental collapse of a young woman in a fight for her life. Kentis and Lau resist the urge to toss in cheap jump scares; when their intended jolts occur, they are organic and have been well-earned. Beyond that, the film is a masterful exercise in moviemaking complexity, told in real time and featuring precious few detectable edits. Planning the shooting must have been daunting, with pressure especially heavy on the actors and cameraman to not mess up. An extensive making-of documentary would make for a fascinating companion piece to the finished product.

As the focal point for the film's full 85-minute running time, Elizabeth Olsen is a rapturous force. One false move, and the illusion of "in-the-moment" reality would be irreparably destroyed. That never happens. Olsen is beyond watchable in only her second film, and second award-worthy performance (following 2011's *Martha Marcy May Marlene*); in her every intuitive motion, she creates a classic protagonist of irresistible depth, resourcefulness and vulnerability, highlighting a wide range of emotions that she can seemingly check on and off at will—quite a plus considering she acts most of it in an elongated single cut. The camera loves her, and the audience doesn't dare look away.

The spare line of dialogue may sound stilted (as when John and Peter call each other "brother" to establish their relationship), but, in all, *Silent House* weaves an intoxicating spell of dread. Intense without having to go down predictable routes to elicit screams, the picture never shrinks from Sarah's ordeal. It is her journey to take, and directors Chris Kentis and Laura Lau wisely insist it be ours, too. Meanwhile, additions to the script are top-notch, some business with the opening and closing of an SUV's hatchback as Sarah sits alone in the passenger seat especially inventive and unsettling. Even the twisty ending works—a surprise since a similar revelation only came off as moronic in the earlier foreign version. The keys to success are in the treatment of the story, the intelligence with which it's crafted, the commitment of the actors, and the understanding that even a deeply flawed project can be fixed with a few judicious nips and tucks. Remake or not, the provocative *Silent House* has been born anew.

Sinister

2012 - Directed by Scott Derrickson

Have you ever been uncontrollably drawn to something you knew you probably shouldn't be seeing? Disturbing and/or violent footage on the Internet? A particularly graphic documentary? Or how about while passing by a terrible, possibly fatal, auto accident on the highway? It is basic human nature to be fascinated by the unknown, by things we cannot understand, and it is this specific brand of voyeurism that is at the blackened, macabre core of *Sinister*. Directed with classically inspired relish by Scott Derrickson and terrifically written with a distinct lack of compromise by Derrickson and C. Robert Cargill, the film is a rarified breed in that it burrows under the skin from the quietly petrifying first frame and stays there for days after. A haunted house movie rooted in such reality that it barely feels like one, Derrickson's cinematic gut-punch (he also helmed 2005's *The Exorcism of Emily Rose*) marries the supernatural with the kind of horrors that run rampant in the everyday world. That he does this so smartly, so methodically and so deliberately helps to inject the gradual pacing with an increasing level of anxiety-laden intrigue matched by our protagonist's experiences. As concerned with creating a suffocating, underlyingly doom-fraught mood as he is with providing "boo!" moments—these are used sparingly, the spooky atmosphere far more effective than any gimmick with a musical stinger—Derrickson shows that he knows exactly what he's doing. *Sinister* lives up to every inference its title alludes to.

Ten years ago, Ellison Oswalt (Ethan Hawke) took the publishing world by storm with *Kentucky Blood*, a revelatory true-crime exposé that inspired the thought-closed case to be reopened. Having exhausted most of his earnings and hungry to match his earlier success, he moves his family to a rural town in Pennsylvania as he hopes to begin investigating and writing his new book. What his wife, Tracy (Juliet Rylance), and children, 12-year-old Trevor (Michael Hall D'Addario) and 8-year-old Ashley (Clare Foley), are unaware of is why they got such a good deal on the property: it is the subject of Ellison's latest work and the location where a family was murdered, ritualistically hung from the tree that still stands in the backyard. The only member not found? The youngest daughter,

Stephanie, abducted and long-presumed dead. Studying such a horrible crime could lead anyone to a few sleepless nights, but Ellison stumbles upon far more than he bargained for when he finds a box of super-8 films in the attic. On each one, innocuously labeled like home movies commemorating barbecues and pool parties, is footage of a different family being first stalked by the camera, then killed. Ellison is shaken by what he sees—is there any wonder why he starts drinking again?—but also thrilled to be onto something potentially far greater and more groundbreaking than a single criminal case. In poring over these snuff films and trying to unravel their eerie connections, however, there is the danger that the evil behind the atrocities—a demonic pagan deity known as Mr. Boogie (Nicholas King), one of the common threads glimpsed on every reel of footage—may somehow be unearthed once more.

Ellison's first mistake—moving into a house where the lives of the former residents were so brutally dispatched—is the only one he makes while still in control of his destiny. From this point forward, there is no escaping a new fate that has been officially locked in. He doesn't realize this, of course, but the viewer gets a fairly good sense of the grim reality to come, having already been shaken by an unforgettable opening scene depicting the blunt, almost clinically straightforward hanging deaths of a mother, a father, a brother and a sister, bags tied over their heads as the nooses around their necks gradually lift them off the ground. Few movies are perfect, and *Sinister* admittedly oversteps the fragile line between subtlety and going too far with a few too many glimpses of corpsy children and a final frame that should have been cut off the film's already absolutely chilling last shot, but this one is nonetheless some kind of twisted work of genius. By not hinging upon a scare-to-minute ratio and allowing a heavy weight of considerable dread to blanket even the most unassuming of scenes, the whole experience is transformed into one lingering, all-encompassing ball of fright.

A sign that *Sinister* is more than just run-of-the-mill horror fare and is, indeed, something rather special: take away all the supernatural elements, and it would still work like gangbusters. Heck, take away the string of family slayings, and the film would continue to hold one's attention with its careful, observational character study of a man struggling to reclaim his former glory at just about any cost. Overcome by his obsessive work practices and striving to make a legacy out of his profession, Ellison grows distant from his family. More than that, he has placed them in real jeopardy while betraying the trust of a wife who never thought her spouse would go to such extremes in the writing of his book. Inclined to rewatch his decade-old talk show appearances when he's not buried deep in his present-day research, Ellison is a man stuck in the past and not ready to see that part of himself go. He views his latest piece of writing as his ticket to all he's been yearning for, which may be why he's not so quick to get the hell out of dodge when he spots a malevolent, witch-like figure in the grainy footage of each family execution. As the hanging victims succumb, the face pops up in the background, watching from the bushes. In a different film, the same figure lurks under the water as each tied-up family member is tugged into their swimming pool and left to drown.

For the most part, Derrickson is very careful about how far he takes things, noting that the mere suggestion that something could happen is sometimes far more disturbing and suspenseful than the times when the attacker pounces. Thus, there are many scenes of curtains illuminated with shadows and a white sheet tacked up on the wall—Ellison's makeshift projector screen—that forever bring tension to otherwise uneventful moments. He also is keenly aware of the importance of sound, the scratchy, skin-crawling score by Christopher Young a cacophony of unearthly sounds, whisperings and ancient chants. In these ways, like John Carpenter and Dario Argento before him, he proves what a legitimate craftsman he is, his instinctual filmmaking and knowledge of the genre every bit as apparent as that of James Wan and Ti West. The lensing by director of photography Christopher Norr is equally outstanding, giving a primal authenticity to the various aged film stocks and subject matter within the horrific home movies.

In *Sinister*, the heinous depravity of the past is rustled awake and lives on, the power of its recorded imagery so potent that it's bound to finally break free (in this way, come to think of it, the film would make a fitting companion piece to 2002's *The Ring*). As Ellison Oswalt, Ethan Hawke runs off with the best role he's had since at least 2004's *Before Sunset*, if not 1999's *Snow Falling on Cedars*, expertly detailing his character's progression from ambitious to consumed to terrified out of his mind about something he's not so sure he can run away from. In her first major feature, Juliet Rylance more than holds her own as wife Tracy, purposefully in the dark about Ellison's book until she starts to realize she should have asked more questions. In a nice twist from the usual in these types of movies, never does anything happen to Tracy that would make her suspect the house is haunted. In some ways, this is even more shuddersome because it's been happening behind her back the whole time. Finally, James Ransone brings a necessary tinge of comic relief as the town sheriff who agrees to help Ellison out with his research while acknowledging that there is no way he would have ever moved under this particular roof. Were it not for him, the film might have become almost too much to take, the difference between a mature, disconcerting, jolt-worthy thrill ride and a strictly depressing excursion in debasement for exploitation's sake. That's not what it is, though—not when it has so much to say about human longing, mortality and those awful things in life we simply cannot turn away from. One of 2012's best, most shiver-inducing releases, *Sinister* proudly joins the upper echelon of horror cinema.

The Sixth Sense

1999 - Directed by M. Night Shyamalan

And the winner of the second-creepiest film of 1999 (after *The Blair Witch Project*) goes to writer-director M. Night Shyamalan's *The Sixth Sense*. To say that the picture is merely creepy, however, is not giving it nearly as much credit as it deserves. A special type of gem that quietly, and gradually, sneaks up on a person, the film immediately absorbs the viewer into the story and characters while aspiring curiosity throughout as to where everything could possibly be leading. So much has been written about *The Sixth Sense* in the years since it was released that one would be hard-pressed to find someone who doesn't yet know the concluding twist. For those not in the know—or, for anyone who remembers seeing the movie in theaters, gloriously untainted—it is virtually impossible to figure out the ending before it comes. Out of left field only in regards to how unexpected it is, the narrative's key revelation is used not as a gimmick, but as a natural progression to what Shyamalan has been covertly setting up all along. In one ingeniously simple scene, every single plot hole is thoroughly patched up, and the film, with that vital turn of the switch, gracefully transitions from mere psychological thriller to something far more profound and ruminant than what one could possibly have anticipated when the opening credits began 113 minutes earlier.

After a stirring prologue in which psychiatrist Dr. Malcolm Crowe (Bruce Willis) and his wife, Anna (Olivia Williams), are paid a visit by one of his past patients, culminating in Malcolm getting shot before the patient commits suicide, the film moves ahead to "The Next Fall." Malcolm has recovered from his injury, but his relationship with Anna has turned into a distant one, the two of them barely speaking to each other anymore. Dr. Crowe's current patient is 9-year-old Cole Sear (Haley Joel Osment), a quiet loner of a boy living with his hard-working single mother, Lynn (Toni Collette). Cole, expected to have a behavioral disorder, tells him right away that he seems like a nice doctor, but one that cannot help him. The boy is hiding a deep, dark, terrifying secret not known by anyone but himself, and, although the original trailers for the film foolishly gave it away, Shyamalan methodically holds on revealing it. Told at an intoxicatingly unhurried tempo, the film takes its time, inspired more by dramatic thrillers of the 1970s than the late '90s.

The aforementioned *The Blair Witch Project*, as with *The Sixth Sense*, couldn't have come at a more opportune time back in the summer of 1999, both films physically showing the audience very little of the actual horrific goings-on, relying on the heavy power of suggestion rather than special-effects extravaganzas. Just look at Jan De Bont's piss-poor remake of *The Haunting*, a $75-million haunted house pic also released around the same time which left nothing to the imagination and, coincidentally, did not have one thoroughly effective moment in its entire running time. The "less-is-more" theory of filmmaking has almost always bred a more fixed, lasting imprint, and it's a tradition that continues to hold true. Shyamalan is wisely very discreet in his storytelling approach to *The Sixth Sense*, and the film never rushes along to the next scene for the insulting reason of keeping the audience awake. If every scene isn't action-packed, that is perfectly fine when material of this nature is in such controlled hands. Indeed, the film progressively draws the viewer into the proceedings as if he or she was reading an intriguing book. When a fleeting moment of visual horror is seen, it is all the more unexpected and emotionally stirring—and *earned*.

The critically important role of the solemn, put-upon Cole was, no doubt, a tricky part to cast because having a sickeningly precocious kid actor who mugs for the camera at every opportunity likely would have ruined the whole film. A then-11-year-old Haley Joel Osment is different, and thankfully so. Simply put, he is a *real* actor, one that, with every line of dialogue and memorable facial expression, is completely believable and sympathetic without being overly cutesy. Incredibly assured but confident even as his character is anything but, Osment is perfect in relaying Cole's personal confusion and terror at the things he is able to see. At the time the film came out, it stood as the best youth performance since 3-year-old Victoire Thivisol in 1997's *Ponette*.

Because Osment is so very good, top-billed veteran of the cast Bruce Willis is unable to hold his own ground as firmly as if a more accomplished actor had been playing this same role. Despite being the best thing Willis had done professionally since 1994's *Pulp Fiction*, there is something about Willis' face that keeps him from selling most of his characters. Seemingly always smirking as if he is in on a joke, the actor segues into "ultra-serious" mode, but does not fully sell some of his line readings. Willis is not bad in the film, but acting alongside the often-brilliant Osment—or, for that matter, the remarkably poignant and compassionate Toni Collette, as Cole's frustrated but caring mother—does him no favors. Also of considerable interest is Olivia Williams, portraying Willis' long-suffering wife, Anna. The part is underwritten and doesn't give her enough to do to equal what she is capable of, but intently watch Williams when she is onscreen to see how an actor can make so much out of so little; the subtle expressions on her face speak volumes over spoken words.

The Sixth Sense shines a bright spotlight on its two main characters, Cole and Dr. Malcolm, and the unlikely bond linking them in this world and the next.

Amazing, too, how the ending has the sheer force to completely blindside when the final, ultimate twist occurs. *The Sixth Sense* is a genuine experience—genuinely scary, genuinely touching, and genuinely thought-provoking—one of those special films released within the confines of the Hollywood studio system that somehow squeezed through the cracks with its original ideas and trust in its audience firmly intact. A late scene between Cole and his mother may even bring some to tears, the emotions striking a truthful note that avoid any semblance of syrupy melodrama. The real kicker, then, is that *The Sixth Sense* isn't really a typical horror movie at all, but actually a contemplative, heart-baring look at the process of life.

Smooth Talk

1985 - Directed by Joyce Chopra

Smooth Talk holds a rich pedigree. Produced on a relatively shoestring budget and originally released in 1985, the film was based upon prolific writer Joyce Carol Oates' stirring 1966 short story, "Where Are You Going, Where Have You Been?"—a staple in college literature courses. It won the prestigious Grand Jury Prize at 1986's inaugural Sundance Film Festival. Upon its limited theatrical release, the picture was met with wide critical acclaim, and ultimately went on to be nominated for five Independent Spirit Awards. Legendary musician James Taylor contributed three tracks to the soundtrack, including "Limousine Driver" (an original song) and the indelibly integrated "Handy Man." Finally, front and center among the cast, was 18-year-old Laura Dern, the fresh-faced offspring of respected actors Bruce Dern and Diane Ladd. Her performance as 15-year-old Connie—by all intents and purposes, her first lead role after a few minor parts—signaled not only the arrival of a versatile, one-of-a-kind new talent, but also the beginning of a long career filled with standout turns (her 2011-2013 HBO series, *Enlightened*, canceled long before its time after two outstanding seasons of television, is a must-see).

Despite all of these accolades and credentials, and despite receiving something of a resurrection on DVD, *Smooth Talk* has seemingly fallen by the wayside in the several decades since its release. It's a shame. The film, written by Tom Cole and directed by Joyce Chopra, is an American masterpiece of modern cinema, at once a blisteringly truthful coming-of-age story, a haunting morality tale, and an uncompromising portrait of the alternately dark and light underpinnings of life as seen through the eyes of a female adolescent.

To watch the movie is to almost be transported into the story as an invisible spectator, observing Connie not as one might a manufactured screen creation but as a real flesh-and-blood person, deeply sympathetic both in spite and because of her internal imperfections and the external missteps she makes along the way. In other words, she stands for you, me, and anyone who has ever been a teenager. That she can be self-absorbed and even a little selfish is not the point; it is the destination that Connie ends up at, her experiences informing her on who she was and transforming her into the stronger, more mature young woman she ultimately becomes, that is crucial to the lingering beauty of *Smooth Talk*.

It is the summer before her sophomore year of high school, and virtually the only thing on Connie's (Laura Dern) mind is the opposite sex. This fact is not lost upon her harried stay-at-home mother, Katherine (Mary Kay Place), who feels underappreciated by her daughter and uses criticisms as a coping mechanism—"I look into your eyes," she says to Connie at one point, "and all I see are a bunch of trashy daydreams." In return, Connie becomes emotionally distant; from her perspective, nothing she can do is right, and her mother's outward preference for elder daughter June (Elizabeth Berridge), a 24-year-old wallflower still living at home, is not lost upon her. Meanwhile, Connie's relationship with her father, Harry (Levon Helm), is on better terms, but they fail to connect. When he talks to her about his contentment in having a family, owning a home, and being his own boss, she has no way of understanding what he means. "I can't wait until I'm old enough to drive," is all Connie can think to offer in return.

Knowledgeable of her blossoming sexuality without really perceiving the consequences of exploiting it, Connie's world starts when she leaves her house. Going day after day to the mall with friends Laura (Margaret Welsh) and Jill (Sarah Inglis), she puts make-up on and redresses herself in the restroom, then parades around the plaza with the sole intention of attracting and flirting with anyone who will give her the time of day. It's harmless enough, at first, but Connie takes a bigger step toward "playing grown-up" when she and Laura venture across the street to Frank's, a burger joint where the older crowd hangs out.

Clad in a revealing skirt and halter-top, it doesn't take Connie more than a couple minutes to capture the attention of a nice guy named Jeff (William Ragsdale), recently out of high school, who invites her for a drive. Parked atop a lovers' lane, the glimmering lights of the town outstretching for miles before them, Connie remarks to Jeff, "I wish I could just travel somewhere." They're the words of someone old enough to recognize the boundless opportunities out there for her, and young enough that her wistful outlook hasn't yet been tainted by the messy realities of life. They share a single kiss, simple and pure, and Jeff returns Connie to the diner to meet up again with Laura. When she returns again a couple nights later and allows a different and slightly older guy, Eddie (David Berridge), to take her to an empty parking garage, they make out for as long as it takes Connie to realize she's not yet ready for what he's expecting of her.

The first hour of *Smooth Talk* is more of a character exploration than a plot-intensive narrative. Chopra meticulously conceives the story this way for a reason, taking the time to set up Connie's humdrum existence and uneventful walks on the wild side so that when her "nothing-bad-can-happen-to-me" beliefs are suddenly pulled out from under her, it makes a startling impact. Angry at her mother yet again and feeling like an outsider, she decides to stay home alone while the rest of them leave for a family barbecue. Connie's lazy day of listening to music, lying out in the sun, and making bead necklaces takes an abrupt left turn when a yellow Pontiac convertible comes barreling down the dirt driveway back to her house. The driver is a dangerously handsome and seductive man (Treat Williams), probably in his early thirties, who calls himself Arnold Friend. He claims he's been watching her from afar—not too far, though, since he reveals details about her life that few know—and wants to take her for a ride. Understandably suspicious of Arnold Friend and his intentions, Connie politely passes on the offer. It rapidly becomes apparent, however, that he won't be taking no for an answer.

What happens next is up to each individual viewer to discover, but, suffice it to say, Arnold Friend talks to Connie in such a way that her innocence and naiveté are stolen away from her. Treat Williams is mesmerizing as the antagonistic Arnold Friend, an intentional question mark of a character with enough smooth swagger and machismo to understand his magnetism. Inspired, at least in part, by serial killer Charles Schmid, the so-called "Pied Piper of Tucson," Williams concurrently plays Arnold as a threatening, spectral figure, possibly capable of committing terrible acts. It is in his careful juggling of these two diverse demeanors that creep under the viewer's skin. Through this frightening experience with Arnold Friend, Connie's rite of passage into adulthood is complete. Her flaws, her mistakes, her broken relationships—they all become glaringly apparent in a heartbreaking climactic moment that signals her growth as a more compassionate human being.

The performances, like the naturalistic writing and in-the-moment direction, are spot-on. Laura Dern is magnificent as Connie, self-assured and vulnerable in equal measures, able to look like a child in one moment and like a worldly woman the next. The character arc that Connie has from the first scene to the last is incalculably huge, and Dern is breathtaking as she navigates the excitement, the loneliness, the alienation, the acceptance and the fear that come with the territory of one's teenage years.

As Connie's mom, Mary Kay Place is just right, capable of expressing the warmth and love she has for her younger daughter, but also infuriating in the error-filled way she tries to get through to her even as she shuts her out. In a quietly touching scene where Katherine listens from an adjoining room to the song (James Taylor's "Handy Man") Connie is playing and silently dances with herself, the door is opened to a side of Katherine the viewer has not seen. Yes, she harps on her daughter and is settling into her middle-aged year, but she hasn't totally broken ties with the remembrances of her own youth. Also making an enduring impression is Elizabeth Berridge, as Connie's sister, June. June is kind to Connie, but she is also envious, recognizing that her baby sister's beauty and personality will carry her further in life than she herself will ever get. "You're gonna have it all, aren't you? And you think you deserve it," June says. In that moment, Connie doesn't yet grasp what she means. By the film's conclusion, she does.

The final two minutes of *Smooth Talk* are note-perfect, subtle and hopeful, emotionally overwhelming but refreshingly unmanipulative, ambiguously suggestive and yet full of clarity. Everything that the film is and stands for masterfully builds to this ending. Bad things can sometimes happen to good people and childhood is fleeting, director Joyce Chopra seems to be saying, but one's own humanity is a nonnegotiable constant. *Smooth Talk* is an unheralded marvel of a motion picture, and one of the more vibrant and authentic depictions of teenage life in memory.

Splice

2010 - Directed by Vincenzo Natali

The clinical twistedness of David Cronenberg and the ready chills of 2001's smashing creature-feature, *Jeepers Creepers,* converge in *Splice*, a barrier-breaking mixture of sci-fi, horror and romantic drama that takes its inspirations seriously even as it goes off on its own wildly creative tangents. Echoes of Mary Shelley's *Frankenstein* tale are also in evidence, but only as a springboard for a timely, archly modern study of the fine line between the benefits of scientific and technological advancements and the potential danger that comes with one's own irresponsible misuse of these things.

Young, ambitious and just a little careless, Clive Nicoli (Adrien Brody) and Elsa Kast (Sarah Polley) are cutting-edge bio-genetic engineers who have created a brand new organism by combining a swirl of different animals' DNA codes. It's a controversial practice, to say the least, but behind closed doors Elsa dares to take their experiment one step further by also adding a human's genetic imprint. Clive warns her of the ethical boundary she is daring to cross, but she makes the excuse that it could be their one real shot at a breakthrough to aid mankind. Besides, she says, "This won't be human—not completely." The fruit of their labor is a human/animal hybrid they name Dren (Delphine Chanéac), growing both physically and intellectually at an exponential rate. Elsa is at first fascinated by the idea of being able to study their creation's entire lifecycle in a compacted period of time, and then she and Clive find themselves connecting to Dren on a deeper level when a sort of parent-child relationship develops. In actuality, they're playing with fire, dealing with a life form they have no research on and no way of knowing what she will ultimately become.

Thank goodness for independent filmmaking. *Splice* was shot in Toronto on a budget of $25-million without the assist of a major Hollywood distributor. Director Vincenzo Natali was able to make the movie he wanted to make, based on a brave, envelope-pushing screenplay he co-wrote with Antoinette Terry Bryant and Doug Taylor. The picture went on to premiere at the 2010 Sundance Film Festival and, through a stroke of surprising fate, was subsequently picked up by executive producer Joel Silver for Warner Bros. Pictures and Dark Castle

Entertainment. The film was released widely in theaters, and fully intact. Prospective viewers who have seen the trailer and other advertising, which misleadingly make the picture appear to be conventional and full of predictable jolts, have no idea what they're in for. Had *Splice* been created all along as a studio project, it's easy to see how protagonists Clive and Elsa might have been stripped of their flaws and not always savory actions, while Dren would have been turned into an evil, one-note villain instead of the carefully layered, deliciously ambiguity-laden character original she is in the finished project. Also gone would have been some majorly shocking and transgressive third-act plot points that will go unmentioned here, turning a spooky horror show into something far more provocative and thematically complex.

The major find of *Splice* is the breathtaking work of Delphine Chanéac, as Dren. Bald, hairless and hauntingly beautiful in the role, Chanéac possesses an ethereal, otherworldly quality that is perfect for a character neither fully human nor animal. With no dialogue and aided by seamless visual effects that rely on giving Dren subtle differentiations from human characteristics—her eyes are wider and slightly more spread apart, while she has a tail complete with stinger, for instance—Chanéac nonetheless develops a full, unforgettable screen creation, one that can be heartbreakingly vulnerable one moment and thoroughly menacing the next. That the viewer is never sure what she is going to do and what she is capable of—her precarious relationship with a cat boils over with portent, while her part-loving, part-antagonistic bond with surrogate mom and dad Elsa and Clive resembles that of a typical teenage girl until it goes several shades grimmer—only increases the icky tension. Unusual in the best way and never less than stunning, Chanéac's performance was one of the best of 2010.

The antiseptic tone of the opening act, temporarily lacking a distinctly emotional throughline, promptly corrects itself once Dren is born and Clive's and Elsa's characters warm to the viewer. Adrien Brody and Sarah Polley give strong turns in their own rights as said co-workers and lovers, their moral lapses and poor judgments eating away at their very lives in far more ways than just via Dren. Brody and Polley feel not only like authentic regular people rather than movie stars, but they are also plausible as scientists; one senses there is more going on behind their eyes than just the reading of a script. Especially intriguing is Elsa's arc as a career woman with little interest at the onset in children growing into someone who loves Dren as a daughter, yet fearful that her own troubled childhood of neglect and abuse is beginning to rub off on her makeshift attempts at parenting. In what is more or less a three-character show—there are a few peripherals, such as Clive's younger brother, Gavin (Brandon McGibbon), but they mostly stay along the sidelines—Natali keeps the narrative tight, taut and claustrophobic. While a little expansion in scope might have been appreciated—save for a farm setting that comes into play in the second half, the movie features next to no exteriors and a cloudy sense of place and even time (is this set in the present or the near-future?)—it doesn't significantly harm one's nail-biting involvement in the story as it plays out.

Is *Splice* making a positive or negative comment on contemporary science and stem-cell research? There are elements within that suggest Natali's instincts could go either way, but a final scene loaded with subtext sneakily points further in one direction. In addition to this is Dren—eerie, scared, curious and capably lethal—an act against nature who didn't ask for this lot in life. Ultimately, the price she must pay is just as big as that of Clive and Elsa. Besides its absorbing ghoulishness—yes, it does work as a strict genre flick if a person doesn't care to dig below the surface—*Splice* is terrifically smart, rife with topics to debate and discuss.

Stake Land

2011 - Directed by Jim Mickle

Writer-director Jim Mickle has a real artist's eye for detail and texture, and he displays this gift time and again during *Stake Land*, a post-apocalyptic drama with the character nuance of 2009's *The Road* and the encroaching threat of 2003's *28 Days Later*. The villains—bloodthirsty vamps with the instincts of wild animals and the physical appearance of clinically insane hospital patients—ensure the film's genre pedigree, but Mickle and co-writer/star Nick Damici fittingly remain focused on a group of survivors struggling to safely make their way up north amidst a desolate, uncertain landscape. They, like the audience, have no way of knowing the degree in which the world has unraveled outside of what they personally see and hear, and this places all involved on the same creepily enigmatic playing field. Above all, *Stake Land* is a thoughtful mood piece more than an action-packed horror movie. Caring about these people, all of them economically written and sympathetic in their authenticity, is easy, so watching their tight unit rapidly splinter as the ravages around them close in becomes all the more tragic.

A quick-spreading viral outbreak has caused the U.S. infrastructure to collapse and the government to be abandoned. It's every man for himself now, as teenager Martin (Connor Paolo) witnesses the deaths of his parents and baby sibling and goes on the run with an armed, self-appointed warrior known only as Mister (Nick Damici). As the two of them make their way up the east coast on their way to New Eden, a rumored safe haven across the Canadian border, they gradually form a makeshift family with the stragglers they pick up. Sister (Kelly McGillis) is a nun whose belief system is being understandably tested, if not dismantled, while Belle (Danielle Harris) is a young pregnant girl who, like Martin, has lost her entire family. With dangers both alive and undead laying in wait, they edge closer to a destination that will either be their savior, or spell their doom.

Filmed primarily in the wilds and isolated small towns of Pennsylvania, *Stake Land* may have been made on a slim budget, but one would never know it based on the striking production values Mickle manages in order to realize his unforgiving vision. There are the occasional necessary suspensions of disbelief in the storytelling—why, for example, is it taking them what looks to be weeks to drive to New Eden, which is established as being roughly 275 miles away and could be gotten to in half a day?—but what perseveres most distinctly and eloquently is the starkly honest snapshot of people who have no choice but to move forward even after the lives they've known are no more. When an exhausted Belle, played with beautiful simplicity by Danielle Harris, can walk no further, Mister chooses to pick her up. "My daddy used to carry me like this when I was little," she says. Mister, not one for mushy nostalgia, promptly tells her he's not her daddy. His selfless actions, however, cannot be denied; no matter what these people have been through, and are still about to face, they cling to their humanity. It's the one thing they have left that separates them from their pursuers.

Movies that rely on narration usually do so because there is a deficiency on the screenplay level and no way to tell a particular story without it. That isn't the case with *Stake Land*, which uses Martin's pensive voice-overs to bring depth to his plight. With dialogue sparse otherwise, the narration acts as a sort of journal or diary to Martin's experiences and the people he meets—strangers at first who grow to mean much more to him—along the way. A quiet sense of loss casts a grim shadow over the picture, lifting it above typical horror-flick theatrics. When *Stake Land* is creepy, it's very creepy, but it's the ghosts who pass through the frames—lost souls who want to carry on and fight to survive, and ultimately do not make it—that hauntingly linger even when they are no more. "One day you'll learn not to dream at all," Mister tells Martin upon meeting him. He's wrong to say such a thing, as Martin eventually learns. Without the ability to dream for the future, what hope does anyone have left?

The Strangers

2008 - Directed by Bryan Bertino

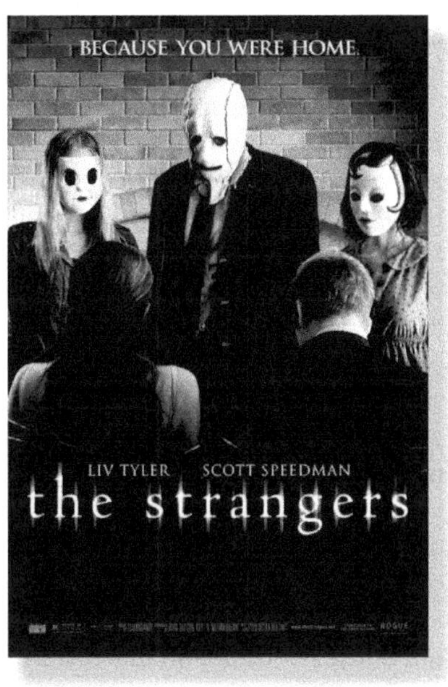

The Strangers was the third film to be released in less than a year, following 2007's *Them* and 2008's *Funny Games*, in which an idyllic country home is besieged by murderous sociopaths. Though the premise is familiar, each one of these pictures is diverse enough in style and technique to stand on its own. As astutely and auspiciously crafted by first-time writer-director Bryan Bertino, *The Strangers* is perhaps the most conventional of the three, following a basic but classic horror-movie formula. That is not to say it's always predictable or pedestrian, because it isn't. Bertino does an expert job of setting up sympathetic and identifiable protagonists and then running them through the wringers as the terror mounts and the unthinkable, yet plausible, odds stack against them.

Following a friend's wedding reception, James Hoyt (Scott Speedman) and Kristen McKay (Liv Tyler) arrive at the Hoyts' secluded summer home. The candles are lit on the dining room table, rose petals are romantically sprinkled over the furniture, and what should be a joyous night together for this couple is instead one drenched in melancholia. Kristen has just turned down James' marriage proposal, and as they try to figure out where they now stand in their relationship a knock at the door interrupts them. What follows is a night that brings to life any number of nightmares one might have about home invasion, as three masked strangers surround their property and prepare to attack.

In the style of *The Texas Chain Saw Massacre*, *The Strangers* opens with an ominous narration alleging that the story about to be told is inspired by actual events. This is only half-true; while Bertino is said to have been influenced by the Manson murders, which claimed the life of Hollywood starlet Sharon Tate and several of her friends in August of 1969, the similarities between that case and this film are superficial, at best. Knowledge of this background information isn't really necessary for the viewer, though it does give the film some increased unsettling undertones.

Either way, *The Strangers* is an immensely creepy thriller, one that plays fair with the audience, treats its characters with unusual intelligence for the genre, and is all the more effective because Bertino chooses to keep the minimalist plot spare and straightforward. The antagonists—a trio of masked killers whom neither James nor Kristen has ever met before—have no motive for their horrific actions, and, save for one instance early on set in shadows, are never revealed without their masks on. This only aids in the purveying mystery of the culprits' identities and backgrounds, and gives the movie's depiction of random attempted homicide a striking sense of reality. Everything that happens could, indeed, happen to any one of us, and when we least expect it.

In introducing James and Kristen as a troubled but likable couple who care for each other, but may want different things for their futures, the film quickly and economically sets up two characters that the viewer cares about. When those very lives are abruptly thrown into a life-or-death situation, James and Kristen defy the odds of most characters in horror flicks who are always doing stupid things at inopportune times and putting themselves in even greater danger. Resourceful and smart even when terrified out of their minds, they exhaust every possibility of escape and rescue—the way Bertino deals with stripping them of the house line and their cell phones is especially crafty—and are still left with nothing more than their own fight-or-flight mechanisms to rely upon.

Helping to keep the tension high for what, in essence, is an 85-minute game of cat and mouse are several virtuoso filmmaking flourishes. The repeated use of a record player to overscore stalking scenes is thoroughly disquieting, while a sequence in which James' best friend, Mike (Glenn Howerton), shows up at the house builds beautifully toward a tragic and unforeseeable sucker-punch. Bertino also remains subtle with his superb use of framing and backgrounds, reminding of 1978's *Halloween* in the way shots are handsomely composed to suggest that danger could be lurking around every corner.

Scott Speedman fulfills the requirements of his role as James Hoyt, even going a little deeper in the first act as he tries to keep his honor and dignity after his marriage proposal is shot down. Still, he plays second-tier to Liv Tyler, whose Kristen McKay is front and center and unquestionably the main character. Tyler is always believable in an emotionally draining performance that is vulnerable, strong-willed and complex; she's a female heroine for any horror fan to be proud of.

The Strangers falters in only two respects. The first has nothing to do with the movie itself, but with its theatrical trailers, which give far too much away and reveal a ridiculous amount of money shots that should have been left hidden. The overly detailed marketing campaign does not ruin the experience of watching the film—not by a long shot—but the mere sight of the frightening masks on display would have had a much bigger impact were they not all over the advertising. The second quibble is the very last shot before the end credits, a would-be ploy to jolt the audience that feels obligatory and leaves in its wake an unanswered question that should have been more finite since the picture is, after all, claiming to be a docudrama. No matter. Gloriously mature and comfortably R-rated, *The Strangers* is a sensational suspenser, sure to please horror buffs and anyone else looking for an alarmingly good time.

Suspiria

1977 - Directed by Dario Argento

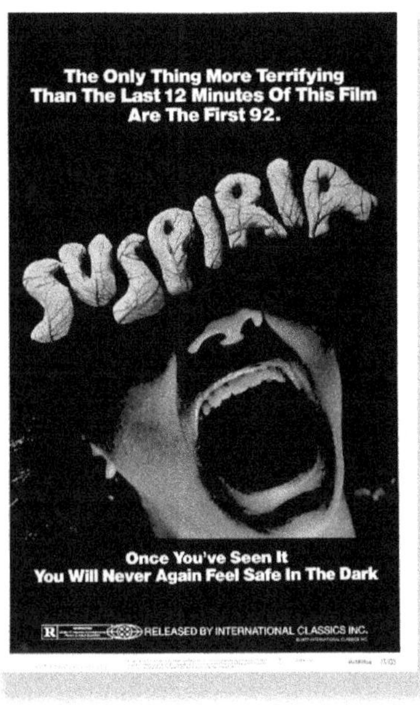

A singularly ravishing, visually mesmerizing genre work reminding of a children's storybook as written and illustrated by Hieronymus Bosch, Dario Argento's *Suspiria* is arguably the Italian horrormeister's most successful motion picture. It is certainly his most aesthetically impressive. Saturated in the kind of atmosphere some of the most talented filmmakers in the business likely can only dream about at night, the film's every shot is worthy of being framed and hung at Manhattan's Museum of Modern Art. Inspired by *Suspiria de Profundis* by Thomas De Quincey, Argento and co-writer Daria Nicolodi's tale of foreign displacement and the black arts has been further injected with the vivid, primary color-based style of 1937's animated milestone, *Snow White and the Seven Dwarfs*. Luciano Tovoli's painterly cinematography—one of the final films to be processed in Technicolor—is nothing short of hypnotic, while the fiendishly guttural music score by Goblin (with aberrant "witch"-whispering vocals from Claudio Simonetti) carries the enraptured viewer through an appropriately alarming soundscape.

It is a dark and stormy night when American ballerina Suzy Bannion (Jessica Harper) lands in Munich, Germany, catching a taxi to the Freiburg dance academy where she has been accepted. Just as she arrives, distraught student Pat (Eva Axén) passes her by as she flees from the building and into the forest. By the next morning, Pat will be dead, having been attacked and brutally disemboweled while seeking shelter at a friend's house. Suzy attempts to settle into her new life away from home—a difficult prospect when she falls mysteriously ill on the first day of classes, then is relegated to a cot in the gymnasium when the dorm rooms are infested with maggots. New friend Sara (Stefania Casini) fills her in on suspicions that the faculty are involved in more behind closed doors than simply teaching dance. Seeking the guidance of psychologist Frank Mandel (Udo Kier), Suzy learns that the academy was founded by the scarcely glimpsed directress, Helena Markos, believed to be a witch.

It has been documented that Dario Argento originally conceived the protagonists in *Suspiria* as 12-year-old girls. When the studio balked at this, he changed them to college age yet did not tweak the script. Thus, much of the dialogue and interplay between Suzy and the rest of the students has an offbeat, childlike tone—all the more fitting, actually, for what is set up as a grim fairy tale. Argento builds a nearly unsurpassed aura of doom over the proceedings, beginning immediately in the opening scene as Suzy is accosted by the wind and rain as she exits the airport. Subliminal imagery runs rampant, from a demonic face horrifyingly showing up in the taxi's glass separator as lightning flashes, to the blink-and-you'll-miss-them shadows of broomstick-riding witches cast across the façade of Munich's Athens-inspired Königsplatz. Audience anxiety slashes like daggers in scenes of immense intensity, as when Suzy and Sara quietly exchange words in the gym as the intimidating directress sleeps just beyond the glowing-red curtain separating the students from the staff. Pat's sprint through the dark forest is equally gorgeous and unnerving, while the murder setpieces—one involving a stain-glass roof and another featuring a pit filled with razor wire—are absolute showstoppers of operatic grisliness.

Jessica Harper is a lithe, almost angelic presence as heroine Suzy Bannion, but she is not an aloof figure. Caught up in a mystery where the key, she believes, are in the words she heard Pat yell ("secret" and "iris") on that first night when they briefly crossed paths, Suzy actively seeks the truth to the baffling goings-on around her. As instructor Miss Tanner and Madame Blanc, Alida Valli and Joan Bennett are perfectly matched, skirting the line between natural sternness and hiding something far more dreadful. And, although his screen time is brief, a strikingly young-looking Udo Kier owns his scene, turning a relatively thankless expository part into something more lingering and charismatic.

Dario Argento was responsible for a number of fine features both prior to and after *Suspiria*, but it is with this particular magnum opus where he innovatively turns genre filmmaking into an undisputable art form. With Sara having disappeared and the rest of the students away at the theatre, Suzy uses the trick her friend showed her, counting the footsteps she hears as a means of being able to retrace their path. This she does, leading her to a hellish discovery as phantasmagoric as it is trenchantly inevitable. *Suspiria* embraces its own skewered logic while weaving a fabled spell that could give rightful nightmares to even the brothers Grimm. From top to bottom, this is sublime filmmaking, alive with imagination.

Sweeney Todd:
The Demon Barber of Fleet Street

2007 - Directed by Tim Burton

An adaptation of the 1979 Tony Award-winning musical by Stephen Sondheim and Hugh Wheeler, *Sweeney Todd: The Demon Barber of Fleet Street* victoriously cuts and thrashes to cinematic life. In what was his most bravura directorial effort in over a decade, Tim Burton proved that he was born to make this film. Instead of merely helming an unoriginal copycat of the Broadway show, Burton and writer John Logan have stayed relatively faithful to the original source material while branching out its energy, scope and haunting deviance in a way that the limits of a stage cannot. There is no denying that this is, indeed, Burton's motion picture, a visually astonishing and imaginative retelling with a *Grand Guignol* sense of the macabre crisscrossing with a narrative vibrantly told mostly through the power of Sondheim's music and lyrics.

Fifteen years ago, Benjamin Barker (Johnny Depp) was torn from his beloved wife and infant daughter, sentenced to imprisonment by the crooked, conniving Judge Turpin (Alan Rickman), who wanted Benjamin's family for himself. Now finally returning to his old home in nineteenth century London, Benjamin has been born a new man calling himself Sweeney Todd. Out for revenge against the man who wronged him, Sweeney is taken in by lonely meat-pie maker Mrs. Lovett (Helena Bonham Carter) and sets up a makeshift barber shop above her eatery. As his madness turns to murder, and then cannibalism—he cuts the throats of his clientele, whose meat subsequently reinvigorate Mrs. Lovett's pies—Sweeney moves ever closer to his number-one target, a louse who unforgivably stole his life while, as it turns out, raising long-lost daughter Johanna (Jayne Wisener) as his own.

It is rare for a film to achieve a feeling of unequivocal, breathtaking transcendence, but *Sweeney Todd: The Demon Barber of Fleet Street* does just that. Told almost entirely via song and image, the story's developments extraordinarily unveil themselves in sequences that bleed seamlessly into one another with nary a moment of downtime or choppiness in sight. The editing by Chris Lebenzon holds an assured fluidity, so much so that the picture approaches qualification as a classical operatic tragedy, while the sparse but successful bids at humor are appropriately as black as the charcoal skies of Burton's London cityscape.

The soundtrack, boomingly reorchestrated by Jonathan Tunick with a ceaseless potency and grandeur that only the cinema can withhold, is marvelous. The musical numbers accompanying them are equally potent and alluring, each setpiece an aesthetic and aural *tour de force*. Of these, highlights include "Pirelli's Miracle Elixir," which introduces the characters of Signor Adolfo Pirelli (Sacha Baron Cohen), a haughty, blackmailing salesman who becomes Sweeney's first victim, and orphaned boy Toby (Edward Sanders), an unwitting accomplice of Sweeney's and Mrs. Lovett's dirty deeds; "Epiphany," wherein Sweeney decides that the whole of London deserves a nasty end and takes to the streets to draw in customers to his barber shop; "Johanna (reprise)," in which the purity of young, starry-eyed Anthony's (Jamie Campbell Bower) love for Johanna is intercut with a montage of Sweeney's out-of-control murderous doings as he longs for the daughter he never got to know, and "Not While I'm Around," a loving ballad between Mrs. Lovett and Toby that takes an evil turn after the boy comes upon their maniacal scheme and can no longer be trusted to keep their secret. The blocking of all the musical scenes is coherent, lively and first-rate, while the cinematography by Dariusz Wolski is forebodingly picturesque, the ashen surroundings boldly contrasting with the generous flow of bright-red blood in the second half.

Performances are spot-on, with perhaps one reservation. Johnny Depp, at last free from the confines of Captain Jack Sparrow, relishes portraying yet another figure who, if he isn't already, is destined for iconic status. Emotionally destroyed inside and hungrily ready for revenge, Depp flawlessly encapsulates Sweeney as a man who starts killing as a means of relieving his heartache before driving over the deep end. Only Depp's acting in the last scene is a miscalculation; it demands high emotions, but Depp plays his reaction to a key discovery with too much reserve for it to have the effect it should.

As Mrs. Lovett, coconspirator to Sweeney's crimes and wannabe love interest, Helena Bonham Carter is the true standout of the piece. While she could be accused of getting the part through biased casting—she was in a relationship with Tim Burton at the time, after all—those suspicions are immediately discounted the second she pops onto the screen. Carter makes the role her own, adding shades of sympathetic depth and longing to her character as she falls in love with a man who will never love her back. Depp and Carter, both of them non-professional singers, have terrific voices well-suited to Sondheim's music. The same goes for a trio of newcomer—Edward Sanders, an endearing, headstrong find as Toby; Jamie Campbell Bower, as Anthony, whose performance of "Johanna" is beautifully carried off, and Jayne Wisener, demure and lovely (and a dead-ringer for Christina Ricci in 1999's *Sleepy Hollow*) as Johanna. Finally, Sacha Baron Cohen steals his few unforgettable scenes as the ill-fated Signor Adolfo Pirelli, his memory long remembered after he is dispatched.

Up until the very ending, *Sweeney Todd: The Demon Barber of Fleet Street* invigoratingly stood as the finest motion picture musical since 2001's *Moulin Rouge*. The last scene, however, is an anticlimactic disappointment—the one flaw in an otherwise speckless production. Whereas the Broadway show concluded with "The Ballad of Sweeney Todd," this song has been taken out here, shedding the climax of a satisfactory denouement and leaving the wrap-ups of three characters—Toby, Anthony and Johanna—dangling and unfinished. Because of this, they come off more as plot constructs than formidable participants in the story, and the abrupt switch to the end credits leaves one feeling like something is missing in translation. Nevertheless, this only puts a temporary damper on what could be, and deserves to be, a modern classic. Thrilling, ghastly, goosebump-inducing and oddly romantic, *Sweeney Todd: The Demon Barber of Fleet Street* is an unqualified genre-buster, not quite like any other horror movie or cinematic musical in memory.

The Texas Chain Saw Massacre

1974 - Directed by Tobe Hooper

The level of ingenuity and skill that went into the making of *The Texas Chain Saw Massacre* astounds even today. Shot on a tiny budget of $83,000 in the blistering summer months of 1973, the film wrangled together a group of up-and-coming young talents behind the scenes—writer-director Tobe Hopper (whose career would take off after this), co-writer Kim Henkel, cinematographer Daniel Pearl (who went on to shoot the inferior 2003 remake), and music composer Wayne Bell (also responsible for 1994's *The Texas Chainsaw Massacre: The Next Generation*). What they ultimately pieced together created a firestorm of controversy. Its release was banned in a number of international territories and its reputation as one of the most violent and gory movies ever made was thereby set into place.

What is amazing, then, is that *The Texas Chain Saw Massacre* has very little blood and the violence comes off as relatively tame by today's standards. The reason so many people mislabeled the film's content was because of its sheer, feel-it-in-the-gut power. Hooper set out to make a motion picture of raw, uncompromising intensity and gritty, unflinching realism, and that is exactly what he achieved. Loosely based on the story of serial killer Ed Gein (who had also inspired 1960's *Psycho*), the film takes the viewer into the mouth of unquenchable insanity and madness and refuses to loosen its grip until the final power tool is silenced by the end credits.

Intermittent camera flashes open the film, the fleeting light revealing the decomposing remains of human corpses. On a radio, a news reporter tells of grave robbers plaguing the dusty Texas area. Who is behind the crimes? Who is taking pictures of the bodies, if, in fact, they are the same ones glimpsed moments before? This information is not disclosed through the course of the film—at least, not concretely—but it efficaciously sets a malevolent tone for the proceedings. So, too, does the music of the opening credits, made up more of a collection of booming, disconcerting sounds and rumbles than a proper orchestral arrangement.

A van carrying two young couples and a nagging tag-along—Sally Hardesty

(Marilyn Burns) and Jerry (Allen Danziger), Pam (Teri McMinn) and Kirk (William Vail), and Sally's wheelchair-bound brother, Franklin (Paul A. Partain)—heads down the open roads of the Texas countryside. After a stop at a cemetery to visit the grave of the Hardestys' grandfather, they set out for his old, abandoned house that Sally and Franklin used to visit as kids. Picking up a hitchhiker (Edwin Neal) whose family runs the nearby slaughterhouse turns out to be their first mistake after he pulls out a scalpel and slices into Franklin's arm. The group promptly kicks him out along the side of the road, but an even bigger nightmare awaits them. Before the day is through, they will run afoul of a clan of cannibalistic lunatics in the business of slaughtering anyone who steps foot on their property.

The plot is fairly barebones, but it is in this hypnotizing simplicity that *The Texas Chain Saw Massacre* rises to a loftier plateau of terror heretofore never quite matched, or done so well, in the annals of cinema. The introduction of the five protagonists in the opening half-hour is almost documentary-like in its view of friends on a road trip together. There isn't an ounce of artifice in the actors' performances, all of them seemingly living out their characters' interactions. This acute naturalism sets them at odds with the landscape before them. The viewer can practically feel the sweaty, sun-drenched atmosphere and sense the heat rising off the asphalt. Their desolation is palpably felt, too—in one shot, the van strolls along the road in a strip of land at the bottom of the screen, the overwhelming infinity of the sky above weighing down upon it. Cinematography, at once appropriately grainy and handsomely composed, and the editing, deliberately paced and intoxicating, plays a large part in raising the tension level. There appears to be a safety net around Sally and her pals for a long time, and things seem to be okay, except they're not.

After arriving at the house, Pam and Kirk head out to find a swimming hole that is supposed to be on the edge of the property. When their search leads them to nothing but dry land, the faint sound of a motor running lures the couple to a farmhouse over the hill. Maybe the residents have some fuel for their van, since the nearby gas station was all out. When no one answers their knocks, Kirk walks inside the front door while Pam waits for him on the swing in the front yard. Is that a squealing pig he hears coming from the open doorway in front of him? He moves deeper into the lair. With sudden, brunt force, a stocky figure (Gunnar Hansen) wearing a mask of human flesh—a man who would grow to be called Leatherface—appears before Kirk, hammers him on the head, and pulls the sliding steel door shut behind them. When Pam gets tired of waiting, she ventures inside, too, literally falling into a living room crudely decorated in filth, chicken feathers and human bones. She won't be leaving any time soon, and Sally's, Franklin's and Jerry's dark fates are right around the corner.

The Texas Chain Saw Massacre is a cutthroat, unendingly bleak masterpiece of horror cinema, one that wears its depravity on its sleeve and isn't without a historical context—Vietnam, peace-loving hippies, the Manson cult and subsequent slayings—to hook its narrative upon. Stimulating in its breathless, brutal nature, unnerving in its out-of-control thematic awfulness, the film finally forces the viewer into Sally's shoes, pushing her insufferable brother in his wheelchair through the underbrush, hopelessly calling out her friends' names in the blackness of night, and then witnessing her wall of security come toppling down with the onslaught of Leatherface and his buzzing chainsaw. The climax, depicting Sally's hellish experiences in the hours before dawn as she screams bloody murder and struggles to stay alive amidst a kaleidoscope of iniquity incarnate and one particularly unsavory dinner, is emotionally draining and, for lack of better words, unimaginably horrific.

Even if Sally survives her ordeal, there is no catharsis for her. She does not turn the tables on her captors. They receive no real comeuppance. And all she has to show for what she goes through is a collapsed mental state that may never heal itself. The brilliance of *The Texas Chain Saw Massacre* is not simply in its coarse yet dazzling filmmaking prowess, or in its forthright goal to shake and stir audiences, but in its brave, chilling admission that the evils in our world never really die. "You think the '70s are messed up," Tobe Hooper looks to be saying. "You ain't seen nothing yet."

The Texas Chainsaw Massacre Part 2

1986 - Directed by Tobe Hooper

Twelve years after *The Texas Chain Saw Massacre* became an instant independent film classic and riled up a lot of close-vested folks with its grim, ultra-realistic depiction of carnage and decay in the Lone Star State, director Tobe Hooper agreed to return for a long-awaited sequel. This wouldn't be any old obligatory continuation, though. As deadly serious as its predecessor is, *The Texas Chainsaw Massacre Part 2* is a ripe and wicked horror-comedy, as black as pitch and every bit as violent as naysayers mistakenly accused the first film of being. Of all the sequels, this is the one that triumphantly stands apart from the pack, daring to be different and actually succeeding against all odds.

When obnoxious Mercedes-driving college kids Buzz (Barry Kinyon) and Rick (Chris Douridas) call into K-OKLA's Red River Rock 'n' Roll request line, they have no sooner begun to harass late-night radio station deejay Stretch (Caroline Williams) when they are attacked on the road by a chainsaw-wielding Leatherface (Bill Johnson). Stretch, hearing the whole incident go down, believes she has the tape to prove it. When revenge-seeking Lieutenant 'Lefty' Enright (Dennis Hopper), older brother of the first picture's Sally and Franklin Hardesty, urges Stretch to play the recording live on her show, she has no idea that the boys' killers will be listening. Narrowly escaping an attack on the station, Stretch follows Leatherface and steel-plated brother Chop-Top (Bill Moseley) back to their underground lair at the abandoned Texas Battleland theme park. She plans to meet Lefty there and smoke the culprits out, but soon finds herself trapped in the catacombs, running for her life from the cannibalistic Sawyer clan.

The Texas Chainsaw Massacre Part 2 may initially turn off fans of the original who are expecting more of the same, but it is in the ballsy decision to do something different that it remains the cult favorite it is today. For one, there are virtually no teenagers in sight. The protagonist is a tough and intelligent, albeit horrified, young woman in her late-twenties. The setting, up until the second half taking place in the nightmarish abode of the Sawyers, appears to be a well-populated part of Texas, with eldest brother Drayton (Jim Siedow) interacting with the locals and even proudly entering (and winning) a chili cookoff contest.

As for Lefty, he is out for vengeance for the death of invalid brother Franklin and will do whatever it takes to bring his killers to the justice they deserve.

The film is just about as macabre as they come and not without tautly embroiled tension, but it also happens to be surprisingly funny and consistently quote-worthy. When the gourmet yuppette host (Judy Kelly) of the cookoff takes a taste of Drayton's chili and stumbles upon a tooth mixed into the beef, Drayton quickly thinks on his feet: "Oh, that's just one of those hard-shelled peppercorns." And, after "far-out fan" Chop-Top makes his presence known at the radio station, raving all along about the snuff tape she's been airing, an edgy Stretch is forced into giving him a tour of the studio that includes such valued items as a rolodex and the "exit" sign. Her failed attempts to bid him goodnight are a riot.

By the time Stretch has fallen into the maze of caves lived in by the Sawyers, the picture turns into a skewed, barbed-wire satire of consumerism and the American Dream, with Drayton and younger siblings Leatherface and Chop-Top playing the parts of a bickering dysfunctional family who also happen to be savage, people-eating maniacs. As Drayton runs around preparing dinner and griping about what fools he has for brothers, Chop-Top dances with the zombified corpse of a fourth brother and annoys skin-wearing sibling Leatherface by chanting, "Bubba's got a girlfriend!" That Leatherface truly wants a girlfriend—and has grown a soft spot for Stretch that he hates to end by slaughtering her—sets him distinctly apart from the two-dimensional, cold-blooded psycho he was portrayed as in 1974.

Tobe Hooper and screenwriter L.M. Kit Carson play all of this with their tongues firmly in cheek, and they continue on this path right up to its grimy, grisly, blood-soaked conclusion. Stretch, affable and good-natured at the onset before calamity ensues, becomes the levelheaded heroine who anchors the film with a much-needed offset of levity. Caroline Williams is a game, dynamite ball of charisma as Stretch, her disarming southern accent and the ability to sweat and get dirtied up while still looking fantastic in a pair of tight jean shorts the cherry on top. When she comes upon the nearly dead body of right-hand man L.G. (Lou Perry), the skin peeled off his face, her tearful reaction is as straight and dramatic as the movie gets.

As Lieutenant Lefty, Dennis Hopper gnaws the scenery and plays the role as if he's a few cards short of a full deck himself. Bill Moseley is brilliant as Chop-Top, in one scene lighting the end of a clothes hanger and scratching away the skin surrounding the steel plate in his head. Moseley is tartly comical and evil in equal measures. And, as head of the family Drayton, Jim Siedow (the one actor reprising his role from the original) is wonderfully, viciously acerbic in his line readings. He's at the end of his ropes with his dim-witted brothers, but he loves them all the same.

Lefty's ultimate confrontation with the Sawyers, getting into a chainsaw fight with Leatherface and cutting up Drayton's crotch real bad ("He sure took care of my hems"), is well-choreographed and gruesomely satisfying. So, too, is the climactic battle between Stretch and Chop-Top set on top of the treacherous rocky cliffs of the theme park's mountain. In the old VHS version of the film, the memorable final shot showed Stretch swinging a chainsaw at the top of the mountain while civilization—a highway filled with passing cars—lurked behind her at the bottom of the frame. On the widescreen version released on DVD and Blu-ray, this is tragically cut off the shot. It's the one instance in memory where full-screen cropping would have been beneficial.

The Texas Chainsaw Massacre Part 2 is as potent a follow-up as one could expect from the series, unapologetically traveling in fresh directions while serving up audiences the gory goods. The cinematography by Richard Kooris is vibrant and alive, taking full advantage of the locations and making particularly effective use of the neon colors at the radio station and the rainbow-colored Christmas lights strung along the walls of the Sawyers' underground hell. The soundtrack is also superb, with choice cuts from The Cramps, Oingo Boingo, Timbuk 3, Concrete Blonde, Lords of the New Church and Stewart Copeland nicely complementing the action. When it comes to humor-laced horror that isn't an outright spoof, there are few films that work quite as well (or with the same amount of bravado) as *The Texas Chainsaw Massacre Part 2*.

Timecrimes

2008 - Directed by Nacho Vigalondo

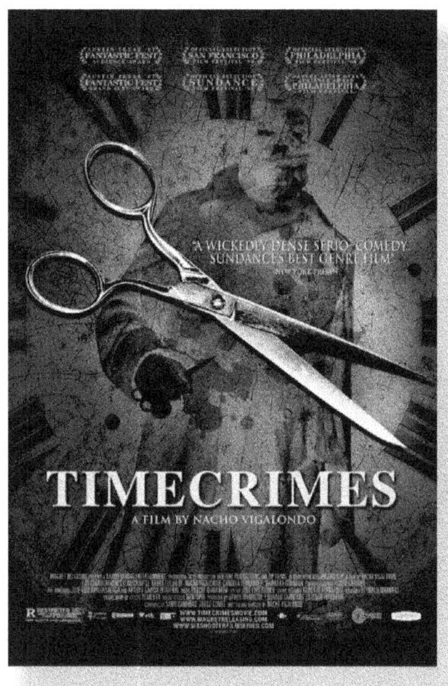

Fans of 2004's mind-bendingly complex time-travel exploration *Primer*, as well as those viewers that found that heady indie film too difficult to follow, should be first in line to see the Spanish-language *Timecrimes* (*Los cronocrímenes*). This genre-jumping, expertly designed thriller, at first set up as a horror tale before moving into different unforeseeable directions, is less cryptic and pretentious than the aforementioned *Primer* while still demanding attention be paid in order to wrap one's mind around its intricacies. In return is a craftily satisfying and wholly absorbing experience.

Hector (Karra Elejalde) and Clara (Candela Fernández) are a happily married couple still fixing up the country home they have recently moved into. When Clara heads into town to run errands, Hector's lawn chair relaxation in the backyard is cut short when, through his binoculars, he spots a nude woman in the woods staring back at him. Going to investigate, Hector is accosted and stabbed by a psychopath with a head wrapped in stained bandages. He narrowly escapes to a nearby gated laboratory where a scientist (Nacho Vigalondo) closes him in a dome-like contraption. When Hector reemerges, he discovers that he has gone back in time by roughly an hour and a half. Spotting a copy of himself—"Hector 2," as the scientist labels him—still sitting in his yard in the lawn chair, Hector is suddenly thrust into an unthinkable situation where he must evade his other self while making sure that the same events occur so that, once again, there will only be one of him in the world.

Motion pictures dealing with the time and space continuum—e.g., *The Time Machine*, the *Back to the Future* trilogy—are usually fascinating, but not always easy to pull off. As with any movie involving time travel, there are small details that don't quite hold up to scrutiny, but *Timecrimes* does a relatively superb job in its attempt to fill in most of the holes. Shot on a low budget and with only four characters, writer-director Nacho Vigalondo's impressive work is a study in minimalism even as the narrative is labyrinthine in the circuitous loop it finds itself within. While difficult to go into too many details—this is one film that the less a first-time viewer knows about it, the better—it should be said that there comes to be a third (and possibly fourth) version of Hector all existing in the same 90-minute time frame. Running into each other, or making one false step, could spell a disastrous paradox.

Before the time-travel material enters the equation, *Timecrimes* has a thirty-minute first act that works deliciously as a trippy, scare-filled horror film. Hector's run-in with the bandaged mystery man in the forest is nightmarish enough, but a sequence where he must make his way up a lighted path amidst the darkness, his only knowledge of where the killer is reliant on the information he receives from the scientist via a walkie-talkie, is utterly chilling in a grasp-the-armrest sort of way. The second and third acts are more technical than emotional, with the stakes raised and time wrapping back around on itself again and again, but no less gripping. The use of the Blondie song, "Picture This," during a few key moments exquisitely adds to the atmosphere.

The ending resolves Hector's plight to a point while leaving a couple unanswered questions—like the matter of a dead body—hanging in the balance. Nevertheless, *Timecrimes* manages to be intellectual as well as never less than entertaining. The story is ingeniously mounted, too, and the tricky cinematography by Flavio Martínez Labiano is both dynamic and menacing. If time travel was an actuality, one suspects that *Timecrimes* would be pretty accurate in its thrilling, frightening, complicated design.

The Town That Dreaded Sundown

1976 - Directed by Charles B. Pierce

The Town That Dreaded Sundown is a film that relies less on a three-act narrative structure than as a wholeheartedly visceral experience where the situations, rather than the characters, stand out. Directed by Charles B. Pierce, the picture is based on a true story that took place in Texarkana, Texas, circa spring 1946, the town's residents coming under siege when two young people are attacked one night at a lovers' lane by an inexplicable hooded killer. They narrowly survive the ordeal, but the people of the town, not used to such violent crimes taking place so close to them, enter into a frenzy, terrified that he might strike again. Exactly twenty-one days later, two more lovers are found in a similar setting—this time viciously murdered. Deputy Sheriff Norman Ramsey (Andrew Prine) and Texas Ranger J.D. Morales (Ben Johnson) are promptly brought onto the case, fearing a possible pattern is starting every three weeks. Just as the killer, nicknamed "The Phantom Killer," seems to shift into overdrive, he vanishes without a trace, never to be seen or heard from again.

Very little is learned about the characters, whether it be the police officers or victims, and, in fact, one of the supporting policemen is played inappropriately as a comic device to most likely lighten up the subject matter. Instead, *The Town That Dreaded Sundown* goes for a quasi-documentary feel throughout, its matter-of-fact portrayal of the crimes a big part of what makes the film so successful. What is so absolutely fascinating about the case is that it was, and still remains, a completely baffling occurrence in which no one ever found out who the culprit was, or what finally happened to him after his reign of terror came to an end.

The film is narrated with a no-nonsense demeanor throughout—a wise choice—bringing added realism to the proceedings. Also helping out is the meticulous way the story is played out, alternating between the investigation and sequences of shocking power as the murders are vividly and brutally reenacted. One particular scene involving a trombone and the prolonged, unsettling torture of a teenage girl in the woods is, no doubt, hair-raisingly tough to watch, but never seems to dip into cheap or pointless exploitation. Another sequence involving the attack on and narrow escape of a woman (former *Gilligan's Island* star Dawn Wells) at home signifies that not even the average townsperson behind locked doors is protected. Because of this, the stakes raise all the more.

By the conclusion of *The Town That Dreaded Sundown*, a brief confrontation between the authorities and the killer occurs, but nothing comes of it, the "Phantom" mysteriously vanishing afterwards as if into thin air. In the closing moments, the viewer is left to ponder not only the whereabouts of the culprit, but the effect that such inconceivable crimes can have on a community. *The Town That Dreaded Sundown* leaves one with such striking moments of stark, raw terror that it puts many less serious horror films to shame. After all, these crimes actually happened, and just the thought of that is petrifying.

Trick 'r Treat

2009 - Directed by Michael Dougherty

As exciting new filmmaker Michael Dougherty (screenwriter of 2006's *Superman Returns*) told the packed audience at New York City's October 13, 2008, Two Boots Pioneer special screening of *Trick 'r Treat*, he was born within days of Halloween and has been enamored with the holiday ever since. It is with this near-religious affinity for All Hallows' Eve that he made his deliciously macabre, exquisitely festive directorial debut. A loving ode to the season of the witch, *Trick 'r Treat* meshes the tone of 1950s E.C. Comics anthologies with the crisscrossing, non-chronological storytelling of *Pulp Fiction*. With inspiration coming from all directions—the animated opening credits are a direct nod to 1982's *Creepshow*, while several choice elements from 1978's *Halloween* make themselves be known—the film is an orgy of ghoulish fun and menace that horror fans the world over should salivate over. For a while, they almost didn't see it. Originally scheduled for a lucrative October 2007 theatrical berth, Warner Bros. and Legendary Pictures saw fit to delay the picture, then pull it from the schedule altogether. Either the heads of these studios were so inept that they didn't realize what kind of a goldmine they were sitting on, or they had a vindictive grudge against Dougherty for some reason. *Trick 'r Treat* did finally see the light of day in 2009, but it was as a direct-to-video release despite getting near-universal acclaim from those critics and general audiences who had seen it—a crime against both film artists and genre enthusiasts alike.

Set entirely on one particularly spooky Halloween night, the film weaves together four interconnecting stories. In the first, greedy prepubescent troublemaker Charlie (Brett Kelly) picks the wrong house to steal candy from. The owner, it turns out, is Steven (Dylan Baker), a school principal who serial kills on the side. Meanwhile, across town, twenty-somethings Maria (Rochelle Aytes) and sister Laurie (Anna Paquin) head with two other sexy friends to the local parade, in hopes of bagging Laurie a date. Lurking among them is a vampiric murderer. The third tale involves a group of trick-or-treaters—Macy (Britt McKillip), Sara (Isabelle Deluce), Schrader (Jean-Luc Bilodeau) and Chip

(Alberto Ghisi)—who decide to play a nasty trick on nerdy classmate Rhonda (Samm Todd). Before the night is out, they will learn more than they bargained for about the town's infamous school bus accident urban legend. And, finally, living next door to Steven is the grumpy old Mr. Kreeg (Brian Cox), a man whose mean ways and lack of Halloween spirit come back to haunt him.

With the exception of John Carpenter's immortal classic, *Halloween, Trick 'r Treat* sets out to become the definitive Halloween movie, the kind that becomes a staple of the holiday, pulled out to watch every October. There isn't a shot to be found that isn't positively dripping with autumnal atmosphere and seasonal chestnuts. Foliage, costumes, scarecrows, jack-o'-lanterns, cornfields, candy—all of these things are beautifully incorporated into the *mise-en-scène* and layer on an undeniable fun moodiness. In scripting the picture, Michael Dougherty took the basis of his animated short entitled *Season's Greetings* and threaded that movie's character of Sam into this one. Sam (Quinn Lord), a fresh creation who is the height of a child and wears a burlap bag over his head, is Halloween's answer to Santa Claus or the Easter Bunny, standing as spectator on the outskirts of the humans' lives and bringing mirth and mayhem to one and all. As befits the holiday, Sam can be cute and mischievous, but he's also got a dark side that should not be messed with.

All four of the respective storylines—five, if you count the prologue in which nagging wife Emma (Leslie Bibb) makes the mistake of uttering aloud, "I hate Halloween"—receive roughly equal screen time and are diverse enough that they stand apart from each other, absorbing in their own way. The neighborhood boogeyman that is Steven is the epitome of all the strangers our parents used to tell us to be cautious of when we went door-to-door begging for treats. His attempts to bury his latest victim in his backyard while young son Billy (Connor Levins) bothers him from the upstairs window is a dark-humored trip. Playing the most twisted onscreen father since his unnerving 1998 role in *Happiness*, Dylan Baker relishes being creepy and setting the viewer off-balance even as he acts the part of an upstanding citizen.

The subplot involving the kids who journey to a fog-entrenched rock quarry where a school bus carrying mentally disturbed students is said to have plummeted features some of the most visually exciting scenes. Their rural walk from their suburban homes to the desolate scene of the crime is like a live-action *It's the Great Pumpkin, Charlie Brown* come to life. The interactions between the kids mirrors authenticity with just a sprinkle of whimsy—newcomer Samm Todd is especially wonderful as outsider Rhonda—and the aesthetics are nothing short of eerily picturesque.

Anna Paquin is the main attraction of the third tale. Dressed as Little Red Riding Hood, she sets out to find a nice guy (or so it seems) and instead encounters a dangerous wolf. The practical effects used in the climax of this segment are scary and refreshing, illuminating how CGI is not always the way to go when setting out to make the viewer believe what they are seeing is really happening. It's a welcome return to the days of the early '80s, when Tom Savini- and Rick Baker-esque ingenuity reigned over the landscape. Last but not least, Brian Cox is entertainingly spiteful as Mr. Kreeg, a Scrooge-like figure in the sunset of his life who gets paid a visit from Halloween mascot Sam. Twisted, violent, tense and blissfully maniacal, these scenes are craftily conceived and expertly pieced together.

If there was any justice in Hollywood, *Trick 'r Treat* would have come out on 2,500 screens and Dougherty would have been able to make a follow-up a year or two later (there are endless possibilities when it comes to anthology movies, after all, without the worry of repeating oneself). What was the hold-up? A scary movie set on Halloween pretty much sells itself, doesn't it? That it's a great film, besides, and has received nothing but positive notices from those who have seen it is the real maddening part. Dougherty's only detectable misstep is a short running time, but that is because the picture is such a joy to watch that the viewer is left wanting another half-hour (and added development) tacked onto its 87 minutes. Moreover, cinematographer Glen MacPherson, production designer Mark Freeborn, art director Tony Wohlgemuth, costume designer Trish Keating and score composer Douglas Pipes outdo themselves, joining together to present one of the most handsome, lushly detailed horror features in years. *Trick 'r Treat* is destined to put the most sour of souls in the Halloween spirit.

Trigger Man

2007 - Directed by Ti West

Writer-director Ti West is one of the twenty-first century's best-kept secrets in genre filmmaking. When it comes to generating the kind of quietly simmering, armrest-clenching suspense he so brilliantly ratchets, there are simply few modern auteurs better than him. High praise, certainly, but the fact that West has thus far been able to achieve breathless levels of intensity while working with budgets that would make a shoestring look thick is quite astounding. His first feature was 2005's *The Roost*, a savvy vampire story involving a rustic barn and bats galore that could put some of the most jaded of horror fans on edge and jumping out of their seats throughout. The more-realistic, just-as-frightening *Trigger Man* is even better, a taut-as-a-vise-grip sophomore effort that is significant of anything but a slump.

Using an unhurried, observational *cinéma vérité* style, Ti West wraps the ADD-free viewer around his finger like a slowly twisting rubber band that starts cutting off circulation. The film opens with the Manhattan skyline, the bricks and steel of society's industrialization at odds with a somewhat similar-looking but very different building that appears later. Sean (Sean Reid), late-20s, drives into the city to pick up old friends Reggie (Reggie Cunningham) and Ray (Ray Sullivan), whom he hasn't seen much of since their lives went in different directions. The three of them head to a woodsy stretch in Delaware for a day of hanging out and hunting for bucks. The slowness of sitting around waiting for something to happen and the unspoken truth that things have changed between them leads to monotony and temporarily flared tempers. Only minutes after the strike of noon, a gunshot will be heard in the vicinity, blood will splatter on Reggie's face, and their presumptions of seclusion and safety will abruptly and cruelly be shattered. Meanwhile, through a clearing in the forest, across a reservoir, looms a long-abandoned factory, its seemingly decrepit desolation quite possibly not so desolate, anymore.

Trigger Man should become a mainstay example of how to pull off minimalist horror. With the sharpness of a woodchipper blade and the precision of a seamstress, Ti West has taken his barebones screenplay—dialogue could probably be compiled together and fit on two script pages—and worked out of it one of the creepiest lingering atmospheres in recent years. A cello- and percussion-based music score by Jeff Grace meticulously underscores the images, making even the simplest shots of people walking through the woods or sitting on logs seem terrifyingly threatening. The crap hits the fan in the second half of *Trigger Man*, but it is before this, just in the way West (who also acts as cinematographer and editor) naturalistically sets up the locations and teases the viewer with the possibility of what might occur to the characters, that the film works just as well.

Early on, as Reggie, Ray and Sean reach their destination and slip on orange hunting vests, they take this precaution as a way of keeping sure that other hunters in the area do not mistake them for prey. The irony is that this is arguably the very reason they transform into the hunted, the garish material standing out and acting as an easy target for a psychopath with a gun. As a horrified Reggie sees both of his companions struck down and fears even moving an inch lest he make himself an easy shot, it is the mere potential that something is about to happen to him at any moment that raises the viewer's blood pressure. And, when Reggie suspects the culprit is lurking over at the dilapidated factory, an unseen force of evil who has almost taken on the role of God's eye, one shudders at the very thought. As much as Reggie and friends Sean and Ray are the leads, it is the factory itself that is the most unforgettable character. An inanimate construction symbolizing the inexplicable darkness of human nature and the world at large, it stands over the proceedings, silent, daring Reggie to come closer.

When more bodies turn up—whoever is shooting, it is clear he/she/they have been doing it for a while—a distraught Reggie finally does get the courage to edge his way toward the building. The climax—twenty minutes of disquieting apprehension, told in only a handful of camera shots and no dialogue—is so effortlessly orchestrated and yet simplistic at the same time that one has to wonder why most big-budgeted horror films have such trouble being the least bit scary. This one delivers all one expects from a genre pic in spades, and it is only in the culminating moment where the shooter is revealed that the pressure diffuses a little. Since the movie is not about who is committing the crimes, but about the very fact that crimes of this cold-blooded nature can, and are, happening, it was not necessary for West to give the shooter a face. That's beside the point.

Trigger Man seems like something Gus Van Sant might have made if his forte was tension-driven thrillers. Sharing the deliberate pacing of Van Sant's exhilarating experimental work—2003's *Elephant*, 2005's *Last Days*, 2008's *Paranoid Park*—West takes his time and allows seemingly authentic life to unfold on camera. By doing this, he is able to capture the subtleties of person-to-person interaction and the intimacy of the human condition with unbatted eyelashes and a truthful clarity. Additionally, West's three central actors, all of them either relative novices or first-timers, benefit from their inexperience. Told to just exist on screen and forget about over-the-top theatrics, the performers dodge artificiality. *Trigger Man* may be slow-paced from an action standpoint, but don't let that fool you; it's as ruthless and nerve-jangling as any motion picture in recent memory.

Troll Hunter

2010 - Directed by André Øvredal

Shot in a faux-documentary style that makes its fantastically ominous happenings all the more real, *Troll Hunter* does for Norwegian mythology what 1999's *The Blair Witch Project* did for getting lost in the woods and 2008's *Cloverfield* did for alien invasions. The tone in savvy director André Øvredal's film is a bit lighter than those aforementioned pics, and, thus, doesn't achieve the same heightened level of stark fear. Boy, is it fun, though, the rocky, woodsy, altogether exotic terrain of its foreign landscape marrying splendidly with its narrative fairy tale gone awry. The characters are more or less a means to an end, but where *Troll Hunter* really cooks is in its bewitching cinematography by Hallvard Bræin and the splendid uses of tension, restraint and eye-poppingly seamless visual effects to weave a riveting, one-of-a-kind spell.

In the wild outskirts of Volda, Norway, a rash of bear killings have led authorities to suspect the work of poachers. A film crew from the university—on-camera journalist Thomas (Glenn Erland Tosterud), sound recordist Johanna (Johanna Mørck) and cameraman Kalle (Tomas Alf Larsen)—think they've found the culprit in Hans (Otto Jespersen), a hunter who works all hours of the night before returning to his trailer home for a day's sleep. When the crew secretly follow him into the heavily forested mountains, they expect to catch him in the act of illegal activities. Instead, they narrowly escape an attack from a giant three-headed creature, just one of many species of troll that the government has been battling to keep on the down-low as Hans tries to control an outbreak. The trolls' kryptonite is ultraviolet light, causing them to either explode or turn to limestone. When a professional scientist/folklorist explains this curious process and why it occurs, it quite surprisingly sounds plausible. Tagging along with Hans thereafter, Thomas and his crew are excited by their findings, but also ignorant of the level of danger they're getting themselves into. When one of them mentions early on the possibility of traveling to Oslo and selling their footage to the BBC, it's a suggestion they probably should take.

Like a pimped-out cinematic telling of the mood-drenched Maelstrom ride at Disney's Epcot, *Troll Hunter* is an ambitious treat of equal parts threat and whimsy. A U.S. remake would be fruitless, the thought of such even more unnecessary than the norm since the story is specific to Norway (it wouldn't work or make sense if transplanted to, say, New York City) and naturally means more to its characters because they are locals and have grown up hearing and not taking seriously the folk yarns about trolls. André Øvredal and his unaffected cast draw the viewer in with the majestic scenery Kalle captures in front of his lens and a gradual increase of intrigue and danger as the characters are drawn into an investigation far bigger than what they could have imagined. The images caught on film of the trolls, leading to a climactic showdown on the top of a desolate mountain with one the size of Godzilla, are nothing short of amazing, the effects work used to bring them to life so vivid and adept that they actually show up most of today's mega-budgeted studio productions. The CGI, blending without question with the live-action surroundings, deserves awards recognition. As with the dinosaurs in 1993's *Jurassic Park*, *Troll Hunter* makes one believe these hairy otherworldly beasts actually exist.

In a curious plot point, the trolls are drawn to Christians like moths to a lamp. When a new camerawoman named Malica (Urmila Berg-Domaas) is picked up along the way, her noted Muslim faith is questioned. Will she be safe? Malica, unaware of what she's about to see, thinks nothing of the question about her religious background and fails to take heed of the warning. It's a missed opportunity, then, that Malica rarely, if ever, is glimpsed again; she is the one from this point forward who is supposed to be behind the camera. Whatever shock and disbelief she may have once the monstrous trolls come calling is left untouched upon. More compellingly explored is a sequence where Hans leads the filmmakers into a large, dark cave they believe to be empty, only to get trapped when a family of trolls return unannounced.

The found-footage genre is just that—comprehensive enough nowadays to have its own genre—and this one purports that the filmmakers have mysteriously disappeared, the only evidence of what they saw and what might have happened to them beginning and ending with the film they shot. *Troll Hunter*, then, is an edited compendium of the 283 alleged hours of footage, and it depicts situations, vistas and images never before seen in quite this manner. An overall darker motion picture could have probably been made—the characters treat their investigative journey with a giddiness that belies the horror until it's almost too late—but there are still plenty of scenes worth setting the hair on a person's arm on end. Bursting with ingenuity and simply stunning to look at, *Troll Hunter* stands as an example next to 2010's shoestring sensation *Monsters* of just how much bang indie filmmakers can get with their bucks. Hollywood should be paying attention.

Vacancy

2007 - Directed by Nimród Antal

Vacancy has a barebones plot, no major twists or revelations, and follows a point-A-to-point-B path with few detours. It's a study in narrative minimalism, really, slowly but surely escalating with a sense of portent that, once it gets going, never lets up. With A-list stars Luke Wilson and Kate Beckinsale gamely getting down and dirty in a genre neither is used to, and director Nimród Antal auspiciously orchestrating a string of tension-drenched setpieces for them to jump into, the 82-minute *Vacancy* doesn't have a moment to spare. By not allowing the film to get bogged down in needless exposition, explanations and motives, Antal and screenwriter Mark L. Smith grab hold of the viewer's jugular and cook up a stylish potboiler as compact as it is well-made.

David (Luke Wilson) and Amy Fox (Kate Beckinsale) are a bickering couple on the verge of ending their marriage and struggling to come to grips with the recent loss of a child. While on one final road trip together, a desolate backways shortcut and a subsequent spot of car trouble forces them to check into the grungy, run-down Pinewood Motel. Let's put it this way: if forced into sleeping overnight either there or at the Bates Motel, most travelers would hedge their bets with Mama's boy Norman. David and Amy have no sooner gotten to their room that they are assaulted by violent banging on the door. Reassured by motel manager Mason (Frank Whaley) that the culprit is probably just a drunk teenager or bum playing a trip on them, David returns to the room, pops in a couple of videotapes, and discovers something much more horrific: real-life snuff films, shot by surveillance cameras in the very motel room he and Amy are in.

Vacancy promptly gets things going with a superb opening titles sequence inspired by Saul Bass, featuring a spine-tingling orchestral score from Paul Haslinger that reminds of something Bernard Herrmann and Alfred Hitchcock might have collaborated on. From there, the picture draws the viewer in with a deliberately paced setup of characters and their own isolation before plowing full speed ahead. The ceaselessly fast, panic-filled second and third acts rarely ease up and, lest the viewer think too long about the improbable last scene, Nimród Antal flashes to the end credits (also paying tribute to Saul Bass' designs, thus arriving full circle from the beginning) before one has time to contemplate what a disappointment the last two minutes are.

Inhabiting the roles of David and Amy, Luke Wilson and Kate Beckinsale are put through physical and emotional obstacles as they are stalked from almost beginning to end by two savage masked killers lurking around the property. It couldn't have been the most relaxing of movie shoots, but Wilson, who is not usually known for dramatic parts, and Beckinsale invest the entirety of their energy into believably meeting the demands. Amidst the crying and running and fighting and tunneling through rat-infested underground caverns, these two actors are able to make David and Amy real people rather than dumb slasher-flick fodder. As might be expected, being faced with a reciprocal life-or-death situation can do wonders for a marriage on the rocks. Perfecting the role of a nerdy but threatening sicko running a black-market snuff film business on the side, Frank Whaley skin-crawlingly relishes his scenes with the voracious appetite of a vampire on the prowl for blood.

Vacancy is reminiscent of a long list of horror-thrillers—among them, 1960's *Psycho*, 2001's *Joyride*, 2003's *Identity*, and, most unlikely but unmistakably, 1983's *Mountaintop Motel Massacre*—but is lean, tight and relentless all on its own. In a story dealing in violent exploitation but not dwelling upon it, director Antal and cinematographer Andrzej Sekula leave it to their masterfully compelling and innovative use of visual compositions to bring out the scare factor. The aforementioned ending is the one sore spot of the film; it feels like a cop-out to what has come before it. Problematic capper aside, *Vacancy* is just the ticket for genre fans starved for a movie that actually thrills. It does that in spades, guaranteeing that a descriptor like "pulse-pounding" is not simply hyperbole.

Vanishing on 7th Street

2011 - Directed by Brad Anderson

Across the early span of his career, director Brad Anderson (2001's *Session 9*, 2005's *The Machinist*, TV's *Masters of Horror* entry "Sounds Like") has exhibited a strong, confident command of genre filmmaking that harkens back to a time when horror-thrillers relied on mood and character over more blatant trappings like violence and bloodshed to weave their effective spells. He does it again with *Vanishing on 7th Street*, a giddily unnerving offering that gets more mileage from its restraint than it ever could by spelling things out and going for more obvious scares (though there is one socko jump-out-of-your-seat moment, too). The plot proper isn't terribly original, but peer beneath the surface and one will find more going on than meets the eye. This, above all else, is where the film should exceed the expectations of audiences who have been trained by commercial Hollywood cinema to turn their brains off rather than consider a story's deeper thematic implications. That *Vanishing on 7th Street* even *has* deeper implications is something of an achievement.

When a mass power outage occurs across Detroit, Michigan—and, one has to assume, the rest of the world—the darkness steals with it the majority of the human population. With the sun rising later and setting sooner with each passing day, three strangers who remain—television news field reporter Luke (Hayden Christensen), physical therapist Rosemary (Thandie Newton), and AMC multiplex projectionist Paul (John Leguizamo)—seek refuge at Sonny's, a corner bar where 12-year-old James (Jacob Latimore) holds court as he feeds the rapidly dwindling electric generator. Struggling to come to terms with the unthinkable as malevolent shadows close in, the four of them eventually figure out the common ground between them: they were all holding or around an independent light source when the blackout occurred. What will happen to them, then, when they no longer are?

Vanishing on 7th Street opens with disquieting eeriness, a mundane evening for movie theater employee Paul turning outright freaky and bizarre when the rest of his co-workers and all the patrons vanish without a trace at the moment of a sudden power outage, their clothes and belongings the only things left behind. Glimpses into Rosemary's and Luke's respective experiences at this crucial moment are also indelible, with Rosemary aghast at the sight of a hospital patient in the midst of open heart surgery who is left horrified and helpless on the operating table before he, too, is snatched up, and Luke waking up the next morning in his apartment beside lit candles before stumbling outside to find a desolate cityscape. Immediately, they begin to get stalked by the shadows on the walls and the darkness surrounding them, pulled off with astonishing efficiency through expertly conceived lighting and visual effects far superior to many other CGI-heavy films with notably larger budgets. It, of course, helps that these elements are critical to the story, used often ingeniously to serve the script and the atmosphere rather than as the frivolous, eye-candied main attractions. Nevertheless, it's one of the main reasons for the picture's suffocating sense of paranoia, the imperiled characters feeling that they are constantly being watched by unknown supernatural forces.

Key flashbacks, all of them aiding in the development of the protagonists, are unobtrusive and minimal, but also powerful. As Luke's extracurricular activities are revealed—he is carrying on an affair with his married co-anchor while still pining for his ex-wife—Rosemary's horror in losing her infant son complements her personal ordeal and James is haunted by a memory of spending time with his bartender mom before she left to find help at a nearby church and never returned. The performances from Hayden Christensen, Thandie Newton, John Leguizamo and newcomer Jacob Latimore are believable and vulnerable, each one distinct but never pre-orchestrated as the lead or some movie-style hero. This is especially wise once they, too, are gradually swept up by the darkness, their disappearances captured with a startling, matter-of-fact nonchalance that leaves everyone in equal danger and duress.

Vanishing on 7th Street is a skillful, compact chiller, unburdened by too many subplots or the tendency to overexplain what is going on. A lesser film would seek answers, but screenwriter Anthony Jaswinski and director Brad Anderson are smart enough to understand their film is more about questions. To tidily provide reason behind the events in the story would be a betrayal of its prophetic aura. Conjecture and one piece of evidence—the word "Croatoan" found written on a wall—linking things to the infamous sixteenth century lost colony of Roanoke Island is provocative while lending further enigmatic inference to the goings-on. Following a middle section that hushes the pacing and the threat before the urgency of the third act takes over, the picture transforms itself into a poignant, borderline-profound metaphor for the mysteries of death and the helplessness with which we fight our inescapable mortality. In spite of the knowledge that all living things must one day pass on, people struggle with the imprint—or lack thereof—they will leave on the world after they are gone. Did they make a difference, or a name for themselves? Will anyone remember in future generations that they even existed? These existential conflicts are, indeed, universal, and the encroaching darkness waiting to pounce on them the moment their light—their very life force—fades is symbolic of nothing less than the grimmest unknown specter of them all. Even with hope more or less gone, they fight. For their survival. For their mark on the earth. That's their nature, and our own.

V/H/S

2012 - Directed by Adam Wingard, David Bruckner, Ti West, Glenn McQuaid, Joe Swanberg, Radio Silence

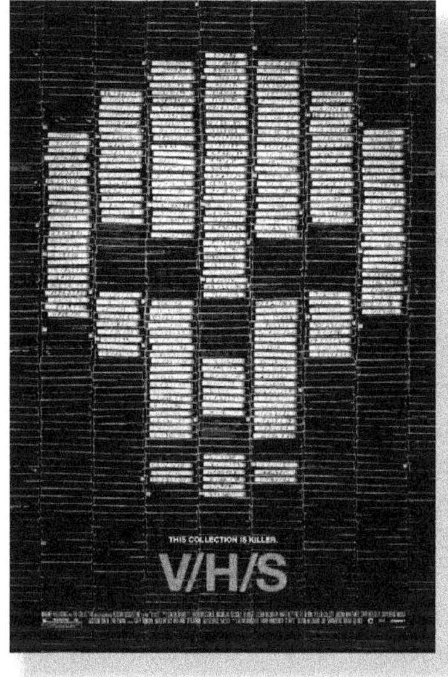

By and large, modern anthological horror pictures are a woefully untapped genre type, viewed by most major film studios as virtually unmarketable. How else to explain writer-director Michael Dougherty's 2009 autumnal spooktacular *Trick 'r Treat*, a film treated for no good reason like a bastard stepchild by studio Warner Bros. and all but sent direct-to-video despite massive critical acclaim? Either Dougherty made an enemy out of some thin-skinned top brass at WB or the distributor honestly—and foolishly—felt that there was no audience for a Halloween-set thriller ingeniously structured to resemble the multilayered, revolving-door timeline of *Pulp Fiction* while tonally matching 1982's perennial part-scary, part-funny classic, *Creepshow*. The truth is that *Trick 'r Treat* would have done huge business had it been sent out to two thousand screens a week or two before October 31st, its intrinsically related subject matter and release date promotion enough to bring in a tidy profit. Partially because there has been such a dearth of this particular brand of horror flick, and also because its creators have come up with a fresh angle with which to present their six short tales of the macabre, *V/H/S* is an inviting addition that has rallied an admiring cult of supporters. With an independent distributor (Magnet Releasing) and a relatively limited initial theatrical release, the film has become a slow but sure word-of-mouth success, and for good reason. Its longevity as the twenty-first century's answer to a style made famous by EC Comics and *The Twilight Zone* is practically guaranteed.

In a wraparound story used to clothesline the rest of the free-standing narratives (each one positioned as found footage on grainy VHS tapes), three adult hooligans involved in recording and then selling their very own random physical and sexual assaults break into a house with the intent to steal a particular videocassette that could earn them a lot of dough. As an older man sits dead in front of the television, they search the house while continually getting drawn to the freaky real-life occurrences documented on the tapes playing on the VCR. The first, "Amateur Night," finds a group of frat guys (led by Mike

Donlan) getting far more than they bargained for when they bring back to their hotel room one particularly off-kilter gal named Lily (Hannah Fierman). Directed by David Bruckner, the chaotic, immature shenanigans of the young men, caught by a secret camera on Donlan's glasses, lead to a payoff that is nightmarish and literally edge-of-your-seat suspenseful, sweetened all the more by a twist to the ending as awe-inspiring as it is creepy.

The second—and best—story of the bunch is "Second Honeymoon," auteur Ti West's deliciously enthralling slow-burn sensibilities impeccably matching this writer's own. A couple, Sam (Joe Swanberg) and Stephanie (Sophia Takal), are taking a road trip across Arizona on old, reliable Route 66, amusing themselves along the way by stopping at tourist trap Wild West Junction and, later, taking in the sights of the Grand Canyon. When a mysterious woman knocks on their motel door one night asking for a ride, Sam politely declines. The whole situation is a strange one, but danger lurks closer than they expect when someone begins breaking into their room during the night, videotaping them sleeping while lightly running a switchblade across their bodies. "Second Honeymoon," which takes on a freaky, entirely unexpected second meaning by the end, is roughly twenty minutes long and mesmerizing for every second of those, unsettling tensions percolating toward a ghastly conclusion. Swanberg and Takal are excellent as the young vacationers, unaware of how abruptly their lives are about to take an unthinkable turn.

Next up on the docket is "Tuesday the 17th," wherein a group of nubile college kids head to the lake for the weekend. Wendy (Norma C. Quinones), however, has an ulterior motive: she plans to use her classmates as bait in an attempt to stop a seemingly unstoppable killer still roaming the woods. Director Glenn McQuaid merges the slasher and supernatural subgenres, delivering expertly upon imaginative kill sequences even as this story does not necessarily add up to much. A good deal more tense and jittery is the fourth yarn, mumblecore director Joe Swanberg's "The Sick Thing That Happened to Emily When She Was Younger." Emily (Helen Rogers) and James (Daniel Kaufman) have begun a cursory Internet relationship on Skype, Emily confiding in James every night as she becomes convinced that her apartment is haunted. Swanberg relies on a foreboding mood and the effectiveness of his jump scares throughout, keeping the viewer consistently on pins and needles. Only the story's final revelation is a letdown. This is one case where the unknown is far scarier than any kind of answer the makers provide.

The final tale is "10/31/98," directed by Radio Silence (a pseudonym for filmmaking quartet Matt Bettinelli-Olpin, Tyler Gillett, Justin Martinez and Chad Villella), and, although it might be the weakest, in *V/H/S* terms that's still pretty good. A bunch of costumed guys head to a Halloween party, but once inside the deceptively desolate house, they discover it's haunted for real. Worse yet, a sacrificial ceremony is occurring in the attic. "10/31/98" has a methodical build and a few solid jolts, but feels a little sloppy and half-finished, as if it wasn't fully developed before it went before the cameras. The same might be said for the wraparound segments, called "Tape 56" and directed by Adam Wingard, threaded in between the five central shorts. There is a downright masterful setup with the introduction of the deceased man in the chair, placed just right in the background as the thieves sit down to watch the tapes, but Wingard botches the landing and doesn't appear to know where to take the premise.

As is apt to be the case with anthologies, not every part of *V/H/S* is equally successful. Taken as a whole, however, it is a grab-bag of clever, diverse frights, each one leading to an untimely death as captured by roving, "you-are-there" POV cameras. Performances are as naturalistic as need be across the board, while make-up and effects work is used to give gristle and crimson to the pseudo-documentary imagery. It's uneven but perfectly fun, an ideal movie to sit and watch in a dark room on a Friday night. With anthology films providing infinite possibilities, this is one case where a sequel—released exactly one year later—was more than welcomed.

V/H/S/2

2013 - Directed by Simon Barrett, Adam Wingard, Gregg Hale, Eduardo Sánchez, Gareth Huw Evans, Timo Tjahjanto, Jason Eisener

When *V/H/S* was released in select theaters and on Video On Demand in September 2012, there was reason to celebrate: not only had a new independent horror franchise been born, but so had an all-but-forgotten genre staple: the anthology. A compilation of short films shot in POV style, each one by an up-and-coming filmmaker, the initial round of tales were tonally all over the place, but such diversity was part of the fun. Though some were better than others (my favorite: Ti West's unnerving, unforgettable slow-burn "Second Honeymoon"), all were solid, recalling a bit of the anything-goes thrill that viewers must have felt when 1982's anthological granddaddy, *Creepshow,* first came out. With a movie like *V/H/S* relying on a grab-bag mentality, it was, indeed, true that a series could easily be made from it. When it came to storylines, the sky was the limit. The only seeming rule: make it scary.

For *V/H/S/2,* a fresh wave of directors get their shot at tweaking first-person narratives while taking ready and willing audiences on a tour of what's really, really scary. Though the wraparound segment, titled "Tape 49" and directed by Simon Barrett, is decidedly flimsy until the whopper of an ending, the meat of the film—the four central shorts—are altogether more inventive and less notably uneven that those in its predecessor. The initial premise of two private investigators (Lawrence Michael Levine, Kelsey Abbott) hired to get to the bottom of a young man's disappearance leads them to an eerily abandoned house filled with buzzing televisions and stacks of VHS tapes. As they put each videocassette in and watch it, they are drawn deeper into the mystery of what happened to the home's MIA resident. Until the payoff, these scenes are weak sauce and more than a little nonsensical—why would one of them call for help in an abandoned house?—but fortunately they don't last long. The rest of the shorts in between are of a very high order.

Kicking things off is "Phase I Clinical Trials," directed by Adam Wingard, wherein a single guy named Herman (Wingard again, doing double-duty on both sides of the camera) receives an artificial eye implant that also poses as a camera, recording his field of vision. All is well until he returns home and almost right away is terrorized by the dead people he sees lurking like specters around every corner. This short is positioned like a funhouse ride, an increasing sense of dread broken up by spooky things popping out. Conventional "boo!" moments in movies can grow old fast, but this one earns every startle and recoil—of which there are many.

The second story finds a way to reinvent the zombie subgenre just when it might be fair for a person to believe there were no unexplored avenues left to go down. "A Ride in the Park," from Eduardo Sánchez and Gregg Hale, sees a bicycler's (Jay Saunders) would-be peaceful ride through a wooded park go downhill fast when he is attacked by an infectious outbreak of the undead. With a camera attached to his helmet, his transformation from man to zombie after getting bitten is both creepy and twistedly funny, leading to a cannibalistic appetite and the crashing of a little girl's birthday party. Sánchez and Hale approach their first-person style with real creativity and resourcefulness; is it any wonder they were responsible, as respective director and producer, for the one that practically started it all, 1999's *The Blair Witch Project*?

If the aforementioned pair of shorts are scary but lighthearted, "Safe Haven," directed by Gareth Huw Evans and Timo Tjahjanto, aims to downright disturb while traveling down an unremittingly bleak tunnel into hopelessness. When a group of documentary filmmakers (among them, Fachry Albar and Hannah Al-Rashid) are invited back to a religious cult leader's (Epy Kusnandar) Borneo compound for an exclusive interview, things take a turn for the worse when the followers go all Jonestown on them. Where things lead from there is best left to be discovered, but it's certainly an experience where no holds are barred and images of an unthinkably graphic, phantasmagoric nature ensure this won't be passing the MPAA's sights with an R rating.

The best is arguably saved for last. Helmed by Jason Eisener, "Alien Abduction Slumber Party" mixes the seat-jumping frights of the former two shorts with the more harrowing tone of the latter as a group of kids left home alone by their parents are terrorized by an alien invasion. Shot mostly from the point of view of the family dog, decked out with a small cam attached to its head, this story never stops moving as it assuredly plants the viewer permanently on the edge of his or her seat. Dexterously menacing creature designs, impeccably innovative cinematography and docu-real performances from a cast of natural young actors are all present and accounted for in this new festively breathless sci-fi/horror mini-classic.

If *V/H/S* got things off to a strong start, *V/H/S/2* steadies its footing while one-upping the original. The interlaced "Tape 49" leaves something to be desired, so thank goodness it takes up no more than about ten minutes of screen time interspersed in tinier chunks throughout. Where *V/H/S/2* works its grisly magic is where it truly counts, the quartet of micro-movies consistently surprising with stylistic ingenuity and storytelling elegance. Never afraid to journey into the blackest of hearts, the filmmakers involved in *V/H/S/2* have given the project their best shot, and it shows. The truth is out there, all right, and horror buffs officially have another good reason to stay at home, curled up in the dark in front of the television on a Friday night.

Warm Bodies

2013 - Directed by Jonathan Levine

Movies about the dead returning to life have been around almost as long as cinema itself, but it is writer-director George A. Romero who popularized an entire subgenre of zombie films with 1968's *Night of the Living Dead* and its subsequent companion pieces, 1978's *Dawn of the Dead* and 1985's *Day of the Dead*. Creepy and at times mordantly humorous, Romero sought to use the idea of the undead roaming the earth as a jumping-off point to bitingly explore modern society and the similarities between the living and the rotting resurrected. In many ways, they were us, and we were them. Following a bit of a lull, the last decade has seen something of a resurgence within popular culture, beginning with Zack Snyder's arguably superior 2004 remake of *Dawn of the Dead* and Edgar Wright's British spoof, *Shaun of the Dead*, continuing on with 2009's fabulously witty distant cousin, *Zombieland,* and the acclaimed AMC television series, *The Walking Dead*, and leading toward the mega-budgeted, Brad Pitt-starring adaptation of *World War Z*. Deserving to not get lost in the shuffle is the deliciously unique, constantly surprising *Warm Bodies*, certain to be unlike any other zombie picture the viewer has ever seen as it dares to explore the inner thoughts and state of mind of a young man who continues to walk around despite no longer having a beating heart. It's blackly comic, particularly in the protagonist's acerbic musings about the condition he and his fellow undead clan have found themselves in ("God, we move slow," he narrates), but also sobering in its view of decomposing creatures who can no longer remember who they were when they were alive, and finally swoon-worthy as our hero discovers it's not too late for him to feel and fall in love.

In a post-apocalyptic world where surviving human beings are protected by an enveloping city wall separating them from the roaming, cannibalistic zombies outside, R (Nicholas Hoult) is one of the grunting, mumbling undead, biding his time in an abandoned airport and internally asking himself the age-old question, "Is this all there is?" With the only thing to look forward to being his eventual transformation into one of the ravenous, skeletal "Boneys," R one day comes upon a small group of people in search of supplies and falls head over heels for

Julie (Teresa Palmer), whose boyfriend, Perry (Dave Franco), he's just munched on. With the only memories R knows being the ones he picks up on as he eats others' brains, R suddenly becomes protective of Julie and takes her to his airplane hangout on the runway. She's naturally horrified at first, then begins to wonder why this zombie is so concerned with saving her rather than eating her. As R struggles to communicate through the words he manages to utter and the music he listens to on his record player, the two become sort of oddball friends. The time ultimately comes when Julie must try to return home—her father, military man Grigio (John Malkovich), is the leader beyond the walls—and R is reluctantly prepared to help her. After all, what kind of future could a zombie possibly have with a living girl? Right?

Faithfully based on the novel by Isaac Marion, *Warm Bodies* confidently blends numerous tones that shouldn't work when put together—satire, horror, pathos, romanticism—but the film is elevated all the more by the peculiar combination. With this blissfully one-of-a-kind paragon, writer-director Jonathan Levine cements his place as one of the most underappreciated American filmmakers working today, not a weak link amongst this and his past efforts, 2008's *All the Boys Love Mandy Lane*, 2008's *The Wackness* and 2011's *50/50*. Even while succinctly commenting on the ways of technology and the modern world—hey, look, all those people who used to rush around the airport lost on their phones aren't much different than the zombies who now mindlessly stagger around the hangars—it is the unlikely relationship between R and Julie where *Warm Bodies* gets its fire. Seemingly more inspired by John Hughes than Romero, the film sees them bond as they spend time together holed up in the airplane, listen and dance to music—there is a lovely montage set to Bruce Springsteen's "Hungry Heart"—and take to the open airport runways as Julie instructs R how to drive. Complications ensue the closer they get to parting ways, but Julie's reaction to learning R killed Perry goes in a refreshing direction. Deep down inside, she admits, she always knew the truth.

One of the joys of the film is its lack of predictability, the narrative evolving in exciting new ways the further it presses on. Because of this, the third act of the film, especially, should not dare be revealed, though it can be mentioned that the twisting of genres continues to be juggled. Sly, good-natured humor referencing everything from *Pretty Woman* to Shakespeare's *Romeo and Juliet* gives way to tense, life-or-death chase sequences and an open-hearted sincerity. When the majority of movie releases are variations on the same old thing, *Warm Bodies* delights in toying with expectations, in reimagining and occasionally trampling over clichés, in serving viewers fresh images and thoughts to pore over, in giving the audience a reason to sit up, take notice, and truly care about the characters on the screen before them.

Nicholas Hoult has impressed in 2009's *A Single Man* and, as a child, in 2002's affectionate *About a Boy*, but it is here, as the increasingly conscionable R, where he graduates to leading-man status. His job couldn't have been easy, a high-wire act of portraying a corpsy, pasty-faced lug but also a viable romantic hero, the closer he gets to Julie the more he starts to genuinely feel again, and Hoult gets the balance just right. It's an exceedingly complex and sympathetic performance worth notice. Playing his object of affection, Teresa Palmer imbues Julie with strength, sweetness and forlorn tinges of loss, an attractive, free-thinking twenty-something woman who has had to give up far more than her controlling father realizes. In concept, there is something admittedly skin-crawling about a living person becoming involved with a living dead guy, but the low-key way it is handled and eventually develops adroitly solves this issue while never once stepping into frothy, frilly, offensively anti-feminist territory like the *Twilight* movies did time and again. Mentioning those Stephanie Meyer adaptations at all seems wrong; *Warm Bodies* is so much smarter, thematically deeper, and charismatic that they warrant nothing more than the most superficial of comparisons. In spry supporting turns, Rob Corddry is M, the closest thing R has to a best friend; Analeigh Tipton brightens up her scenes as Julie's self-deprecating pal and confidante, Nora; Dave Franco exits early as the ill-fated Perry, his role filling out as R gets a front-row seat to Perry's life with each handful of brain he eats, and John Malkovich gives unanticipated shades to Grigio, a protective father whose cynical world views need to change.

A touching story of rebirth, of dreams fulfilled, of lives saved by the powers of love and togetherness, *Warm Bodies* is a wake-up call against terminal apathy while offering hope for a better tomorrow. Jonathan Levine has declaratively carved out a place for himself as a writer-director with a clear voice, the compassion he lends to his characters an ideal foil for his provocative underlying messages, attuned observational comedy, and sublime music choices. A prime example of how an immaculate soundtrack can serve to promote a film to an even loftier level, Levine imagines John Waite's 1980s power ballad, "Missing You," as R's mournful anthem of the former life he's lost, while other cuts not previously mentioned ("Patience" by Guns N' Roses, "Shelter from the Storm" by Bob Dylan, "Shell Suite" by Chad Valley, and "Yamaha" by Delta Spirit, among them) are just as indelibly used. Together, gradually but surely, R and Julie (and, by extension, Nicholas Hoult and Teresa Palmer) form an offbeat connection that is transcendent, carrying the picture to a conclusion as organic as it is uncanny, as sweeping as it is emotionally potent. It's so thrilling when all the elements of a film come together just right. Chill-inducing cadavers be damned, *Warm Bodies* is sheer bliss.

We Need to Talk About Kevin

2011 - Directed by Lynne Ramsay

There have been innumerable films made turning children and teens into vessels to be feared rather than fawned over (2007's *Joshua* is one grim unsung treasure that comes immediately to mind), and ever since the tragic 1999 events at Columbine High School there have been almost as many exploring the cause-and-effect—or lack of solid answers—behind school violence (among them, 2003's unforgettable *Elephant* and 2008's *The Life Before Her Eyes*). More recently, 2011's stirring, overlooked *Beautiful Boy* starred Maria Bello and Michael Sheen as parents left lost and reeling after their son shoots up his college campus before turning the gun on himself. What could they have done? How did they not notice the warning signals? And, most of all, why? For *We Need to Talk About Kevin*, based upon the novel by Lionel Shriver, writer-director Lynne Ramsay takes a challenging, thematically provocative stance on an old topic by telling it solely from the point of view of a mother who wonders if she might have had something to do with the way her psychologically disturbed son turned out. For that matter, how much of what she sees is true, and how much is skewed by her own preconceived judgments and harshly critical biases? In a freakish nightmare there's no waking up from, her only choice is to live with the guilt, with the remorse, and with the nagging questions she'll never know the answers to.

Without wasting a second of screen time, Ramsay and co-writer Rory Stewart Kinnear have impeccably crafted a narrative that, in its immaculate construction, crisscrosses through time like a free-floating stream of consciousness. One minute we are at an overseas tomato festival, picking up with Eva Khatchadourian (Tilda Swinton) while she's still young and the possibilities of the world seem endless. Then we're planted in front of a construction site, the overwhelming sound of a worker drilling into the road just what Eva needs to drown out the incessant crying of her fussy infant son, Kevin. Eva also has a precocious, eyepatch-wearing daughter, Celia (Ashley Gerasimovich), and in the next scene the cold, calculating 15-year-old Kevin (Ezra Miller) is a 6-year-old boy (Jasper Newell) who tests his mom until she shoves him in frustration and hurts his arm. Even at such a young age, Kevin might as well be a professional liar, enabling

Eva not to protect her but to jab his claws in her all the more. Years later, Eva's sprawling suburban home and spacious backyard have been traded in for a ratty, compact box of a house in a depressed, lower-income neighborhood. Her family, including husband Franklin (John C. Reilly), don't appear to be around anymore, and the façade of her home has been marked with damning splashes of red paint, makeshift blood all the better to taint Eva with the plaguing wounds of her past.

It would be easy to label Kevin as evil, a young boy rotten to the core and dead inside. There is no denying that he's mentally unstable with sociopathic tendencies. But would he have turned out this way had Eva ever wholeheartedly accepted him? At birth, she looks at him as something that has encroached upon her life. He cries a lot, and so he isn't an easy baby. As a little boy, he refuses to potty-train and wears diapers long past when he should. Old enough to see the feelings of discomfort, even disdain, in his mother's eyes, Kevin matures, but never stops testing her. As a brother, he's passive-aggressive, and, as a son to his father, he likes to put on an act of normalcy. With Eva, though, it's different. She's not a terrible person—she tries to connect with him, taking him to play putt-putt and out to dinner, just the two of them—but it always ends in hurt feelings and, coming from the perceptive Kevin, painful unleashed truths. When, in one scene, Eva unleashes a harsh tirade on obese people, it has nothing to do with anything other than her prickly own interior. She's not always the warmest of people, either. It's hard to say if Eva loves Kevin the way a parent normally loves a child, but maybe so; how else to explain her prison visits to see him after he rips her, his, and an entire town's world apart?

We Need to Talk About Kevin provides a collection of nonlinear snapshots and trusts the viewer to put it all together alongside the heroine. The film is enlivened with spontaneity because of this unorthodox approach, and also a classical, hallucinatory horror vibe in the vein of 1968's *Rosemary's Baby*. The difference is that Kevin is not Satan's spawn, but a human boy with an ocean of troubles. For Eva, whatever ultimately comes to pass has left her alone, slightly disheveled and piercingly vulnerable. She gets a job at a travel agency called Travel R Us and overworks while trying to blend in with the wallpaper. On Halloween, cloaked revelers dressed as demons and ghosts stalk her movements (scored frighteningly to Buddy Holly's "Everyday"), though it's never cemented whether or not this is her psyche haunting her or really happening. At a company Christmas party, a would-be pleasant time turns rancid when a co-worker (Alex Manette) comes onto Eva as she sits off to the side of the room like a sheepish schoolgirl, then verbally assaults her when she politely turns down his invite to dance. The mere act of walking down the street is a tough one for Eva these days; in a town that knows all too well who she is, she's destined to run into someone with connections to her, and how that goes is up for grabs.

From trading genders in 1993's *Orlando* to learning fluent Italian for 2010's *I Am Love*, Tilda Swinton has always been, and continues to be, absolutely fearless. Having no qualms about baring body and soul if the role requires it, she tosses out any chances for artifice and becomes the characters she plays. As Eva,

Swinton is the focus of just about every scene and she's mesmerizing. Not the kind of actor who needs to be liked all the time, she instead portrays a person with so much gray area the other color has drained out of her being. Battered and clinging to a rock wall with no ledges, she is knocked down repeatedly in scenes of extraordinarily rhapsodic discomfort. Swinton plays the part as her own judge and jury, casting stones that finally begin to bounce back at her. In his calculated, detached, super-intelligent reading of the title figure, Ezra Miller emulates to eerie perfection that strange sensation of someone standing behind you, one step away from breathing down your neck. There doesn't seem to be any humanity in his actions or thoughts—his reaction to his mom walking in on him masturbating is skin-crawling—which makes the fact that he is human more disconcerting. Supporting performances are as naturalistic as photographer Seamus McGarvey's *cinéma vérité* lensing, with John C. Reilly approaching Franklin as a father and husband more apt to trust his kids than his wife—a grievous mistake—and young Ashley Gerasimovich casting a light of contrasting innocence on Celia that Kevin has never known.

We Need to Talk About Kevin is utterly chilling more for its restraint in what it suggests without necessarily showing. From a missing hamster, to the circumstances surrounding Celia's eyepatch, to an archery set Franklin gives his son, well-versed moviegoers will no doubt wait in expectation for thriller conventions to follow. Ramsay goes a different route while deepening the grave aura of unease, careful to also see the flip side. Out of tragedy, one's propensity for compassion sometimes flourishes; a scene where Eva holds the hand of a distraught mother whose child is also locked up is something she never would have done in the past. More than that, however, the film is profoundly devastating as the story of lives ruined over nothing. When, in one of the final scenes, Eva finally asks Kevin why he did what he did, his answer is more telling than it might at first seem: "I used to think I knew, but now I'm not so sure." What a waste. *We Need to Talk About Kevin* has a fitting title; once seen, it will be impossible for viewers to hold back on their conversations about it.

Wolf Creek

2005 - Directed by Greg Mclean

The writing-directing debut of Greg Mclean, *Wolf Creek* shares certain similarities with 2003's *High Tension*. For American audiences, both are low-budget foreign imports—*High Tension* was from France, *Wolf Creek* is Australian—picked up by major studios and given wide theatrical releases. For much of their running times, both pit two intelligent, traumatized young women against a human antagonist who dresses, looks and basically acts like everyone else. That he is also an insane psychopath who gets off on the gruesome slaughter of innocent strangers is a significant characteristic where each picture excels. *High Tension* ultimately revealed itself to have far more than this up its sleeve, presenting a devastating tale that was as much about unrequited "forbidden" love as it was a yarn strictly of blood and guts. If *Wolf Creek* lacks the sociological undercurrents of *High Tension* and, thus, isn't quite on the same level, it makes no matter. After suffering through Hollywood's early-2000s PG-13 kiddie-horror onslaught and often unnecessary and inferior fad toward remakes, the gritty, starkly uncompromising *Wolf Creek* comes as a breath of fresh air—or, a breath of freshly coughed-up blood.

The premise is simple, never bogging down in extraneous subplots and played-out climactic twists. Liz (Cassandra Magrath) and Kristy (Kestie Morassi) are British confidantes nearing the end of their two-week backpacking tour across Australia. One of their final destinations is Wolf Creek, a desolate site in the Outback where a meteorite once hit, creating a giant crater within the earth's land. Their means of transportation comes in the form of Ben (Nathan Phillips), an Aussie native with a car whom they've recently made friends with. Their trip to Wolf Creek runs smoothly enough until it is time to leave. Soon after discovering that their watches have all stopped at the same time, the car won't start. Much-needed help arrives from Mick (John Jarratt), a pleasant Outbacker who agrees to tow their car and fix it free of charge. This seeming good Samaritan, who Kristy compares at one point to *Crocodile Dundee*, eventually reveals himself to be far from helpful. His game of choice is not wildlife, it turns out, but stranded motorists, and Liz, Kristy and Ben are next on his list.

Greg Mclean spends nearly a full hour on setup, a risky proposition that might have grown tedious if it weren't for the unhurried care and mounting intrigue he brings to this elongated opening act. By concentrating on the charms and realism of his characters and their naturalistic, laid-back relationships with each other, the crucial turn toward mortal danger means a great deal more to the viewer. And, when one of them meets an abrupt, premature end, their loss is more emphatically felt afterwards. Liz and Kristy aren't blonde bimbos running around in skimpy lingerie, but look and act like actual, freethinking people. The same goes for Ben, who isn't a priggish alpha male, but more low-key and sweet-natured. When an early stop at a roadside cafe leads to disrespectful, chauvinistic remarks from the burly locals, Ben decides to avoid getting into a big fight with them because he weighs his options before acting and knows it isn't worth it.

Once *Wolf Creek* makes a sudden turn toward sheer panic and terror, Mclean aims squarely for the jugular—or, as the case may be, lower spine. Far from a glossy motion picture starring the hottest young flavor-of-the-week television stars, Mclean has cast virtual unknowns Cassandra Magrath, Kestie Morassi and Nathan Phillips, each of them unaffected, likable performers whose very authenticity only adds urgency and puts more at stake when they wake up to a living nightmare. As deliberately paced as the first hour is—essential to making the visceral impact Mclean strives for in the second half—the last forty minutes are tightly edited, breathlessly intense, and graphically violent in rattlingly unexpected ways. In a change of events for the genre, the three protagonists do the smart thing at all times, their minds always working in logical ways that fit their horrific situation as opposed to, for example, lingering too long as the supposedly dead killer lies on the floor. In turn, their deaths do not arise out of their own stupidity, but because their dire circumstances prove impossible to overcome.

In one of the most frightening depictions of human evil in recent memory, John Jarratt is downright brilliant, his endearing personality acting as an unforgettable counterpoint to his grisly, monstrous actions. His first few scenes achieve a heightened level of creepiness and surprise from his mastery of body language, speech, and what he doesn't say, but infers. Usually movie villains are at their most effective when they are silent, but not this time; Jarratt turns his role as serial killer into an art that rivals Anthony Hopkins' portrayal of Hannibal Lecter.

"Inspired by a true story"—that of convicted New South Wales serial killer Ivan Milat—but strong enough to not need this declaration, *Wolf Creek* begins with a statistic that "30,000 people go missing in the Australian Outback each year. 90% are found within a month. Some are never seen again." With that in the back of the audience's mind, the film makes for a scarily plausible example of how people around the world can so easily be abducted and killed, their whereabouts forever left as a mystery. The novel and very specific setting of the Outback—scenically beautiful but endlessly sparse and vast—only ups the believability of these characters' plight; with nothing and nobody around for miles, how can they hope to escape a killer's wrath? *Wolf Creek* is a supremely well-made and unrelenting thriller, putting to shame a whole lot of comparable works that cost three, four or five times as much to make, but don't even have half the filmmaking prowess and brutal inspiration behind them. With *Wolf Creek*, a brazen new talent in writer-director Greg Mclean was born.

The Woman

2011 - Directed by Lucky McKee

In *The Woman*, the suburban ennui of 1999's *American Beauty* collides head-on with the graphically violent nature of 2003's *High Tension*, and the results are nothing short of excitingly unique, deeply disturbing and seductively macabre. For writer-director Lucky McKee, this was his comeback picture after years of not being able to match up to his striking solo debut feature, 2003's breathtaking dark parable, *May*. There was an oft-delayed, tossed-aside studio film in the interim (2006's misguided *The Woods*), a quirky episode of *Masters of Horror* entitled "Sick Girl," and an effective if little-seen Jack Ketchum adaptation, 2008's *Red*. As it turns out, McKee's second collaboration with author Ketchum (who co-writes the screenplay and the novel from which this picture is based upon) is the lucky charm, the two of them conspiring on a tone and premise and mash-up of genres that have never quite been tackled and achieved with this much ingenuity and tragic reverence. Is it horror? Is it drama? Is it black comedy? *The Woman* is all of the above and none of them at all, defying pat descriptions and easy conclusions. Whatever it is, it won't be easily forgotten.

From the outside, the Cleek family appears perfectly ordinary, living peacefully on a nice piece of land and happily attending neighborhood barbecues. Father Chris (Sean Bridgers) is a respected small-town lawyer. Wife Belle (Angela Bettis) is a homemaker still caring for 3-year-old daughter Darlin' (Shyla Molhusen) during the day. They have two other teenage children, obedient if brooding high schooler Peggy (Lauren Ashley Carter) and chip-off-the-old-block middle schooler Brian (Zach Rand). The more one peers past this façade, however, the more things start to look unsettled and just plain off about them. Audience suspicions raise all the more when Chris heads off on a hunting trip and returns with a feral adult woman (Pollyanna McIntosh) he's found living in the forest. He ties her up in the storm cellar—and it's a good thing, too, since she's wild enough to bite off and eat half of his finger when it gets too close to her mouth—and wastes no time in showing her off to the rest of the family. Chris' goal is to teach her how to be "civilized," an example of hypocrisy if there ever was one as his despicable actions reveal how little he himself understands about the word.

It is a constant guessing game where *The Woman* is headed, and is all the better for it. Too often in today's landscape of formulaic filmmaking, the viewer can predict almost from the start where each movie will end up. Such is the sad but true case of paint-by-numbers Hollywood greenlighting. McKee and Ketchum, mavericks not afraid of jumping ship from the straight and narrow, make certain that this doesn't happen. Carefully, methodically, they uncover layers heretofore unseen, the Cleeks beginning as blank canvases of normalcy until a grimmer picture begins to show up with each new stroke. When Belle non-confrontationally questions her husband about keeping some strange woman in the cellar, he hits her before she's finished the sentence. Chris insists on harshly power-washing the dirt and grime off the woman when scrubbing her won't do. At night when he thinks everyone is asleep, he tiptoes down to his underground lair to be with her. At school, Brian puts gum in his classmate's hairbrush so that he can attempt to come to her rescue, and at home he drills a hole in the cellar door so he can spy on the tied-up woman's naked body. Meanwhile, Peggy becomes increasingly withdrawn at school, torn apart by a home life she doesn't feel she can do anything about. When her young math teacher, Ms. Raton (Carlee Baker), spots all the tell-tale signs that Peg might be pregnant, her decision whether or not to take this information to the parents could likely decide the fate of the rest of her life.

As a portrait of a criminally dysfunctional family—just what is Chris doing with those chained-up dogs in the shed?—the film wavers between amusingly offbeat and emotionally shattering. When humor leaks into scenes—after knocking Belle out and sitting her up at the kitchen table, Chris makes the excuse to a visitor that she's simply "power-napping"—it is natural and unforced, never overwhelming or making jest of what is, at heart, a horrific fairy tale that happens to be set in modern-day suburbia. Throughout, McKee twists conventional movie wisdom that would point to the woman as the villain by having the viewer waver sympathies to her side as Chris and Brian display sociopathic tendencies and Belle and Peggy choose not to do anything about what they know is wrong. Darlin', the youngest and purest of the clan, carries with her an innocent spirit still, sitting by the cellar door and playing music on her tape recorder to keep the captured woman company. In a family where the rest of the members have either been negatively influenced by the father's awful ways or beaten into submission, only Darlin' still has a chance at a life unaffected by the horrors she has seen.

Pollyanna McIntosh is chillingly credible as the title character, first seen in 2010's loosely connected companion piece, *The Offspring*. Uttering few comprehensible words, McIntosh gets to the soul of this mystery woman, sparking a guttural cry for all the confusion, pain and vengeance-yearning anger the Cleeks are putting her through. It seems understandable to fear her since she represents a certain unknown, but vying for our attentions is also the desire to see her tear apart a rotten family just as we know she is capable of doing. As Chris, Sean Bridgers is disquieting in his own right by so convincingly essaying the kind of evil soul that exists in one's everyday surroundings. With a bright career and a tidy home, Chris believes he's untouchable. Belle knows different, letting out her grievances by the third act in a scene that turns from triumphant to doomed within seconds. Angela Bettis' anguished performance in the role is brave and unshakable, Belle's desire to see things change ultimately coming too little, too late to alter her and her family members' fatalistic destinations.

The Woman leads to a knife-cuttingly tense climax, one that alternates from justified to unfair and back again, the viewer recoiling in apprehension and then rooting for certain characters to get what's coming to them. Taking yet another turn, the final moments transcend the havoc on display for a closing image as provocatively loaded with suggestion as it is eerily resplendent. Heavily scored with a soundtrack of original songs by Sean Spillane—a folksy-pop crisscrosser—the picture's catchy, melodic sounds always seem to fit emotionally even as they often stand in contrast to what is occurring on the screen. Finally, the post-credits coda is an ideally wondrous capper, a blending of live-action and animated effects that gets to the poetic center of its foreboding and whimsy. In *The Woman*, the American Dream goes terribly wrong, ripped wide open by a sharp pair of pliers, a husband and son's sickly raging libidos, a wild woman out to make them pay, and a secret in the doghouse probably not named Rover. Why can't more films be as proudly one-of-a-kind as this one? Lucky McKee makes it look so easy.

The Woman in Black

2012 - Directed by James Watkins

Daniel Radcliffe ably sheds his Harry Potter persona very nearly instantaneously in *The Woman in Black*, a shiveringly handsome adaptation of the 1983 novella by Susan Hill. Pitting one unwelcome visitor against a ghostly mansion of horrors is a formula older than movies themselves, but director James Watkins (he of 2008's chilling *Eden Lake*) exhibits such an artful know-how for scaring the pants off his audience that it doesn't matter. With just a couple of exceptions where he tips his hand a little too obviously toward spelled-out manipulation, Watkins keeps things absorbingly creepy in a subdued fashion until just the right moments when he's ready to pounce. When he does, watch out. It isn't every day that a film causes the hair on one's legs to stand up on end. *The Woman in Black* achieves this more than once.

1920s London. With mounting unpaid bills and a job dangling in the balance, young widowed lawyer Arthur Kipps (Daniel Radcliffe) bids farewell to 4-year-old son Joseph (Misha Handley) and the boy's nanny (Jessica Raine) and travels to the lonesome village of Crythin Gifford in Northeast England. Mrs. Drablow (Alisa Khazanova), the last surviving resident of the desolate Eel Marsh House, has recently passed, and it is up to Arthur to go through all of her papers and locate the most current version of her will. The job will take a week, but the property, separated from civilization by a forever rising and falling marshland, isn't exactly the kind of place one dreams of holidaying. A spectral woman cloaked in noir prowls the property, vengeance for the young son who was taken away from her and allowed to drown decades before the only thing on her mind.

Arthur, whose beloved wife died during childbirth, is an upstanding if sad-faced man whose livelihood depends on him getting his job done at the foreboding Eel Marsh. Though he begins seeing things he cannot explain almost immediately, it is his sticky financial circumstances that explain away why he doesn't just pick up and go at the first sight of the title character, seen standing motionless out by the fog-shrouded garden. Treated by all of the townspeople as a leper until a kind wealthy couple, Mr. and Mrs. Daily (Ciarán Hinds and Janet McTeer), invite him in, Arthur appreciates the gesture even as he is unable to miss the unbearable grief they're still going through over the death of their only son. Midway through his trip, Arthur finally makes the decision to stay put and work through the night. As spooky as the surroundings are during the day, he has no idea what's about to go bump after dark.

A mood piece with style and heart (perhaps too much heart), *The Woman in Black* is elegantly written by Jane Goldman and the cinematography by Tim Maurice-Jones richly atmospheric. Produced by the updated Hammer Films production company and shot primarily at the classic Pinewood Studios, the film looks and feels like every inch the part of a 1960s or '70s supernatural thriller. It might be a tad scarier than most of those, though, with Watkins taking expert advantage of putting his audience through the urgent paces of what reminds of a ghostly funhouse carnival ride. Enigmatic sound effects spaced through eerie silences lead to sock-'em jolts and a devilish use of props, from a creaky rocking chair to a nursery filled with old wind-up toys that could give anyone a case of the willies. It's all very well set-up as the woman of the title lurks around shadowy corners and in obscured doorways, biding her time and building up anger over how she was wronged in life.

Having graduated from Hogwarts once and for all, Daniel Radcliffe—twenty-two years old at the time of filming—has taken the sorts of professional chances that help to move a child actor into adulthood and other roles and opportunities. Also an acclaimed Broadway performer, Radcliffe takes on his first grown-up film turn without any threatened signs of awkwardness. The actor, particularly intense with a bristly face and dark brows, commands the frame while remaining wholly sympathetic (and this is especially fortunate since he is often playing scenes by himself). Ciarán Hinds lends strong support as Mr. Daily, a friendly companion whose goodness, for once, isn't a ruse for more malevolent intentions. As for the woman in black herself, Liz White essays one of the more memorably freaky screen villainesses since Samara in 2002's admittedly very similar *The Ring*.

The Woman in Black is set up as a mystery on top of being a horror tale, but, even for people not familiar with the literary source, its supposed twists will come off as foregone conclusions. That hardly matters in the long run since the film is more an emotional experience than an intellectual or plot-based one, but it's worth mentioning. To that end, there is at least one minor leap in logic that must be gotten over (involving the corpse of the woman in black's drowned son), and the last scene is too treacly for its own good, like something out of 1993's Halloween-set Disney feature, *Hocus Pocus*. Nevertheless, if the core function of a horror picture is to frighten and leave on edge, *The Woman in Black* hits the bull's-eye for the duration of its running time. Uncommonly smart not only in what it does, but how it does it, this bleak cinematic fable cuts to the cathartic quick.

Would You Rather

2013 - Directed by David Guy Levy

1985's *Clue* is stripped of its giddy absurdist humor and replaced by a deadly, unsparing seriousness in *Would You Rather*, a gripping horror-drama that's far more ruminative than *Saw*, but destined to draw a comparison because of its onscreen game of wits and violence. Working from Steffen Schlachtenhaufen's slyly devious screenplay, director David Guy Levy exhibits a smart balance between restraint and forthrightness, showing enough to cause viewers to repeatedly flinch, but never crossing the line into gross-out schlock. Above all, a supreme lack of comfort is the name of the game, the atrocities being forced upon its players cruelly fetishistic and then outright unthinkable. "What did I ever do to you?" one distraught character asks the corrupt head of ceremonies Shepard Lambrick (Jeffrey Combs) late in the picture. The answer, left unspoken, is nothing at all, and that's precisely why *Would You Rather* grows so rapidly disturbing.

Ever since their parents passed away, the responsible Iris (Brittany Snow) has struggled to take care of her cancer-afflicted teenage brother, Raleigh (Logan Miller). Financially stretched thin and in desperate need of help, Iris is approached by Shepard Lambrick, a wealthy medical entrepreneur who invites her to his mansion to participate in a game. The winner will be taken care of and Raleigh will be moved to the front of the bone marrow transplant list. Though suspicious, Iris accepts, joining a group of fellow contestants that include a recovering alcoholic (John Heard), a gambling addict (Robb Wells), a paralyzed elderly lady (June Squibb), an Iraqi war vet (Charlie Hofheimer) and a cutthroat single mother (Sasha Grey). Once the festivities begin, there is no escaping, as a game of "Would You Rather" transforms into a fight to be the sole survivor.

Would You Rather is an instant contender for feel-bad movie of the year—of any year—but please do not read this as a criticism. The film's unforgiving plot requires that it be dark and downbeat, and director Levy refuses to pull back from this bleak tone as Iris and at least some of the other players cling to their morality for as long as they can before there is no choice left but to knowingly kill the fellow players. With flight not a possibility—when one person tries to get up to leave, they are promptly shot in the head—they must fight to live. In Iris' case, she also has a brother whose life hangs in the balance. Relatively harmless but telling challenges—Iris gives up her almost lifelong vegetarianism when she is offered $10,000 to eat a steak and foie gras—segue to choices between stabbing someone's thigh and beating another three times with a whipping stick, between attempting to survive two minutes underwater and a mystery challenge randomly handed out in envelopes. It's a beyond-frightening situation, but the game isn't just used as shock value and instead takes the time to explore the awful things people are capable of when they seemingly have no other choice.

When *Would You Rather* stays put around its fateful dining room table of terror (which is most of the time), it is nothing short of riveting. When it moves away for a subplot where Iris' guilty doctor (Lawrence Gilliard Jr.)—a former survivor of Lambrick's competition—tries to put a stop to the current game, it feels contrived, then pointless, as it goes nowhere. At least these brief scenes are over quickly, paving the way for the immediate dastardly quandary at hand. A committed, emotionally available Brittany Snow, as Iris, and an unforgettably calm and disquieting Jeffrey Combs, as Lambrick, lead an exceptional ensemble cast who linger like spirits in one's memory even after their lifeless bodies are dragged from the room. No matter who wins the game, the cost of surviving in *Would You Rather* is destined to permeate and pollute their consciousness for as long as they live. In many ways, the victor is destined to suffer the most—a notion hauntingly made all the more certain by an ending that slaps you in the face, and makes sure you feel it.

Wrong Turn

2003 - Directed by Rob Schmidt

Taking its cue from such down-and-dirty '70s horror films as 1974's *The Texas Chain Saw Massacre* and 1977's *The Hills Have Eyes*, *Wrong Turn* is a grisly, effective little number that wisely does not bog itself down with needlessly overplotted exposition and last-minute story twists. If it does not as closely capture the look and feel of those aforementioned cult classics the way 2003's *House of 1000 Corpses* did, it is still a tense and frightful good time. Tautly directed by Rob Schmidt and written with clear knowledge of the backwoods slasher genre by Alan McElroy, *Wrong Turn* is simple, straightforward and destined to hit horror fans where it hurts. All others need not apply.

On his way to Raleigh, N.C., for a job interview, Chris Flynn (Desmond Harrington) gets stuck in backed-up highway traffic and opts to bypass it by taking the back roads of West Virginia. Before he can make it back to the main thoroughfare, he accidentally hits a van carrying a group of would-be campers—engaged lovebirds Carly (Emmanuelle Chriqui) and Scott (Jeremy Sisto), couple Francine (Lindy Booth) and Evan (Kevin Zegers), and Jessie (Eliza Dushku), who is just getting over a relationship. With their van's tires flattened after having run over barbed wire and Chris' car totaled, Chris, Jessie, Carly and Scott go to find a phone. Unfortunately, the first house they come upon—a ramshackle cabin in the middle of the wilderness—belongs to three grotesquely deformed inbred cannibals. Don't you hate when that happens?

Once the twenty-something friends come face to face with their worst nightmare at the 30-minute mark, *Wrong Turn* transcends its shaky first act by turning into a fast and scary nonstop chase picture. As the six characters run for their lives and are whittled down one by one by the deranged backwoods clan, Schmidt does an admirable job in escalating the suspense to an occasionally almost unbearable altitude. A setpiece involving a looming watchtower and a daring escape across tree branches at least one hundred feet in the air is easily the film's high point, ingeniously constructed and edited. The sudden slaughter of one of the main characters in this sequence is imaginative, gruesome and even a little moving—rare for a horror movie that keeps its character development at a decided minimum.

Schmidt also knows just how to handle his three villains, keeping them in the shadows enough so that when they are finally seen more clearly, their visceral effect on the viewer is heavily palpable. Kudos to producer Stan Winston's perfectly chilling makeup effects, gruesome and frightening without being too exaggerated. Other technical credits are top-notch, with the detailed production design by Alicia Keywan; gritty and atmospheric cinematography of the Ontario wilderness (posing as West Virginia) by John S. Bartley, and memorable music score by Elia Cmiral standing out.

The cast, headed by Eliza Dushku, Desmond Harrington, Emmanuelle Chriqui and Jeremy Sisto do their jobs professionally and with little fault outside of their lack of depth. To be fair, if one was being chased by three hillbilly cannibals, there probably wouldn't be too many chances for intimate scenes of character-building. Watching the extreme physical demands the actors have to go through is almost wrenching; the shoot was clearly not an easy one, and it shows.

Beginning around the time Rob Zombie's *House of 1000 Corpses* was made, there was a refreshing, resurgent turn in the horror genre away from the self-referential likes of *Scream*-style efforts and back to the sort of grimy, realistic, no-holds-barred cult B-movies of the '70s and early '80s. Save for one reference to 1972's *Deliverance*, *Wrong Turn* takes itself and the horrific situation it puts its characters in seriously. Even when the film occasionally does not pay off as well as it should (as in the slightly disappointing and too-short climax), one has to still admire the makers for what they set out to do. And more often than not, Schmidt does it very well. Perhaps the most resounding endorsement of *Wrong Turn* is the convincing case it makes for avoiding road trips through the West Virginia wilderness. Suffice it to say, camping and nature hikes are clearly out of the question.

Xtro

1983 - Directed by Harry Bromley Davenport

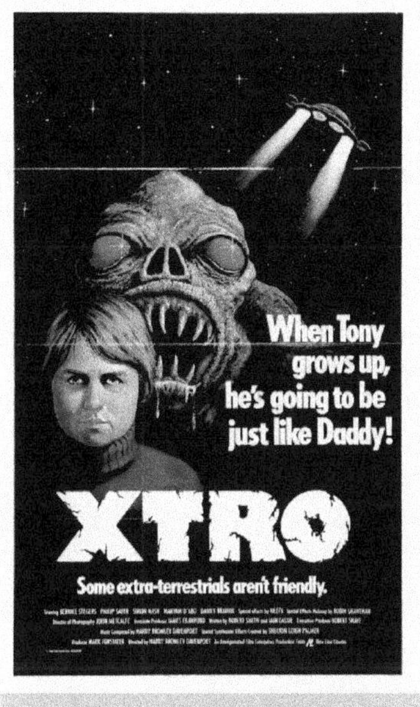

Xtro is an innovative, nihilistic bit of sci-fi/horror nastiness that freaked me out as a child. One could argue I was perhaps too young to be watching it at the time, but watch it I did, and the image of a young boy and a midget clown incubating the body of a young woman with black sacs of alien fetuses stayed with me. Seeing the film again as an adult, it is easy to understand why it would make such an impression on a kid too young to understand what was going on. Then again, *Xtro* still doesn't make a heck of a lot of sense, but that's part of its charm. It's perverse, it's sickening, and it's so far outside the stratosphere of conventional moviemaking that one cannot help but admire its chance-taking.

Three years after young Tony Phillips (Simon Nash) was the only witness to his father, Sam's (Philip Sayer), alien abduction, he has still not been able to free himself of nightmares about that fateful day. No one has believed Tony's claims and, in the interim, caring mother Rachel (Bernice Stegers) has moved on and moved in with photographer Joe (Danny Brainin). When Sam suddenly returns, claiming that he doesn't remember anything since the day he went missing, Rachel finds herself torn between her son's father and the new man in her life. More diabolical things are afoot, however, as Sam sets out to infect Tony with his alien seed and begin harvesting alien life forms.

Audaciously directed by Harry Bromley Davenport, *Xtro* is even wonkier than it sounds. The complete antithesis of *E.T. The Extra-Terrestrial*, which had been released about eight months prior, the film is crude, slimy and surrealistic, boasting ingeniously sinister effects work that outshines its low budget. Answers to the hows and whys of the plot are sketchy, at best, the movie working as a disturbing, phantasmagoric mood piece rather than as a concrete narrative.

Would you believe it that *Xtro* features a spider-crawling alien creature crashing to Earth and transferring itself into the body of a woman at a cottage, who, in turn, gives birth to a grown man? Or how about a father, now an extraterrestrial, sucking his son's bare shoulder and transplanting him with the same alien gene? There are also toys that turn into life-size beings, from a sidekick clown who does the young boy's murderous bidding, to a plastic soldier who does away with the crabby old lady living downstairs. A snake in a salad, goopy face-peeling and an ill-fated nanny, Analise (Maryam d'Abo), whose fertility is abused in unthinkable ways only skim the surface of the places *Xtro* goes to shock and gross out audiences. It's downright Lynchian before David Lynch was even on the map.

If *Xtro* defies the standards of straight forward storytelling, it does not lose sight of Rachel's humanity. She is the closest thing the film has to a protagonist, and the turmoil she faces as she stands to lose everyone she's ever loved is displayed with bereaved emotion by British actress Bernice Stegers. She's quite good in the part, and the one element that lifts the film from being the empty stylistic exercise it might have otherwise become. *Xtro* may be morbid, unsettling and even upsetting—it pushes upon boundaries and then crosses them—but it's a bona fide original in the genre. No one could ever accuse it of just being more of the same.

You're Next

2013 - Directed by Adam Wingard

An understandable sensation in the Midnight Madness section of the 2011 Toronto International Film Festival, dynamite horror indie *You're Next* was promptly bought by Lionsgate before sitting on the shelf for nearly two years. The wait might have been long, but for a movie that allegedly cost under a million dollars to make and garnered a wide theatrical rollout on 2,400 screens, it can only be considered a huge success no matter how much it grossed (for the record, just under $20-million). Inspiringly directed by Adam Wingard and cunningly penned by Simon Barrett (collaborators on the spooky jack-in-the-box "Phase I Clinical Trials" segment of 2013's *V/H/S/2*), *You're Next* is an exciting piece of work, a film that revitalizes the home-invasion thriller in unexpectedly vibrant ways while giving masterfully sly nods to vintage '70s and '80s Carpenter-esque synth scores and quintessential classics such as 1974's *The Texas Chain Saw Massacre*, 1978's *Halloween* and 1984's *A Nightmare on Elm Street*. Not content to simply ape other films, Wingard and Barrett cook up a unique identity in their stylish approach to the material and their treatment of characters who would be interesting enough for the viewer to want to watch even if they were transplanted into, say, a straight family drama. If that weren't enough, Sharni Vinson instantly belongs in the same company as Jamie Lee Curtis, Heather Langenkamp and Neve Campbell, a willful, determined, dynamic horror heroine for the ages.

Paul (Rob Moran) and Aubrey Davison (Barbara Crampton) have invited their four grown children—Crispian (AJ Bowen), Drake (Joe Swanberg), Aimee (Amy Seimetz) and Felix (Nicholas Tucci)—to celebrate their thirty-fifth wedding anniversary. With their significant others in tow, they convene at their family's secluded mansion in the country. It doesn't take long for sibling bickering to commence at dinner, but their petty arguments are rudely interrupted when an arrow pierces the head of one of the guests. Accosted by three masked figures—a lamb, a tiger and a fox—the family becomes trapped prey, the body count skyrocketing among them as they're systematically sliced and diced. Things look bleak for sure, but Crispian's graduate student girlfriend, Erin (Sharni

Vinson), has a little secret about her past that might make her these killer's most formidable match.

Oftentimes, slasher pictures of this nature hit close to home—everyone can relate to fears of strangers invading one's private space and lives—while becoming subjective studies in doom and gloom. *You're Next* is seriously intense at times and the premise is a naturally dark one, made all the more persuasive by the unusually realistic ways the different family members react when faced with such wrenching circumstances, but the experience of watching it is far from glum. Poppy and assured, the film introduces its characters with economical snapshots of lives in progress—a loaded dysfunctional history between the family members brings added weight to the goings-on—before preparing to attack. Once the killers appear, there is scarcely any letting up. And, when the tables turn midway through and Erin comes clean about why she's so knowledgeable about extreme situations such as this, the movie transforms again into a brutal, thrilling crowd-pleaser.

Contrary to popular opinion, it's fun seeing people in horror flicks who are savvy and smart, making more right decisions than wrong when their lives are in danger. At the same time, there is a certain human fallibility that comes into play. Thus, while Erin tries to assess the situation rationally, Drake's wife, Kelly (Sarah Myers), is hasty in her decision to get out of the house and seek help from the closest neighbors. Drake and Crispian, who are always at each other's throat, make a go at putting their disagreements aside. Meanwhile, mother Aubrey closes down in shock and grief when one of her kids is killed, while Aimee—always trying to compensate and please her parents and siblings—makes a brave but stupid decision that could cost her dearly. As for patriarch Paul, he wants revenge, his ideas about safety shaken to their core when he makes a discovery that the intruders have been hiding in their abode for days, patiently lying in wait. It's a fascinating dichotomy between loved ones and acquaintances that gives a welcome extra layer to what, in lesser, more frequent instances, is apt to devolve into a thematically empty chopping-block procession.

Sharni Vinson gives what should be a breakthrough performance as Erin. A lot is asked of her in this role, which requires emotional vulnerability as well as physical and intellectual aptness, and she more or less carries the film through the rousing second half. There isn't a moment where the viewer isn't on her side, one's sympathy at attention. It warrants mentioning that Erin may be learned in the ways of survival, but she is far from invincible. Her struggle, as it were, is ours. The unconventional rest of the cast will probably not be familiar to casual filmgoers, but anyone who knows their current indie directors, character actors and horror veterans are certain to be delighted by this line-up. AJ Bowen is becoming a current-day horror staple, and his part as eldest brother Crispian is the juiciest of his career, to date. Joe Swanberg is perfectly smarmy as Crispian's judgmental brother, Drake. Usually seen playing downbeat, downtrodden types, Amy Seimetz impressively changes things up as Aimee, her bouncy exterior a defense mechanism to shield her insecurities having grown up in a family of boys and never measuring up. Rob Moran plays it low-key but all the more memorable for it as father Rob, just trying to hold on and protect his wife and kids as well as he can. And, as mother Aubrey, it is a treat to see Barbara Crampton (best-known for her work with Stuart Gordon in 1984's *Re-Animator* and 1986's *From Beyond*) onscreen again, her shattering portrayal of motherly anguish at the sight of what she cares for the most falling apart a lingering force even after she's exited the scene.

You're Next opens with a post-coital prologue that finds a dumpy middle-aged guy (Larry Fessenden) heading to take a shower while his younger, casually unimpressed girlfriend (Kate Lyn Sheil) makes her way downstairs. Partially naked with only an unbuttoned shirt barely covering her breasts, she is left exposed by the living room's looming floor-to-ceiling glass windows as she sits and listens to a song from the CD player. Suffice it to say, these two are not long for this world, yet the haunting, echoey 1977 pop-rock ditty—Dwight Twilley Band's "Looking for the Magic"—continues on repeat. Returning again and again at different points in the film, this sonic leitmotif is ingenious verging on unforgettable. There is something insanely eerie about up-tempo music playing over and over in a lonesome home occupied by no one other than two undiscovered dead bodies, and Wingard milks this for every ounce of jittery effectiveness it's worth. One could say the same in general about the pic's entirety, so superbly conceived and carried out, so draped in tension yet also naturally funny in its tonal command, that it seems nearly impossible not to walk out of the film on a nervy, satisfied high. Horror cinema fans, a word of advice: rally together and absolutely do not let *You're Next* pass you by.

Zodiac

2007 - Directed by David Fincher

Zodiac marked a departure for director David Fincher, he of such unremittingly dark and visually eye-popping thrillers as 1995's *Seven*, 1999's *Fight Club* and 2002's *Panic Room*. Less a sensationalized serial murder picture than a talk-heavy, scrupulously researched investigation procedural, the film delves into the frustrating decades-long hunt for the Zodiac, an enigmatic killer who terrorized the San Francisco area in the late 1960s and early '70s. Clocking in at a whopping, epic-sized 160 minutes, *Zodiac* is an absorbing, hugely ambitious, richly textured entertainment, the kind that rarely get made anymore.

Based in part on the book by former *San Francisco Chronicle* cartoonist Robert Graysmith, *Zodiac* primarily follows three real-life people whose lives were progressively haunted by the seemingly unsolvable mystery surrounding the identity of the self-proclaimed Zodiac Killer: hard-living newspaper reporter Paul Avery (Robert Downey Jr.), assigned to the story after the Zodiac began sending cryptic letters, warnings and codes to the *San Francisco Chronicle*; SFPD Inspector David Toschi (Mark Ruffalo), prime investigator on the case, and Robert Graysmith himself (Jake Gyllenhaal), a lowly cartoonist who becomes interested and later obsessed with finding out the truth long after the murders and letters subside. With only circumstantial evidence to go on, however, these three people's hope for resolution begins to dim as the years pass them by.

In what could almost be a companion piece to 1999's *Summer of Sam*, Spike Lee's spellbindingly complex exploration into the sweltering season of the Son of Sam killings in 1970s New York City, *Zodiac* is likewise a fascinating look at a particular time and place as it relates to the fear and paranoia of a madman on the loose. While the former film centered on fictional characters who just happened to be living in the area during the Son of Sam reign, Fincher zeroes in on those most closely related to the investigation into the Zodiac. Everyday citizens of the Bay area, as well as the families of the victims, only appear in the periphery. *Zodiac* isn't so much about them, or the murders themselves, as it is about professional men swept up, encumbered and ultimately almost destroyed by their inability to piece the puzzle together in order to figure out whodunit.

Fincher's unusually low-key approach to the material works here, because the story he has set out to tell favors the human condition over slam-bang action sequences. The setpieces of the crimes are detailed as well (they all occur during the movie's first act), and the results are nothing short of chilling in their stark, straightforward brutality. The opening scene, in which a young couple are shot at a lovers' lane on the Fourth of July, unforgettably jump-starts the story and is made all the more indelible by the brilliant use of the song, "Hurdy Gurdy Man," by Donovan. The depiction of the masked Zodiac's stabbings of another couple picnicking alongside Napa County's Lake Berryessa is equally effective, with the lone sound of a nearby woodpecker minimalistically ratcheting up the tension. Finally, a scene in which a mother (Ione Skye) narrowly escapes with her baby from the clutches of a man who might or might not be the Zodiac is shiver-inducing.

Other than these fleeting steps into horror territory, *Zodiac* is very much an expositional drama that journeys in-depth into an investigation that drags on for over a decade before threatening to go cold for good. First and foremost an actors' film, the ensemble cast is uniformly superlative. Jake Gyllenhaal's rock-solid portrayal of Robert Graysmith is the one the viewer latches onto the most, as his career and home life with wife Melanie (Chloë Sevigny) and three children suffer at the expense of a fixation over the Zodiac case. Graysmith eventually went on to pen two successful books on the subject, but his personal story is a sad one that shows what he had to, at least temporarily, sacrifice.

Mark Ruffalo is quietly compelling in the role of police detective David Toschi, the toll the case takes on him staying a largely interior one. And, as self-destructive reporter Paul Avery, Robert Downey Jr. mesmerizingly layers his role with a buoyant personality masking the emotional wounds and feelings of regret underneath. Further mention should go to John Carroll Lynch, excellent as number-one suspect Arthur Leigh Allen, and Chloë Sevigny, doing a lot with little as Robert's neglected wife, Melanie.

Deliberately paced but tantalizingly immersive for every second, *Zodiac* earns the right to slowly simmer as all avenues of the story and investigation pull the viewer in. Kudos, too, to Fincher's and screenwriter James Vanderbilt's devotion to historical accuracy; they don't simply throw in exploitation or excess to pep things up, trusting that the facts can often be more intriguing than fiction. In turn, suspense arrives not by way of violence or exploitation, but from the nagging notion that these horrible crimes may never be solved, leaving the perpetrator a free man who has managed to elude authorities with the same ease as getting out of bed in the morning. Truth be told, *Zodiac* is so riveting and rife with further material left untapped that keeping its initial three-hour-plus length probably wouldn't have been such a horrible idea at all.

Zombieland

2009 - Directed by Ruben Fleischer

"Mad cow became mad person became mad zombie" is how quick-footed, virginal twenty-something Columbus (Jesse Eisenberg) describes the worldwide epidemic that started with diseased hamburger and has now turned all but a random few into the cannibalistic undead. Thus begins *Zombieland*, a gleefully whacked-out horror-comedy that is funnier and scarier than 2004's cult classic, *Shaun of the Dead*. Making their devilishly good feature debuts, director Ruben Fleischer and screenwriters Rhett Reese and Paul Wernick show full control of their tricky tone—sarcastic but serious when need be—and a loose plot that makes up for a lack of motivation and resolution through its sheer narrative originality.

Columbus has managed to survive the takeover—so far—by following a series of practical rules, including being good at cardio, avoiding public bathrooms, wearing his seatbelt, checking the backseat, and always double-tapping his latest zombie kill with an extra shot to the head. As he makes his way across a desolate landscape of abandoned cars and silent roads headed for his hometown in Ohio to see if his parents are still living, he joins forces with the straight-talking Tallahassee (Woody Harrelson) and, later, two con-playing sisters, Wichita (Emma Stone) and Little Rock (Abigail Breslin). When word comes that Ohio is a wasteland, Columbus opts to stay with his new pack as Wichita and Little Rock set their sights on the California coast. Just outside of Los Angeles sits Pacific Playland, an amusement park that, from what they hear, is zombie-free. They really ought to know better.

Zombieland opens like a comic-tinged version of 2004's *Dawn of the Dead* and then consistently surprises as it moves forward, reinventing itself again and again as the characters travel on and the ever-changing setting flutters by. The opening credits sequence—slow-motion shots of the world falling apart scored to Metallica's "For Whom the Bell Tolls"—is mesmerizing. A single shot involving an evil clown peering under a bathroom stall is so startling and creepy it might induce gasps in the coulrophobic. A flashback to the inaugural outbreak goes from romantic to foreboding to ghastly as Columbus wakes in his apartment to find his beautiful neighbor (Amber Heard) frothing at the mouth and hungry for his flesh. Wichita and Little Rock, cautious at first of getting close to anyone else, make multiple attempts at stealing Columbus' and Tallahassee's truck—they succeed the first time—before deciding the guys are not so bad and agreeing to carpool with them. A montage of the foursome's disparate car conversations as they each take turns driving is a hoot.

Once they arrive in Los Angeles, driving down a Hollywood Boulevard populated only by costumed zombified workers in front of Grauman's Chinese Theater, their travels take them to the thought-deserted mansion of Tallahassee's idol, Bill Murray. The extended setpiece that follows is one of the most deliriously ingenious and fall-down-funny in ages, featuring one priceless idea, interchange and one-liner after the next. For a roughly ten-minute segment, *Zombieland* surpasses merely auspicious and moves into the terrain of the downright brilliant. The action-oriented, guns-blasting climax taking place at Pacific Playland is also loads of fun, like the ending of 1983's *National Lampoon's Vacation* if the Griswolds had to contend with blasting away swarms of zombies while partaking in the thrill rides. Nothing is exactly solved by the end—the planet, after all, is decidedly apocalyptic—but the film does make the valid point that real family is what you make of it, not reliant on blood relations.

Prior to his game-changing turn as whip-smart, backstabbing Facebook founder Mark Zuckerberg in 2010's *The Social Network*, Jesse Eisenberg, along with Michael Cera, had the market cornered for characters who are supposed to be unassuming, non-threatening underdogs. In *Zombieland*, he is the logic-bound glue that holds all else together as Columbus. His developing friendship with Tallahassee, sibling-like relationship with Little Rock, and romantic feelings for Wichita are all well-established. As the Twinkie-seeking Tallahassee, Woody Harrelson is all-business at first and then lightens up and grows lovable himself once he gets to better know his road buddies. When revealed, a tragedy from his life that he is still trying to deal with brings welcome dramatic layers to his macho exterior. As Wichita, Emma Stone is an edgy but inwardly sweet foil for Eisenberg's Columbus, and Abigail Breslin lets her hair down and embraces her gun-toting, tough-girl side as 12-year-old Little Rock. Playing himself (to what extent will be left for viewers to discover), Bill Murray is worth applauding for having a self-deprecating sense of humor and making the most of, quite possibly, one of modern cinema's best screen cameos.

Playing like a useful survival guide to an undead outbreak, a guts-filled horror film that turns George A. Romero on his head, and a knowing, occasionally referential screwball comedy, *Zombieland* is a zippy blast. Enthusiastic and acerbic, the writing and handful of characters keep on keepin' on while depth remains light and mostly on the surface. The joy and creativity brought to the project is what is most appreciable, Fleischer and cinematographer Michael Bonvillain injecting candy colors, innovation and veritable threat into what could have just been another predictable study in dystopian destruction. Escaping a zombie uprising might be hazardous business, but *Zombieland* also makes it ridiculously entertaining.

ACKNOWLEDGMENTS

There are many people who contributed and inspired me, whether they realize it or not, on my journey toward completing this book. It was a lot of hard work and has been, more or less, fifteen years in the making, but it would have never happened without the experiences I've had, the people I've met, and the nudges I have been given to steer me in the right direction.

First and foremost, I must thank Patrick Jennings for his unyielding love, support and encouragement over the last thirteen years. He has been my biggest champion, stood by me through good times and bad, been my invaluable web producer, and given up countless free nights to accompany me to a lot—and I mean *a lot*—of advance film screenings. Luckily, he loves movies as much as I do.

To my mom and dad, Carol and Ronald Putman, you, too, have always had faith in me and told me that I could do whatever I set my mind to. Your guidance and love have made me the person I am today. Even when I was five years old and insisted on going to Video Villa every Saturday morning to rent movies, you were accepting of my crazy hobby—even if it meant renting *The Care Bears Movie* alongside *Friday the 13th* as the world's strangest double feature. You are the best parents a person could ever hope to have. I love you both.

To my wonderful sister, Ronni Renee Putman, a great mother in her own right who has never been afraid to tell me what she honestly thinks. We may not always have the same taste in movies, but if I were to start singing any of the songs from *The New Adventures of Pippi Longstocking*, it is a safe bet that she would join in without hesitation.

When thinking back on all of the teachers I had growing up, there was one special instructor who truly stood out. My seventh-grade English teacher, Mary Haller, was passionate about what she did and always let me know how much value she saw in my work. In my yearbook, she wrote to me to "keep writing." I have.

There are many more shout-outs well worth mentioning. Thank you to my entire extended family and all my friends. To my grandma, Thelma Poole, who would always take me to Little Professor Book Center when I was growing up and let me pick out a new book to read every week. Also, to Rebecca Baugher, Bradd Bowman, Bobby Burns, Joel Copling, Jason Flynt, Lora Fowler, Jay Franzak, Rick Gibbons and Jacqueline M. Gadomski-Gibbons, Gwendolyn Grastorf, Tyler, Bailey and Josh Griffin, Joseph, Melissa, Helena and Eli Gryder, Azeezaly Jaffer, Paulette Jennings, Mike and Jill Jennings, Scott, Katie, Calvin and Carter Jennings, Mark "Sparky" and Kitty McKenzie, Sharon McKinney, Tom and Charlene Miller,

Matt Moyer, Paul and Sarah Puglisi, Andy, Kellie, Hunter and Makenzie Putman, Gene and Marti Putman, Larry and Marina Putman, Robert and Jenny Putman, Rhudel "Pap" Putman, Scott and Rachel Putman, Steve Reeves, Becky Rice, Katie Richardson, Shirley Richardson, Scott Shackleford and Insley Schaden-Shackleford, Megan Swank, Vi Tagala, Patricia Twentey, Chad Weimer, Angela Wilson, Ariana Wisniewski, Jack and Claire Wynn, and anyone else I may have overlooked. Thank you to Leeann Bonaventura, Carla Brooks, Glenn Byrd, Ardandia Campbell-Williams, and everyone at MedImmune.

To Nell Minow, thank you for all of your invaluable knowledge and early guidance in getting the ball rolling on this project. Your support means the world to me. To the rest of my film critic friends, colleagues and fellow WAFCA members, including (but not limited to) Michelle Alexandria, Jen Chaney, Sandie Angulo Chen, Lauren Bradshaw, Arch Campbell, Leslie Combemale, Rebecca Cusey, Brandon Fibbs, Cynthia Fuchs, Jack Giroux, Tim Gordon, Roxana Hadadi, Christian Hamaker, John Hanlon, Travis Hopson, Jane Horwitz, Joshua Hylton, Jim Judy, Jeffrey Lyles, Kevin McCarthy, John Nolan, Tricia Olszewski, Kyle Osborne, Eddie Pasa, Matthew Razak, Dean Rogers, Elias and Andrea Savada, Lauren Veniziani, and Willie Waffle. To Gloria Jones and the team at Allied-THA, Renée Tsao and the team at PR Collaborative, and to Jeff Nelson and Cliff MacMillan at Scream Factory, for bringing such loving care and attention to the horror genre. Thanks, also, to the many readers of my film reviews and friends that I have made over the years.

Special thanks to Scott Derrickson, for your very kind words.

And, finally, I would be remiss not to thank my big brother, Rhudel "Rudy" Putman II. He is no longer with us, but the impact he made on my life's path cannot be measured in words. He not only helped to mold my ceaseless love for cinema, but he was my best friend and confidante. I may have been ten years younger than him, but he never treated me as anything less than his equal. He is greatly missed, and thought about every single day.

Dustin Putman
Ashburn, Virginia
September 15, 2013

www.ingramcontent.com/pod-product-compliance
Lightning Source LLC
Chambersburg PA
CBHW060233100426
42742CB00011B/1520

9780615774022